WORKING I
A New Perspective on

Front Cover: The painting by Honoré Daumier (1810-1879) is both a sympathetic image of motherhood and a dramatic symbol of the burden of labour

WORKING LIFE
A NEW PERSPECTIVE ON LABOUR LAW

KEITH EWING

THE INSTITUTE OF EMPLOYMENT RIGHTS
LAWRENCE & WISHART, LONDON

Lawrence & Wishart
99a Wallis Road, London E9 5LN
in association with the
Institute of Employment Rights
160 Falcon Road, London SW11 2LN

First published 1996

Copyright © Institute of Employment Rights
1996

The authors have asserted their right under the
Copyright, Designs and Patents Act, 1988, to be
identified as authors of this work.

All rights reserved. Apart from fair dealing for
the purpose of private study, research, criticism
or review, no part of this publication may be
reproduced, stored in a retrieval system, or
transmitted, in any form or by any means,
electronic, electrical, chemical, mechanical,
optical, photocopying, recording or otherwise,
without the prior permission of the copyright
owner.

ISBN 0 85315 829 0

Brtitish Library Cataloguing
in Publication data
A catalogue record for this book
is available from the British Library

Typesetting Art Services, Norwich
Printed and bound in Great Britain
by Biddles Ltd, Guildford.

CONTENTS

Chapter Nine: Job Security and Unfair Dismissal   286

FOREWORD

Elected to power in 1979, the Conservatives have waged a relentless war against trade unions and working people. Using slogans like 'removing burdens from business' and 'giving unions back to their members' the Tories began a programme of legislative changes aimed at deregulating the labour market and weakening the ability of unions to resist the onslaught on workers' rights.

The end result for British workers has been a disaster. Working life in Britain is now characterised by a growing feeling of insecurity, increased income inequality, the dilution of employment protection rights and the loss, for many, of a democratic voice at work. A growing number of people live in poverty, while at the same time Britain has continued to slide down the world economic performance table.

It is important that the labour and trade union movement now develops an alternative and democratic approach to working life. We want a perspective that has at its heart the aspirations of working people. We need to rebuild our workplace relations by developing decent labour standards and by promoting collective bargaining, having regard to best practices throughout Europe and taking on board our obligations under international laws.

The ideas in this study, based as they are on the principles of equality of opportunity, social justice, workplace democracy, civil liberties and fairness at work, present us with the building blocks for a new and positive framework of employment law. It focuses attention on the issues policy makers need to consider and identifies a role for law in helping to rebuild institutions and people's lives.

The Institute of Employment Rights is an independent think-tank supported by the trade union movement. It brings together leading academics, lawyers and trade unionists to discuss ideas on the future of employment law. This study is a fine example of their work.

I warmly welcome this initiative and hope the study stimulates the debate needed to develop a new agenda for the next millenium.

This is not to say that UNISON supports all the ideas contained in this report - I would be surprised if anyone reading the book agreed with every aspect. But it raises the issues, provides European comparisons and presents detailed information about international law. We owe a debt of gratitude to the Institute and all those involved for taking on the task.

Rodney Bickerstaffe
General Secretary
UNISON

PREFACE

A strong and vibrant trade union movement is a precondition of a free and democratic society. So too is a comprehensive framework of statutory rights promoting equality of opportunity, social justice and fairness at work. Yet it is common knowledge that over the last 17 years trade union freedom has been eroded by a complex but uncompromising government attack, an attack which has led to condemnation of Britain at the bar of international law. It is common knowledge also that the erosion of our rights of citizenship at the workplace has been accompanied by an increase in income inequality and job insecurity, and continued mass unemployment.

In the light of these developments, the Institute for Employment Rights, as a think-tank for the labour movement, embarked upon a project to explore the possible content of a comprehensive code by which workers' rights could better be protected by law. With the support of the Annual General Meeting, the Executive Committee decided towards the end of 1994 to commission such a project and to this end a Project Management Group was appointed to oversee its work, with accountability to the Executive Committee itself. The Executive Committee also appointed a Project Co-ordinator and a Director of Research, and authorised the appointment of a Research Officer.

The project was launched towards the end of 1994, and work began in January 1995. The Institute decided that the project should be open and inclusive, and that an attempt should be made to draw upon the reservoir of knowledge and experience in the trade union, legal, and academic communities. The Institute was immensely flattered by and very grateful to the wealth of talent of those who agreed to take part. It was also agreed that we should consult trade unionists at every stage in the process in order to ensure that the project was broadly in tune with their hopes and aspirations. The Institute has endeavoured to follow these guidelines at every stage.

At the initial meeting of the Project Management Group, it was decided that the first step was to prepare an introductory document which would explore the principles which should underpin the detailed work. A draft of that document, *Just the Job?*, was presented for consideration by participants in the project at a meeting of more than 40 trade union officials, academics and legal practitioners held at the TUC in May 1995. The document proposed that future strategy should be based on five key principles, and that it should be set in the context of international and EU labour standards. These themes were found to be broadly acceptable and the document was formally launched in October 1995.

Just the Job? was the subject of wide ranging consultation in the trade union movement. Members of the Project Management Group attended meetings throughout the country, and the ideas were presented at fringe meetings at the TUC Annual Congress, the TGWU Biennial Delegate Conference and at a number of other trade union gatherings. Presentations were also made at a number of events organised by Liberty in the Summer of 1995. The ideas were very warmly received and the Institute has been greatly encouraged by the fact that they have now made their way onto the 1996 annual conference agenda of a number of trade unions, where the discussion will continue.

Prior to the meeting at the TUC in May 1995, the Institute invited a large number of people to participate in the project. It was decided that it would be most useful to establish a number of Specialist Working Groups of roughly six members, each to drive the work of the project. The groups dealt with a range of issues, namely The Employment Relationship, Trade Unions and Collective Bargaining, Equal Opportunities, The Right to Strike, Termination of the Employment Relationship, and The Protection and Enforcement of Rights.

Three of the groups were chaired by trade union officials, and three by academics. Each group contained members who were trade unionists, legal practitioners and academics. The groups met on at least three occasions (and some groups met on four or more occasions) to consider the development of ideas and draft paperwork which was contributed by different members of the teams. Every meeting was attended by the Project Co-ordinator, the Director of Research and the Research Officer. The first drafts of the different groups were considered at a plenary session of all the participants, held at the TUC in December 1995.

Since December work has continued revising the text in the light of the comments received at various meetings and in written submissions by a number of organisations and individuals. The opportunity was also taken to respond to some of the points which had been made in the course of our consultations in the Autumn of 1995, and indeed at the December seminar itself. As the text came closer to completion the Institute held a final consultative seminar of trade unionists at NATFHE in April 1996, attended by over one hundred and twenty people from the trade union movement and academic and legal communities. Final revisions to the text have taken place to reflect some of the very helpful contributions made at that meeting. The Institute wishes to thank all those who have taken part in the project. These include financial sponsors without whom the project could never have been contemplated; the participants in the different specialist working groups who worked tirelessly and without reward; the consultants who were always ready with advice and support; the trade unionists who took part in the meetings and seminars, and responded so warmly and enthusiastically to the idea of the project; and members of the Institute Executive Committee whose wisdom and determination was greatly appreciated at all times.

A large number of people have been involved in this project in a number of different capacities, and although not everyone can be presumed to agree with everything which appears on the following pages, the Institute pays tribute to their willingness to be open minded and tolerant in the desire to produce an agenda for change. They have been willing to strike an optimistic and forward looking note at a time when the mood of defeatism seems all too pervasive. If nothing else, it is hoped that this report will unequivocally demonstrate that the spirit of resignation on the issue of workers' and trade union rights is premature, and that there is a labour movement in this country brimming with ideas for reform and hungry for change.

KD Ewing
Director of Research

John Hendy, QC
Chairman

C. Jones
Director

LIST OF PARTICIPANTS

Chairman of the Institute
John Hendy QC, Old Square Chambers

Director of Research
Professor K.D. Ewing, Professor of Public Law, King's College,
University of London

Research Officer
Hannah Reed, Institute of Employment Rights

Project Co-ordinator
Carolyn Jones, Director, Institute of Employment Rights

Members of Specialist Working Groups and Consultants
Simon Auerbach, Pattinson and Brewer, Solicitors
Adrienne Aziz, Assistant General Secretary, AUT
Professor Brian Bercusson, Professor of European Law, University
of Manchester
Catherine Barnard, Lecturer in Law and Fellow of Trinity College,
University of Cambridge
Colin Bourn, Director, International Centre for Management, Law
and Industrial Relations, University of Leicester
Damian Brown, Barrister, Old Square Chambers
Stephen Cavalier, Brian Thompson & Partners, Solicitors
Mike Clancy, Area Secretary, EMA
Professor Jon Clark, Professor of Industrial Relations, University
of Southampton
Graham Clayton, Senior Solicitor, NUT
Celia Cleave, Regional Legal Officer, GMB
David Cockburn, Pattinson & Brewer, Solicitors
Professor Hugh Collins, Law Department, London School of
Economics, University of London
Steve Cottingham, Brian Thompson & Partners, Solicitors
Bryn Davies, Campaign for Pension Fund Democracy
Simon Deakin, Lecturer in Law and Fellow of Peterhouse,
University of Cambridge
Professor Brian Doyle, Faculty of Law, University of Liverpool
Professor Barry Fitzpatrick, School of Public Policy, Economics
and Law, University of Ulster

Michael Ford, Barrister, Doughty Street Chambers
John Foster, General Secretary, NUJ
Sandra Fredman, Reader in Law, Exeter College,
    University of Oxford
Professor Bob Fryer, Principal of Northern College
Steve Gibbons, Head of Employment Law, Income Data Services,
    Ltd
Tess Gill, Barrister, Old Square Chambers
Phil James, Professor of Employment Relations, Middlesex
    University
Brian Langstaffe QC, Cloisters Chambers
Professor Roy Lewis, Barrister, Old Square Chambers &
    University of Southampton
Aileen McColgan, Lecturer in Law, King's College, University of
    London
Kevin Maguire, Industrial Editor, *Daily Mirror*
Sonia McKay, Employment Law Researcher, Labour Research
    Department
Bronwyn McKenna, Assistant Director of Legal Services,
    UNISON
Jeremy McMullen QC, Old Square Chambers
Jonathan Michie, Fellow and Director of Studies in Economics at
    Robinson College, University of Cambridge
Qudsia Mirza, Lecturer in Law, University of East London
Peter Morris, Director of Policy and Research, UNISON
Jim Mortimer, Chairman of ACAS (1971-1974)
Professor Brian Napier, Barrister & Advocate, Visiting Professor
    of Law, Queen Mary and Westfield College, University of
    London
Joe O'Hara, National Legal Officer, GMB
Bruce Piper, Director of Legal Services, UNISON
Margaret Prosser, National Organiser, TGWU
Rod Robertson, National Development Officer, UNISON
Barbara Switzer, Assistant General Secretary, MSF
Roger Welch, Senior Lecturer in Law, Anglia Polytechnic
    University
Fraser Whitehead, Russel, Jones and Walker, Solicitors
Frank Wilkinson, Senior Research Officer, Department of Applied
    Economics, University of Cambridge
David Wilson, NUJ

Donations towards the project have been received from:

Trade Unions and Trade Union Branches

ANSA, AUT, FBU, FBU REGION 10, GMB,
GMB / APEX GRAPHIC DESIGN, GMB LEEDS
GMB PLYMOUTH, GMB SCOTLAND, GPMU,
GMPU CHILTERN & THAMES, GPMU MID COUNTIES,
GPMU S & W GRAPHIC, MSF LONDON CRAFT,
MSF LONDON REGIONAL COUNCIL,
NCTU, NUJ, NUJ BELFAST, NUJ EDINBURGH & DISTRICT,
NUJ LONDON CENTRAL, NUJ OXFORD & DISTRICT,
NUJ SCOTTISH OFFICE, NUKFAT, NUM,
NUT BRIGHTON & HOVE, PRISON SERVICE UNION,
SERTUC, TGWU 4/259, TGWU 5/908, TGWU 6/765, TGWU 7/21,
TGWU ACTS 1/524, TGWU SCOTLAND,
TGWU SE & E ANGLIA, UCATT / FTAT LIVERPOOL
UNIFI, UNISON, UNISON BEDFORDSHIRE,
UNISON DURHAM, UNISON KENT,
UNISON LEICESTERSHIRE, UNISON OLDHAM,
UNISON OXFORD BROOKES, UNISON GRAMPIAN,
UNISON ROTHERHAM, UNISON SALFORD,
UNISON WAKEFIELD, UNISON SUFFOLK, USDAW,
USDAW NORTH WEST.

Charitable Trusts and Individuals

S. BARR,
CAMBRIDGE POLITICAL ECONOMY SOCIETY TRUST,
A. S. DANDO, TESS GILL, HAMLYN TRUST,
KAZUHIKO HAYASHI, DENNIS McWILLIAMS,
CHRISTINE ODDY MEP, SCOTTISH CHURCHES MISSION,
JACK THORNLEY.

INTRODUCTION

1.1   Since 1979 successive Conservative governments have moved gradually to dismantle the structure of labour law carefully built up in the 1970s. We have seen the erosion of the measures designed to underpin the process of collective bargaining and the deregulation of employment protection legislation. Although the strategy has been one of gradual change, it has been pursued vigorously, with no fewer than eight major pieces of legislation being introduced between 1980 and 1993, excluding the Trade Union and Labour Relations (Consolidation) Act 1992.

1.2   What is the alternative to this calculated assault on the rights of workers and trade unions? Taking the view that it is now time for the labour movement to begin developing its own agenda, the Institute of Employment Rights decided in 1994 to embark upon a project which would begin to answer that question. The aim is to provide suggestions for a coherent framework of labour law which will strengthen legal rights for people at work and offer a vision radically different from the regime which has governed the workplaces of this country since 1979. In developing this framework it is clearly important to embrace international and EC labour standards, but it is equally important that this should be done in the context of a framework of principle which both reflects and builds upon these standards.

1.3   In the pages which follow it is proposed that a new settlement for labour law should be underpinned by a number of principles. Drawing directly or indirectly from the ILO, and in particular the Declaration of Philadelphia of 1944, which is supposed to inspire the policies of the members, five such principles have been identified, respectively

> equality of opportunity
> social justice
> workplace democracy
> protection of civil liberties
> fairness at work

These principles are fairly fluid, and may be said to merge into each other. Some may see equality of opportunity as an aspect of social justice; or the protection of civil liberties as an aspect of workplace democracy. But for ease of presentation, we shall refer to these as five discrete, if overlapping, principles.

1.4   These principles were presented in a discussion document, *Just the Job?* published in October 1995 as part of our design better to inform public opinion on the question of labour law reform, and to offer some educational material for trade unionists and others who may be involved in the debate, in whatever capacity. In that document we also proposed that these principles should be built upon three secure pillars. The first of these is collective bargaining, as a method for the implementation of labour standards which is desirable in principle and effective in practice. The second is a comprehensive code of statutory rights to underpin the bargaining process, to facilitate the work of trade unions and to confer minimum standards on workers generally. The third is a new conceptual framework for the employment relationship as we move towards the 21st century, to replace the current law with its values rooted in the Victorian workplace, and beyond.

1.5   Our proposals for the future development of labour law cover a wide range of issues. But before beginning to examine these in chapter 2 with an account of the employment relationship, it is necessary in this introduction to say something of the context within which these proposals are set. In particular it is necessary to address the economic and social background to our proposals, both in terms of the legacy of deregulatory policies pursued since 1979 on the one hand, and the powerful economic arguments now emerging in favour of re-regulation on the other. It is necessary also to address the international and European context within which our proposals are set. In our view, a substantial element of re-regulation (and new forms of regulation) is necessary if we are to swim with the tide of international labour standards and European Labour Law. We begin this examination of the contextual background with an account of the failures of economic deregulation.

Deregulation: A Social and Economic Failure

1.6   From the end of the Second World War until the mid-1970s, the consensus in advanced industrial countries was that an effective floor of employment rights was both socially and economically beneficial. Decent standards of pay and working conditions were regarded as having a central part to play in reducing exploitation and poverty and in encouraging the more productive use of labour. Since the mid-1970s the climate of opinion, particularly amongst economists, has swung towards the view that such regulations impede the working of the labour markets, thereby preventing necessary adjustments to changed economic environments and causing unemployment. Since 1979 this view has become the predominant influence on government policy towards the labour market in Britain, and has provided a justification for the numerous measures taken to weaken trade unions, dismantle large parts of the legal floor of labour market rights, and to reduce entitlements to social security.

(a) The Costs of Deregulation

1.7   Measuring the unemployment consequences of the policy shifts of the 1980s and 1990s raises major problems. Since 1979, no fewer than 30 changes have been made to the way unemployment is officially counted, all but one of which have reduced recorded unemployment. The official definition of unemployment has also been changed from persons registered as unemployed to the current definition of those out of work claiming unemployment benefits of various kinds. Between 1979 and 1993, claimant unemployment increased from around 1 million to 2.8 million. The Unemployment Unit has estimated that on the basis of those registered as unemployed, unemployment increased from around 1.4 million in 1979 to more than 4 million in 1993. These estimates receive support from a study by Wells which shows a level of unemployment in early 1994 'closer to the Unemployment Unit's total of 4 million than to the official claimant count of under 3 million'.[1]

1.8   The record of deregulatory policies is no better if employment, rather than unemployment, is taken as the measure of success. It is a myth that the policies pursued in the 1980s and 1990s have led to substantial job growth in comparison to previous decades. Official figures show that by 1983 total employment - a figure which includes employees, the self-employed and members of the armed forces - had fallen by 1.7 million from its 1979 peak. It then recovered slowly but after 1989 a second intense depression again reduced the number of jobs to 0.6 million below its 1979 level. Employment was

---

1.   J Wells, 'The Missing Million' (1994) (Summer) *European Labour Forum.*

also restructured during this period, with a decline in the number of full-time, secure jobs. Between 1979 and 1993 male full-time employment fell by 2.3 million; this was only partly compensated for by an increase of 0.5 million in male part-time jobs. Meanwhile, female employment increased by 1.3 million, although only 196,000 of these jobs were full-time. Overall, in this period the number of employees fell by 1.7 million and self-employment increased by 1.1 million (0.4 million of whom were part-time). Much of the 'new' self-employment resulted from government incentive schemes for the unemployed, and is very low paid.[2]

1.9   As unemployment has grown and employment has become increasingly part-time and/or casual, pay, and more generally income, have become more unequally distributed. Between 1977 and 1992 the average real wages of the bottom 10 per cent of male earners were static; the median or mid-point increase was 27 per cent; while for the top tenth of earners, the average increase was 44 per cent.[3] During this period the earnings of non-manual workers rose more quickly than those of manual workers and full-timers' earnings rose more quickly than those of part-time workers. Of the self-employed in 1993, more than 20 per cent had incomes which were below half the average income for all individuals.[4] The rise in inequality of earnings, together with cuts in social security provision, has contributed to a sharp increase in household poverty. Official sources show that between 1979 and 1993 the lowest decile of households saw no increase in their income before housing costs are taken into account, whereas the highest decile had a rise of 45 per cent. When housing costs are taken into account, the lowest decile had a drop in real income of 17 per cent, compared to an increase of 62 per cent for the highest decile.

1.10   The degree of job insecurity and dissatisfaction arising from these developments is not easy to measure. Some part-time jobs are stable and secure, and some individuals may welcome the flexibility offered by part-time work and self-employment. Conversely, many full-time jobs pay very low wages and offer only partial guarantees of

---

2. *Joseph Rowntree Foundation Inquiry into Income and Wealth* Vol. 2 (1995), p 53.
3. A Goodman and S Webb, 'For Richer, for Poorer: the Changing Distribution of Income in the UK, 1961-1991' (1994) 15 *Fiscal Studies* 28.
4. Department of Social Security, *Households with Below Average Incomes* (1995).

continuing employment. The essential question here is how insecurity affects different groups and to what extent it is growing. There is little doubt that an ever-growing number of workers are affected by insecurity. One recent assessment is that 13.5 million workers in the British economy are now in a 'primary' sector of the labour force which, on the whole, enjoys secure and well remunerated full-time employment, with a further 6.5 million in an 'intermediate' category of those who, while not having a full-time job, are nevertheless relatively well-paid and secure.[5] This leaves a further 9 million 'disadvantaged' workers without secure or well-paid employment. Of this 9 million, 4.9 million are in employment and 4.1 million are without employment; the latter figure includes, in addition to the claimant unemployed, 'discouraged' workers who do not figure in the unemployment count because they are not actively seeking work, and a further group of individuals who would like a job but who are not available for paid employment by reasons of sickness or family responsibilities. Thus 'around seventy per cent of the labour force are financially comfortable and reasonably secure, while thirty per cent live in either insecurity or comparative poverty'.[6]

1.11 For a short time in the mid-1980s Britain was thought to have achieved economic prosperity and political stability, a result many were quick to ascribe to the neo-liberal reform agenda. The growth in employment from the mid-1980s was widely cited as convincing evidence for the success of labour market deregulation. But as we have just seen, the growth in employment was mainly accounted for by low paid, insecure jobs with poor working conditions. The political stability briefly attained at that time is largely explained by the contribution made by the exploitation of a growing 'underclass' to the 'contentment' of the more affluent members of society.[7] But it is also clear that many of the previously protected white collar and managerial jobs are now becoming more precarious, as large-scale

---

5. K Coutts and R Rowthorn, *Employment in the United Kingdom: Trends and Prospects,* ESRC Centre for Business Research, University of Cambridge, Working Paper No. 3 (1995).
6. *Ibid.*, at p6. This analysis, if anything, errs on the side of caution; it does not seek to assess how many of those in the 'primary' segment, who are apparently secure, perceive their position as being under threat, as more firms use redundancy as a measure of first and not of last resort. The important point is that the ratio of disadvantaged to advantaged workers has increased over the past 15 years and continues to do so.
7. J.K. Galbraith, *The Culture of Contentment* (1992).

redundancies and casualisation penetrate deeper into the 'primary' employment sectors. Reversing the downwards spiral of deregulation is a priority for all those affected by these processes.

(b) The Economic Functions of Labour Standards

1.12   The downwards spiral described above can only be reversed by a radical change in policy direction. The adoption of an effective system of labour market regulation is an essential precondition of an economy based on a high rate of innovation, high productivity, high quality in production, and full employment based on decent wages and terms and conditions. What Britain thus needs is a programme of re-regulation of the labour market, designed not only to reverse the trend towards greater social and labour market inequality, but also to promote economic efficiency. It would also serve to end the costly and self-defeating reliance on wage subsidies as a means of alleviating low pay.

1.13   **Labour standards and productive efficiency**. The ability of any one firm to adopt a high-productivity route to competitive success is limited if its rivals are able to compete on the basis of low pay and poor working conditions. This is why labour-market regulation is an essential component of any industrial policy which has enhanced competitiveness as its goal. Basic levels of protection in such areas as wages, working time and conditions of employment aim to forestall destructive competition by setting a floor below which terms and conditions may not fall. Effective labour standards constitute, therefore, a form of discipline for firms, requiring them to engage in continuous improvements to products and techniques in order to stay competitive. The existence of a pool of undervalued labour, on the other hand, offers a means by which firms can compensate for organisational and other managerial inadequacies, for example by delaying the scrapping of obsolete equipment. The survival of the more technologically and managerially backward firms also helps prevent more progressive firms from expanding their share of the market. The overall effect is a lower average level of productivity and a slower rate of introduction of new techniques and products. Labour standards help to avert such a situation by promoting co-operation between firms in joint product development, the pooling and sharing of resources for gaining access to new markets, and generally improving performance. Co-operation requires minimum levels of stability in social relations, security, and mutual trust. None of these are easy to secure on any broad scale unless there is some form of collective understanding which assures each competitor that undercutting wages and other destructive competition are not to be tolerated.

1.14 **Labour standards and worker efficiency**. Labour standards also affect the quality of labour. Standards do not simply permit but also effectively require firms to adopt strategies based on enhancing the quality of labour inputs through improvements to health and safety protection, training and skills development. It is now widely recognised that high-trust work organisation is necessary to secure worker co-operation in technical development, product enhancement and continuous quality control. Worker involvement is the key to such development, but this cannot be relied on where there is no long term commitment by employers to their work-force and no assurance that workers' interests will not be summarily sacrificed to those of other interest groups in the firm, such as shareholders and creditors. The effectiveness of the modern business enterprise depends on providing workers with rights which give them a voice alongside those of other interest groups: this involves, at the very least, guarantees of effective collective representation and participation for workers. Participatory standards - standards providing for the collective representation of both employers and workers - enable collective interests to be expressed and mechanisms put in place for the resolution of disputes. Moreover, poor pay and working conditions and the absence of job security also have a negative impact on incentives for training. One orthodox economic explanation for low pay is that it results from lack of training and that higher pay will further discourage employers from investing in training. But experience shows that low paying employers are the least likely to train; they are more often in the business of exploiting rather than creating human capital. Moreover, jobs with poor terms and conditions of employment are unlikely to be afforded high social status whatever their skill level, and this will help discourage individuals from acquiring the necessary entry qualifications by undertaking education and training.

1.15 **Labour standards, consumption and employment growth**. The more even distribution of economic opportunities resulting from the imposition of effective labour standards will also improve the prospects for employment generation by its effect on the level and structure of consumption. The redistribution of income from the rich, who save a high proportion of their income, to the poor, most of whose income is consumed, will raise the level of demand in the economy generally and generate employment. In the longer term, a more equal distribution of income will make more generally affordable a healthier diet and one which is more environmentally friendly, thereby creating the conditions for improving the quality of life and for increasing the level of economic and employment growth which is sustainable. Standards are also needed to ensure that economic opportunities are as widely shared as possible. It is essential to bring about the successful redeployment of workers displaced by technical progress and changing patterns of consumer demand. This requires a macro-economic policy which incorporates a full-employment target over the medium term; adequate and widely available facilities for retraining; the minimisation of artificial barriers to entry into particular occupations; and an effective strategy on working time. Such measures are required both to maintain demand in the labour market and to prevent the establishment and growth of social and economic disadvantage.

1.16 **Labour standards and the public purse.** Labour standards have the important role of avoiding the use of social security and/or the tax system to subsidise low pay. Such subsidisation often succeeds only in transferring income to low-paying employers, thereby exacerbating the problem which the transfers were intended to deal with. Family credit creates a set of perverse incentives: employers are encouraged to pay lower wages, while means-testing discourages workers from pressing for or seeking out higher wages by imposing a high marginal tax rate on any wage increases which they might secure. At the same time, the taxpayer is faced with a growing burden on public expenditure. In April 1989, for example, there were 286,000 claims for family credit at a weekly cost of around £7 million. By January 1994 the number of claims had risen to 521,000 at a weekly cost of £24 million. Annual expenditure on family credit in 1993-94 was well over £1 billion and by 1994-95 it had increased further to almost £1.5 billion.[8] This figure can be expected to continue to grow sharply over the next few years if low wages continue to decline and if plans to extend similar benefit payments to families without children (through the 'employment top-up') are implemented. There are further costs to the policy of promoting 'non-standard' forms of work. The proliferation of part-time work at low rates of pay and self-employment means that the tax base is being eroded. In construction, which saw a considerable increase in self-employment in the 1980s, both (lawful) tax avoidance and (illegal) tax evasion have become widespread. The resulting loss to government revenues

---

8. Department of Social Security, *Social Security Statistics 1994-1995*, Tables A1.01, A1.02.

has been estimated at between £2 and £4 billion annually. The tax regime for construction has also contributed to a policy of cut-throat competition over labour costs which is undermining training and leading to skills shortages.[9]

International Labour Standards

1.17 When they eventually leave office, the Conservatives will bequeath a deregulated labour law; a disorganised system of collective industrial relations; and serious labour market inequality. The first step in the process of reconstruction will be to consider the standards and obligations of international and EU labour law. These both inform us of the extent to which domestic labour law now falls below accepted international minima, and at the same time indicate the degree of regulation necessary if these obligations are to be taken seriously. Broadly, there are three sets of standards which must now be addressed. These are respectively those established by the International Labour Organisation (ILO), the Council of Europe, and the European Union (EU). The first two are considered in this section, while the last is considered in the next.

(a) The ILO
1.18 Since its creation in 1919 as part of the peace settlement at the end of the First World War, the ILO has developed a wealth of international labour standards which cover a broad range of topics. By the end of 1995 the Organisation had adopted no fewer than 177 Conventions and 184 Recommendations. It is well known that Britain played a key role both in the creation of the ILO and in the development of many of the Conventions and Recommendations. Indeed, much of our early social legislation provided the Organisation with models for some of its earliest instruments. It is also the case that Britain has been willing to ratify a high number of Conventions, and that our record on ratification was amongst the best in the world. Since 1979, however, Britain's relationship with the ILO has seriously deteriorated in a number of ways: by the denunciation of a number of Conventions; by the failure to adopt new instruments; and by the breach of Conventions by which we continue to be bound.
1.19 It is clear as a result that a process of post-Conservative reconstruction will, so far as ILO Conventions are concerned, require

9. M. Harvey, *Towards the Insecurity Society: The Tax Trap of Self-Employment*, London 1995.

attention to be given to three issues. The first is the possibility of ratifying the Conventions which have been denounced, including in particular the Minimum Wage-Fixing Convention, 1928 (Convention 26). A second question is whether a new government ought to ratify any of the Conventions made since 1979. Although there are no fewer than 23 such Conventions (of which only one has been ratified by the UK), the most significant include the Occupational Safety and Health Convention, 1981 (Convention 155), the Workers with Family Responsibilities Convention, 1981 (Convention 156) and the Termination of Employment Convention, 1982 (Convention 158). All of these deal in some way with problems already addressed to some extent by our domestic labour law, but in different ways go beyond the boundaries of protection which national law currently provides.

1.20 The third, and perhaps the most pressing issue in the reconstruction, will be to ensure that domestic law complies with the obligations by which we continue to be bound. The ILO supervisory agencies have indicated on a number of occasions that the UK is in breach of Conventions 87 (the Freedom of Association and Protection of the Right to Organise Convention, 1948) and 98 (the Right to Organise and Collective Bargaining Convention, 1949) in particular, and their recommendations would require as a minimum:

* the extension of measures designed to protect trade unionists from victimisation and discrimination, including the restoration of trade union rights at GCHQ;
* the removal of restraints on trade union autonomy, in particular the restrictions on the right of trade unions to discipline and expel strike-breakers;
* the removal of restrictions on the freedom to strike and the introduction of a number of measures designed to protect the individual striker.

1.21 Clearly the most controversial of these is the last, though it by no means follows that all restrictions on the freedom to strike would have to be removed in order to comply with ILO Convention 87. It would, for example, be possible to retain the obligation for trade unions to ballot their members before industrial action, though it would not be necessary to do so. But it is equally clear that a number of other restrictions will have to be removed if British law is fully to comply with Convention 87. Thus, the ILO Committee of Experts found Britain in breach in the following respects

* the removal of all legal protection for secondary and sympathy action;
* the narrowing of the definition of a trade dispute to include only disputes between workers and their employers;
* the exclusion of immunity for protest strikes against government policy on the one hand, and in support of overseas workers on the other.

1.22 Alongside the issue of trade union immunities, both the ILO Committee of Experts and the Committee on Freedom of Association have criticised British law for its failure to protect striking workers from dismissal. While the Committee of Experts recognised that British law offered a limited measure of protection, in the sense that unfair dismissal proceedings may be brought in the event of the selective dismissal of workers engaged in industrial action, it was not adequate for the purposes of Convention 87 as employers were still able with impunity to dismiss the entire workforce and to re-hire workers on a selective basis once a period of three months had elapsed. These views were endorsed by the Freedom of Association Committee in a complaint referred to it after the dismissal of striking seafarers in 1988. The Committee also criticised the provisions of the Employment Act 1990 permitting the selective dismissal of workers engaged in unofficial industrial action.

(b) The Council of Europe
1.23 Established at the end of the Second World War, the Council of Europe is the product of an early attempt at European integration. Its original mandate anticipated activity not only in the field of human rights, but also in the pursuit of agreement and common action between its Member States in economic, social, legal and administrative matters. In practice, however, the role of the Council in political and economic affairs has proved minimal, having been surpassed by the European Union. Nevertheless, significant advances have been made in the field of human rights, with both the European Convention on Human Rights and Fundamental Freedoms of 1950 (ECHR) on the one hand, and the European Social Charter of 1961 on the other, being created under the auspices of the Council.
1.24 For present purposes the latter is the more significant, with the ECHR being a limited source of protection for trade unions and their members. But this is not to diminish the importance of the

Convention as a framework of principle which can contribute to the development of a new agenda for labour law, in a number of ways. So far as the Social Charter is concerned, however, this draws much inspiration from ILO standards and enshrines fundamental freedoms such as the right to work; the right to just conditions of work; the right to a fair remuneration; and the right to organise and to bargain collectively. Perhaps most significantly, the Charter was the first international treaty explicitly to recognise the right to strike. The purpose of the Charter, however, is by no means confined to the protection of workers' rights. Many of its provisions seek also to establish general standards in the field of social policy, dealing with such matters as the protection of health, the right to social security, and the provision of welfare services.

1.25 Under the terms of the Social Charter a State must undertake to consider itself bound by at least ten out of the nineteen articles that make up Part II, or by forty five out of the seventy two numbered paragraphs. In addition, a State must agree to accept in entirety at least five of the seven core articles of the Charter. These are specified as those dealing with the right to work; the right to organise; the right to bargain collectively; the right to social security; the right to social and medical assistance; the right of the family to social, legal and economic protection; and the protection of migrant workers. But wide-ranging though these measures are, the integrity of the rights protected is undermined to some extent by the weakness of the enforcement machinery which relies on the scrutiny of biennial reports submitted by governments. Unlike the European Convention on Human Rights, there is no right of individual petition, and no hearing of complaints by bodies such as the European Court of Human Rights, although in November 1995, an additional protocol was added to the Charter providing, upon ratification by the Member States, for a system of collective complaints by international and national organisations of employers and trade unions and international non-governmental organisations.

1.26 Yet limited though their powers may be, in the 1980s and early 1990s the supervisory agencies responsible for the Charter have found Britain to be in violation of its terms on a number of grounds. In its latest Report (at the time of writing) the Committee of Independent Experts found that Britain was in violation of no less than fifteen of its sixty obligations under the Charter. In addition, the Committee deferred its conclusion as to Britain's compliance under five other paragraphs, pending the receipt of information from the government.[10] Yet although the failure to comply with the Charter is wide-ranging and the need for regulation correspondingly extensive, two particular issues stand out above all others, the first relating to pay, regulated by Article 4, and the second to the rights to organise, collective bargaining and strike, regulated by Articles 5 and 6. Both of these issues will need to be addressed by legislation if Britain is to be seen to be taking its obligations under the Social Charter seriously.

1.27   By Article 4(1) of the Charter the UK is required to recognise the rights of workers to a remuneration such as will give them and their families a decent standard of living. In its most recent Report the Committee of Independent Experts noted that Britain failed to comply with this most fundamental measure on the ground that as many as 21 per cent of all workers earned pay below the Council of Europe's decency threshold of 68 per cent of the national average wage. Admittedly this represented an improvement on 1989 when as many as 25 per cent of all workers and at least 50 per cent of all female workers were said to fall below the decency threshold.[11] Also on the matter of pay, the Committee of Independent Experts criticised the fact that low rates of pay amongst adults in the United Kingdom have had detrimental knock on effects for young people, whose average rates of pay have been said to be unfair. Questions have also been raised about the failure to comply with Article 4 (2) which seeks to guarantee the right to enhanced payments for overtime.

1.28   So far as trade union rights are concerned, the Committee of Independent Experts has endorsed many of the findings of the ILO bodies in relation to the trade union rights. This is true, for example, of the right to strike (which is expressly protected by Article 6(4), though not without limitation). Thus, in its last two Reports, the Experts found that Britain was in breach of Article 6(4) on two grounds, relating respectively to the lack of protection for workers dismissed in the course of industrial action on the one hand, and to the erosion of the immunities from civil liability for trade unions and their officials on the other. In its latest Report, the Committee endorsed the recommendations of the ILO Committee of Experts regarding amendments that must be made in order to bring Britain back into compliance with its international obligations on the right to strike. In particular the Committee highlighted lack of immunity for secondary

10. Council of Europe, European Social Charter, Committee of Independent Experts, Conclusions XIII-1, XIII-2.
11. Council of Europe, European Social Charter, Committee of Independent Experts, Conclusions XII-1, pp 92-4; and Conclusions XIII-1, p 12.

action, or for industrial action organised in support of individuals dismissed while taking part in unofficial action.

The European Union and Labour Law

1.29 Although the European Union is a continuing source of controversy in British politics, it is nevertheless difficult to escape the conclusion that Britain is now embedded in a wider legal and political community extending beyond the frontiers of the nation state. The social dimension of the Union, like other areas of its activity, is in a process of evolution. Yet it is already clear that we no longer have full control over the social policy agenda pursued by the Westminster Parliament. While the impact of the EU should not be exaggerated, nor should it be under-estimated, with developments at European level proving to be a welcome relief from the labour law deconstruction and deregulation since 1979. Indeed the extent to which Europe now operates as a counter offensive against the deregulatory pressures of British governments is indicated by the fact that the Trade Union Reform and Employment Rights Act 1993 was needed to implement no fewer than seven EC directives.

(a) European Labour Law
1.30 Although manifestly not established to protect the interests of workers, the EC Treaty nevertheless addresses social policy issues. Article 117 provides that Member States 'agree upon the need to promote improved working conditions and an improved standard of living for workers'; Article 118 provides that the European Commission 'shall have the task of promoting close co-operation between Member States in the social field', particularly in relation to prescribed matters which include labour law and working conditions; and Article 119 provides that each Member State shall 'ensure and subsequently maintain the application of the principle that men and women should receive equal pay for equal work'. But with the exception of the last of these measures they do not confer any directly effective rights for workers or their organisations. Nor do they authorise the Community institutions to introduce legislation in the social field, generally to be done under the authority of Article 100 which permits the making of directives in areas which 'directly affect the establishment or functioning of the common market'.[12]

---

12. See also Article 235 authorising the Council, acting unanimously on a proposal from the Commission, otherwise to promote 'one of the objectives of the Community'.

1.31 The early period in the history of the EU is said to have been dominated by a free market or neo-liberal philosophy, and it was not until the 1970s that significant social policy initiatives were taken for the first time, dealing respectively with equal opportunities and business restructuring (collective redundancies, transfer of undertakings, and insolvency). These led in turn to important changes in domestic law, both in terms of the improvement of existing protections and the creation of new ones, including the right of trade unions to be consulted before redundancies take place, the protection of workers in the event of the business for which they work being transferred, and the right of women to equal pay with men for work of equal value (and vice versa). In the 1980s, however, there were few concrete achievements, partly as a result of the veto of the Thatcher governments which were able as a result to prevent any significant labour market regulation at the community level, such as measures for the protection of part-time and temporary workers, which would contradict developments at home.

1.32 Many of these early 'Social Market' initiatives have been made much more effective as a result of the intervention of the European Court of Justice, while the role of the domestic courts in the implementation of these European Social Policy initiatives is not to be underestimated. In recent years, the ECJ has required the removal of financial limits imposed by domestic law on compensation for sex discrimination; it has ensured that public sector workers are protected by the Acquired Rights Directive (77/187/EEC) and its domestic progeny when their business has been transferred; and most recently it held that the employers' duty to consult with workers' representatives before collective redundancies or business transfers is not met by statutory provisions which require the employer to consult only with the representatives of recognised trade unions.[13] In the same spirit, the House of Lords decided in 1994 that the statutory restrictions on the rights of part-time workers to seek remedies for redundancy and unfair dismissal was in breach of the EC sex discrimination law.[14]

---

13. See respectively *Marshall v Southampton and South West Hampshire Health Authority* (No 2) [1993] ICR 893; *Sophie Redmond Stichting v Bartol* [1992] IRLR 366; *Rask v ISS Kantineservice A/S* [1993] IRLR 133; *European Commission v UK* [1994] IRLR 392,412.
14. *R v Secretary of State for Employment, ex parte Equal Opportunities Commission* [1994] 2 WLR 409.

(b) The Community Charter of the Fundamental Rights of Workers

1.33 In 1989, 11 of the then 12 Member States adopted the Community Charter of the Fundamental Social Rights of Workers. The Charter addresses a wide range of issues, including freedom of movement; employment and remuneration (including a requirement that all employment 'shall be fairly remunerated'); the improvement of living and working conditions; social protection for workers; freedom of association and collective bargaining; vocational training; equal treatment for men and women; information, consultation and participation for workers; health and safety at the workplace; and provision for disabled persons. Although the Charter had no formal legal status as such, it was nevertheless 'a new point of departure ', expressing the 'political will' that 'the completion of the internal market should not be achieved without taking the "social dimension" into account'.[15]

1.34 The Charter was accompanied by a Social Action Programme 'aimed at giving tangible expression'[16] to its principles, with all 47 initiatives announced in the Action Programme having been presented by the Commission. Not all of these required legislative action, but many did and as a result a number of new Directives were introduced. The process of implementing the Action Programme has been assisted by two major constitutional changes to the EC Treaty. The first of these, by the Single European Act of 1986, introduced Article 118A, thereby requiring a qualified majority only for the adoption by the Council of Ministers of measures designed to encourage improvements 'especially in the working environment, as regards the health and safety of workers'. This was used as the basis for the adoption of a number of instruments, including not only measures in the traditional areas of health and safety, but also the Pregnant Workers' Directive of 1992 (92/85/EEC), implemented in Britain by the Trade Union Reform and Employment Rights Act 1993.

1.35 More controversially, the Working Time Directive (93/104/EC) was adopted under the authority of Article 118A, thereby permitting the Member States to override the British veto. The Working Time Directive is important for a number or reasons. The first relates to its substance, with the Directive prescribing minimum daily rest periods, rest breaks, weekly rest periods, maximum weekly

---

15. European Commission, *European Social Policy: Options for the Union*. A Green Paper (COM (93) 551), p 10.
16. *Ibid.*

working time, annual leave entitlements, and the regulation of night work. Some of these measures are of the first importance, including a prescribed average working week not exceeding 48 hours as well as at least 4 weeks paid annual leave. But apart from thus extending the base of social protection, the Directive is important also in terms of the role anticipated for collective bargaining not only for the setting and implementation of standards, but also in permitting derogations, subject to certain prescribed conditions being met.

(c) The Maastricht Protocol and Agreement

1.36   The other major constitutional change is the Protocol on Social Policy concluded at Maastricht in 1992. This authorised 11 (of the then 12) Member States to use the institutions and procedures of the EC Treaty designed to implement an Agreement on Social Policy, concluded to develop 'the path laid down in the 1989 Social Charter'. It now covers 14 of the present 15 Member States, the exception being the UK. Under the Agreement, the Council was empowered to adopt, by qualified majority voting, directives and other instruments in a number of areas, including health and safety, working conditions, information and consultation of workers, and equality between men and women with regard to labour market opportunities. In a number of other areas the Council is empowered to act unanimously (though without Britain) on a proposal from the Commission, these including social security and social protection of workers; protection of workers on dismissal; and representation and the collective defence of workers' interests.

1.37   Article 2 (6) of the Agreement expressly provides, however, that it does not apply to 'pay, the right of association, the right to strike or the right to impose lock-outs'. This mirrors the provisions of the Action Programme of 1989 which offered no Community level instrument for dealing with what are perhaps the most fundamental of all labour law issues. Had rights been strengthened in these areas they would underpin some of the other provisions of the Maastricht Agreement. Of particular interest is Article 2(4), which provides that a Member State may entrust management and labour, at their joint request, with the implementation of directives. Of perhaps even greater interest are Article 3, which provides for the consultation of the social partners by the Commission 'before submitting proposals in the social policy field', and Article 4, which anticipates the possibility of norm setting at the Community level by collective bargaining. Thus social dialogue between management and labour may lead to 'contractual relations including collective agreements' which in turn may be implemented 'by a Council decision on a proposal from the Commission'.

1.38   The first measure to be introduced under the Agreement on Social policy is the EC Works Councils Directive (94/45/EC). This deals with the establishment of works councils in companies with at least 1000 employees in the European Union and with at least more than 150 employees in two or more member states. The initiative for setting up consultative machinery may be taken either by management or by 100 or more employees or their representatives. A special negotiating body representing the workers in the different Member States will then be elected or appointed, to determine with management 'the scope, composition, functions and term of office of the European Works Council or the arrangements for implementing a procedure for the information and consultation of employees'. In the event of a failure of the parties to agree on matters such as the composition, timing and functions of the EWC, a framework of minimum requirements is laid down as an Annex to the Directive, as most recently in the case of the Framework Agreement on Parental Leave.

(d) Implications for British Labour Law

1.39   Developments at EU level clearly have a number of important implications for British labour law. Although there are many who are critical of the scope of the EU Social Policy agenda on labour law matters (for example the exclusion of freedom of association and collective bargaining) and the lack of speed with which progress is being made, it remains the case that the EU has kept social policy issues on the political agenda and that significant steps have been taken in the fields of equal opportunities, health and safety and workplace consultation. And while it is true that for a number of reasons the immediate prospects for social policy appear uncertain,[17] there are nevertheless outstanding issues still waiting to be implemented, notably the Working Time Directive of 1993 and the European Works Council Directive of 1994 which could have a not insignificant bearing on the structure of domestic labour law in the future.

1.40   Yet the consequences of EU standards extend well beyond the need to introduce legislation to implement Community obligations. There are also more direct implications and opportunities for trade unionism and collective bargaining, including the need to

---

17. But see the suggestions for future legislative action in *European Commission, European Social Policy. A Way Forward for the Union.* A White Paper (COM (94) 333), pp 31-3.

adapt to new forms of workplace organisation; the extension of social dialogue as a source of community instruments; and the use of collective bargaining as a means of implementing community obligations and derogating from directives. These measures may help to stimulate trade union organisation, but they also suggest a need for strong trade union organisation and collective bargaining infrastructure if Britain is to play a full part in the development and implementation of European Social Policy. It would be fanciful at best to contemplate the possibility of standards being imposed by collective bargaining at European level when there is an absence of machinery for their effective implementation at home.

Conclusion

1.41   We propose then that labour law in the future should seek to promote five guiding principles. As a starting point it is necessary to ensure full and effective compliance with international labour standards, particularly those of the Council of Europe and the ILO. It is necessary also to ensure that our labour law complies with the requirements of EU labour law, but also that we are in a position effectively to implement European social policy. It may be necessary still further to entrench international labour standards as part of the constitutional law and practice of this country, though constitutional entrenchment of these treaties (however they are enforced) will not in itself provide the necessary framework of labour law which would promote our underlying principles, and our concern also to promote an efficient economy. The constitutional framework would be a useful starting point, but we turn now to consider the type of legislative framework which would be necessary if our goals are to be realised

Summary of Recommendations

1   Labour law should be underpinned by five key principles which seek to promote equality of opportunity, social justice, workplace democracy, civil liberties, and fairness at work.

2   There is a need for re-regulation of the labour market in order to reverse the trend towards greater social and economic inequality, but also to promote economic efficiency.

3   High labour standards are necessary to promote productive efficiency, worker efficiency, consumption and employment growth.

4   There is a need to ensure that British law complies with international standards established by the ILO and the Council of Europe, particularly ILO Conventions 87 and 98.

5   There is a need to re-ratify ILO Conventions denounced since 1979 and to review the ILO Conventions made since 1979, with a view to increasing the number ratified by the UK.

6   Britain must play a full part in the development of European Social Policy, and to this end must become a party to the Maastricht Agreement on Social Policy.

7   There is a need to ensure that British law complies with EC labour standards, and to this end measures such as the Working Time Directive should be implemented without delay.

8   International labour standards and European labour form an important background to, but are no substitute for, a comprehensive statutory framework of rights for workers and trade unions.

THE EMPLOYMENT RELATIONSHIP

2.1   The way in which the employment relationship is defined for legal purposes is of paramount importance in ensuring the effective application of employment rights. It serves to identify the categories of workers to which the substantive provisions of labour law apply, and to resolve conflicts between different sources of labour law, such as those between legislation and collective bargaining. The chosen model of the employment relationship must be one which is capable of providing a firm foundation to employment legislation, but must also be adaptable to a range of different needs and circumstances. The following specific issues need to be considered:

*   Which groups of workers should labour law aim to protect?
*   What should be the role of legislation and collective bargaining as sources of terms and conditions of employment?

These questions will be examined in this and the following two chapters. But in order to put our discussion in context, we begin by briefly outlining relevant developments in the law and practice of the employment relationship and then examine some general considerations relating to the legal form which the employment relationship may take.

The Need for Reform

2.2   The most striking feature of the law governing the employment relationship in Britain has long been its disorganised, uncodified quality. As long ago as 1898, the Webbs observed that the 'policy of prescribing minimum conditions, below which no employer may be allowed to drive even his most necessitous operatives, has been only imperfectly carried out', and argued for 'a systematic and comprehensive Labour Code, prescribing the minimum conditions under which the community can afford to allow industry to be carried on; and including not merely definite precautions of sanitation and safety, and maximum hours of toil, but also a minimum of weekly earnings'.[1] At the end of the twentieth century, the situation is in many ways remarkably similar. There is still no general minimum wage, no statute on working time and a patchwork quilt of regulation on health and safety, much of which continues to be specific to particular industries and occupations. The conceptual basis of the employment relationship remains the common law of the contract of employment, notwithstanding the growth, in the 1960s and 1970s, of employment protection legislation governing termination of employment, redundancy compensation and rights to income protection during periods of sickness, lay-off and maternity.

2.3 Extensive and complex as the employment protection legislation is, it in no sense constitutes a comprehensive framework for protection of the individual worker. Not only are certain essential issues such as minimum wages and maximum working hours not touched on at all in this body of law, but large numbers of individuals find themselves excluded from the protective scope of the legislation by strict qualifying conditions. The absence of laws on such key issues is the consequence, in part, of the reluctance of the state to legislate in areas already covered by collective bargaining between employers or employers' associations and trade unions. Direct statutory intervention on pay and hours was reserved for sectors of the economy in which voluntary collective bargaining was considered incomplete or ineffective (hence the wages councils), or for areas of regulation, such as health and safety, which had remained beyond the scope of joint regulation in industry (as in the case of the Factories Acts). This type of 'selective regulation' worked satisfactorily, in the eyes of many, as long as voluntary collective bargaining remained an effective source of protection in most industries and occupations. That is now no longer the case. The decline in multi-employer collective bargaining, which has been particularly rapid since the mid-1980s, and the resulting concentration of joint regulation on individual companies and establishments, means that collective agreements currently cover less than half the workforce, down from an estimated 70 per cent in 1980.

2.4 The other major cause of the present situation is the deregulatory policy pursued by the Government since 1979. This has led, as we have seen, to the denunciation of several ILO Conventions and the abolition of the wages councils, leaving agriculture as the only sector covered by a legally binding minimum wage. Controls over the working hours of women in industrial

---

1. S & B Webb, *Industrial Democracy* (1920 ed., p 767).

employment have also been repealed, together with limits placed on the hours of young persons. Statute now provides for maximum working hours only for those under the school leaving age (which under certain circumstances may be as low as 15 years, 8 months). Following the passage of the Deregulation and Contracting Out Act 1994, powers have been granted to repeal large parts of regulatory legislation by parliamentary order. As a consequence of these and related changes, Britain now makes the weakest provision for labour standards of any western industrialised country with the possible exception of the USA, with which it was ranked equally for this purpose by the OECD in 1994. However, even the USA has a statutory minimum wage at federal level and in many states, and even the United States has in place legislation designed to enable a majority union to secure recognition (or 'certification') from an unwilling employer, relatively ineffective though this legislation may be.

2.5   Changes beyond the law have also had important implications for the effectiveness of protective regulation. As numbers employed on a part-time or fixed-term contract basis have increased, so has the difficulty of applying employment protection legislation, which operates most effectively in the context of a full-time working week and a contract of indefinite (or 'permanent') duration. This is partly a problem of definition, since fewer workers now fall under the scope of the legislation in question, and partly of regulatory design, since the legislation tends to assume that full-time, continuous work is the norm. It is on this basis that the legislation in effect defends a notion of the 'normal' or 'standard' employment relationship, by requiring the employer to compensate the employee for interruptions to work and for the premature termination of the relationship. However, this type of relationship is becoming progressively confined to a minority of more secure, 'core' workers. Even in the case of many full-time workers, other forms of flexibility are undermining the basis on which employment protection legislation has been constructed. These include the practice of varying working hours on a daily or weekly basis, the extension of working hours without the payment of overtime premia, and the introduction of 'annualised' hours.

2.6   At the other extreme, the growing use of 'zero-hours contracts' means that many workers are now required to be available to the employer without any guarantee that they will either be called on to work or, if not, compensated for time spent at the employer's disposal in this way. Distance-working, in its various forms, is becoming more common, as is the practice of workers being contracted not directly to an employer, but through intermediaries such as employment agencies. Taken together, these developments mean that new forms of protection need to be devised, to cope with the growing variety of working arrangements which we are now seeing and with the blurring of clear divisions between working time and private time, and between the workplace and the home. In short, a major task of reconstruction in the area of basic employment rights would seem to be called for, to make up for the currently weakened state of voluntary collective bargaining and for the repeal of the selective statutory regulation under the Wages Councils Acts and Factories Acts. It should be the aim of labour law reform to establish a codified framework of basic rights for the employment relationship. At the same time, the goal of re-regulating the employment relationship is complicated by changes in the nature of employment itself.

Reformulating the Employment Relationship

2.7   The profound changes in the workforce and in the labour market which we are currently witnessing would seem to require an equally profound transformation in labour law's conception of the employment relationship. Traditionally, labour law has taken the individual *contract of employment* as the focus of its intervention. This has meant, on the one hand, accepting the contractual basis of employment, with its focus on the bilateral relationship of employer and employee, and, on the other hand, seeking to regulate the contract by superimposing on it a set of statutory obligations (or collectively-agreed terms and conditions) aimed at constraining the power of the employer. In the process, labour law has had to assimilate a large body of common law doctrine concerning such matters as the definition of employee status, the application of collective agreements, and the construction of the parties' mutual rights and obligations during performance, some express and some implied. Much of this common law doctrine has been in conflict with the protective goals of labour law. The tension which this has produced has hindered the development of a coherent body of principle within labour law and has often made it unnecessarily difficult to apply the law in practice. This tendency appears to be stronger in the case of labour law in Britain than in some other European systems, where the role of contractual concepts has been a more marginal one.

2.8   The starting point for any reform would be to recognise the worker's rights as citizen, as is the case in the labour law systems of several other EC Member States, as well as increasingly within

EU law itself (inspired by international law texts including the Constitution of the International Labour Organisation). A number of countries recognise the social and economic rights of the worker at a constitutional level. The Italian Constitution acknowledges 'all citizens' right to work' as one of a number of 'Basic Principles', and the Title of 'Economic Relations' contains references to the right to an equitable wage, the right to equal pay for equal work between men and women, the right to social assistance, the right to trade union organisation and the right to strike. The French Constitution also embodies the right to work, the right to strike and the principle of trade union freedom. Of similar importance in certain other systems are constitutional provisions which are general in character but which have acquired a particular meaning when applied to the employment relationship. The Basic Law of the German Federal Republic guarantees the 'Protection of human dignity' and states that 'Everyone shall have the right to the free development of his personality in so far as he does not violate the rights of others or offend against the constitutional order'. These provisions, together with Article 4 on freedom of opinion, conscience and religion, Article 5 on freedom of expression, and Article 6 on the protection of marriage and the family, have had an extensive influence on labour law.

2.9   Such developments are not as far removed from British experience as they might seem, notwithstanding that the UK will continue to lack, for the foreseeable future, the kind of constitutional provisions found in other Member States. British labour law already contains a model of the employment relationship which is closer to the concept of the worker as citizen than it is to the traditional contract of employment. This is found in UK anti-discrimination legislation, which in addition to protecting 'employees' employed under contracts of employment also benefits certain self-employed workers who contract to supply their personal labour or services to another, as well as applicants for employment. Rather than focusing exclusively on the contract of employment, then, this legislation takes a broader view which in addition to regulating rights at work is also concerned with the worker's rights to equal access to employment, training and professional development, and hence with rights at the level of the labour market. The example of UK anti-discrimination legislation also serves as a reminder that even with a constitutional framework which denies a place to a 'bill of rights' or similar basic text, it is possible to use legislation for the purpose of expressing certain fundamental rights, such as, in this case, the right to equality of treatment regardless of an individual's race or gender. We therefore propose that legislation should enunciate a set of fundamental guiding principles, to be applied by the courts in the interpretation of more detailed legislation and in the resolution of individual disputes. The principles would be those identified above (see paragraph 1.3), namely equality of opportunity; social justice; workplace democracy; protection of civil liberties; and fairness at work.

2.10   Within such a framework which builds upon the worker's rights as citizen, it is not clear what role there would be for the contract of employment, as traditionally conceived. It is clear to us that within the model of the employment relationship which we have in mind, the traditional contract of employment would cease to be the starting point for analysis. What we have in mind is an employment relationship which would contain certain guaranteed and inalienable rights and would be regulated by legislation and by collective bargaining on the various models described in the following chapters. This is not to deny that there may be scope for individual agreement on matters not covered by legislation or collective bargaining. Nor is it to deny that there may be workers in a position to conclude agreements with employers which exceed the requirements of statutes or collective agreements. However, the concept of a contract of employment which reserves to the employer implied, far-ranging powers of direction and control would cease to apply, being displaced by the notion of an 'employment relationship' based on reciprocal rights and obligations of both parties. We are of the view that as we move into the twenty first century it would be quixotic at best to continue to bed the employment relationship in a legal form developed in an earlier epoch.

2.11   What would this mean in practice? In the first place, clearly several attributes of contract would remain. This is true, for example, of the notion of an agreement to constitute or form the initial relationship. There would thus still be a need for an agreement to establish the relationship, though it may be that the terms of the relationship would be determined largely by collective bargaining and legislation rather than by the parties themselves. This is not to say that there would be no scope for personal agreement on terms between the parties to the relationship, as already explained; but this would be a secondary rather than a primary source of the terms governing the relationship. A further difference concerns the important role of terms implied by common law. At present, terms such as the duty of co-operation operate largely in favour of the employer. Such terms are a legacy of an earlier era of 'master and servant' relations. The rigidly hierarchical model of employment which they presuppose has no place in a modern system of labour law. Why, for example, should the employer have authority to introduce new technology without consultation or to require schoolteachers to cover for absent colleagues without expressly contracting for such powers? To the extent that the employment relationship is equivocal on any such point and in need of interpretation, this should be a task undertaken by an autonomous system of labour adjudication in which the adjudicator is directed expressly to have regard to a number of fundamental principles. As well as the five principles expressly referred to in paragraph 1.3 above, these would include the right to equality of treatment, the right to the dignity of the individual, and the right to autonomy at work.

Categories of Workers Protected by Labour Law

2.12 A principal benefit of adopting a broader definition of the employment relationship would be to extend the coverage of protective legislation to workers who are currently excluded from protection or whose status is in doubt. The scope of existing employment protection legislation is limited by the use of a narrow definition of employment status. Much of the Employment Rights Act 1996 applies only to those who are *employees*, that is to say those 'employed under a contract of employment' which for this purpose includes a contract of service or apprenticeship. This provision has been interpreted in such a way as to put in doubt the status of *casual workers* and *homeworkers*, amongst others. Nor does it cover those who work as *trainees*, for example under the Youth Training Scheme, without being *apprentices* in the strict sense of that term. Even where workers such as homeworkers or casual workers are able to show that they are employees for the purposes of the legislation, they are likely to encounter a second hurdle namely that most employment protection rights require a minimum period of continuity of service. Because of the casual nature of their employment this may be difficult to establish in some cases.

(a) 'Workers' and 'Employees'
2.13 Some of the legislation currently in force applies more widely to a *worker*, rather than to an *employee*. Under the Trade Union and Labour Relations (Consolidation) Act 1992 a 'worker' is described as (inter alia) 'an individual who works, or normally works or seeks to work - (a) under a contract of employment, or (b) any other contract whereby he undertakes to do or perform personally

any work or services for another party to the contract who is not a professional client of his...'. Sex and race discrimination legislation applies to 'employment under a contract of service or of apprenticeship or a contract personally to execute any work or labour' (Equal Pay Act 1970, section 1(6)(a); Sex Discrimination Act 1975, section 82; and Race Relations Act 1976, section 78); this legislation also protects applicants for employment, trainees (whether or not they have a contract of apprenticeship) and agency workers in their relationship with the user of their services. The Health and Safety at Work Act 1974 and the measures first introduced by the Wages Act 1986 also contain broad definitions of employment status. It is also true that in none of this legislation is there a concept of continuity of service or a requirement of a minimum period of employment.

2.14   The extended concept of the 'worker' which is already used in certain statutes can form the basis for a more effective, generally-applicable concept of the *employment relationship*. We propose that the core of rights contained in labour legislation should apply to an employment relationship defined for this purpose to mean anyone who undertakes personally to execute work or labour for another and is economically dependent on the business of the other. It would not, however, apply to the genuinely self-employed, that is to say those who contract to supply labour or services through a business of their own on which they are economically dependent; and secondly, those who contract to supply an end product without contracting to supply their own personal services or labour in producing or procuring it. If, however, our proposal for a new legal base for the employment relationship is rejected, we would propose that the scope of labour law should at the very least be extended to include *(i) those currently classified as 'employees', who work under a contract of employment; and (ii) those currently classified as 'workers', who work under a contract personally to execute work or labour and are economically dependent on the business of the other*. This should be wide enough to include trainees and apprentices on the one hand, and homeworkers on the other, though express provision could be made to include both. In appropriate circumstances (such as equal treatment legislation and certain collective rights, such as the right to strike) those who normally work or who are seeking work under one of the above arrangements would also be included in the scope of protection.

(b) Qualifying Periods

2.15   This wide definition of employment would have general and universal application in the field of labour law. As we have seen, however, there is a second hurdle to the effective operation of employment rights, namely the requirement of a minimum period of continuous service. The significance of the concept of continuity of employment has already been diminished by the decisions of the House of Lords in *R v Secretary of State for Employment, ex parte the Equal Opportunities Commission* [1994] 2-WLR 409 and of the Court of Appeal in *R v Secretary of State for Employment, ex parte Seymour-Smith* [1995] IRLR 465. Following the first of these decisions, the 8 and 16 hour weekly thresholds were abolished. The second decision puts in doubt the two-year qualifying period for unfair dismissal; at the time of writing the decision of the House of Lords is awaited. Whatever the outcome, it is clear that the application, in this context, of the principle of equal treatment of the sexes in EC law has limited the role of the strict qualifying conditions which previously excluded part-time workers and those without continuous service. We propose that the role of continuity of employment be confined, for the most part, to defining the proportion or extent of certain employment protection rights, by reference to service completed, as opposed to excluding certain categories of workers altogether as at present.

2.16 We are of the view that in principle the vast majority of employment rights under the Code would apply from day 1 of the employment relationship. There may be a case for a short minimum threshold period to deal with residual cases of very short-term service, where the application of employment protection legislation would impose undue administrative costs on the employer. But if this view were to prevail we would be concerned that a barrier would be erected which would make it difficult in many cases for casual workers and homeworkers to cross. Thus if a minimum period of one month were to be retained for access to statutory rights (as is currently the position with the written statement of particulars which the employer must issue to employees) it is possible to contemplate the situation where someone is recruited by an employer to work for periods of time each less than four weeks at a single stretch, but the arrangement continuing in this way over a period of years. In this type of case the worker in question might never accumulate sufficient continuity of service and so always fall outside the protection of the legislation. We therefore propose that in those cases where a minimum qualifying period is retained it should be possible for a worker to aggregate discrete periods of employment with the employer in order to accumulate sufficient continuity of service. This is a point to which we return in greater detail in paragraph 2.32 below.

Special Regulation of Particular Forms of Employment

2.17 A feature of most mainland European systems of labour law is the special regulation of particular forms of employment such as part-time work, fixed-term employment, homeworking and temporary or agency work. Agency work is also subject to such regulation in Britain (under the Employment Agencies Act 1973 and associated regulations, as amended by the Deregulation and Contracting-Out Act 1994), and homeworking was until the repeal of wages councils legislation in 1993. Fixed-term contract work and agency work are also regulated by the Temporary Workers Directive (91/383/EEC). The case for making specific provision for these forms of work is that regulations principally designed with full-time, indefinite duration employment in mind may be inappropriate for other forms of work, or may need to be supplemented in some respects. Further consideration should be given to extending the principle of specific regulation for flexible forms of work. The guiding principles should be those of proportionality in the benefits and protection accorded to individuals, and non-discrimination in the legal analysis and treatment of different forms of work.

(a) Self-Employment

2.18 As already pointed out those individuals who are economically dependent on their own business, as opposed to that of an employer, would not normally be protected by labour law (though this does not rule out a role for competition law, for example, in protecting small businesses and subcontractors against unjust terms or late payment of debts). Nor should labour law, as opposed to commercial law or competition law, be concerned with contracts to supply goods or services between companies or individuals which do not involve any element of personal service on either side. Indeed labour law standards would not normally be expected to apply on the one hand to those who contract to supply labour or services through a business of their own on which they are economically dependent, or on the other hand to those who contract to supply an end product without contracting to supply their own personal services or labour in producing or procuring it. At the same time, it should be clearly provided that labour law protection could not be evaded merely by the choice of the parties concerned or by a simple declaration of self-employment on the part of the worker. The scope for such evasion is currently restricted by the Employment Rights Act 1996, section 203, but there is a case for strengthening the precise formulation of the provisions in question. Nor should it be possible for labour law protection to be deflected by an individual worker's decision to supply his or her labour through an intermediary company, while still, in practice, being subject to the direction of the ultimate employer.

(b) Part-Time Workers

2.19   The removal of the 8 and 16 hour thresholds in employment protection law is an important step which should ensure access by part-time workers to the employment protection legislation. But these reforms apply only to statutory rights in the sense that part-time workers will be entitled, for example, to receive a written statement of terms and conditions of employment, and will have a right not to be unfairly dismissed and to receive a redundancy payment. Yet there are many outstanding issues which need to be addressed relating in the main to contractual benefits and contractual terms and conditions. It is true that the different contractual terms for full-time and part-time workers may not be unlawful as violating the principle of equal treatment in EC law, but this does not exclude the possibility of specific regulation of the position of part-time workers and the introduction of specific measures designed to ensure that they are entitled to the same benefits and advantages as full-time workers in the enterprise where they may be employed, albeit on a pro rata basis.

2.20   It is well known that a number of initiatives have been taken at the European level to seek to extend the legal protection of atypical workers including part-time workers. Two directives proposed in 1991 would have provided part-time workers (defined to mean 'employment relationships involving shorter working hours than statutory, collectively agreed or usual working hours') equal treatment on a range of matters with other workers in respect of employment and working conditions. This includes on the one hand access to vocational training and the social services normally made available to other workers, and on the other hand 'entitlements to annual holidays, dismissal allowances and seniority allowances'. There were also important proposals for employers to consult with workers' representatives when proposing to 'have recourse to' part-time staff, for employers to draw up regular reports on part-time employment, and for part-time staff to be informed of any full-time vacancies which may arise. Although these measures were stillborn, a new initiative has recently been taken by the European Commission.

2.21   We propose that legislation should be introduced in this country to ensure that part-time workers are extended equal treatment with their full-time colleagues. It is open to question, however, whether a definition of a part-time worker is necessary and whether it would be enough simply to say that all workers regardless of hours worked are entitled to be treated equally (on prescribed matters) on a pro rata basis. It is open to question also whether it is necessary to specify in respect of what incidents of the employment relationship this should apply. In our view, the principle of equal treatment between full-time and part-time workers should apply in respect of all aspects of the employment relationship unless a case can be made for the exclusion of any particular matter either generally or specifically in the case of a particular industry or sector, in which case it should be the subject of collective bargaining. We also propose the adoption of obligations of the kind contemplated by the 1991 draft directives in terms of consultation with workers' representatives about the use of part-time workers and the regular reporting about the role of part-time workers in the enterprise.

(c) Agency Workers

2.22 A growing area of concern relates to the role of employment agencies. The role and form of regulation is complicated by the fact that the nature and activities of employment agencies may vary. On the one hand the agent may operate as a true agency, that is to say for the purposes of recruiting workers who then form a direct and conventional relationship with an employer, who pays a fee to the agency for the service provided in finding staff. But on the other hand the agency may employ the worker who is supplied to a third party, in which case the traditional functions of the employer are split between two entities: the functions of payment and control are found in the agency, operating itself as a business, but the services provided by the employee are enjoyed by another - the client, who pays a fee to the agency for this benefit. There is evidence that the phenomenon of agency employment in this latter form is increasing, partly as a result of legislation and judicial decisions which have extended greater rights for part-time employees and other staff. The employer who chooses to use staff who are legally employed by an agency is, in effect, 'contracting-out' the responsibilities he or she otherwise would have as a (direct) employer, while continuing to retain the benefits he or she derives from the performance of work by the individuals concerned.

2.23 Why should this matter? In some cases, it may not. The use of agency labour is a perfectly appropriate way of meeting short-term fluctuations in demand. But there are signs that the use of agency labour may be spreading beyond this and other 'traditional' areas of fluctuating labour demand. It may be, in some instances, becoming the permanent basis on which certain types of labour are provided. This raises important issues for those concerned with ensuring minimum labour standards and organisational rights in the workplace. If legislation imposes minimum standards on employment, then this usually operates by way of requiring observance of these standards by an employer. For example, if statute imposes a minimum wage set in terms of £x per hour, either generally or by reference to a particular sector, this would usually be expressed in terms of obliging an employer, either in general or in the relevant sector, to pay a certain amount to those whom he or she employs. But if a user of labour in the relevant sector chooses to buy in labour services via an agency, then there is no contractual link between the user and provider of labour services on which the minimum standard can bite. Instead, the minimum standard has to be imposed on the contract which the worker has with the agency which provides his or her services to the user.

2.24 There can be little doubt that, as statutory controls on employment conditions are seen as more onerous by employers, the use of agency labour becomes an increasingly attractive alternative way of delegating responsibility for the observance of such standards to another. It is not, however, just a matter of the availability of statutory rights. Trade unionism in these circumstances will face a much more difficult challenge. And, of course, the obligations which an employer owes to staff in respect of trade union activities cannot be required of him or her by those who are in law employed by another. A further problem may arise because of the way agencies use technology to compile lists of individuals available for work. Computers make it easy to hold large databases of staff and these may be compiled on a nation-wide basis. If the situation should arise where, in any particular sector, one or more agencies become established as the leading providers of staff to employers (as, for example, may currently be happening in relation to part-time teaching staff in the further education sector) then inclusion on an agency's database becomes, in effect, a requirement of obtaining work in that capacity. In such a situation, where agencies will be controlling entry into employment, there is a need to ensure that their decisions are responsibly and fairly taken. For example, individuals should not find themselves excluded on grounds of trade union activities.

2.25 While agencies do useful and valuable work in matching needs and availability, there is scope for the better regulation of their activities and for the better protection of workers whom they engage. One way of supervising the activities of employment agencies is by developing a mechanism already in existence. The Employment Agencies Act 1973 provides for the regulation of the conduct of employment agencies, but the controls imposed could be taken further - for example to limit exclusions from recruitment on specified grounds and to require the observance of minimum terms for the employment of staff. It is already the case that under the Sex Discrimination Act 1975 and the Race Relations Act 1976 employment agencies may not discriminate on the grounds of sex or race respectively in the provision of any of their services, which presumably means services to workers as well as clients. There is a case for monitoring the position to determine whether provisions of this kind need to be extended to ensure that people are not excluded from an agency list unreasonably, particularly where the agency occupies a monopoly or dominant position in a particular labour market.

2.26 This in turn raises questions about the nature of the employment relationship which agency workers have and who is responsible for the observance and application of minimum employment standards. We are of the view that where workers are supplied by an agency, there should be a statutory presumption that the worker in question is engaged in an employment relationship by both the agency and the client which will thus both be directly responsible jointly and severally for all liabilities arising from any employment relationship. The presumption could easily be rebutted in the case of an agency of the first kind described in paragraph 2.25 above. The possibility that both the client and the agency may be liable is particularly important in the case of termination of an engagement by the client. At the present time if the client terminates the services of the worker without good cause, he or she may have no remedy in respect of the dismissal unless he or she were an employee of the client, which may not always be easy to show. Although the worker might (though might not) be an employee of the agency, he or she would have to resign from the agency in order to pursue a remedy and might not in any event be successful where the fault lay with the client. A provision that an agency worker is deemed to have an employment relationship with both the agency and the client will go a long way to ensure that there is better protection.

(d) Casual Workers and Homeworkers

2.27 A specific problem arises in the case of those workers who have no fixed hours of work, but who may be called upon by the employer as and when work is available. This is a category most likely to include casual workers and homeworkers, who as we have seen encounter problems establishing that they are 'employees' for the purposes of the employment protection legislation as it is currently drafted. The adoption of our proposal for an 'employment relationship' to replace the contract of employment, failing which the extension of the coverage from 'employees' to 'workers', would go a long way towards ensuring that these workers were within the protective environment of labour law. This would not, however, resolve all the problems likely to be encountered, particularly if a qualifying period for any of the aspects of the legislation were to be retained. If on the other hand there is no qualifying period, employers will almost certainly complain that they are being exposed to unacceptable liability. The position is in fact extremely tricky, raising difficult questions about the balance to be struck between fairness and flexibility. Just how far should casual workers be protected?

2.28 On the one hand if there is no qualifying period for the purposes of statutory entitlements, could this mean as a result that a casual worker would be eligible for all the benefits under the legislation, notwithstanding the casual nature of the engagement? This is likely to be felt particularly acutely in the area of unfair dismissal if it was to mean that an action for unfair dismissal could be brought at the end of each casual engagement, even though there is a possibility that the engagement will be renewed at some indeterminate time in the future. It might be appropriate to avoid this risk and to mitigate the worrying implications for employers. Thus at least in a dismissal case the adjudicating body could be directed to have regard to the casual nature of the employment in determining whether any dismissal was fair or unfair. Industrial tribunals are already directed to have regard to the size and administrative resources of the business in determining the fairness or unfairness of a dismissal (Employment Rights Act 1996, section 98). An additional obligation of this kind would allow the adjudicating body to strike a fair balance between the conflicting needs of both parties, so that it would be unlikely (though not impossible) that a dismissal would be held to be unfair by virtue only of the fact that a casual relationship had been terminated.

2.29 On the other hand, if there is a minimum qualifying period for the purposes of statutory entitlements, this could operate to exclude casual workers who may have been engaged by an employer intermittently over a number of years, without any single engagement and without the most recent engagement exceeding the minimum qualifying period for access to the employment protection measure in question. Under the current regime in some cases it may be possible to treat any gaps between periods of service as not breaking and indeed as counting towards continuity of service (Employment Rights Act 1996, section 212). This would require the worker to show that he or she was absent 'on account of a temporary cessation of work', which may be possible in some but unlikely in all cases. The problem could, however, be resolved by adopting our recommendation in paragraph 2.16 that a worker be permitted to *aggregate* periods of service (perhaps within a defined period) with an employer in order to meet the qualifying threshold, rather than be required as now to show a minimum period of *continuous* service. This ought to be possible in respect of any statutory right where a minimum qualifying period is retained.

2.30 It would, of course, always be possible to have in place a special regime for casual workers. Regardless of whether or not a qualifying period for any purpose is retained (and assuming that it does not exceed several months) it would be possible to provide that the right to bring an action in respect of the disputed matter does not apply in respect of a person who was engaged for a period which was not likely to exceed, say, 12 weeks. In principle this could apply to some though not all statutory provisions, with a number of exceptions relating, for example, to the statutory minimum wage, race and sex discrimination and dismissals relating to trade union membership. Although casual workers would be regarded as 'workers', such a regime would nevertheless operate to deny such workers access to many provisions of employment legislation, particularly if on the one hand there was also no opportunity to aggregate periods of service, and if on the other hand the adjudicating bodies were directed to have regard to the casual nature of the relationship. We are strongly of the view, however, that an exclusion of this kind would not be justifiable in principle and would tend to exclude a category of workers who are perfectly entitled to expect that they will be protected by the law.

(e) Fixed Term Contracts

2.31 A final issue for consideration concerns the legitimacy of employing workers on fixed-term contracts. As the law currently stands, there are no obstacles to the parties to the employment relationship agreeing to a contract for a fixed term or duration. The law provides that upon the expiry of that term, the failure to renew the contract is a dismissal (although not necessarily an unfair one);

however, the parties are free to contract out of the protections provided by the law on unfair dismissal and on redundancy compensation, in return for the employer granting the employee a minimum fixed term of one year and two years respectively. Again, no reason or justification for doing so need be offered. The supposed quid pro quo for contracting-out - the guarantee of a minimum duration of one or two years - is illusory, since the employer remains free to insert a term into the contract entitling him or her to determine the contract by notice before the term has expired. Nor (a few exceptions aside) can any claim for unfair dismissal or redundancy be brought if the employee, at the time of the dismissal, has not amassed two years of continuous employment (subject to the review of the two-year qualifying period by the House of Lords in *R v Secretary of State, ex parte Seymour-Smith* [1995] IRLR 465, which at the time of writing is yet to take place).

2.32 This situation is unsatisfactory: employers are provided with a relatively cost-free means of avoiding some of the key provisions of employment protection legislation. The insertion of waiver clauses into terms and conditions of service is standard practice in large areas of the public sector, while the practice is growing in the private sector of dismissing workers a short time before they acquire the two years' service necessary to bring a normal unfair dismissal claim. To some extent, these problems will be mitigated by any reduction of the qualifying period. But as a general principle we see no justification for a legal regime which permits employers to require workers to sign away their legal rights as a condition of employment. As was pointed out to us in one of our meetings the waiver clause is a device which authorises the employer to act unfairly. We agree with this view and propose that it should not be possible for workers to contract out of the legislation whether the employment is for an indefinite duration or for a fixed term. In making this proposal we appreciate the bona fide reasons which drive some employers to adopt the practice of the fixed term contract with waiver clauses. We are not convinced, however, that they bring greater security to the good employer acting fairly than would in any event be permitted by the courts and tribunals.

Summary of Recommendations

1 It should be the aim of labour law reform to establish a codified framework of basic rights for the employment relationship.

2 There is a need for a far-reaching reform in the way the employment relationship is constituted and regulated, in order to avoid the pitfalls of the traditional concept of the contract of employment.

3 The starting point for such a reform would be the notion of the *worker's rights as citizen* which is recognised in the labour law systems of several other EC Member States, as well as increasingly within EC law itself.

4 The employment relationship should be reconstituted on a new conceptual basis, under which the primary sources of norms would be collective agreements and legislation.

5 Labour law should apply to an *employment relationship* defined for this purpose to mean anyone who undertakes personally to execute work or labour for another and is economically dependent on the business of the other.

6 Labour law should not apply to the genuinely self-employed, that is to say those who contract to supply labour or services through a business of their own on which they are economically dependent, or those who contract to supply an end product without contracting to supply their own personal services or labour in producing or procuring it.

7 In the absence of a new legal base for the employment relationship, the scope of labour law should be extended generally to include *(i) those currently classified as 'employees', who work under a contract of employment; and (ii) those currently classified as 'workers', who work under a contract personally to execute work or labour and are economically dependent on the business of the other.*

8 Express provision should be made to ensure that trainees and homeworkers are covered by any general definition of a worker for the purposes of the legislation.

9 Specific regulation is required to deal with the growing variety of working arrangements which are developing and with the

blurring of clear divisions between working time and private time, and between the workplace and the home.

10 The vast majority of employment rights should apply from day 1 of the employment relationship. There may be a case for a short minimum threshold period to deal with residual cases of very short-term service.

11 Where a minimum qualifying period is retained it should be possible for a worker to aggregate discrete periods of employment with the employer in order to accumulate sufficient continuity of service.

12 It should be clearly provided that all protective terms of the employment relationship (whatever their source) apply to all workers regardless of length of service and regardless of the number of hours worked. Where appropriate, benefits should be conferred pro rata on part-time workers and those with short term service.

13 There may be a case for specific regulation for flexible forms of work, but any such regulation should be guided by the principles of proportionality in the benefits and protection accorded to individuals, and non-discrimination in the treatment of different forms of work.

14 Where workers are supplied by an agency there should be a statutory presumption that the worker in question is engaged in an employment relationship by both the agency and the client, the two of which will thus both be directly responsible jointly and severally for all liabilities arising.

15 It should not be possible for workers to waive their statutory rights. Therefore it should not be possible to contract out of the legislation, whether the employment is for an indefinite duration or for a fixed term.

SETTING EMPLOYMENT STANDARDS

3.1   How can labour standards best be established? In a recent consultation document on *A New Economic Future for Britain*, Labour's Economic Policy Commission proposed that 'The government has the responsibility for defining minimum standards, including through legislation'. But this is also a responsibility which traditionally has been discharged by collective bargaining, both here and in other European countries, and is a responsibility which it is contemplated will continue to be conducted by collective bargaining by the architects of European Social Policy, as the Working Time Directive (93/104/EC) makes abundantly clear. This provides not only for the setting of standards by collective agreements but also for the derogation from prescribed standards by collective agreements. There are, however, a number of matters which will need urgently to be addressed if collective bargaining rather than regulatory legislation is to continue to be the dominant method of standard-setting in British workplaces.

Collective Bargaining: Decline and Decentralisation

(a) General Trends
3.2   The first of these matters relates to the declining coverage and decentralisation of collective bargaining, with only a minority of British workers now covered by agreements. The decline in collective bargaining coverage has in fact been one of the most significant developments in the last 17 years, and appears to be without parallel in any of the other OECD countries, a recent survey concluding that 'the decline in collective bargaining has been most pronounced in Great Britain'.[1] Collective bargaining coverage in Britain has fallen from an estimated 70 per cent in 1980 to an estimated 47 per cent in 1990 and the position is in fact worse when we take into account

---

1   'Collective Bargaining: Levels and Coverage', in *OECD Employment Outlook 1994*, chapter 5.

that at least another 11 or 12 per cent were covered by wages council orders, pushing joint regulation up in excess of an estimated 80 per cent, perhaps as high as 85 per cent. On this basis coverage has in fact fallen to an estimated 47 per cent from an estimated 80-85 per cent since 1980. But not only is our decline the sharpest, we are as a result among the OECD countries with the lowest levels of collective bargaining coverage. To put the matter in perspective, coverage in Australia stood at 80 per cent, Finland 95 per cent, France 92 per cent, and Germany 90 per cent.

3.3   Related to this is the decentralisation of collective bargaining, now extending from the private sector into the public sector as well. This has seen the break up of national or sectoral bargaining arrangements (with only 1 in 10 workers in the private sector now thought to be covered by multi-employer bargaining arrangements) and a greater emphasis on enterprise based bargaining. One reason why this is important is that collective bargaining decentralisation is sometimes associated with low levels of coverage, with a recent OECD study pointing out that '[c]ountries characterised by single-employer bargaining tend to have lower coverage rates compared with countries where bargaining is conducted at higher levels and where employer organisations and union federations are strong'. Although decentralisation is also a feature of bargaining developments in other countries, 'there has been great variation between countries in the nature and extent of decentralisation of industrial relations and of employers' flexibility initiatives'.[2] But few countries it seems have gone as far as we have, and even as late as 1994 the OECD survey could record that 'in a majority of OECD countries the sectoral level has remained the principal arena for wage determination'.[3]

(b) The Reasons for Decentralisation
3.4   The decline in sector level bargaining, which has been

---

2   A Ferner and R Hyman, *Industrial Relations in the New Europe*, (1992), p xxi.

3   So, for example, in Germany decentralisation has taken place in the form of devolved bargaining which has been accommodated 'within existing procedures at enterprise level, and has been embedded within a solid structure of national and industry-level arrangements'. This is in marked contrast to Britain where decentralisation, in contrast to most European countries, has been paralleled by what Crouch refers to as a 'collapse of associational control', and hence 'multi-employer bargaining'. See Ferner and Hyman, *op. cit.*

developing since the 1960s, has taken two forms. First, as already indicated, there has been the complete abolition in many sectors of multi-employer agreements, a trend that has gathered pace since 1979. In parts of the private sector this trend away from multi-employer bargaining has since 1979 coincided, to some extent, with another. This is a tendency for employers to create more devolved and decentralised arrangements organised on the individual workplace, division or business unit. Where this has occurred, however, the employers concerned nevertheless retain considerable central control over pay settlements. But even where multi-employer bargaining has remained, a second symptom of decentralisation has been the reduction in the regulatory effect of agreements, most notably through a movement towards the specification of 'minimum' rather than 'actual' pay rates.

3.5 This two-fold process of decentralisation has been influenced by a variety of factors. Notable among them have been a desire on the part of employers to bring their bargaining and human resource strategies into line with more devolved management structures; a wish to link pay more closely to rewards; a desire to develop locally more flexible working patterns; and in the public sector, political initiatives and pressures designed to create less centralised institutional structures, introduce greater competition and allow pay better to reflect local labour market and operational conditions. Such developments have influenced both the level at which bargaining takes place and the content of the agreements concluded. Where multi-employer bargaining has been dismantled or where larger employers have withdrawn from such bargaining, initiatives have often been taken substantially to revise grading systems and working patterns, and introduce a variety of incentive pay arrangements, both within and between different parts of the business. The same is true, although probably to a lesser degree, where single-employer arrangements have been decentralised.

(c) The Equivocal Benefits of Decentralisation

3.6 These changes may be of financial benefit to the employers concerned in terms of contributing to increased labour flexibility and productivity, greater employee commitment, and reduced unit labour costs. However, the changes may not always have beneficial consequences in the longer run. In particular, the decentralisation of bargaining may:

* reduce the power of unions and hence enable employers to worsen terms and conditions of employment and to compete more through low labour costs rather than more efficient capital investment;
* by leading to a multiplication in the number of 'pay decision points', create the potential for an inflationary pay spiral in tight labour market conditions, a consideration which may explain, for example, why NHS Trusts are consulting other trusts when determining local pay; and
* in the case of the decentralisation of single-employer bargaining arrangements, act, as part of a more general devolution of human resource management, to reinforce the already ad-hoc and short-term nature of human resource management within many UK-based organisations.

3.7   Nor can the desirability of decentralisation be assessed purely on the grounds of the financial benefits to particular companies. The issue also raises important questions about the quality and standards of living of workers and families. Two related points arise here. The devolution of bargaining structures, by creating more isolated and smaller bargaining units, creates a greater potential for derecognition and may make membership loss more likely to arise as a result of member disillusionment and direct employer pressure. Secondly, as already pointed out, the abolition of multi-employer arrangements acts to reduce the degree of union regulation in the labour market, because such agreements have always also tended to affect pay and conditions in both non-union and non-affiliated organisations. Indeed, as the OECD study points out, the density of collective bargaining coverage is likely to be significantly lower in countries with decentralised bargaining systems. In view of these and other problems associated with decentralised bargaining arrangements we recommend that steps be taken to re-establish multi-employer bargaining structures.

The European Dimension

(a) European Social Policy

3.8   An important dimension in the current debate is European Social Policy where we find a number of sometimes conflicting pressures at work. On the one hand, there is little if any legal support for the making of Community instruments for the protection of trade unions and collective bargaining. Although these matters are dealt with in the Community Charter of the Fundamental Social Rights of

Workers of 1989, the procedures provided by the Maastricht Agreement on Social Policy do not apply to 'the right of association, the right to strike or the right to impose lock-outs', though they do apply to the 'representation and collective defence of the interests of workers and employers, including co-determination'. Indeed to the extent that there is direct legal support for workplace or worker representation this has been largely on the basis of company or enterprise rather than sectoral based initiatives, and it has been on the basis also of forms of representation which do not guarantee a role for independent trade unions. This last point was most vividly illustrated by the requirement to consult workers' representatives in the event of a collective redundancy or transfer of an undertaking even where there is no recognised trade union, an obligation which was used by the British government to undermine the rights of trade unions in the Collective Redundancies and Transfer of Undertakings (Protection of Employment) (Amendment) Regulations 1995 (SI 1995/2587).

3.9   On the other hand, however, another thread which is clearly emerging is the possibility of making and implementing Community instruments by a process of social dialogue or collective bargaining. It may seem strange that the Community should anticipate the use of collective bargaining for the making of standards and that the Commission should anticipate the use of collective bargaining for the implementation of standards without seeking also to put in place an infrastructure of Community law which would better facilitate both of these developments at national level. Nevertheless, the process of social dialogue as a source of Community law is now clearly established by the Maastricht Agreement on Social Policy while it seems to have been widely accepted before then that collective agreements could be used to implement Directives, a practice which was adopted in a number of European countries including Denmark and Italy. It would, however, be extremely difficult for collective bargaining to be used as an effective way of transposing EC Directives in this country in view of the erosion of sectoral bargaining arrangements, which is an important precondition of such a strategy, as also is the capacity to extend agreements to the non-unionised sector.

(b) Social Dialogue

3.10 The Agreement on Social Policy imposes a duty on the Commission to promote the consultation of management and labour at Community level and to take measures to facilitate their dialogue.

To this end, the Commission is required to consult the social partners 'on the possible direction of Community action' as well as on the content of any proposed Community action. It is also provided, however, that where management and labour so desire, 'the dialogue between them at Community level may lead to contractual relations, including agreements'. Agreements concluded in this way may be implemented in one of two ways, 'either in accordance with the procedures and practices specific to management and labour and the Member States' or in some cases 'at the joint request of the signatory parties, by a Council decision on a proposal from the Commission'. The latter method of enforcement can be used only in respect of matters which are covered by Article 2 of the Agreement, this including health and safety, working conditions, equality between men and women, and protection from dismissal. A Declaration appended to the Agreement expressly provides, however, that there is no obligation on Member States to apply the agreements directly or to work out rules for their transposition.

3.11   At the time of writing one agreement has been made under this procedure though it has not yet been implemented. This is the Framework Agreement on Parental Leave (96/34/EC), which provides for three months parental leave (for each parent) following the birth or adoption of a child, the right of workers to return to their job after parental leave, and time off work for urgent family reasons. The Agreement leaves much of the detail to be implemented by legislation and/or collective bargaining, but in the case of Britain it is clear that these decisions would have to be taken by Parliament which, in the absence of an adequate collective bargaining infrastructure, will be the principal vehicle for the implementation of this and other instruments made under the procedure, which at the time of writing does not of course apply to the United Kingdom. Many will regard it as paradoxical that we should be bound to rely mainly on legislation (primary or secondary) to implement the fruits of the collective bargaining process.

(c) The Transposition of Community Instruments
3.12   Under Community law it is thus possible not only for standards to be made by collective bargaining, but also for standards to be implemented by collective bargaining. This is true of several instruments including, for example, the Working Time Directive (93/104/EC) which lays down minimum standards in terms of minimum daily rest periods, rest breaks, weekly rest periods, maximum weekly working time, and annual leave. The Directive provides that it may

be implemented either by laws or by agreement between the two sides of industry. It also provides for the possible derogation from standards 'by means of collective agreements or agreements concluded between the two sides of industry at national or regional level or, in conformity with the rules laid down by them, by means of collective agreements'. That is to say 'Derogations at enterprise level are to be shaped by framework agreements at national or regional level'.[4] In Member States where there is no statutory system for collective bargaining at national or regional level, derogations may also be allowed by collective agreements concluded between the two sides of industry 'at the appropriate collective level'.

3.13 It is not suggested that it would be impracticable to implement this or other Directives without sectoral bargaining arrangements. It is clearly possible for legislation again to be the primary vehicle for the carriage of Directives into domestic law in the usual way and for derogations to be made at enterprise level by collective agreements, this increasingly being the appropriate collective level in this country for the concluding of such agreements. But although this would be feasible and indeed inevitable unless there are reforms to the bargaining machinery, this would be to impose a heavy load on legislation, and it would encourage the adoption and application of the barest of minimum standards. It would also be a wasted opportunity for the social partners in each sector to take responsibility for the transposition of these obligations in their own sector, in a manner which more accurately reflects the needs and experience of employers and workers in the sector in question. Transposition in this way is not necessarily secured at the expense of flexibility within enterprises, for it is clearly contemplated that the possibility for further derogations can be devolved by the terms of a sectoral agreement to individual enterprises.

Rebuilding Collective Bargaining Structures: Initiatives and Opportunities

(a) Strategies for Reform

3.14 If collective bargaining is thus to re-assert a dominant role it may need, as a matter of urgency, some form of State support, and in view of the extent of the decline, the scale of that support may have to be substantial. But this raises a second problem which relates

---

4 B Bercusson, *Working Time in Britain: Towards a European Model*, (1994).

to the form of State support. If the goal is to expand the coverage, the obvious solution would be to seek to turn the tide and re-assert the importance of sectoral bargaining arrangements, while also retaining arrangements which already exist. Such a strategy appears to have a number of possible benefits in the sense that it would contribute in no small way to the principles of equality of opportunity (to the extent that there is evidence that the gender pay gap may be smaller in countries with more centralised bargaining arrangements), social justice (to the extent that workers covered by collective bargaining are on average more favoured than those who are not covered and to the extent that there is thus likely to be a higher level of coverage of a wide range of benefits), and workplace democracy (to the extent that it is suggested by some commentators that centralised pay determination is likely to reduce employer resistance to a trade union presence in the company, perhaps more likely still if devolved flexibility bargaining were to be permitted.

3.15   This is not to deny that there are other ways of restoring trade unionism and collective bargaining. Another possible strategy is to adopt the enterprise based recognition strategy currently favoured by the TUC in its policy document, *Your Voice at Work*, published in 1995, in which it is proposed that new rights of representation and recognition should be introduced for trade unions, · the nature of these rights depending to some extent on the level of support or membership which the union has in a particular enterprise. This is an important initiative and indeed, in chapter 7, we make broadly similar proposals, albeit with significant differences of emphasis. Yet although this strategy is clearly of the first importance in seeking to promote our principle of workplace democracy, we are concerned that it may not be the most efficient way of extending the frontiers of collective bargaining and the benefits which collective bargaining will bring in its wake for those who are currently excluded from the process. So although there is clearly a role for such a strategy, it may well be that the enterprise based strategy for collective bargaining is best seen as supplementary to a model based on more direct measures designed to stimulate sectoral bargaining or standard setting arrangements.

(b) Enterprise-based Initiatives: Some Problems

3.16   The limitations of an enterprise based initiative are perhaps self evident. In the first place it requires a tremendous investment of resources by trade unions to organise individual workplaces, an effort all the greater for the fact that one in five workers is now employed in businesses which employ no more than ten people. Secondly an enterprise based approach requires a tremendous effort of resources for potentially little reward: under the TUC proposals a union will be entitled to bargaining rights only if it has majority support; anything less will yield consultation rights only. And thirdly an attempt by an enterprise based approach to pick off employers one at a time is bound to meet employer resistance and in turn litigation which is calculated to draw the teeth of any such strategy. It is also the case that comparative evidence provides a salutary warning. Is it only a coincidence that the only major OECD countries with levels of collective bargaining density lower than the UK are also countries with a legal strategy based largely on an enterprise based model? Thus collective bargaining density stands at 18 per cent in the United States, 23 per cent in Japan, and 38 per cent in Canada, reinforcing the concerns that an enterprise based strategy as the primary vehicle for the extension of collective bargaining is not calculated to be an unqualified success.

3.17   There is thus a strong case on efficiency and equity-related grounds for taking steps to counter recent moves towards the greater decentralisation of collective bargaining structures and the undesirable consequences flowing from it. These steps should ideally place limits on the degree to which terms and conditions can be driven downwards and would enhance the institutional position of trade unions. They should also seek to eliminate destructive wage competition between firms. There are a number of ways by which this could be done, and here we explore three possibilities. The first is by the extension of 'minimum standards agreements'; the second is by an adaptation and refinement of what we believe to be the current proposal for a Low Pay strategy; and the third is the introduction of some mandatory sectoral bargaining obligation which might be particularly appropriate in the public sector and the privatised utilities, participation in which might be made obligatory on the part of individual companies. We do not offer these suggestions necessarily as separate options, for the cumulative impact of them all operating simultaneously would be helpful. We therefore propose that all three strategies should be actively pursued.

(c) Minimum Standards Agreements

3.18   The first possibility is for the extension throughout industry of collective agreements setting down minimum standards (the minimum standards agreements strategy). If this could be successfully engineered, perhaps with appropriate incentives, it would be especially desirable for a number of obvious reasons. A recent example of such an initiative is provided by reports that the TUC was seeking meetings with the leading employers' organisations (the CBI, the Institute of Directors, the Institute of Management, and the British Chambers of Commerce) with a view to setting minimum standards at work in order to prevent good employers being undercut by the bad, and to explore ways by which employers and trade unions can implement standards agreed at European level. In the case of the latter this was said to include the making of agreements on matters such as parental leave and working time, with the law operating as a safety net. The aim is to provide a floor below which no worker would be allowed to fall[5], the strategy being explored more fully in the TUC's 1996 paper, *Rebuilding Job Security*. This is self evidently also an important initiative which provides clear evidence of the value of multi-employer initiatives as means of promoting social justice in the workplace and transposing European standards.

3.19   But it remains to be seen how far voluntary initiatives of this kind can be taken, and at least one of the employers' organisations mentioned is reported as having responded in a sceptical vein. Apart from the fact that the initiative grows out of an enterprise based initiative, the problem is that agreements of this kind are most likely to be concluded by those employers who least need to have them in the sense that it is they who are already observing more than adequate standards. There is thus the question of how any minimum standards agreement of this kind could be introduced into sectors where they are most likely to be needed but most likely to be resisted, and where they are introduced how they could be extended to employers who have no wish to be bound by their terms. At least in the latter case it may be difficult to contemplate the extension of agreements without some form of legal intervention in the form of the procedures once contained in Schedule 11 of the Employment Protection Act 1975. And it is difficult to be optimistic about the operation of such legal support which is not being used to extend national agreements into the unorganised sector but much more elusive 'general' or 'common' standards.

(d) The Low Pay Strategy

3.20   Also relevant in this context is the low pay strategy which is proposed by the Labour Party. Although the precise details at the time of writing are uncertain, this involves the creation of a Low Pay Commission with responsibility for fixing a statutory minimum wage.

---

5   *Financial Times*, 29 February 1996.

Proposals published at the time of writing suggest that the Commission will be tripartite in composition, its members presumably appointed by the Secretary of State, and suggest also that its recommendations as for example on the level of the minimum wage, will not necessarily be binding on the government. It is unclear whether the Commission will be asked to set a single flat rate of universal application, or whether it will be empowered or indeed required to set sectoral, occupational or geographical variations. It is also unclear whether it will be empowered to deal with matters other than pay. Is it possible, for example, to regulate pay without regulating in some way the question of working time? Questions will also arise as to the legal status and enforcement of the Commission's recommended minimum, though if adopted by the government any recommendation could presumably be implemented by way of statutory instrument and constitute an enforceable minimum below which no one would be permitted to fall.

3.21 Although not conceived to do so, the low pay strategy is capable of metamorphosing into something much more ambitious and much more comprehensive in order to deal with the problem of declining collective bargaining coverage and in order to relieve the State of its responsibility of direct regulation of working conditions through legislation. There are thus two opportunities provided by this strategy. The first relates to the issues which the Commission is asked to deal with. As already suggested, these need not necessarily be confined to pay, for even if the Commission is to concentrate its efforts on the low paid, there is no evidence to suggest that pay is the only matter for which the vulnerable need standards to be regulated by a body such as the Commission. Obvious candidates for inclusion would be working time and parental leave. The second opportunity relates to the possibility that this Commission could perform these tasks through what might be called sectoral chambers or councils, so that rather than having a flat rate or common term for every worker in the country, there are sectoral variations which are sensitive to the needs of the each particular industry or sector. If this approach were adopted it would be possible to build up the sectoral chambers or councils slowly with the emphasis initially on those sectors where there is no effective collective bargaining.

(e) Rebuilding National Bargaining Arrangements

3.22 A third possibility is legislation requiring multi-employer bargaining arrangements to be established. A refinement of this, which could perhaps be combined with other strategies, is to require national bargaining to be conducted in the public sector and selected industries, notably the privatised utilities. Yet despite the social benefits, despite the fact that it happens elsewhere, and despite the importance of collective bargaining as a method of workplace regulation, it would be very ambitious to seek to re-assert the primary role of sectoral bargaining more generally. In the first place it would require a commitment to reconstruction as great as that demonstrated in 1917, but without the spectre of Communism haunting Europe to drive the engine of reform. Secondly, it would mean setting up collective bargaining machinery in every industry, at a time when organisation on the employers' side appears to have weakened if not disintegrated. Thirdly, it would mean confronting rather than appeasing the resistance of employers at a time when there is no ideological stomach for such a fight and no obvious political capital to be gained in picking one.

3.23 These problems indicate that a determined effort to re-assert the primacy of sectoral bargaining in Britain would be a heavy load for our voluntary system to bear and a great deal to contemplate. In the absence of a strong political commitment, it is open to question whether it could be done without the support and co-operation of employers, and there is no evidence of any enthusiasm on their part for such structures. Indeed the opposite appears to be the case, with William Brown pointing out for example that '[e]mployers' determination to remain with single-employer bargaining if they are to have any sort of bargaining is strongly implied by their rejection of existing forms of employer collaboration'.[6] Further evidence of employer resistance to the idea was indicated some time ago in the CBI report of 1991 on UK Inflation Performance which was clearly of the view that it would be unrealistic to turn back the tide given the trend towards decentralisation in the 1980s. Despite the admitted advantages of a highly centralised system of pay bargaining, they thought it more sensible and in keeping with current practices and institutions, to enhance wage flexibility by moving more rapidly towards decentralisation in pay determination, taking advantage in the process of the weakened market power of trade unions. Mindful of these difficulties, we nevertheless propose that steps be taken to

---

6. W Brown, 'The Contraction of Collective Bargaining' (1993)
   31 BJIR 189.

explore the possibility of rebuilding national bargaining arrangements.

Sectoral Employment Commissions

3.24 There are thus a number of steps which could be contemplated with a view to re-establishing sectoral determination of working conditions. There are also a number of problems standing in the way of any such initiative. A more radical approach still, perhaps more accurately reflecting the urgency of the current situation, is to build on all three of these possible initiatives in order to construct more directly by legislation the conditions in which sectoral regulation may take place. We have in mind here the possibility of sectoral bodies being established by statute, provisionally to be called Sectoral Employment Commissions, both empowered and obliged to regulate the working conditions in the industries in questions. We recognise that such a proposal will be regarded by some as radical and far reaching. We recognise also that such a proposal would have to confront some quite formidable practical hurdles in order to be capable of implementation and that these difficulties should not be underestimated. So be it. We regard the current position of decline and under-coverage of collective bargaining to be one which requires such radical steps with an accompanying determination to see them implemented.

3.25 It is important here to consider at least some of the problems which would have to be faced before an initiative of this kind could be introduced. First and most obviously, the economy would need to be divided into a number of sectors for this purpose, a huge administrative task particularly when the economy does not neatly divide into identifiable sectors. Quite apart from the mechanics of the operation who would be its engineer? Secondly, there is the question of who would sit on these commissions and what would happen if employers refused to participate: would the procedure be mandatory or consensual? Thirdly, there is the question of the functions and duties of these Commissions and what would happen if they were unable to reach an agreement on any particular matter: who would resolve any disagreements between the parties? Fourthly, there is the question of the status of any agreement or award which is made, and the related question of to whom it would apply: would it apply to everyone in the sector in question or only to union members or only to workers of employers in some way engaged in the process? And finally, there is the question of flexibility: would employers and workers be bound by a rigid framework when their own local needs called for a different set of arrangements?

(a) A Comprehensive and Universal System of Regulation

3.26   What we have in mind is a framework which introduces a procedure for the joint regulation of working conditions for every sector of the economy. In this sense the proposals are for a structure which is comprehensive and compulsory rather than selective and voluntary in its operation. It would clearly be possible for a procedure of this kind to operate so that a Sectoral Employment Commission would be set up only where there is no meaningful collective bargaining in the sector in question, as was the case with the wages councils, now abolished. In this way the procedure would operate as a fall-back to benefit those workers not otherwise protected by collective bargaining arrangements. It would also be possible for the procedure to operate on the basis of a request from either representative trade unions or employers (or jointly by both) for the setting up of a Commission. Where this was done it would be necessary to ensure that there was also some procedure in place for those sectors where there are adequate collective bargaining arrangements to ensure that the fruits of the bargaining process were enjoyed equally by all those employed in the sector in question. This would mean the re-introduction of a procedure such as that contained in Schedule 11 of the Employment Protection Act 1975.

3.27   Although it would thus be possible to move cautiously in this way our proposals eschew such an approach in favour of a comprehensive scheme which aims to ensure that every worker is covered by some form of mechanism for the joint regulation of working conditions. Where such sectoral schemes already exist we would anticipate that they would form the basis of any sectoral commission under our proposed legislation. There would thus be a minimum of disruption, with a possible extension of the jurisdiction of existing voluntary bodies. Where there are industries with active and effective enterprise bargaining, this would continue largely unaffected by our proposals in the sense that the minimum standards laid down by the Commissions would always be capable of improvement by autonomous enterprise based collective bargaining. Although we propose a universal and comprehensive structure, we do not anticipate that the Commissions would necessarily all operate in the same way, any more than did the old National Joint Industrial Councils. Much would depend on the level of maturity of the relationship between the parties concerned. Some would operate as collective bargaining fora, especially where a particular Commission simply reflected an existing collective bargaining structure. Others would not and would simply be standard setting bodies, perhaps with differences to be resolved on a regular basis by a third party.

(b) Sectoral Division of the Economy

3.28 Perhaps the most difficult question which this procedure presents is how to identify the different economic sectors for the purpose of regulating terms and conditions of employment. This is a matter on which we had some initial reservations and about which we consulted widely at home and overseas. Our initial doubts were, however, overcome by the strength of some of the points which were put to us. Quite apart from the desirability of this initiative in principle, it was suggested that any practical problems could easily be exaggerated but just as easily be overcome. Thus it was pointed out that initiatives of this kind had already been adopted in this country and that there were at one time no fewer than 63 joint industrial councils and 33 wages councils, operating for the most part on a sectoral basis. It was also pointed out that initiatives of this kind have been introduced in other countries with some degree of success.

3.29 In the light of the foregoing we believe that, given the political will, it would be possible to construct effective sectoral machinery for the regulation of working conditions for every worker in the country. We accept that there will be difficulties in identifying distinct sectors of the economy, that any attempt to do so will inevitably be rather arbitrary, and that there will be difficulty in classifying the service sector in particular. These problems are not, however, in our view strong enough to outweigh the advantages of sectoral regulation of working conditions. We, therefore, propose that a statutory framework should be introduced and that a statutory obligation be imposed on ACAS, failing which on a new public body, the Industrial Relations Commission, to divide the workforce into sectors for the purpose of the joint regulation of working conditions. In our view, any such Industrial Relations Commission should be tripartite in nature, its members to be appointed by the Secretary of State with representation of both sides of industry, its work to be completed within one year of its appointment. Steps should be taken to eliminate, avoid or mitigate the danger of judicial review of the work of the Commission, which should be restricted in accordance with our proposals in paragraph 10.24 below.

(c) Composition of the Sectoral Employment Commissions

3.30   It would be the duty of ACAS or the Industrial Relations Commission to appoint the members of the Sectoral Employment Commissions. We propose that these should be bilateral in nature, with representatives of the employers and workers in the industries in question. In the case of employer representation, we anticipate that where there is an employers' association in the industry in question, at least some if not all of the representatives would be nominated by the employers' association. For this purpose, we note that in 1995 there were 114 employers' associations listed with the Certification Officer and at least another 114 unlisted. Where there is no employers' association or one which is not representative of the industry as a whole, it would be open to the Commission to seek representatives from representative employers, and it is for consideration whether the Commission should be directed to ensure that there was adequate representation of small businesses on any Sectoral Employment Commission.

3.31   On the workers' side, we would anticipate that the workers' representatives would be drawn from organisations representative of workers in the industry in question. Essentially this means trade unions and in most cases it may mean more than one trade union being represented on the Sectoral Employment Commission in question. An obvious objection to trade union representation in all cases is that in some industries only a minority of workers may be trade union members, while in others the level of membership may be infinitesimal. In these cases it may be said that the trade unions have no mandate to conclude agreements which will apply to the workforce as a whole. We recognise that some may see this as a matter for concern, but are fortified first by the view that it would misunderstand the role of the trade union in the process, and secondly by the evidence from other countries where not dissimilar arrangements exist. In this forum trade unions are acting in a regulatory rather than a representative capacity in the same way as would any employer who participates and who would not as a result have a mandate to speak for other employers in the sector in question.

(d) The Functions of the Sectoral Employment Commissions

3.32   So far as the functions of the Commissions are concerned, we anticipate that these would be wide-ranging. Primarily the duties would be fivefold:

*   The setting of minimum terms and conditions of employment

* The transposition of EC Directives
* The development of equal opportunities policies and strategies
* The training of people employed or intending to be employed in the industry
* The provision and regulation of pensions for those employed in the industry

In many of these areas the Commissions would build upon statutory minima which would apply to all employment relationships, and which would continue to be particularly important for those workers, who for one reason or another, fell outside the scope of one or more Sectoral Employment Commission. Statutory standards of the type described in chapter 4 would also be important to regulate activities other than those prescribed matters with which the Commissions would be required to deal.

3.33 The five duties of the Sectoral Employment Commissions could be increased over time, though it should not be overlooked that they are already extensive. Under the first heading they could be required to deal with matters such as

* specifying a single minimum hourly rate of pay and overtime premium;
* establishing a framework for the design of performance related pay systems;
* laying down minimum standards concerning such matters as hours of work, holidays, and sick pay;
* establishing procedures for the introduction of new technology; and
* developing framework procedures for dealing with grievances and discipline

We have already given some indication of the instruments which could be implemented under the second heading, including most notably the Working Time Directive (93/104/EC) and the Framework Agreement on Parental Leave (96/34/EC). Clearly this list of matters could expand significantly if the spate of European law is to continue, though we acknowledge that there would necessarily continue to be an important role for legislation in the transposition of community standards. So far as issues relating to equal opportunities, training at work and pensions are concerned, these are dealt with in more detail in chapters 4 and 5 below.

(e) The Resolution of Disputes

3.34 It is possible that the list of issues covered in paragraph
3.33 above should not necessarily be dealt with in the same way.
Thus, it may be that some of these matters should be mandatory,
that is to say that the Commissions should be required to regulate
on the matters in question regardless of the views of the parties
concerned. This could be true of a minimum wage, training and
occupational pensions. The remaining issues could be elective, that
is to say that the Commissions would be required to deal with them
only at the request of one of the parties. Therefore, it would be open
to the trade unions on a Sectoral Employment Commission to insist,
for example, that the Commission deal with occupational sick pay.
There would, however, be no obligation on the part of a Commission
to set minimum standards on any of these elective issues, unless
there was an interest in doing so by one or other of the parties: it
would thus be open to the parties to agree in effect that some matters
are to be dealt with at the level of the enterprise. (It is also for
consideration whether the transposition of EC Directives should be
mandatory or elective, and, if the latter, whether the government
should have a power to direct a commission to set a standard.)

3.35 In the case of mandatory issues, the Commission would
thus be required to set minimum standards. In the case of elective
issues, we anticipate that it would be open to either party represented
on the Commission to raise matters for consideration and to seek to
strike a fresh agreement on the matters falling within the jurisdiction
of the Commission. But what happens if the parties fail to reach an
agreement after an issue has been raised for consideration? In order
to deal with disagreements of this kind we anticipate that each
Commission should be encouraged to develop its own procedures for
resolving disputes, failing which any failure to agree on any matter
falling within the jurisdiction of a Commission could be referred by
either party to the Central Arbitration Committee for resolution. An
award of the Central Arbitration Committee would have the same
status as a sectoral employment agreement and could be varied only
by such an agreement or by another award of the CAC. It would also
be open to either a trade union or the employers to take whatever
sanctions seemed appropriate to press or resist any claims, subject to
any restrictions on doing so which may be contained in chapter 7 below.

*(f) The Scope and Effect of Sectoral Employment
Agreements and Awards*

3.36 A further question which arises for consideration relates to the scope of the sectoral employment agreements. In our view the terms of the agreement should not apply only to those employed by employers, or members of the trade unions, who are in some way participating in the process, but should apply to everyone working in the sector in question. The agreements would operate in the same way as wages council orders under the Wages Councils Act 1979 to the extent that they applied to everyone covered by the order in question. There would thus be no need at this point for the reintroduction of something along the lines of Schedule 11 of the Employment Protection Act 1975 to ensure the extension of sectoral employment agreements: they would apply automatically to everyone working in the industry in question without any further formality. This is not to say, however, that there may not be a case for a modified Schedule 11 type of procedure where the general level of wages in any particular trade or industry exceeds the norm established in a sectoral employment agreement, a point to which we return in paragraph 3.38.

3.37   So far as the legal effect of a sectoral employment agreement is concerned, we do not propose that the agreement itself should be a legally binding agreement on those who make it. There is little to be gained by such a requirement. We do, however, recommend that the terms of the agreement should be automatically enforceable, as terms of the employment relationship, by anyone to whom it applies, and enforceable as such by the individual worker or by a trade union acting on his or her behalf. This would be the case, for example, in respect of any terms relating to pay, working time and holiday entitlement. We recognise, however, that there may be terms of sectoral employment agreements which impose duties on employers but which may not be designed to confer identifiable rights directly on individual workers. This would be true, for example, of any procedures for implementing equal opportunities programmes, or for the provision of facilities for training, or perhaps aspects of the arrangements made for pensions. In these cases it ought to be possible for an interested worker, trade union or employer to seek an order of the Labour Court to compel the employer to comply with his or her obligations under the agreement.

(g) Sectoral Employment Agreements and Workplace Flexibility

3.38   The final question relates to the possibility of derogation from the terms of the sectoral employment agreement. Here we propose that the terms of a sectoral employment agreementshould be such that they impose a non-derogable minimum below which workers in the sector in question should not be permitted to fall. Clearly there would be no objection in principle for any employer to provide a level of benefits in excess of the agreed minimum and we would not wish to prevent such practices developing. We would, however, add two caveats, the first being that any departure from the agreed minimum should be consistent with the principles of equality of opportunity, a matter to which we return in chapter 5 below. And secondly, there is the question of departures taking place from the agreed norm to such an extent that the 'general level' in terms of pay or other conditions was in excess of the prescribed minimum. As already suggested, in these cases it ought to be possible for those workers left behind to invoke a procedure like the old Schedule 11 procedure to pull themselves up to the general level in question. Ideally this is not a problem which any Commission should allow to develop and indeed any drift of this kind is something to which their attention should be drawn in setting new terms.

3.39 The real problem, however, is not the question of more favourable terms being imposed by an employer, but the reverse, that is to say whether it would be possible for an employer to vary the employment relationship by observing less favourable terms than those set down in the sectoral employment agreement. This is clearly a matter of some difficulty but we see no objection to it in principle provided a number of safeguards are met. In practice a flexibility package may improve on some matters in the sectoral employment agreement and offer less favourable provision on others. We see no reason why packages of this kind should not be negotiated collectively at local level. There may also be good reason related to immediate market conditions why a particular employer may wish to derogate downwards from the agreed minima and again we would not necessarily wish to say that this should be prohibited if the alternative was to be redundancy. We would, however, propose that any derogation downwards from the agreed minima, to any extent should be permitted only by a collective agreement with an independent trade union, in accordance with the procedure described in chapter 7 below.

Conclusion

3.40 We are of the view that fundamental steps are required to reform the institutional framework within which standards are set at the work-place. There is a need above all for the more centralised determination of working conditions on a sectoral basis to help ensure the widespread coverage of minimum terms which are relevant to the sector in question. To this end we believe that a number of initiatives should be encouraged, though we are also of the view that there is a need for a more radical initiative of the kind which we set out in this chapter. It is only in this way we believe that we can ensure universal coverage of benefits and at the same time give a much needed shot in the arm to the collective bargaining process. Clearly there will be objections that in seeking to re-establish this type of structure we are swimming against the international tide which is moving inexorably in the direction of deregulation, decentralisation and enterprise flexibility.

3.41   We are not unmindful of this concern, though we note that the Social Dialogue procedures in the Maastricht Agreement go some way to indicate that there is still seen to be an important role for more centralised standard-setting arrangements. We are, however, acutely aware that the tide has already advanced much further in this country than in others in mainland Europe. Our concern is to establish a procedure which will create a decency threshold below which no worker should be allowed to fall and from which enterprise based collective bargaining would be possible to introduce whatever flexibility was required. Our concern then is to combine decency with flexibility, but in a manner which will give trade unions a key role in the setting of employment standards, trade unions providing the only institutional form which provides a genuine opportunity for workers to have an effective say in determining the terms and conditions by which they are employed and ensuring that agreed terms and conditions are complied with.

Summary of Recommendations

1   Steps should be taken to re-establish multi-employer bargaining structures.

2   Steps should be taken to promote the extension by voluntary means of Minimum Standards Agreements throughout different industrial sectors.

3   When it is established that collectively agreed terms and conditions of employment are commonly applied in a particular sector, it should be possible for a trade union to seek the extension of the common terms to all workers in the sector in question.

4   The proposed Low Pay Commission should be adapted to permit the establishment of minimum rates of pay and the regulation of other issues (such as working time) on a sectoral basis. Any terms and conditions determined by the Commission should apply to all workers in the sector in question.

5   National pay bargaining should be required in all public sector activities, and sectoral bargaining should be required in the privatised utilities, such as water, electricity and gas. National agreements should apply automatically to all workers in the sector in question.

6   In the longer term every worker in this country should be covered by a collective agreement concluded at the sectoral level. With this in mind there should be established by statute Sectoral Employment Commissions with responsibility to promote collective bargaining and to regulate minimum terms and conditions of employment within specific industrial sectors of the economy.

7   A statutory framework should be introduced and a statutory obligation imposed on ACAS, failing which a new public body, the Industrial Relations Commission, to divide the workforce into sectors for the purpose of the joint regulation of working conditions. The arrangement would be universal and comprehensive in its nature but would incorporate existing bargaining arrangements.

8   The Industrial Relations Commission should be tripartite in nature, its members to be appointed by the Secretary of State for Employment with representation from both sides of industry, its work to be completed within one year of its appointment.

9   The Sectoral Employment Commissions should be bipartite in nature with representatives of employers on the one hand and workers on the other. Employers' representatives would be nominated by representative employers' associations where these existed and workers' representatives would be nominated by trade unions in the sector in question.

10 Steps should be taken to ensure the proper representation of small businesses in each Sectoral Employment Commission, and of workers who are employed by small businesses.

11 Sectoral Employment Commissions would have responsibility
for the following matters

* The setting of minimum terms and conditions of employment
* The transposition of EC Directives
* The development of equal opportunities policies and
  strategies
* The training of people employed or intending to be employed
  in the industry
* The provision and regulation of pensions for those employed
  in the industry

In addition to these prescribed matters, the Commissions
would have the option to deal with any other matter which the
members thought appropriate.

12 The terms of any Sectoral Employment Agreement should
apply automatically to govern the employment relationship of
any worker employed in the sector to which the agreement
relates. The terms would be enforceable as such by individual
workers or by trade unions acting on their behalf.

13 To the extent that a Sectoral Employment Agreement imposes
obligations on employers which do not directly govern the
employment relationship, these should be enforceable by the
Labour Court at the suit of a worker, a trade union or another
employer.

14 The terms set by the Sectoral Employment Agreements would
be minimum standards only. It would be possible for an
employer and worker to agree to an improvement on the
sectoral minimum in any respect, provided that the conditions
relating to equality of opportunity in chapter 5 below are met.

15 It should be possible to derogate downwards from the agreed
minima to any extent, but only by a collective agreement with
an independent trade union, in accordance with the procedure
described in chapter 7 below.

STATUTORY REGULATION OF THE EMPLOYMENT RELATIONSHIP

4.1   This chapter is concerned with the substance of the minimum statutory standards which ought to govern all employment relationships. In the previous chapter we proposed that so far as possible terms and conditions of employment should be set mainly by collective bargaining or by some kind of joint regulation involving trade unions and employers. But even if this was successful in restoring the levels of collective bargaining density, this would not exclude the role of legislation in directly setting minimum standards with which all employers would be required to comply. In the first place, it would be desirable to set a benchmark which would guide those involved in the bargaining or standard setting process; secondly, it would be necessary to deal with those employers, who for one reason or another are excluded from the process; and thirdly, there is the need to address matters which may be excluded from the bargaining or standard setting agenda. It is also the case that the procedures we have in mind in the foregoing chapter would take time to establish and that in the meantime there would be a need to set minimum standards by legislation.

The Statement of Written Particulars

4.2   Under the Employment Rights Act 1996, an employer has a duty to provide each of its employees with a written statement of particulars of employment. This obligation was reinforced by the provisions of the EC Directive on an employer's obligation to inform employees of the conditions applicable to the contract or relationship of employment (91/533/EEC), which required a number of amendments made to the UK legislation in 1993. Under the law as it now stands employers are required to issue employees with a statement within eight weeks of beginning work, which must include details about a wide range of issues relating to the employment relationship. It should contain particulars of the names of the parties, the date when the employment began, and the date when the employee's period of continuous employment began. The statement should also contain particulars relating to remuneration, working time, holidays, sickness and injury, notice required to terminate the relationship, the job title or a brief description of the work for which the employee is employed, the place of work, and any collective agreements which apply to the employment, as well as other information. Apart from the fact that the obligation to issue a statement applies only to employees, the only major exclusion is in respect of those who are employed for less than a month.

4.3   In our view this is an appropriate and important measure which can only help to increase transparency in the employment relationship. It is true that the 1993 reforms produced a rather complex set of interlocking requirements, which it may be possible to simplify without going against the Directive. But in principle we are of the view that there should be more information about the terms of the relationship rather than less, and at various points throughout the text we highlight information which ought to be included in the written statement issued to workers. In terms of the information which is currently required, we are of the view that employers should be required to give particulars of the job title *and* a description of the work which the worker is engaged to perform. There should be no choice of one or the other, and the description should not be 'brief'. We are also of the view that it should not be possible for the employer to reserve in the statement or elsewhere a residual power to require the worker to perform any other unspecified task, whether it relates to the job or not. In terms of new information, this would apply, for example, to training opportunities, matters relating to workers' civil liberties, equal opportunities policies, and rights in respect of trade union membership, activities and representation.

The Regulation of Wages and Remuneration

(a) A Statutory Minimum Wage

4.4   Article 4(1) of the Council of Europe's Social Charter of 1961, which is binding on the UK, provides that member states should recognise 'the right of workers to a remuneration such as will give them and their families a decent standard of living'. In interpreting Article 4(1), the Committee of Independent Experts appointed under the Social Charter has developed the notion of a 'decency threshold' of 68 per cent of average earnings as a benchmark level for legally-binding minimum wages. Prior to abolition in 1993, the rates set by the UK wages councils were well below this level, in a range of between 40 and 50 per cent of the average wage of blue-collar workers. Also important is Article 5 of the European Community Charter of Fundamental Social Rights which states that 'all employments shall be fairly remunerated ... in accordance with the arrangements applying in each country' and goes on to provide, inter alia, that 'workers shall be assured of an equitable wage, i.e. a wage sufficient to enable them to have a decent standard of living'. Although there is no immediate prospect of the EC adopting a legally-binding measure on minimum wages which might give effect to Article 5 in the near future, in part since issues of 'pay' are excluded from the procedure for adopting legal instruments under the Social Policy Agreement of the Maastricht Treaty, the principle contained in Article 5 is one which should command respect.[1]

(b) Setting and Enforcing the Statutory Minimum Wage

4.5   The level at which a national minimum wage is set is clearly the responsibility of the government. Although we propose that the Council of Europe decency threshold should be taken as a benchmark, we also recognise that this is a goal to be achieved over the medium to long term. In the short term, however, questions will arise as to the precise level at which the minimum wage is to be set. Current political proposals include the creation of a Low Pay Commission (which we would prefer to call a Fair Wages Commission), although substantially the same result could be achieved by the government convening an annual meeting of interested parties to review the rate of the minimum wage. But whatever institutional framework is adopted, we propose that the national minimum wage should be set by government, following consultation with, and if possible the agreement of, the TUC and the CBI. Ideally the TUC and the CBI would conclude an agreement which the government (although formally not bound to do so) would implement by way of legislation. We propose that the minimum wage be reviewed annually and that it would be possible to implement any revision by secondary legislation.

---

1   Further guidance may be found in the Commission Opinion on an Equitable Wage of September 1993 which calls on Member States to improve the collection and dissemination of information and to consider legislation to ensure that the right to an equitable wage is protected, with particular reference to the avoidance of discrimination, the treatment of homeworkers and mechanisms for the establishment of negotiated minima and the strengthening of collective bargaining arrangements.

4.6   In terms of setting the minimum wage, a number of questions arise for consideration. First, should there be sectoral variations with a national minimum fall back? We already indicated in chapter 3 the potential of such an initiative. Secondly, should there be different rates for young workers? This is permissible under international standards, and is common in systems with statutory minimum wage regulation. However, any decision to set separate rates must be sensitive to issues of equity and to the danger of young workers being exploited as a source of cheap labour. Thirdly, there is also the question of working time. We propose that there should be an overtime rate where workers are employed in any week for more than a prescribed number of hours, the overtime rate being a minimum of one and a half times the statutory minimum wage. Finally, there is the question of part-time workers who in our view should qualify on a pro rata basis with other workers, which in our view means that they would be entitled to premium payments for working longer than their normal hours.

4.7   So far as enforcement of the national minimum wage is concerned, this would be a right to which every worker would be entitled to rely on and to enforce. We deal with the enforcement of rights in chapter 10. Here it may be enough to say that the primary method of enforcement would be by way of complaint to a Labour Inspector who, after making inquiries, would be empowered to make a compensation order to cover back pay where there is evidence that the statutory minimum wage has been not been paid. Any order of the Labour Inspector would be enforceable in the same way as an order of a court and there would be a right of appeal from the Labour Inspector to the Labour Court. Labour Inspectors would have the right to intervene on their own initiative (perhaps following a routine inspection of the premises) or when called upon to do so by a worker or any other interested party.

(c) Fair Wages

4.8   Under Schedule 11 of the Employment Protection Act 1975 (repealed in 1980), unions (or employers' associations) could lodge claims for 'recognised terms and conditions', and, in their absence, for 'the general level of terms and conditions'. Recognised terms and conditions were effectively those laid down in relevant collective agreements. Given the decline in multi-employer bargaining, the potential for such claims to be revived under a new Schedule 11 procedure has been reduced. In chapter 3, however, we propose the introduction of measures which would have the effect of rebuilding multi-employer bargaining arrangements. We propose that minimum standards should be established in this way, leaving open the possibility either that some employers will seek to evade these agreements, or that bargaining will take place beyond the terms of the agreement so that the pay provisions of sectoral agreements may bear little relationship to actual earnings. In these cases we see a potentially important though perhaps residual role for a fair wages strategy which allows for the extension of collective agreements or for the extension of the going rate or general level in the industry in question.

4.9   We therefore propose that a Schedule 11 framework be re-introduced, which would enable complaints to be brought by unions *and* individual workers. The re-introduction of a right to claim that terms and conditions are below the prevailing 'general level' in a sector in particular would provide a valuable means of affording protection to vulnerable groups of workers and also of enabling unions to assist members in workplaces where they have not managed to obtain recognition. However, three issues surrounding the utilisation and operation of the procedure require further consideration:

*   should the right of complaint provided to individual workers be restricted to those not covered by enterprise bargaining arrangements?
*   should the general level be assessed in relation to the terms and conditions applying in workplaces where unions are recognised for bargaining purposes or in relation to those applying in all relevant workplaces?
*   to what extent could the relevant adjudicating body take into account factors such as the profitability of plants and companies, employers' product market prospects, and questions of labour efficiency?

These are matters which require further discussion and analysis. However, they do not detract from the central proposition that a legal mechanism of some kind may be needed to reduce excessive earnings disparities between firms within sectors.

The Protection of Wages

4.10   An important function of labour legislation is to protect workers' wages. The need for protection arises in two quite different situations: the first relates to arbitrary deductions from pay by the employer; and the second relates to the right to recover unpaid wages (and other benefits due) in the event of the employer's insolvency. In both cases there is a clear need for the present legal position to be reformed and for the rights of workers to be made more secure.

(a) Deductions from Wages

4.11 Protection against arbitrary deductions is presently performed inadequately by Part II of the Employment Rights Act 1996. This generally permits deductions as long as they are supported by a contract term the effect of which is notified to the worker in writing before the deduction is made. This offers little protection to some of the most vulnerable workers in the labour force who will often be in no position to agree to the employer imposing terms of this kind and in no position to refuse to authorise deductions to be made. Workers in the retail trades are slightly better protected, since in their case a ceiling to deductions equivalent to 10 per cent of the worker's weekly or monthly pay (as appropriate) is imposed. However, there is no meaningful limit on the number of occasions on which a deduction of up to this amount may be made, as long as the employer has contractual authority for the power to make the deduction.

4.12 The payment of wages is governed by ILO Convention 95 (the Protection of Wages Convention, 1949), denounced by the UK prior to the passage of the Wages Act 1986. The Convention contains important standards governing the payment of the agreed wage, the control of deductions, intervals between payments and payment in kind. Notwithstanding the UK's denunciation, this provides a useful model for a strengthened wage protection measure. In addition, ILO Recommendation 85 (the Protection of Wages Recommendation, 1949) offers guidance on the circumstances under which deductions should be permitted. Article 1 provides that 'All necessary measures should be taken to limit deductions from wages to the extent deemed necessary to safeguard the maintenance of the worker and his family', and Article 2 provides, inter alia, that deductions in respect of loss or damage sustained by the employer 'should be fair and not exceed the actual amount' in question. In our view the relevant ILO standards should form the basis for legislation protecting workers against arbitrary deductions from pay and ensuring that wages are paid on a regular periodic basis. Practices of payment in kind should be strictly regulated.

(b) Employer's Insolvency

4.13 Present legislation provides a number of protections for employees of companies which become insolvent. First, under the

Insolvency Act 1986, employees are classed as preferred creditors whose claims rank above those of the general body of unsecured creditors. Claims in respect of accrued wages for a period of four months, subject to an upper limit of £800, are protected in this way. However, even these claims will be defeated by secured creditors, such as those holding a fixed charge over the company's assets. Secondly, certain statutory and contractual claims of employees may be met from the National Insurance Fund, which then inherits the original claim against the employer (Employment Rights Act 1996, sections 166-170 and 182-190). These include certain arrears of wages and statutory entitlements to redundancy compensation. However, in relation to unfair dismissal only the basic award is currently protected by this means.

4.14 Notwithstanding the existence of statutory protections which are specific to the situation of insolvency, insolvency may easily have the effect of depriving employees of the full value of certain contractual and statutory entitlements. One option for reform would be to strengthen worker protection, by providing, for example, that claims for arrears for wages should rank above those of all other unsecured creditors. However, issues of equity in the distribution of losses arising from insolvency also need to be carefully considered. The workers in the insolvent company are not the only group which may lose out; other unsecured creditors may include suppliers and customers whose own viability may rest on recovering a significant part of the debt owed to them. It is not obvious that favouring the workers of the insolvent company over all other unsecured creditors is always the fairest solution, particularly when those other creditors have workers of their own whose jobs are at risk. This is not to imply that the present arrangements are adequate in all respects; simply that any attempt at reform must balance a range of competing interests and considerations.

4.15 The protection of workers as preferred creditors under the Insolvency Act 1986, while important, is rather weak, and there is a case for strengthening it. The current upper limit on protection of £800 has not been increased since 1986, despite rises in earnings since that date. The limit should be increased to an amount which takes inflation into account. In addition, the Secretary of State should be required to increase this threshold annually in line with the rise in average earnings. Neither of these changes could be seen as an illegitimate restriction on the rights of other unsecured creditors; unless the present limit is raised, its real value will continue to decline until the protection becomes effectively worthless. An alternative to strengthening the position of workers is to extend the range of matters over which claims may be made against the National Insurance Fund. In effect , this route to protection spreads the costs of insolvency among all those employers and workers who pay national insurance contributions. This is not to say that the Fund could or should meet all the losses of workers in situations of insolvency. Nevertheless, some reforms here would be appropriate. Matters which could be considered would include raising the threshold on the weekly limit of wages for the purpose of earnings in respect of which claims can be made, and allowing workers to recover in respect of the compensatory, additional and special awards in unfair dismissal.

Income Security during Interruption from Work

4.16 Present legislation ensures that employees receive a minimum degree of income protection in the event of interruptions to work by reason of sickness (statutory sick pay) or lay-off (guaranteed pay). Two major problems arise with regard to this body of law (in addition to its inordinate complexity). First, entitlements in the area of employment protection legislation tend to cancel out entitlements to social security benefits which would otherwise arise. The relationship between employment rights and social security rights is in urgent need of clarification. Secondly, the rules in this area have proved difficult to apply in the case of part-time work, regular short-time working and job-sharing. This is because the legislation tends to assume that it is dealing with a case of full-time, five-day-a-week working; other forms of employment are, as a consequence, less well protected against unexpected interruptions to work.

(a) Sickness
4.17 Rights to statutory sick pay cancel out, for the most part, any rights the worker might have under social security legislation, and are also set off against contractual entitlements. Similarly, a worker entitled to guaranteed pay in respect of a day without work is thereby disqualified from claiming unemployment benefit (or, now, the jobseeker's allowance) for the same day. In principle, there are advantages to this approach: in the case of short-term interruptions, it is artificial to regard the employment relationship as at an end. There is also a case in terms of equity for making the individual employer responsible for making payments of wages and salary for

such short periods. On the other hand, the devolution of liabilities from the state (or the social security system) to individual employers may place on the latter costs which they are not able effectively to meet. This has been a consequence of legislation since the mid-1970s, when the responsibility for income maintenance during lay-off was formally transferred from the state to employers; more recently, the state social insurance system has ceased to meet the costs of statutory sick pay and statutory maternity pay to the same extent as when these forms of payment were first introduced.

4.18   For the immediate future, statutory sick pay will continue to be administered, as at present, by individual employers, with some element of reimbursement through the system of national insurance contributions. Public expenditure constraints make it unlikely that reimbursement could be returned to the 100 per cent level. In the longer-term, the form taken by statutory sick pay will depend on the nature of any wider changes to the national insurance system. It is possible that statutory sick pay will be completely separated from any element of state social insurance. On the other hand, if the state encourages new forms of collective occupational provision in the area of retirement pensions (see below, paragraphs 4.85 - 4.95), this new framework could also provide the basis for an expanded system of occupational sickness benefits for workers.

(b) Guaranteed Payments

4.19   An employee meeting the qualifying conditions is currently entitled to guaranteed pay in respect of a 'workless day' which must be a day on which he or she would normally have been required to work under their contract of employment (Employment Rights Act 1996, sections 28-35). This causes difficulty for workers who do not have clear contractual expectations of receiving work (such as those employed under 'zero hours contracts'). Equally, where an employer and a worker agree to a reduction in normal weekly working hours in response to a reduction in demand, this may also have the effect of rendering inapplicable the notion of the workless day. To deal with these and associated problems, the legislation on guaranteed pay should be amended so that the notion of the 'normal working week' is more effectively established. This should refer to the number of hours that the worker is normally expected to work, and not necessarily to those which he or she is contracted to work at any given time.

4.20   Unemployment benefit (or the 'insurance-based' jobseeker's allowance) is not generally available to subsidise regular short-time working or part-time working, thanks to the 'full extent normal' rule and the 'normal idle day rule', subject only to an earnings disregard of £12 per week. Even where these two rules do not apply, legislation puts an absolute bar on the insurance-based jobseeker's allowance being paid in a week where the employee's earnings exceed the lower earnings limit for national insurance contributions (£58 in 1995-96). These rules are designed to avoid a situation in which the social insurance system subsidises regular short-time working, but their effect is to make extremely difficult for those seeking to re-enter employment to do so on the basis of part-time work or job-sharing arrangements, while still retaining a portion of their benefits. By contrast, 'partial unemployment' schemes in many other EC countries make it possible for certain social security benefits to be combined with the receipt of earnings from employment, for short periods. The option of partial unemployment schemes is one which should be considered for the UK. Although there are implications for public expenditure and for issues of equity in the treatment of different groups of workers, the use of such schemes could be justified as a way to assist the re-integration of the long-term unemployed into regular work.

The Regulation of Working Time

(a) The British Tradition

4.21   The goals of working time legislation include improving health and safety at work; ensuring the preservation of leisure and family time for workers; and the redistribution of employment, through hours reductions and work sharing. These goals are achieved in a number of ways. In addition to setting maximum daily, weekly or annual working hours, legislation may also set premia for nightwork, shiftwork and overtime work, as well as regulating the conditions under which such work is carried out. Sector-level bargaining, rather than legislation, has been the major source of such regulation of working time for most workers in Britain. The decline of sectoral bargaining, together with the repeal of the minimal controls which remained in the Factories Acts, have left many workers with no protection at all in this area. Currently there is no legal right to a limit on working time, other than residual protection from health and safety law, nor is there a legal right to overtime premia for excessive hours. Such rights depend on the terms of the individual worker's contract and of any relevant collective agreement.

4.22   Even before the recent deregulatory changes, the UK model of regulation through collective bargaining was weak in terms of substance when compared to most mainland European systems. UK collective agreements have not sought to impose absolute upper limits on overtime working; nor have they laid down the precise form and limits of shift work. Instead, most sector-level agreements have been confined to setting overtime and shift premium payments. In themselves these premia do not provide employers with much of a disincentive to limit overtime working, in particular since they have normally been multiples (such as time-and-a-half or double time) of the national basic wage rate, and not of the higher basic rate which might be set by plant or company-level agreements. This is one reason why overtime and shift working in Britain has been particularly prevalent for full-time workers, compared to practice in other EC Member States.

(b) European Standards

4.23 The standards contained in EC Directive 93/104 provide a starting point for the re-regulation of working time in Britain. At the same time, it should be borne in mind that the Directive only sets minimum standards, upon which Member States may improve. In certain important respects, a level of regulation over and above that provided by the Directive should be considered. The limits on working time which are contained in Directive 93/104 should be incorporated into UK domestic law, together with the Directive's provisions concerning the regulation of nightwork and shiftwork. The Directive's requirement of four weeks' annual paid leave should also be implemented. This should be done through legislation in the first instance, given the weak state of multi-employer collective bargaining in most sectors. The Directive envisages:

* a minimum daily rest period of eleven consecutive hours out of every 24;
* rest breaks every 6 hours during the working day, the details to be set by collective bargaining or, failing that, national legislation;
* a weekly rest period of 35 consecutive hours per week (24 hours, in addition to the eleven hours of minimum daily rest), which 'shall in principle include Sunday' but which may be reduced to 24 hours in total where 'objective, technical or work organisation conditions so justify'; and
* a maximum average working week, including overtime of 48 hours.

4.24 In addition, the Directive lays down the following standards with regard to nightwork and unsocial hours working.

* The Directive provides for a limit to normal average nightwork of 8 hours in any 24 hour period, and an absolute limit of 8 hours in any 24 if the work involves special hazards, heavy physical or mental strain. Nightworkers are also to be entitled to periodic, free health assessments. Member States must ensure that employers report their use of nightwork to the relevant health and safety authorities, and may subject night work to guarantees or conditions to be laid down by legislation and/or practice. Nightwork is defined for these purposes as a period of not less than seven hours including at least the period from midnight to 5 a.m.

* In organising working patterns of shifts, employers must also take into account 'the general principle of adapting work to the worker, with a view, in particular, to alleviating monotonous work and work at a predetermined work-rate, depending on the type of activity, and of safety and health requirements, especially as regards breaks during working time'. This is based on the important principle of the 'humanisation of work'.

* These limits to working time and nightwork are subject to the concept of the 'reference period' over which actual working hours may be averaged out. In particular, Member States are permitted to lay down a reference period of up to 14 days in respect of the minimum period of weekly rest and one of four months in respect of the maximum working week of 48 hours. The nightwork standards may be qualified by a reference period set after consultation with the two sides of industry or by a national or regional level collective agreement.

The Directive also provides for minimum annual paid leave.

* Annual paid leave of four weeks is the minimum required by the Directive. This period of leave may not be commuted into a payment of wages or salary in lieu of holiday.

(c) Derogations and Exclusions

4.25 The Directive envisages an active role for collective bargaining at sector and company or plant level as a means of achieving regulated derogations from these norms in the interests of flexibility. The importance of collective bargaining as a source of implementing working time controls in a flexible manner should be recognised in domestic UK legislation. As laid down in the Directive, derogations from the limits on normal working time and on shiftwork and nightwork would be conditional upon compensatory periods of rest for the workers concerned. The participation of a representative trade union would also be required. No derogations should be permitted from the right to annual paid leave, as the Directive itself intends. In other respects the Directive goes further in permitting exceptions and derogations than may be desirable. For example, certain types of activity are altogether excluded from the scope of the Directive. These include 'air, rail, road, sea, inland waterway and lake transport, sea fishing, other work at sea and the activities of doctors in training'. These exceptions, particularly the latter, are anomalous, in particular given the possibility of achieving flexibility through collective bargaining or other means. The exclusions contained in Directive 93/104 should be reviewed to see how far, if at all, they can be justified on objective economic grounds.

4.26   The Directive also permits derogations to be made from the 48 hour maximum working week by individual agreement, on condition that regular records are kept of workers employed beyond this limit. This provision operates for a period of seven years after the Directive is due to come into force on 23 November 1996. The Directive also allows a Member State to delay the right to paid annual leave of four weeks for a period three years from 1996, substituting, for this period, a minimum of 3 weeks' annual paid leave. These derogations should be closely examined to see whether they are necessary on social and economic grounds. The provision for individual workers to derogate from the maximum limit of 48 hours per week should also be assessed by reference to its workability. It could lead to the fragmentation of existing pay and working time arrangements under collective agreements, thereby undermining good industrial relations and the achievement of flexibility through collective negotiation.

(d) 'Zero-Hours' Contracts

4.27   The regulation of 'zero-hours' contracts needs careful consideration. Under Directive 93/104, 'working time' means 'any period during which the worker is working, at the employer's disposal and carrying out his activity of duties, in accordance with national law and/or practice', and a rest period is 'any period which is not working time'. It is not completely clear whether time spent on call falls under this definition, and whether, therefore, a zero-hours contract worker could claim that these hours should count towards the relevant daily and weekly limits. The ambiguity could be resolved through domestic legislation, which is permitted to set standards which are more protective than those laid down in the Directive itself.

There are at least three ways by which this could be done, with different strategies being adopted depending on whether the desire is to regulate the practice of 'zero hours' contracts and to strike at some of its worst abuses, or effectively proscribe it altogether. Whichever route is chosen will depend upon whether the advantages to workers of a regulated system of on call contracts are thought to outweigh its disadvantages.

4.28   In the first place, the employer could be required to specify a guaranteed minimum number of hours in the written statement of particulars. The worker would be entitled to be paid for hours on call as well as for the hours actually worked. A worker who had exceeded the guaranteed minimum could not be required to work any additional hours and could not be dismissed for refusing to do so. Secondly, it would be possible to provide that where the terms of the employment relationship do not prescribe a fixed number of hours, a prescribed minimum number will be deemed to exist, for all of which the worker would be entitled to be paid, provided that he or she was required to be on call, even though this prescribed number of hours was not in fact worked. Thirdly, and most radically, it could be provided that all hours spent on-call under a 'zero-hours' contract should be counted as working time. This means that they would count towards the relevant limits on working hours and that they would attract the right of the worker to be paid at least the applicable hourly rate of the minimum wage for the time in question. It could also be provided, whichever model is adopted, that a worker can be required to attend for work only after a prescribed minimum period of notice is given by the employer.

A Safe and Healthy Working Environment

4.29   In 1994/95, 381 people died as a result of work-related accidents, and a considerably larger number die as a result of illnesses caused or exacerbated by their work activities. More generally, figures from the 1990 Labour Force Survey suggest that during the year 1990-91 those in employment (employees and the self-employed) suffered at least 1.4 million accidents and that these incidents caused the loss of an estimated 21 million working days. Calculations prepared for the Health and Safety Executive (HSE) moreover suggest that work-related accidents cost employers £900 million per annum and the economy as a whole between one and two per cent of gross domestic product. There are then both moral and financial reasons to take action to reduce the current toll that work inflicts on workers.

4.30   In many respects the legal duties imposed on employers under the Health and Safety at Work Act (HASAWA 1974) and supporting 'relevant statutory provisions' are adequate. Nevertheless, important weaknesses remain. Attention is focused here on some of the more general and wide-ranging areas where reforms are needed. Thought should also be given to a better organisation of the legislation in this area. Although the HASAWA 1974 forms the core of the statutory framework for occupational health and safety, in many ways it is now the provisions of the Management of Health and Safety at Work Regulations 1992 (SI 1992/2051), broadly implementing the EU Framework Directive on Health and Safety (89/391/EEC), which now lays down the general legal framework relating to the management of health and safety. It may be that the time has come radically to overhaul, and even possibly replace, the 1974 statute so that it truly does lay down the central duties and rights of employers and workers.

(a) Occupational Health and Safety Services and Safety Policies

4.31   At present the law says little about the expertise that employers need to have in the field of occupational health and safety. The main general requirement in this area, laid down under the Management of Health and Safety at Work (MHSW) Regulations 1992, is for employers to appoint one or more competent persons to assist them in the development of protective and preventive measures. The definition of competence used for this purpose is, however, very general. Employers have to comply with a large and complex body of statutory duties, and frequently manage highly technical and hazardous work processes. It is highly questionable whether the approach to defining competence in the MHSW Regulations provides an adequate means of ensuring that they have the expertise in place to deal with the challenges flowing from these two factors. A much better way forward would be to introduce requirements, as is done in much of the rest of the EC, to oblige employers to have access to qualified occupational health and safety services. The adoption of such an approach could particularly have beneficial consequences in small firms, where accident rates in manufacturing are relatively high.

4.32   Under section 2(3) of the HASAWA 1974, employers with five or more employees are required to prepare a safety policy. Health and Safety Executive inspectors have since the advent of this requirement placed considerable emphasis on the presence and content of these documents. However, at present section 2(3) says nothing about the need for policies to be 'adequate' and gives relatively little guidance on what they should contain. As a result inspectors face difficulties in taking enforcement action in respect of policy documents which are seriously flawed. This weakness of section 2(3) is one which needs to be remedied in order to enable it to do what it was intended to - that is encourage employers to develop a coherent and organised approach to the management of occupational health and safety. The law should therefore prescribe in greater detail the minimum acceptable contents of employers' safety policies by, for example, specifically requiring policies to identify the manager with overall responsibility for health and safety, detail safety rules and procedures, and outline the arrangements in place for appointing competent persons, conducting risk assessments and providing training and workforce consultation.

(b) Protective Measures and Work Design

4.33   Under the HASAWA 1974 and the MHSW Regulations 1992 no specific statutory guidance is given as to the principles which should inform the selection of preventive and protective measures. This contrasts with the position under the Control of Substances Hazardous to Health Regulations 1988 (SI 1988/1657), where emphasis is placed on the removal of risks, and the control of risks at source. There seems to be no good reason why this approach should not also be incorporated into the MHSW Regulations 1992, rather than their supporting Approved Code of Practice. Indeed the absence from the regulations arguably constitutes a failure to transpose the requirements of Article 6(2) of the EC's Framework Directive into British law. It also sits oddly with the requirements of some other EC inspired regulations. A good example of this regulation is 4(1)(a) of the Manual Handling Regulations 1992 (SI 1992/2792) which specifically requires employers, so far as is reasonably practicable, to 'avoid the need for his employees to undertake any manual handling operations at work which involves a risk of their being injured.'

4.34   Relatively little attention has been paid to the way in which harm may be caused by the design of jobs. Upper limb disorder and stress are the two areas where it has been increasingly recognised that the way in which jobs are designed can have important consequences for worker well being. In theory, the general duties laid down under section 2 of the HASAWA 1974 do extend to encompass the protection of workers from these conditions. However, there does seem a case for more specific requirements to be imposed in this area. The importance of work design issues has in effect already been acknowledged in the EC Framework Directive (89/391/EEC) and in the EC Directives on Display Screen Equipment (90/270/EEC) and Working Time (93/104/EC). The first of these contains provisions which require employers, wherever possible, to recognise the principle of adapting the work to the individual worker. Unfortunately, these have been relegated to the Approved Code of Practice supporting the MHSW Regulations. This needs to be replaced by the introduction of an explicit regulatory duty. More generally, legislation should specifically acknowledge the duty of employers to protect workers from psycho-social harm and in this way make clear that quality of life issues form part of the agenda of occupational health and safety.

(c) Transparency and Enforcement

4.35 At present companies do not have to provide any information about their health and safety arrangements and performance to shareholders or the public. Yet concerns about adverse publicity clearly can encourage organisations to accord a greater priority to the protection of workers. It would therefore be desirable to introduce an obligation, possibly under section 235 of the Companies Act 1985, requiring companies to provide information in their annual reports on their health and safety arrangements, including specialist advisory and treatment services, trends in accident and ill health statistics, and cases where enforcement action has been taken against them. Such an obligation would clearly need to be supplemented by the introduction of similar requirements on public sector organisations. It may also be desirable to extend the proposed requirements to encompass the provision of information on successful personal injury claims made against employers.

4.36 It has long been recognised that Health and Safety Executive and local authority inspectorates do not have the resources adequately to enforce the present statutory framework for occupational health and safety. This lack of resources is clearly something that urgently needs to be addressed. However, several other steps could be taken to improve the position. At present proceedings can effectively be brought only by enforcement bodies. Provision is admittedly made for other persons to initiate proceedings with the approval of the Director of Public Prosecutions. However, as far as is known, no such approval has so far been given. This reliance on external initiation confronts two problems: first, the lack of resources of local authorities and the HSE which has already been mentioned; and secondly, the HSE's traditional preference to rely on persuasion and use formal enforcement methods only as a last resort. Clearly there is some scope for the HSE to take a more rigorous approach to enforcement. However, there is a danger that if this is taken too far the benefits of the current enforcement approach in terms of maintaining good working relationships with employers will be lost. A further option that therefore merits consideration is to make it easier for workers and their unions to bring private proceedings.

(d) Remedies and Sanctions

4.37   Section 37(1) of the HASAWA 1974 enables proceedings to be brought against directors and other senior office holders of a body corporate where an offence has been committed with their consent or connivance or was attributable to their neglect. The problem with this provision is that it is of little practical value in bringing prosecutions against such officials in large organisations because of the problem of showing a causal link between their actions and those of the body corporate. As a result senior managers at present are frequently able to make decisions, notably budgetary ones, which have adverse consequences for worker protection, and escape any personal liability for those consequences. A solution to this problem would be to introduce a form of no-fault liability for senior management and/or members of the board of directors where a company is found to have recklessly exposed employees to serious risk of personal injury. Clearly if such a form of liability were to be introduced some decision would have to be made as to whom this liability would apply. The most straightforward solution here would be to require an employer to nominate a director as having overall responsibility for health and safety.

4.38   At present employers can be convicted summarily or on indictment. In the former case the standard maximum penalty is £5,000. However, this rises to £20,000 if the case concerns a breach of sections 2-6 of the HASAWA 1974 or a failure to comply with an enforcement notice. In addition imprisonment of up to six months can be ordered where an enforcement notice has been breached. The rationale for this complex set of formulae is unclear. A clearer and more logical approach than the present one would be simply to provide for a maximum of six months' imprisonment and a fine of £20,000 to be imposed in respect of all types of health and safety offence. Moreover this change is desirable not only on the grounds of logic and clarity: it could also act to encourage magistrates to increase the level of fines imposed on employers found guilty of breaching their statutory duties. That such an increase is needed is borne out by official figures for the year 1994/95. These show that the average penalty per conviction, including cases taken on indictment, amounted to just £2,645 - an extraordinary low level given that prosecutions are only brought in respect of serious breaches of the law.

Civil Liberties at the Workplace

4.39　Workers should have the right to protection of their civil liberties from violation by the employer and others in the workplace. While the likelihood that workers' rights will be violated is reduced where there is strong workplace representation, this does not deny that there is a role for a statutory framework of rights which respects the civil liberties of workers. The question then arises of which rights should be protected within such a statutory framework? A useful starting point are the provisions of the European Convention on Human Rights. While, as a matter of international law, the Convention applies mainly to the regulation of the activities of government, its principles are equally relevant to private relationships, especially the relationship between employer and worker. Four of the articles from the Convention seem particularly applicable in the context of the workplace. These are Article 8, which protects the right to privacy; Article 9 which protects freedom of conscience and religion; Article 10 which protects the right to freedom of expression; and Article 11 which protects the right to freedom of assembly and association. In some respects each of these rights are covered by proposals contained in other chapters. There are, however, several outstanding matters which should be addressed here. These relate in particular to data protection, surveillance, 'whistleblowing' and political activities.

(a) Data Protection

4.40　Turning first to the right to protection of personal information concerning individual workers, such protection would involve the regulation of the types of personal information which employers are permitted to store; the right for workers to be informed of and have access to information that is being held about them by employers and others; and restrictions on personal information which employers and others are permitted to provide to third parties about workers. The rights currently provided to data subjects (individuals about whom data is held) by the Data Protection Act 1984 are both limited and substantially ineffectual. Data subjects have the right to receive a copy of the information about them which is held on computer; the right to challenge the information if it is inaccurate and where appropriate to have the information corrected or erased; and finally the right to claim compensation for damage arising from inaccurate data or from loss or unauthorised destruction or disclosure of personal data. The data user, however, as a general rule, is not obliged under the Act to inform the data subject, nor to seek his or her consent before processing information. The data subject also has only limited control over the subsequent disclosure, processing or use of data about him or her.

4.41 On 24th October 1995 the Data Protection Directive (95/46/EC) was adopted. The implementation of the Directive will require substantial changes to British labour law in a number of areas. First, the Directive introduces rules about the legitimacy of processing which are new to the United Kingdom. The Directive provides that the processing of personal information will only be legitimate and therefore lawful in a limited number of circumstances, including where the data subject has given consent, where it is necessary for the performance or creation of a contract to which the data subject is a party, or for compliance with either national or Community law. The Directive also provides that processing will be lawful where it is necessary in the legitimate interests of the data user, or third parties to whom the data is to be disclosed, but only where these interests are not overridden by the interests of the data subject. As a result the circumstances in which data processing is lawful are far fewer than those permitted by the Data Protection Act 1984. Most important is the overriding interest provided for the data subject, which undoubtedly represents a significant extension in the level of protection provided to data subjects.

4.42 The Directive imposes strict limits on the processing and use of data revealing racial or ethnic origin, political opinions, religious or philosophical beliefs, trade union membership, and the processing of data concerning health or sex life. These restrictions extend to information relating to the physical and mental health of an individual, be it past, present or future, and to drug or alcohol use and information about an individual's sex life. Under the terms of the Directive the processing of such data is generally prohibited. Exceptions are only permitted where the individual has given express consent; where processing is necessary in the vital interests of the data subject; where it is part of the legitimate activities of non-profit making associations and only relates to their members; and where the information has been made manifestly public by the data subject or its processing is necessary in the course of a legal claim. One further exception is permitted, which is of particular relevance to labour law, and that is where processing of sensitive data 'is necessary for the purposes of carrying out the obligations and specific rights of the controller in the field of employment law in so far as it is authorized by national law providing for adequate safeguards.' This exception will allow for instances where employers retain records on trade union membership for check-off and other related purposes, or where employers monitor the participation rate of ethnic minorities in the workplace.

4.43   Unlike the Data Protection Act 1984, the Directive imposes on data users a duty actively to inform an individual of information that is being processed about him or her. In contrast, the Data Protection Act 1984 is dependent on enquiries made by individuals themselves. In addition, a data subject has the right to receive from the data user confirmation of whether data is being processed about him or her, and an intelligible copy of the data held. Further, the Directive provides the right for information which is incomplete or inaccurate to be rectified or erased. Where such erasure or rectification is appropriate, any third parties to whom the relevant data had been passed must be informed, unless this would involve disproportionate effort. Additionally, data protection legislation can no longer be restricted to information which is processed automatically, as the Directive also applies to manually processed information. This extension of protection is particularly welcome in order to enable the monitoring and regulation of activities by groups such as the Economic League, which in the past avoided scrutiny by confining their records to paper.

4.44   The restrictions on the collection, storage, and use of personal data by employers and others, which are contained in Directive 95/46, should be incorporated into UK law. In line with the provisions of the Directive all workers should have the right to object to and to block the illegitimate processing of their personal data. The processing of sensitive data revealing a worker's racial or ethnic origin, political opinions, religious or philosophical beliefs, trade union membership, and concerning a worker's health or sex life should only be permitted by an employer in circumstances specified in the Directive and where the interests of the worker are safeguarded. All workers should have the right to be informed by the employer of the personal data being processed about them, the purposes for which the data is held and the parties to whom it will be disclosed. All workers should continue to have a right of access to this data and the right to have it corrected or erased where appropriate. Moreover, data protection legislation should be amended to extend to manually processed files.

(b) Surveillance

4.45 The right to privacy is not only about the storage, access to and use of personal information. Invasion of privacy in the workplace is perhaps greatest where employers electronically monitor their workers. Advances in technology mean that workers are increasingly monitored by a wide range of techniques, including keyboard, telephone and video-surveillance technologies. A recent example was provided by UNISON which claims that postroom workers at a London hospital were being 'spied on', staff having 'discovered four lenses, connected to a video recorder, concealed in the ceiling of the hospital's postroom'. A regional officer of the union was quoted as having said that there was 'no innocuous reason for the cameras', and concern was expressed that 'no law exists to stop management spying on the staff' despite the fact that their 'civil liberties were being jeopardised'. The incident gave rise to calls for 'guidelines for the use of surveillance equipment in the NHS', though there may be a case for the more general application of any such guidelines were they to be introduced.

4.46 The Data Protection Directive introduces protection in two different but related areas which may be relevant to some forms of workplace surveillance. First, the Directive establishes the principle that no decision which significantly affects the rights and interests of an individual should be made solely by computer. The extension of protection in this area could have significant implications for both selection processes and disciplinary procedures adopted by employers. Potentially, for example, it could prohibit employers from rejecting job applicants solely on the basis of the results of a computerised psychological evaluation test, or from dismissing a typist or word processing operator solely on the grounds that he or she failed to meet a computer assessed hourly work quota. During consideration of the Directive, the European Parliament proposed an amendment which would have allowed automated decisions to be taken if the person concerned had consented or had entered into a contract to that effect. This was not adopted, however, as it was recognised that if the two sides were not on equal terms neither consent nor the hope of a contract could provide sufficient safeguards.

4.47 Rather, the Directive provides that decisions based solely on automatic assessment, e.g. scoring techniques, may only be taken in the workplace where it leads to a positive effect for the worker. Where the result of automatic assessment is negative, the legitimate interests of the worker must be safeguarded. This provision, which is based upon French law, finds no comparison in the Data Protection Act 1984. Indeed, the Data Protection Tribunal has found that the 1984 Act is concerned only with processing and not with the use of information derived from processing. Unfortunately, the protection offered by the Directive is weakened by that fact that the involvement of any element of human decision making in an automated process may have the effect of removing such decisions from the scope of the Directive. Having said this, the extended definition of 'processing' used in the Directive, which includes the use of information, may still provide additional protection to that expressly provided in the Directive, and certainly beyond that provided by the 1984 Act.

4.48 Recent technical advances have made it possible for employers to subject workers to a variety of forms of surveillance with a view to assessing performance and preventing crime. These surveillance techniques include the instalment of close circuit television and surveillance cameras, the reading of a worker's electronic mail, monitoring telephone calls, and experimentation with electrical devices which permit employers to identify the location of employees. Any measures introduced to deal with such developments should of course balance the rights of the individual worker to privacy and the legitimate operational requirements of the employer. Paragraph 14 of the recital to the Data Protection Directive suggests that the definition of 'personal data' used in the Directive should be interpreted as including both image and sound. The use of such a broad definition may bring new surveillance techniques within the scope of the Directive. As a result employers may be required to inform workers when they are being surveyed and the courts will be enabled to assess whether such surveillance is necessary and legitimate.

4.49 In line with the Directive, no worker or prospective worker should be subject to a decision adversely affecting his or her rights or interests which is based solely on automatic assessment. Exceptions to this principle should only be permitted where there are adequate measures to safeguard an individual's interests. This would not, however, be enough to deal with all the problems which are likely to arise in the context of workplace monitoring. Consequently in our view electronic monitoring of workers should be permissible only where the employer can demonstrate a sufficient cause which makes the use of such devices necessary, having regard to their impact on the worker's right to privacy. It should be open to workers to refer such matters to a Labour Inspector who after hearing both sides should be empowered, if he or she upholds a complaint, to issue an order requiring the use of any method or device to be discontinued.

(c) 'Whistleblowing'

4.50 The issue of freedom of expression for workers within the enterprise is difficult and controversial in the sense that the liberty of the individual must be balanced against the needs of the employer. It is undoubtedly necessary for employers to keep some forms of information confidential in order to protect trade secrets, their commercial position in a competitive marketplace, or to fulfil duties of confidentiality to third parties. But this does not mean that classical civil liberties should not have a role to play in the government and management of the enterprise. There is no reason why in appropriate cases workers should not be free to speak out against intolerable practices, and indeed it is in the public interest for workers in certain circumstances to disclose malpractice or mismanagement or to draw attention to poor working conditions which contravene statutorily recognised minimum standards. Yet the disclosure of confidential information obtained in the course of employment can have severe consequences for the individual. These can include actions in the civil courts for breach of confidence, and for some categories of civil servants, prosecution for breach of the Official Secrets Acts 1911-1989. However, most common will be disciplinary measures including dismissal.

4.51 Express terms which prohibit the disclosure of confidential information obtained in the workplace are increasingly common in a wide range of industries, including the public sector and most notably the NHS. Research undertaken in 1995 by the Labour Research Department shows as many as one in five disciplinary procedures 'specifically barred employees from disclosing confidential information regardless of the circumstances and threatened instant dismissal to employees who disregarded the rule'. In the absence of an express term to this effect, workers may still be prohibited from disclosing information as the result of the duty of confidentiality implied into the contract of employment. Since the Court of Appeal's ruling in *Initial Services v Putterill* [1968] 1 QB 368 an exception is made where there is 'any misconduct of such a nature that it ought in the public interest to be disclosed to others.' While disclosures of illegal or irregular conduct, or matters relating to the health and safety of workers or the general public, are almost certainly covered by the exception, it is unclear whether the same is true of disclosures of mismanagement. This limitation has particular effect for those employed in the public sector, who may wish to draw attention to matters of concern about the efficacy of government reforms or falling standards of service.

4.52 In our view measures should be introduced which, while not imposing a duty on workers to speak out about malpractice in the workplace, encourage workers to raise issues of concern in a constructive manner. A series of practical measures can be adopted which will assist in creating an environment within the workplace where workers feel able to speak out, without fear of retaliation. First, it is important that the issue of whistleblowing is recognised and openly discussed in the workplace. We therefore propose that employers should be required to provide their workers with a policy statement on the reporting of improprieties at work and the arrangements that exist for carrying out those policies. The terms of the policy statement should be developed in discussion with recognised or representative trade unions.

4.53 Secondly, it is important that appropriate channels of communication should be created, through which workers may raise their concerns about impropriety. We therefore propose that employers should be required to specify 'a person to whom workers should apply for the purpose of raising concern about impropriety within their employment' as part of the written statement of particulars which, by virtue of what is now the Employment Rights Act 1996, must be supplied to workers. Due to the fact that some workers may wish to raise concerns over the acts or omissions of their line managers, it is important that written statements should allow for alternative channels of communication. Where an employer fails to include such a term within the written statement a worker, or trade union representing the worker concerned, may refer the matter to the Labour Inspector for resolution. As will be discussed below, the introduction of these measures should not preclude a worker in certain circumstances from disclosing information to an external party.

4.54 Thirdly, it is important that legislation should expressly recognise the right of workers to disclose information obtained in the course of employment, if at the time they had reasonable grounds to believe that the information was accurate and they reasonably believed that disclosure of the information was in the public interest. In order to avoid uncertainty in the application of this right, the legislation should clearly specify what constitutes disclosure in the public interest. While the definition of public interest used should build on the existing common law, it should not be confined to matters relating to illegality, malpractice or health and safety. We therefore propose that disclosures made in the public interest should be defined to include disclosures relating to a criminal offence or breach of any statutory duty or other legal obligation; improper or unauthorised use of public or other funds; abuse of authority; miscarriages of justice; maladministration; danger to the health and safety of any individual or to the environment; or other misconduct, malpractice or mismanagement.

4.55   Having addressed how the public interest is to be defined, it is necessary to consider to whom information, obtained in the course of employment, may be disclosed. The principal question which arises relates to the circumstances in which a worker should be entitled to disclose information to an external party without first following established internal procedures. While in many cases it will be appropriate for a worker to raise matters of concern internally, there will undoubtedly be instances, where the worker considers that the only effective action that can be taken is to expose the information externally, either to a regulatory body or even the press. An appropriate balance can be reached by proposing that workers be required to comply with established internal procedures for raising concerns, unless it was reasonable for them to assume either that such steps would be ineffective or that the matter is of such urgency as to warrant the immediate external disclosure of the information. In cases where information is disclosed to external parties, there should be a presumption that the worker acted in a reasonable manner, unless the employer is able to show clearly to the contrary.

4.56   In order to make these proposals effective it is necessary to ensure that any worker who exercises the rights in question is protected from dismissal by the employer, and not subjected to any detriment. Consequently it should be unlawful to subject a worker to any detriment for having lawfully disclosed information about the business by which he or she is employed, and it should be automatically unfair to dismiss anyone for 'whistleblowing' within the scope of the foregoing proposals, and any term of an employment relationship which restricts the right of workers in this area should be void and unenforceable. It should also be presumed in any legal proceedings that any disclosure was in the public interest and that the onus should lie on the employer to show that the disclosure of the information concerned did not fall under any of the prescribed headings and therefore was not in the public interest.

(d) Political Activities

4.57 As a general rule, the law does not prohibit individual workers from associating together for political purposes. Restrictions, however, are imposed by statute and administrative practice on the political freedoms of certain categories of workers, in particular the civil service, local government officers and the police. The retention of such measures should only be permitted where it is reasonable and necessary to do so in the public interest, for example, where it is necessary to protect the impartiality of public servants in the exercise of their duties or the political neutrality of advice provided by civil servants to Ministers of State. Regulations which extend beyond these boundaries should be removed. Particularly controversial in this respect are the political restrictions on local government officers which were introduced by the Local Government and Housing Act 1989 following the report of the Widdicombe Committee of Inquiry into the Conduct of Local Authority Business which had, however, recommended more modest measures than those which were eventually adopted by the government.

4.58 Section 1 of the 1989 Act imposes a number of disqualifications and restrictions on staff who hold 'politically restricted' posts. A person who holds such a post in one local authority is disqualified from becoming or remaining a member of any other local authority, and is disqualified from being a member of Parliament. Perhaps more significantly, the 'terms of appointment or conditions of employment of every person holding a politically restricted post under a local authority (including persons appointed to such posts before the coming into force of this section) shall be deemed to incorporate such requirements for restricting his political activities as may be prescribed . . . by regulations made by the Secretary of State'. A politically restricted post is one referred to in section 2 and includes a number of senior officers as well as other staff whose rate of remuneration exceeds a prescribed amount. A politically restricted post may also include one which pays less than the prescribed amount if the duties of the person holding the post include the giving of advice on a regular basis to the authority and/or speaking on behalf of the authority to journalists.

4.59 The prohibited activities of local government officers in politically restricted posts are specified in the Local Government Officers (Political Restrictions) Regulations 1990 (SI 1990/851). These are listed in a schedule of 10 rather detailed paragraphs which regulate the conduct of employees who are parliamentary candidates, or candidates for the European Parliament or a local authority. More controversially, an employee in a politically restricted post is prohibited from acting as an election agent, or as an officer of a political party or of any branch of a political party. A person in a politically restricted post is also prohibited from canvassing on behalf of a political party or candidate for election. But the restrictions go even wider still, for an affected employee may not 'speak to the public at large or to a section of the public with the apparent intention of affecting public support for a political party', though an affected employee may display posters in their homes or cars. Artistic freedom is also a victim of the restrictions which apply to the publication of any written or artistic work 'if the work appears to be intended to affect public support for a political party'.

4.60 Trade unions in local government are understandably concerned about these measures which significantly restrict the civil and political liberties of their members, a concern which is strengthened by the government's dismissal of such claims as nonsense. What made the legislation particularly difficult to defend was that it did not extend only to new recruits but applied immediately to existing personnel, thereby taking away existing rights. This was done without compensation, even on the meagre scale provided at GCHQ. It is unsurprising that the restrictions should thus be challenged in the courts on the ground that the Regulations violated the right to freedom of expression, by reference to article 10(1) of the European Convention on Human Rights, and as such could be justified only on the ground that they could be shown to be necessary in a democratic society. It is perhaps just as unsurprising that the application should fail, with the Court of Appeal taking the view that the Regulations did not conflict with the policy or purpose of the 1989 Act (*NALGO v Secretary of State for the Environment*, The Times Law Reports, 2 December 1992).

4.61 It is unclear whether the restrictions constitute a breach of article 10 of the European Convention. This is a question which the domestic courts are rarely permitted to ask in view of the fact that the Convention is not part of domestic law and as such directly enforceable by the domestic courts. But regardless of how the matter may be dealt by the European Court of Human Rights we are of the view that there is much substance in the complaints of the union which were raised before the Court of Appeal. It seems to us unreasonable to impose new terms on officers already in post, but more importantly it is particularly unreasonable that restrictions should be imposed which restrict legitimate trade union activities by the members of public service trade unions, particularly in light of the uncontradicted claim that local government employees had in the past been able to provide impartial advice. There is no reason in our view why those who work in the public sector should be denied basic civil and political liberties, and we propose that the current restrictions on the political activities of local government officers should be removed and only reintroduced to any extent if there is clear and compelling evidence of a need to do so.

Training Opportunities at Work

4.62 It is increasingly clear that the skills level of a workforce is a central determinant of macro-economic performance. Yet it is equally clear that markets are not very effective providers of the necessary skills. Training is a good example of the sort of free rider problem which markets generally cannot solve. In a labour market where workers are able to choose for whom they work, it is typically cheaper for each economically rational employer to seek to poach workers trained by others. By the same token, there is a limited incentive for employers to train workers in anything other than firm-specific skills, only to lose them to competitors. The problem is probably most acute in the context of general skills which provide individuals with the means to adapt to different forms of work and technology. No employer is likely to pay for them to acquire those skills.

4.63 Governments since 1979 have introduced a variety of measures designed at least in part to improve the supply side of labour. The inadequacies of the initiatives may owe something to the ideological tension. But whatever the explanations for the relative failure, there is clearly a great deal of room for improvement. It seems that training in the UK lags behind its principal competitors at all levels, from education to the workplace. Yet training should not just aim at improving macro-economic performance; it can and should also be a means of implementing an egalitarian social policy and of redressing the inequalities which continue to dominate the labour market. Proper opportunities for education and training can to some extent compensate for the prior inequalities of resources or opportunity, which continue to correlate all too closely with social class, sex and race. It can also be a means of enabling those with genuine or perceived disabilities to gain access to jobs otherwise barred to them. Although this political goal has been absent from recent government training policy, it should not be forgotten in the future.

(a) The Present Position

4.64 In the context of a politics dominated by the belief that management should be left free to manage, it is unremarkable that training policy has placed virtually no requirements on, and given almost no incentives to, the individual employer to train its workers. In the absence of an express term, an employer is under no contractual obligation to train workers or to allow workers to undertake training for new jobs (although there is some limited duty when a 'job' remains but new technology is introduced: see *Cresswell v Inland Revenue* [1984] 2 All ER 713). Apart from duties in the context of health and safety, such as regulation 11 of the Management of Health and Safety at Work Regulations 1992 (SI 1992/2051), statute places no such duties on an employer. On the contrary, the introduction of measures lowering the costs of shedding the workforce, exemplified by the gradual reduction in real terms of redundancy and unfair dismissal compensation, may mean that it is more economically rational for an employer faced with the introduction of new technologies (for example) to dismiss its workers and to employ others trained by outside agencies. The decision to train or not is a largely unconstrained management prerogative - with the consequent emergence of the free rider problem to which we have already referred.

4.65 As a result, the promotion of training has thus increasingly been left to outside agencies. But apart from the obvious example of state education, prior to the 1960s there was limited government intervention. The Industrial Training Act 1964 imposed a training levy on employers and allowed the establishment of industrial training boards, with trade union representation, to promote training in individual sectors. Recognition that the boards were not tending to develop general, as opposed to industry-specific, skills led to increased state involvement in the form of the Employment Training Act 1973. Reflecting a corporatist philosophy of economic steering, it established state agencies to conduct training, including the tripartite Manpower Services Commission. But forced to deal with short term causes of the recession and hampered by poor funding, it devoted insufficient attention to the long term needs of the economy and the workforce.

4.66 These corporatist schemes have progressively been removed since 1979. In their place has emerged an approach dominated by employer interests and, increasingly, the control of the unemployed. From 1983 the Manpower Services Commission administered the Youth Training Scheme as an attempt to address the growing problem of young persons' unemployment. At the time it appeared that the government was as much concerned with keeping young persons' wage expectations at a low level, in keeping with the neo-liberal ideas of the time, as it was with training. Later measures, such as the 1988 Job Training Scheme and the pilot compulsory four week training schemes introduced in 1994 for 18 to 24 year olds out of work for one year, displayed a central wish to discipline the long-term unemployed (who would, according to neo-liberal theory, then exert a disciplining force on the wages of those in employment); any concern with the quality of training offered has been very much secondary. The evidence suggests that YTS training, for example, has had a negligible impact on young persons' skills: at worst, it may simply have encouraged some people to leave full-time education.

4.67 Running in tandem with these developments was the removal of trade union influence at the institutional level from training schemes. The dismantling the industrial training boards began with the Employment Act 1980. After seeing its functions whittled away the successor to the Manpower Services Commission, the Training Commission, was abolished in 1990. In the place of these more or less tripartite bodies have emerged Training and Enterprise Councils ('TECs'), dominated by employer interests. Thus, two-thirds of the representatives on each board must be local business leaders from the private sector. As well as providing training responsive to local needs, the TECs administer government training programmes, including the youth training schemes. An example of the employer-led focus of current training is the 'Investors In People' programme, launched in 1990 and again operated by the TECs. Backed only by vague exhortations to companies to develop their employees, its effect has as a result been limited. The seven million people in the UK who have no qualifications at all bear testimony to the relative failure of the TEC schemes.

4.68 Many criticisms can be directed at the current programme, only some of which are touched on here. Most fundamentally, the funding of training remains too low. This includes the inadequate resources given to education in the UK. But no radical steps have been taken redress matters after schooling is completed. At the same time, existing initiatives are too readily dominated by short-term employer interests rather than the needs of the trainees for the future. At the institutional level, the domination of the TECs by local employer interests means that they tend to service the short-term skill shortages of local employers rather than address the more important skills shortages in the workforce generally. It is plausible that the nature of their funding has the consequence that they neglect those whose training is expensive, such as persons with special needs, language difficulties or disabled workers. Finally, the Government's obsession of disciplining the unemployed has meant that training scheme placements are often viewed as undesirable, low status jobs by participants - hardly the best way to encourage them to acquire what are meant to be necessary skills.

(b) Reform

4.69   Training policy involves issues, such as general education, which extend far beyond the duties owed by an employer to its workers. For that reason, only some suggestions are put forward here. But at the heart of any egalitarian and progressive training policy should be a concern both to improve macro-economic performance and to promote fairness, in the widest sense, among workers and the unemployed. As part of these goals, it is suggested that a comprehensive training policy needs to address a number of issues. As a starting point, however, we propose that employers should be under a general training duty to ensure that their workers are adequately trained and have the skills required for the jobs they are required to do. We also propose that trade unions should be centrally involved in future training policy, at all levels. In particular trade unions have a role to play in developing a training programme at the level of the enterprise, in order to assist the employer in fulfilling its general training duty.

4.70   So far as the role of trade unions in the enterprise is concerned, this can be encouraged in a number of ways. In the first place, there should be an obligation on the part of employers to consult with recognised or representative trade unions in the enterprise with a view to agreeing and developing a general training strategy for the enterprise. Secondly, this general duty should be supplemented by specific training duties, for example to consult with the workforce representatives in the context of introducing new methods of working or new technologies, as recommended by the Manpower Services Commission as long ago as 1985. It would also be appropriate to impose specific duties on the employer in relation to job security which is particularly vulnerable to erosion in a period of rapid technological change. Apart from a specific duty to consult trade union representatives in a redundancy situation on the question of retraining it might also be provided that where an employer cannot show that the costs of training greatly outweigh the costs of redundancies, any dismissal would be automatically unfair, notwithstanding the fact that the job had disappeared.

4.71 Although training at enterprise level is clearly important, as we have already indicated there is a need also for training initiatives at the sectoral level as well. It is equally important that trade unions should be involved at this level, for too much focus on individual company interests can sacrifice the long term skills which both workers and the economy in general may need. Consequently, we propose that steps should be taken to encourage collective bargaining on training matters at the sectoral level, and in the previous chapter we have provided some account of the institutional structures upon which any initiative could build. We also propose that initiatives of this kind should be financed by a training levy of employers which would be payable by all employers in the industry in question, with the amount of the levy to be set by the respective Sectoral Employment Commission, should this proposal be adopted. The amount of the levy payable by each employer would vary according to the number of workers employed, and it is for consideration whether small businesses should be exempt from the levy or assessable at a lower rate.

4.72 There is a training responsibility beyond the level of the firm and beyond the level of the different industries. There is also a government responsibility, which could be discharged in two ways. The most basic requirement is a fuller investment in education to guarantee that each school leaver possesses certain core competencies, such as literacy. Although education policy is beyond our immediate brief, we are concerned nevertheless that steps should be taken as part of general education policy to provide opportunities for adults to enter or re-enter the formal education sector. But apart from responsibility to provide education for work, there is a second responsibility of the State which is to co-ordinate training needs within the economy as a whole, in order to identify areas of need and to ensure that steps are taken to meet these needs. We propose that consideration should be given to the creation of a body such as a Training Commission, a tripartite public body with training responsibilities of a strategic nature whose members would include not only trade unions and employers but also representatives of local authorities and others in the education field.

4.73 Finally, in terms of the rights of individual workers we propose that workers should have a statutory right to time off with pay to undergo training which is necessary for the job they are employed to do. We also propose that workers should have a statutory right to reasonable time off from their employment in order to undertake further study in order to extend their skills and qualifications. It is for consideration to what extent the time off should be with pay, and the extent to which State grants, tax incentives or loans could be used to provide financial support to individuals, reflecting the public interest at stake. We further propose that where a worker is faced with redundancy, he or she could have an additional right to take time off to engage in training, and again it is for consideration how far the cost should be borne by workers themselves (possibly with the help of tax relief or loans), employers (perhaps subsidised by public funds) or more directly by the State.

Fairness at Work

4.74   The right to be treated fairly at work is already recognised by the common law (to the extent that there is an implied term of the contract of employment that the employer will not treat employees 'arbitrarily, capriciously or inequitably' in matters of pay (*Gardner (FC) Ltd v Beresford* [1978] IRLR 63), or that they will not 'without reasonable and proper cause' act in a way 'calculated to destroy the relationship of confidence and trust between employer and employee' (*Woods v W M Car Services (Peterborough) Ltd* [1982] ICR 692), and by legislation (to the extent that there is a right not to be unfairly dismissed in the Employment Rights Act 1996). In both cases, however, the scope of the principle is limited, in the case of the common law by the fact that the implied terms are often unenforceable without the employee first leaving the job and the economic security which it provides, and in the case of the legislation by the fact that it applies only to decisions relating to dismissal.

4.75   If we are serious about the right of workers not to be treated unfairly at work, it is for consideration whether the principle of fairness should be extended, and if so how this might be done. There are really two questions for consideration: the first is the application of the principle of fairness during the subsistence of the employment relationship, and the second is the application of the principle on termination of the relationship, a matter considered at greater length in chapter 9. So far as the former issue is concerned, we have been concerned to ask whether the protection against unfair treatment should depend upon the implied terms of the contract of employment, particularly when these terms are for all practical purposes often unenforceable. There may well be a case for statutory protection against unfair treatment at work generally, just as there is statutory protection for discriminatory treatment on the basis of race and sex covering a wide range of employer decisions. Our immediate concerns, however, are to ensure that within the workplace there is a forum for the effective resolution of grievances on the one hand, that there are in place procedures to prevent employers unilaterally altering working conditions on the other, and that workers have an opportunity to challenge unfair disciplinary measures taken against them.

(a) Grievance Procedures

4.76 A key feature of any properly functioning workplace committed to the principle of fairness is a properly constituted and accessible grievance procedure, through which workers can raise their concerns and have them dealt with by the employer. Yet at the present time there is very little legal regulation of grievance procedures. It is true that the written statement of terms and conditions of employment which employers are required to issue to employees under the Employment Rights Act 1996, section 1 must contain particulars of a person to whom 'the employee can apply for the purpose of seeking redress of any grievance relating to his employment'. The difficulty with this, however, is that an employer is merely required to provided information about a procedure which he or she has imposed. There is no regulation of the content of the procedure or any requirement that it should be jointly agreed with workers' representatives. Nor indeed is there a procedure available to employers on the model of the ACAS Disciplinary Procedure which industrial tribunals may take into account in legal proceedings.

4.77 Apart from this statutory duty a further obligation on employers may exist at common law. In an important decision of the Employment Appeal Tribunal in *W A Goold (Pearmak) Ltd v McConnell* [1995] IRLR 516 the statutory duty to refer to grievance procedures in the written statement of particulars was cited as a clear indication that Parliament had 'considered that good industrial relations requires employers to provide their employees with a method of dealing with grievances in a proper and timeous fashion'. This led in turn to the conclusion that 'there was an implied term in the contract of employment that the employers would reasonably and promptly afford a reasonable opportunity to their employees to obtain redress of any grievance they may have'. It is unclear how widely this term will extend though there is no reason to believe that it will be confined to the facts of this particular case. But even so, it is of limited value in the sense that despite being of great importance in principle, in practice the employee's only remedy for the employer's failure to respond to a grievance may be to resign and to claim that he or she has been constructively dismissed.

4.78   We are of the view that the position relating to grievance procedures needs to be revised and improved. It is not in our view sufficient that employers should be at liberty unilaterally to determine the content of these procedures, subject only to whatever demands may be imposed indirectly by the law of unfair dismissal. We therefore propose that employers should be required to have a grievance procedure in place which must be agreed with the representatives of a recognised or representative trade union, failing which a procedure approved by a Labour Inspector which should comply with minimum standards set down in a Code of Practice to be drafted by ACAS. An acceptable grievance procedure should (i) specify with whom a grievance may be raised in the first instance and to whom any appeal or reference for further consideration should be made. It should (ii) indicate that the worker is entitled to be represented in any written or oral stage in the procedure by a trade union representative. And it should (iii) indicate what steps are to be taken in the event of the grievance being unresolved, contemplating the possibility of some form of external review as a final stage. In the absence of such a procedure a worker should be entitled to refer a grievance in the first instance to a Labour Adjudicator, as proposed in chapter 10.

(b) Changing Terms and Conditions

4.79   The unilateral variation of established terms and conditions of employment by employers has become a common problem in certain industries in recent years. Two problems arise, the first being the introduction of changes under the authority of express or implied terms of the contract of employment, and the second being the unilateral imposition of changes to an existing contract. The position is made worse by what appears to be the increasingly common use of 'Reserve clauses' which purport to grant to employers open-ended powers to modify and abrogate terms and conditions of employment. Yet even in the absence of terms of this kind (the legal status of which are uncertain) workers may often be powerless to assert their legal rights under the contract. It is true that unilateral variations by employers are likely to amount to a repudiatory breach of individual contracts of employment, but it is not clear in all cases what sanctions are then available to an individual worker. An injunction to restrain the employer from breaking the contract is unlikely to be available; damages or compensation may be awarded for wrongful or unfair dismissal; but this may be of little assistance to a worker who wishes to retain his or her job. In some cases an employee dismissed for refusing to submit to new terms and conditions may well find that the dismissal is fair and that no remedy is available.

4.80 Some of the issues relating to the problem of unilateral variation would be resolved if many of our proposals elsewhere in this text were to be adopted. Under the provisions considered above, variation around the standards laid down in the legislation or collective agreements governing the employment relationship would not be permitted, except in so far as the legislation itself authorised such derogation. Even then, as in the case of working time, such derogation would be conditional upon the involvement of recognised or representative trade unions, and would have to involve compensatory payments or rest periods for the workers affected. It does not follow, however, that the problem would be eliminated completely, for there is the possibility of the unilateral variation of individual agreements which confer benefits beyond those prescribed by collective agreements or by statute, and there is also the more worrying problem of the situation which would prevail if our proposals were not to be adopted. There is thus a need for a more effective procedure which would prevent employers from unilaterally imposing changes to working conditions without any effective remedies being available to the workers affected. We are not suggesting of course that working conditions should never be changed. What we are suggesting, however, is that change should be introduced only after proper procedures and due formality have been observed.

4.81 There is in the first place a case for regarding 'Reserve clauses' as void on the grounds of the uncertainty they introduce into the employment relationship. This would require the employer to indicate to workers the terms of their engagement with reasonable certainty in the statement of written particulars. Secondly, however, it ought to be possible also to nullify unlawful variations to the terms of the employment relationship. We propose in the first instance that a complaint about a unilateral variation of employment conditions should be made to a Labour Inspector who in turn should be empowered to make an order to the effect that an unlawful variation was void, thereby reinstating the original terms. Appeal against the Labour Inspector's ruling would be heard by a Labour Court or other appropriate body for resolving disputes over terms and conditions of employment. We also propose that steps should be taken to prevent employers dismissing workers because they refuse to submit to a variation of terms and conditions of the employment relationship (unless, for example, the change takes place as a result of collective bargaining or as a result of a new sectoral employment agreement or award). This is a matter which we deal with more fully in chapter 9 below. For the present it is enough to anticipate our proposal that it should be automatically unfair to dismiss someone because he or she refuses to agree to a variation of working conditions.

(c) Disciplinary Procedures

4.82   Under the law as it currently stands there is also inadequate regulation of the disciplinary powers of employers. It is true that the written statement of terms and conditions of employment which employers are required to issue to employees under the Employment Rights Act 1996, section 1, should include a note specifying any disciplinary rules applicable to the employee. This is an obligation on employers which we propose should be retained. But as in the case of grievance procedures, there is no regulation of the content of these procedures, though unlike grievance procedures there is an ACAS Code of Practice which lays down recommended minimum standards. The Code of Practice may be taken into account in legal proceedings, but it is not directly enforceable by an aggrieved employee. It is also the case that the burgeoning case law on unfair dismissal has established a number of guidelines with which employers would have to comply in terms of their disciplinary procedures if they wished to avoid liability for an unfair disciplinary dismissal. The courts have quite rightly emphasised the need for a hearing of the employee before the dismissal takes place and of the need to ensure that the decision to dismiss is 'reasonable'.

4.83   The question of disciplinary procedures before dismissal is a matter which we consider in chapter 9 below. Our concern here relates to the position of workers faced with disciplinary action short of dismissal which may take the form of a financial penalty or a downgrading or demotion. In these cases the aggrieved worker might have one of two options. The first would be to seek a remedy for breach of contract or for a breach of the Employment Rights Act 1996, Part II where the disciplinary action by the employer is not authorised by the contract of employment or sanctioned in accordance with the procedures first introduced by the Wages Act 1986. But if these requirements are met, there is of course nothing that can be done. Secondly, it would be possible to contemplate the possibility of resignation from the job and for the worker to claim that he or she had been constructively dismissed. But again it would be necessary to show that the employer had acted in breach of contract and in any event it is not clear why a worker should have to resign in order to establish his or her right to be treated fairly by an employer exercising disciplinary powers. It is against this background that we propose that there should be more direct regulation of the exercise of employer's disciplinary powers in cases other than dismissal.

4.84 In our view it should be open to a worker to challenge a disciplinary decision against him or her. In the first place, a decision would be unfair if it failed to comply with the employer's disciplinary procedure, which should be based on an agreement with a recognised or representative trade union, failing which is one which has been approved by a Labour Inspector guided by a Code of Practice. In the absence of either of the foregoing the employer would be advised to follow the terms of the relevant Code of Practice as a guide to fairness; otherwise the disciplinary action could be unfair simply on the ground of an unfair procedure. Secondly, we propose that a decision should be considered to be unfair even where it follows the prescribed procedure if it can be said that the penalty (even if authorised) is disproportionate to the 'offence' which the worker has been found to have committed. This would have the effect of ensuring that employers not only follow their procedures but reach conclusions which are seen to be fair and reasonable. In terms of enforcing this right not to be disciplined unfairly, we propose that any complaints could be raised in the first instance with a Labour Adjudicator, along the lines discussed more fully in chapter 10.

Pensions: Income Security in Retirement

4.85 For most people there is a close relationship between their employment and the provision of a decent pension. The most important sources of retirement income are the State scheme on the one hand, and occupational pension schemes sponsored by employers on the other, both of which provide pensions which depend largely on years of work and, to a more limited extent, levels of earnings. Unfortunately, the current structure of retirement provision, characterised by limited State provision, an unplanned patchwork of employer sponsored schemes, and voluntary savings by those who can afford it, delivers an inadequate income to a large proportion of pensioners.

4.86 It is true that many workers still do well, particularly those who belong to an occupational scheme for most or all of their working life. But the present structure of providing pensions in the United Kingdom means that millions of people cannot expect an adequate pension; and if no changes are made to the present structure then the number of those with inadequate benefits is set to increase. The general characteristics that the millions of workers who are set to receive inadequate pensions tend to share are that their pay is below average; they work for small businesses; and they have temporary or part-time employment. All that such workers, the great majority of whom are women, can expect by way of a pension are currently inadequate benefits provided through the State. Outside Government, few people disagree with the need to improve the income of the poorest pensioners both now and in the future, but views vary as to the best way by which this can be achieved. The fundamental question is what should be the role of the State? But even when this has been resolved there is still the question of the role of collective bargaining in going beyond the level of pension ensured by the State.

(a) The Role of the State

4.87   As far as the role of the State is concerned there are on one side of the debate those who see a continuing and important role for a State scheme, funded on a pay-as-you-go basis, providing everyone with an adequate minimum pension plus an earnings-related pension for those workers not in a satisfactory employer sponsored scheme. At the other end of the spectrum, the State is seen as having only a residual role, which is simply to ensure that everyone makes their own arrangements for retirement and to provide benefits on a means tested basis for those who for one reason or another are unable to do so. Those who argue that the provision of an adequate State scheme is not viable generally base their argument on the question of cost and the burden which it is claimed it will place on future generations of workers. The answer, they believe, is compulsory additional savings which will provide workers with a pension on top of the inadequate flat rate benefit provided for them by the State. The idea of compulsory savings is generally coupled with the introduction of some form of minimum guaranteed pension from the State, on a means tested basis, to deal with those who have been unable to build up an adequate pension.

4.88   There are a number of differences in the form of the compulsory second tier pension that different people have suggested but the variation is more in the detail than in the principle. Thus the Commission for Social Justice, the National

Association of Pension Funds, Frank Field MP and, most recently, the Retirement Income Inquiry have all proposed some form of compulsory savings arrangement on top of the State pension for those workers who are not already in an employer sponsored scheme. The Commission for Social Justice favoured industry-wide schemes run jointly by employers and employees, while the Retirement Income Inquiry has suggested a new National Pension Scheme run independently of the Government. What now finds little favour is the widespread use of personal pensions as they are seen to be too expensive to sell and administer, particularly for the lower paid who are the main losers under the present system. Also currently out of favour is the compulsory second tier pension already in existence, namely the State Earnings Related Pension Scheme (SERPS). Following government cuts, this will now only provide pensions that are a quarter or less of those originally envisaged, and indeed only 17 per cent of the workforce are now accruing full SERPS benefits.

4.89   In our view the most important role for the State in this area is to ensure the structure and benefit levels, both for the basic pension and for the State Earnings Related Pension Schemes (SERPS), that will ensure an adequate pension for all workers. Secondly, the State needs to establish minimum standards for private pension provision, whether this is in addition to or in substitute for State benefits. As far as social security legislation is concerned the aim must be to ensure that all workers receive an adequate income when they retire and that the necessary mechanisms are in place, whether public or private, to make such an objective feasible. Any system which fails to deliver this objective is unacceptable. We also see virtue in basing the system on tried and tested structures which as far as possible avoid the indignities and inefficiencies of means testing. We therefore propose:

*   First, all workers should be guaranteed a minimum acceptable level of income in their retirement by means of a flat rate benefit paid at a level in excess of the present inadequate basic pension. We believe that this income should be provided by the State, paid to all workers as of right and increased in line with general living standards.
*   Secondly, workers should be ensured of a reasonable income in their retirement which is above this basic level and is related to their income while at work. We consider that

for many workers this can be ensured through the restoration and revitalisation of SERPS, but we accept that there is also a role for well-funded occupational schemes as a substitute for SERPS, providing that members are guaranteed that they will be no worse off than had they stayed in SERPS.

(b) Industry-Wide Pension Schemes

4.90 Alongside the restoration of SERPS we propose the expansion of private provision to ensure benefits in excess of the State's minimum. The problem is that the coverage of occupational pension schemes sponsored by a single employer has hit a ceiling, with no significant increase in coverage for almost thirty years. On the other hand personal pensions have been shown to be too expensive and uncertain for the low paid and insecure worker. To expand the coverage of pensions we therefore favour the development of what are generally known as industry-wide pension schemes. The basic idea is that workers should take the initiative to supply for themselves the structures which will provide the pension they need to supplement minimum benefits guaranteed by the State. By acting collectively they will be able to keep costs down to an acceptable level, while providing the opportunity to negotiate the essential contributions form their employers.

4.91   The key characteristics of industry schemes are that they will:

* be established through statutory based collective bargaining between groups of employers and appropriate trade unions;
* operate collectively, covering many employers within a distinct area of employment, defined either by trade and/or geography;
* have fixed contribution rates payable by employers and members, which can be changed only be agreement;
* have benefits based on an appropriate final pay target, to which bonuses will be added, depending upon investment performance;
* be democratic, run by committees with representatives of participating employers but a majority elected by the members; and
* have administrators and investment manager(s) appointed by the control committees.

4.92   This approach to extending the coverage of private pension provision is relatively new to the UK although there are a limited number of examples where the approach has worked successfully. But it has been extremely successful in widening the scope of pension provision in countries as diverse as Australia and Denmark, where , significantly, there have not only been strong trade unions but also strong sectroral institutions for the regulation of working conditions (though paradoxically these are now under attack in Australia). But it is only through such collective bargaining that pension schemes can overcome the problem of coverage, adequacy and expense that beset other forms of provision. It also means that they will achieve a high level of legitimacy in the eyes of potential members. For employers they will offer an easy and relatively inexpensive way of obtaining the advantages of occupational provision, without putting themselves out of line with what other employers are prepared to offer.

4.93   We therefore propose that there should be legislation that will:

* give trade unions the right to represent their members in collective bargaining with employers over the terms of their pension arrangements;
* encourage by legislation the development of industry-wide pensions; and
* require a majority of pension scheme trustees to be nominated by members, rather than the one third provided for in the Pensions Act 1995.

We have already proposed in chapter 3 that the proper forum for the negotiation of industry wide pension provision should be the Sectoral Employment Commissions which we propose should be established.

Transfer of Undertakings

(a) The Impact of European Law
4.94   There can be no dispute that the Transfer of Undertakings (Protection of Employment) Regulations 1981 (and the Acquired Rights Directive (1977/187/EEC) which they implement) have been potent forces in the preservation of job security in recent years. The regulations have proved particularly significant in cushioning the impact of the government's programmes of market testing and compulsory competitive tendering, which have driven many thousands of employees from the public to the private sector. Thanks to TUPE employees have in many cases been able to take not only their jobs with them to their new employments but also many (if not all) of their former conditions of employment. TUPE of course does not just protect workers who move from public to private sector

employment; it also protects all employees who find the identity of their employer has changed, typically as a consequence of a business purchase. In essence it operates by defeating the old common law rule that a change in the identity of the employer brings the contract of employment to an end.

4.95 The development of TUPE and the ARD in the 1990s has been attributable, paradoxically, to the activism of the judges, both in the UK and in the ECJ. It is they who have taken a firm lead both in defining the scope of the regulations and content, often in the teeth of opposition from government and employers' organisations. It was English case law which established that the Regulations might apply to transfers where no assets are transferred (*Dines v Initial Health Care Services Ltd* [1994] IRLR 336), and, most recently, it is the same force that has limited the opportunity of an employer to obtain effective agreements to post-transfer variations in contract affected by a TUPE transfer: *Wilson v St Helens Borough Council* [1996] IRLR 320. While the judges of the European Court of Justice have been responsible for the decisions of principle relating to the Acquired Rights Directive which have guided British judges in their approach to TUPE it is our own judges who can take credit for the enthusiastic application and development of these decisions in the domestic setting.

4.96 Summarising the effect of a large number of decided cases, it is possible to say that in general (and subject to exceptions in special cases) most instances of the contracting-out of specific areas of work will now give rise to transfers subject to TUPE, as will transfers of work between successive contractors. All this has been to the general discomfiture of government, which has generally opposed any widening of the scope of TUPE on the often-heard complaint that to do so imposes unwarranted burdens on business; more particularly, the government has been concerned that the preservation of employees' rights via TUPE and the ARD should not impede its objectives for introducing competition into the public sector. While, however, it has made much of the advantages of competition in achieving better value for money much less has been heard in support of the proposition that it is acceptable to achieve lower prices at the cost of reducing the employment entitlements of the typically low-paid staff responsible for providing services.

4.97 While TUPE is primarily thought of as ensuring the direct protection of employees, it also has an important collective dimension. It operates by encouraging collective representation, although it gives no effective protection to collective agreements when transfers take place. In transfer situations, employers are required to give certain information in advance and to consult with the representatives of employees. Following a ruling of the ECJ, that obligation cannot be restricted to situations where representation takes place via recognised trade unions. Since March 1996, the government, in purported compliance with the ECJ ruling has widened the duty to consult. The obligation now exists where there are elected representatives of the workers, in addition to where there are recognised unions representing affected employees (the Collective Redundancies and Transfer of Undertakings (Protection of Employment) (Amendment) Regulations 1995 (SI 1995/2587)). Controversially, however, an employer may under the new rules comply with the duty to consult by dealing with elected representatives even where a recognised union is also present in the workplace. In other words, the change in the law allows employers to avoid dealing with recognised unions if they can find, as an alternative, elected representatives.

4.98 The Transfer of Undertakings Regulations have acquired a particular relevance in the special context of compulsory competitive tendering. But even if compulsory competitive tendering were to be abolished, there would still be an important role for the regulations in protecting workers in the case of voluntary competitive tendering or in the case of other business mergers and transfers. As a result it is important to identify areas where the law needs to be consolidated and improved to retain and enhance the measures already in place. For despite the many advances made, there are still difficulties in using TUPE as an effective means of defending employment rights. Not least is the complexity of the law and the problems this poses for employees seeking to know and claim their rights. In 1995 the European Commission brought forward proposals for revisions to the Acquired Rights Directive. The proposed revision was opposed by the ETUC and other groups and now appears to be moribund following lack of progress in the European Parliament. But the proposals were examined in the UK by the Select Committee on the European Communities (*Transfer of Undertakings: Acquired Rights*, Session 1995-96, 5th Report, HL Paper 38) and the evidence presented to this Committee from a wide spectrum of interested bodies provides a useful insight into the workings and shortcomings of the present law.

(b) Questions for Reform

4.99 At present the Regulations have no application where a change in employer is brought about by way of share transfer. Here, technically, there is no change in the employer's identity - the corporate personality of the company remains unchanged - but the change of ownership can have profound implications for policy and for the position of individuals employed. At the very least, there is an argument for giving representatives a right to be consulted on such transfers, in order to allow the views of the workforce to be made clear to the new controllers of the company. A problem of a rather different nature relates to employees who find themselves caught between transferor and transferee employers, neither of whom wishes to take responsibility as employer for them; in such circumstances the employee has little choice but to sue both and leave the identification issue to the court or tribunal. The UK has not taken advantage of the provision in the ARD allowing imposition of a continuing liability on the transferor post-transfer with the result that the transfer has the effect of passing on all liability to the transferee. The Commission has recommended that there should be at least some joint liability - and this would certainly be helpful to workers who find that, for one reason or another, a transferee employer is either inaccessible or not worth suing.

4.100 A matter of some concern is the practice of hiving down as a way of avoiding the application of the regulations. Hiving down occurs where a receiver transfers the business in question to a subsidiary while retaining the employees in the employment of the insolvent company. The subsidiary is later sold , free of the employees, to a third party. Regulation 4 of TUPE allows this to happen by providing that no transfer of employment takes place when the business is sold from the original employer to the subsidiary. The earliest the transfer can take place is immediately before the new owner buys the business or takes a controlling shareholding in the subsidiary. As a result, the receiver can dismiss the employees before the business is sold on, ensuring that at no point they become employed by the subsidiary. Regulation 4 is an exception to the normal rule on transfers, and would seem to contradict the goal of protecting employment which underlies the Acquired Rights Directive. The European Court of Justice has held that the Directive should apply in normal situations where an insolvency practitioner is attempting to effect the rescue of the business, but not where an insolvency procedure is concerned solely with the liquidation of assets. There is a case for amending Regulation 4 of TUPE so as to reflect this particular distinction, thereby restricting the potential use of regulation 4 as a means of side-stepping the protection provided by the Regulations.

4.101 Probably the most regrettable exclusion from the protection offered by TUPE is in relation to pensions. The ARD allows for the exclusion of rights under occupational pension schemes, and the UK has taken advantage of that in TUPE, Regulation 7. Recently it has been held that the exclusion of pension rights under TUPE is consistent with the ARD (*Adams v Lancashire County Council and BET Catering Services Ltd* [1996] IRLR 153) but of course it remains open for the UK to go further than the minimum requirements of the Directive. The exclusion of pensions from the rights protected on transfer is probably the single most important limitation on the effectiveness of the Regulations from a worker's point of view. Although there is recognition by some employers that, notwithstanding the pension exclusion, a transferor employer is obliged (under pain of facing constructive dismissal claims) to show that the transferee will provide equivalent pension protections, there is little certainty about what this means. What is, judged by reference to the position of the workforce as a group, 'broadly comparable' from an actuarial point of view, may well mean that some individuals, depending on their personal circumstances do better, and some do worse. A definition of 'broadly comparable' in terms of individual benefits would be a welcome improvement.

4.102 While the cases of the last five years show the potential that both the ARD and TUPE have for safeguarding employment rights at a critical time for an employee, it cannot be certain that the positive support provided by the courts will continue. Already the European Court of Justice has shown signs of wishing to limit the application of the ARD in ways which could impact upon many instances of outsourcing in the UK. Whether the next president of the Employment Appeal Tribunal will continue the kind of approach favoured by Mr Justice Mummery remains to be seen. In these circumstances amendment of the legislation is the safer way to ensure that gains achieved are not lost; any such amendment, it may be hoped, will take account of the fact that the standards set by the ARD constitute minimum and not maximum levels of protection. We therefore propose that the regulations should be amended and adapted to cover a change of ownership of a company; that a worker should be permitted to pursue an appropriate remedy against either the transferee or the transferor; that the restrictions relating to hiving down should be narrowed; that employers should be required to make no less favourable pension provision for workers acquired by a transfer and that the nature of this obligation should be clarified; and that a worker should have a clear statutory right not to suffer any detriment arising out of a transfer. We return to the question of consultation in chapter 7.

Summary of Recommendations

1 A core of statutory rights in a number of areas should apply to every employment relationship as a matter of law.

2 Derogations from statutory standards should be permitted only where they are the subject of collective bargaining at either sector, company or plant level, involving recognised or representative trade unions.

3 All workers should be entitled to a statutory minimum wage, with the Council of Europe decency threshold providing a benchmark for the statutory minimum rate.

4 The statutory minimum wage should be set and reviewed annually by government, following the recommendations of a Fair Wages Commission which would include representatives of the TUC and the CBI.

5 Workers should be entitled to an overtime rate where they are employed in any week for more than a prescribed number of hours, the overtime rate being a minimum of one and a half times the statutory minimum wage.

6 Workers should be protected against arbitrary deductions from pay and legislation should seek to ensure that wages are paid on a regular periodic basis. Payment in kind should be strictly regulated.

7 Workers should enjoy greater protection in the event of their employer's insolvency. The upper limit on the protection of workers' wages should be increased.

8 Workers should have a greater opportunity to recover outstanding sums owed by an insolvent employer from the National Insurance Fund.

9 Workers should have the right not to work for more than 48 hours a week. The limits on working time which are contained in the Working Time Directive (93/104/EC) should be incorporated into domestic UK law, together with the Directive's provisions concerning the regulation of nightwork and shiftwork.

10 The exclusions and derogations contained in and permitted by the Working Time Directive should be reviewed to see how far, if at all, they can be justified on objective economic and social grounds. The provision for individual workers to derogate from the maximum limit of 48 hours per week should be reviewed.

11 Workers should have the right to a statutory minimum of four weeks' paid holidays annually. This would be in addition to time off for family reasons or trade union activities.

12 Employers should be required to have access to qualified occupational health and safety services in developing health and safety strategies, and legislation should prescribe in greater detail the minimum acceptable contents of employers' safety policies.

13 Companies should be required to provide information in their annual reports on their health and safety arrangements, including specialist advisory and treatment services, trends in accident and ill health statistics, and cases where enforcement action has been taken against them.

14 Legislation should specifically acknowledge the duty of employers to protect workers from psycho-social harm and in this way make clear that quality of life issues form part of the agenda of occupational health and safety.

15 A form of no-fault liability should be introduced for senior management and/or members of the board of directors where a company is found to have recklessly exposed workers to serious risk of personal injury.

16 Criminal penalties under health and safety legislation should be made more rational, and it should be easier for workers and their unions to bring private proceedings.

17 Workers should have the right to control the collection, storage, and use of personal data by employers and others, including data held manually. The protections contained in the Data Protection Directive should be incorporated into UK law.

18 The processing of sensitive data revealing a worker's racial or ethnic origin, political opinions, religious or philosophical beliefs, trade union membership, and concerning a worker's health or sex life should only be permitted by an employer in

circumstances specified in the Directive and where the interests of the worker are safeguarded.

19 All workers should have the right to be informed by the employer of the personal data being processed about them, the purposes for which the data is held and the parties to whom it will be disclosed. All workers should have a right of access to this data and the right to have it corrected or erased where appropriate.

20 Electronic monitoring of workers should be permissible only where the employer can demonstrate a sufficient cause which makes the use of such devices necessary, having regard to their impact on the worker's right to privacy.

21 Workers should have the right to speak out about malpractice in the workplace, in accordance with clear statutory guidance. Employers should be required to provide workers with a policy statement on the reporting of improprieties at work and the arrangements that exist for carrying out those policies.

22 There should be no restrictions on the political activities of public servants unless such restrictions can be shown to be necessary in the public interest. Regulations which extend beyond these boundaries should be prohibited.

23 Employers should be under a general training duty, to be developed in consultation with recognised or representative trade unions, to ensure that their workers are adequately trained and have the skills required for the jobs they are employed to do.

24 Workers should have a statutory right (i) to time off with pay to undergo training in the job which they are employed to do, (ii) to reasonable time off from their employment in order to extend their skills and qualifications, and (iii) a right to take time off to engage in training when faced with redundancy.

25 Employers should be required to have a grievance procedure in place which must be agreed with the representatives of a recognised or representative trade union, failing which a procedure approved by a Labour Inspector which should comply with minimum standards set down in a Code of Practice to be drafted by ACAS.

26 Workers should have a right to a speedy remedy to prevent employers changing working conditions without agreement. It should be automatically unfair to dismiss someone because he or she refuses to agree to a variation of working conditions.

27 Workers should have the right to challenge a disciplinary decision against them on the ground that the action in question is unfair, whatever form the disciplinary sanction may take.

28 All workers should be guaranteed a minimum acceptable level of income in their retirement by means of a flat rate benefit paid at a level in excess of the present inadequate basic pension. This income should be provided by the State, paid to all workers as of right and increased in line with general living standards.

29 All workers should be ensured a reasonable income in their retirement which is above the basic level and is related to their income while at work. For many workers this could be ensured through the restoration and revitalisation of SERPS, with well-founded occupational schemes as a substitute.

30 Alongside the restoration of SERPS, there should be an expansion of private provision to ensure benefits in excess of the State's minimum. This should be provided by collectively agreed schemes negotiated and regulated at sectoral level.

31 The Transfer of Undertakings (Protection of Employment) Regulations 1981 should be amended and adapted to cover a change of ownership of a company, and a worker should be permitted to pursue an appropriate remedy under the regulations against either the transferor or the transferee.

32 The Transfer of Undertakings (Protection of Employment) Regulations 1981 should be amended to require employers to make no less favourable pension provision for workers acquired by a transfer, and the nature of this obligation should be clarified; a worker should have a clear statutory right not to suffer any detriment arising out of a transfer.

EQUAL OPPORTUNITIES

5.1   It is commonplace to observe that the life chances of people in Britain differ widely. Health, gender, race and the social and economic class of one's parents all influence, if not determine, one's chances in life. To provide equality of opportunity is to open up the chances in life of the individuals who compose the disadvantaged groups in society. Although our main concern is with the role of law in promoting equality of opportunity at work, it should not be overlooked that general economic and social policies aimed at reducing inequality also have an important part to play. The most important aspect of general economic policy in reducing inequality and expanding opportunities is that of reducing levels of unemployment. Current unemployment levels are 8.5 per cent, according to the claimant count, but just under half of all unemployed men and nearly a third of all unemployed women have been out of work for a year or more. Any policy which succeeds in stimulating employment must create greater equality of opportunity.

5.2   A second priority is to reverse the trend towards increasing inequality of income amongst the working population. Increasing inequality of income has been seen as a price which might have to be paid for the reduction of unemployment, but this argument now appears highly questionable. A suitable minimum wage policy should materially assist the position of the low-paid and thereby do much to further the aim of greater equality of opportunity. Any consideration of wages policy should be in conformity with the EC Commission Opinion on the Equitable Wage, which would mean 'that all workers should receive a reward for work done which in the context of the society in which they live and work is fair and sufficient to enable them to have a decent standard of living.' To this end the Commission have recommended

'further legislation including legislation on discrimination, in particular on grounds of gender, race, ethnic origin or religion;

means of ensuring fair treatment of workers in all age groups and for homeworkers; [and] mechanisms for the establishment of negotiated minima and the strengthening of collective bargaining arrangements'

5.3   A third priority must be to strengthen the framework of statutory employment rights, reducing the admittedly discriminatory effects of extended qualification periods and providing more accessible means of redress. Central to any attempt to enlarge equality of opportunity must be the abandonment of the contractual test of employee status, which, together with long qualification periods, excludes many vulnerable or marginal workers from most forms of employment protection legislation. In so far as this would increase the security of employment of the less skilled and the more vulnerable workers, it would be a major step towards greater equality of life chances. An EC draft Directive on part-time and temporary work has been withdrawn, but consultation is expected to take place between the social partners on the issue. Should this procedure result in agreement or legislation, these standards should be adhered to by the UK, as disparities between the terms and conditions of full-timers and part-timers have a well established indirectly discriminatory effect on women.

5.4   But although a strategy designed to promote equality of opportunity cannot fail to take account of general considerations of this kind, it is also the case that such a strategy also needs carefully directed legal support. In our view this legislation should seek to proceed along three parallel paths: first, it should seek to eliminate discriminatory employment practices; second, it should seek to remove barriers to effective labour market participation; and third, it should seek to promote the right of fair participation in work. In developing these strategies we are also of the view that legislation should be specifically targeted to particular groups who suffer discrimination, disadvantage and exclusion. In other words we reject the view that the problem of discrimination can best be addressed by a single piece of legislation of general application. In our view there is a need to recognise that the patterns of disadvantage and discrimination vary and that legislation can best respond by addressing the problems encountered by different victims of discrimination and disadvantage.

Disability, Discrimination and Equality of Opportunity

5.5   The personal experience of disability in modern societies is frequently characterised by social discrimination, segregation and exclusion. Persons with disabilities are often marginalised and subjected to disadvantage in educational provision, health and welfare services, transport systems, the built environment, the political process, and in social and leisure activities. Above all, disabled people are especially vulnerable to employment discrimination, lack of equal employment opportunities and a denial of basic employment rights. While impairments or disabilities can of themselves produce 'handicaps' to full participation in the labour market, all too often disabled workers are not permitted a chance to demonstrate their abilities or to prove their worth. Rather their employment expectations are cut short and are predetermined by the negative behaviour and attitudes of employers and co-workers. Prejudice, ignorance and fear constantly inform discriminatory employment policies and practices, while disability discrimination has become institutionalised or systemic in the workplace.

(a) Disability, Discrimination and the Labour Market

5.6   According to the Office of Population, Censuses and Surveys (OPCS) research data, disabled persons appear to represent approximately 4-6 per cent of the economically active adult population. Yet only a minority of disabled adults are in work, and this compares unfavourably with the general population. Whereas an estimated 69 per cent of the population under pension age are working, only an estimated 31 per cent of disabled adults are similarly situated. The OPCS research suggests that 10-15 per cent of disabled adults are unemployed, whereas a Social and Community Planning Research (SCPR) study found that 22 per cent of occupationally handicapped, economically active disabled persons were looking for or wanted to work. The economic activity of persons with disabilities varies according to occupational category, socio-economic status and educational or vocational qualifications. Disabled workers are nearly twice as likely as non-disabled workers to lack formal educational qualifications, while manual occupational status and low levels of qualifications tend to be associated with an increased incidence of disabled unemployment.

5.7   Undoubtedly disability has some effect upon the employment and unemployment status of disabled workers. Physical limitations caused by impairment or disability might have a degree of influence upon the chance of getting work and the type of work available to such persons. Thereafter it may well affect working hours and earned income. In the SCPR survey referred to above, 10 per cent of respondents reported facing prejudice and ignorance among employers concerning disability. There was also evidence that, where a disabled person became disabled while in employment, his or her chances of retaining employment were greater if the onset of illness or disability could be concealed from the employer. Length of service and the size of the employing organisation were also relevant factors. Larger firms were more likely to make efforts to retain the newly-disabled worker in post. Managerial or professional employees too had a greater chance of being retained, while skilled or unskilled manual employees were least likely to be kept on. Nearly a quarter of non-retained workers in these situations had not worked again and the remainder had taken an appreciable time to find fresh employment.

5.8   A number of problems faced by disabled workers in attempting to enter employment can be identified. First, they must surmount physical and vocational obstacles during rehabilitation and training. Secondly, disabled persons must overcome the barriers confronted in architectural designs and transportation systems. Thirdly, they will encounter resistance by employers to hiring persons with disabilities. Fourthly, disabled job-seekers experience self-doubt as a product of previous prejudice. Fifthly, they must master the tests created by inflexible medical examinations, which many employers use without questioning their value and utility. It is contended that disability-informed discrimination in many guises plays an important hand in affairs. But a crucial cause of disabled unemployment is employer attitudes and stereotyped prejudices. Discrimination against disabled persons often takes the form of prejudice.

5.9   Prejudice feeds the stereotypical, stigmatised view of disabled persons, exaggerates the negative connotations of impairment, and excludes or devalues other measures of social worth or attributes. The assumption is that disability means inability and consequently many jobs are assumed to be beyond the capacity of disabled workers. In research undertaken for the then Department of Employment and published in 1990, it was found that as many as 40 per cent of employers believed that there were no problems facing them in employing disabled persons. However, when prompted, a number of problems were perceived by 91 per cent of employers. The unsuitability of available jobs, problems with the suitability of the workplace premises, and lack of disabled applicants were the problems most frequently mentioned, although other problems anticipated included problems of getting to work (because the workplace was inaccessible) and shift working. There is clear evidence that employer ambivalence towards disabled people is frequently displaced by antipathy and prejudice.

(b) The Disability Discrimination Act 1995

5.10 Following the controversy surrounding the defeat of the Civil Rights (Disabled Persons) Bill in May 1994 - when the then Minister for Disabled People, Nicholas Scott, effectively talked the Bill out on the floor of the House of Commons - the Government eventually conceded the need for anti-discrimination legislation. Although welcome, and although much improved in Parliament, the Disability Discrimination Act 1995 nevertheless falls short of providing adequate protection and support for disabled workers. A number of problems have been identified, relating first to the definition of disability, secondly to the meaning of discrimination, thirdly to the exceptions and qualifications in the Act, and fourthly to questions of enforcement and remedies, with the Act contrasting unfavourably in a number of important respects with the less than satisfactory legislation dealing with race and gender.

5.11 So far as the definition of 'disability' and 'disabled person' are concerned, these are fundamentally based upon a medical model of impairment. They take little or no account of the social model of disability which seeks to explain disability by reference to the disabling effects of the social, economic and built environment. It is anticipated that many disabled persons will fall through the definitional net and will either fail to establish their status to pursue the right not to be discriminated against or will have to marshal complex and expensive expert medical evidence in order to be able to do so. The failure to take account of the social model of disability also means that, while someone with a history or record of disability will be covered by the law in respect of present discrimination based on past disabilities, the legislation will not protect those individuals wrongly or erroneously perceived to be, treated or reputed to be disabled. Similarly, discrimination based upon association with a disabled person is not explicitly prohibited.

5.12 The meaning of discrimination adopted by the Act is a novel and hybrid one. It does not distinguish between direct and indirect discrimination and thus does not make express provision for adverse effects or adverse impact discrimination. Nevertheless, the Government stated its view that most forms of indirect discrimination experienced by disabled persons will be caught by the hybrid definition, but there is a price to pay for that. Accordingly, disability discrimination is defined as less favourable treatment for a reason which relates to a disabled person's disability and which the discriminator cannot show to be justified. Less favourable treatment is only justified if the reason for it is both material to the circumstances of the particular case and substantial. The hybrid definition of discrimination used in the Act imports a justification defence into both the direct and indirect forms of discriminatory treatment. This flies in the face of existing discrimination theory and practice.

5.13   In terms of exceptions and qualifications, it is true that the Act introduces a welcome duty upon employers to make reasonable adjustments to the workplace and to working practices or policies so as to accommodate disabled persons, a duty not found in such explicit terms in other discrimination statutes. However, financial and other costs (including disruption to any of the employer's activities) have been raised as among the criteria by which the reasonableness of an adjustment might be judged. A matter of equal concern is the total exemption of small businesses from the reach of the Act which means that the anti-discrimination and reasonable adjustment mandates will not affect an employer employing less than 20 people.

5.14   So far as remedies and enforcement are concerned, the remediable framework of the Act, although a mirror image of the Sex Discrimination Act 1975 and the Race Relations Act 1976, is limited to empowering industrial tribunals to make declarations, to award compensation, and to make recommendations. There is no power to make positive orders such as might require an employer to afford to a disabled complainant an employment opportunity which has been denied or refused by virtue of a discriminatory act. There is, moreover, the obvious lack of an enforcement strategy. There is to be no Disability Rights Commission comparable with the Equal Opportunities Commission or Commission for Racial Equality. The National Disability Council is to be a purely advisory body, with no powers to provide aid or assistance to complainants nor to take strategic action to investigate examples of disability discrimination. Its remit in the employment field is severely limited in any event.

(c) A Framework for Reform

5.15   Although the Disability Discrimination Act thus goes some way towards providing a right to disabled workers to compete in the labour market free from disability-related discrimination, it falls short of the comprehensive disability rights legislation demanded by disabled people and disability rights activists. It provides a starting point for the development of disability rights. But there is clearly much to be done. In our view it is necessary first to have in place legislation which prohibits discrimination against disabled workers, but also legislation which genuinely promotes labour market participation by disabled workers by removing structural constraints thereto. In implementing such a strategy, questions arise in relation to the workers who are to be supported by the legislation, defining what is meant by discrimination for this purpose, and the duties which should be imposed on the employer.

5.16 So far as the protected class of workers is concerned, we propose that

* the definition of disability must be both a broad and inclusive one based upon a social, rather than medical, model of disability;
* any measures or devices used to mitigate the effects of impairment or disability should be discounted in identifying disability status;
* contagious diseases should normally be covered by the definition; workers with HIV/AIDS should also be within the protected class, as should individuals who are erroneously perceived, treated or reputed to be HIV seropositive;
* the protected class must also include those who are not presently disabled but who have a previous history of disability or who are wrongly perceived as being disabled or who are identified (perhaps by genetic testing and forecasting) as being prone to or at risk of future illness or disability.

We also propose that discrimination based upon a person's association with a member of the protected class shall be unlawful; and that the burden of proving that a complainant is not a member of the protected class or has not suffered discrimination should be upon the party who asserts otherwise.

5.17 Turning to the definition of discrimination, we propose that

* an employer should not be permitted to discriminate against a disabled person who, with or without reasonable accommodation, can perform the essential functions of the employment position that such an individual holds or desires;

* in deciding what functions are essential, due consideration should be given to the employer's judgement, but the employer's view should not be conclusive;
* in determining a disabled person's employment opportunities, no account should be taken of disability, what might happen in the future or any impact on health insurance or related costs; rather an employer should only be allowed to discriminate on the basis of personal merit and suitability for the job;
* both direct and indirect discrimination should be prohibited;
* discrimination should therefore be defined as including both less favourable treatment by reason of disability, and the application of a requirement, condition, policy or practice which is such that a smaller number of persons with a disability can comply, and which cannot be shown to be justified;
* the use of qualification standards, employment tests and selection criteria should be unlawful if they tend to screen out disabled persons, unless these can be shown to be essential to the job in question.

5.18 We also propose that an employer might defend direct discrimination only by showing lack of a causal connection between the alleged less favourable treatment and the complainant's disability. Indirect discrimination should only be defensible where the employer can objectively justify the use of a bona fide, job-related occupational requirement, condition or qualification or, exceptionally, an overriding business need. Another key issue which needs to be addressed relates to the question of harassment of disabled workers. Protection from harassment is not satisfactorily dealt with by anti-discrimination legislation because it requires a comparison between the treatment of a disabled worker and that of an able bodied worker. We propose that there should be specific statutory provisions setting out a right not to be harassed. This is dealt with in paragraphs 5.94 - 5.98 below. Similarly we propose that the provisions on victimisation should be amended in line with the proposals on sex discrimination (see paragraphs 5.25 - 5.26 below).

5.19 In order to reinforce the protection against discrimination, consideration should be given to the use of medical examinations as a means of screening out disabled persons from employment. We propose that employers should be prohibited from conducting a medical examination of any employment applicant, except for the single purpose of ascertaining ability to perform job-related functions.

Once an offer of employment had been made, a medical examination could be required before the new recruit commenced employment duties and the employer could make the employment offer conditional upon the results of the medical examination. Safeguards would have to built into the use of post-selection, pre-placement medical examinations, which should only be permitted if all successful applicants are subjected to such a medical examination. Once in employment, we propose that workers should not be required to undergo a medical examination at the behest of the employer, except to ascertain a worker's continuing ability to perform job-related functions (although voluntary medical examinations may be conducted as part of an occupational health programme).

5.20   Although we believe that these measures would go a long way to promote equality of opportunity for disabled workers, there is more which needs to be done. It is not enough that the law should seek only to prohibit discrimination. Also important if equality of opportunity is to be promoted is the duty of the employer to take steps to facilitate opportunities for disabled workers. Apart from a commitment to training, we propose that employers should be under a duty to make reasonable accommodation for disabled persons by making alterations to the workplace or by adjusting policies and practices which have an adverse effect upon disabled applicants or workers. A failure or refusal to make reasonable accommodation would be an act of unlawful discrimination and an employer could not plead any available defences to disability discrimination unless he or she had made reasonable efforts to discharge a duty to make reasonable accommodation. The duty to make reasonable accommodation, and indeed all our proposals on disability, would apply to all employers, with no exemption being provided for small businesses. We propose, however, that a failure to make reasonable accommodation would be nevertheless subject to a defence of undue hardship and the burden of proving undue hardship should be on the employer, taking account of the nature and cost of the accommodation. The employer would be expected to have considered the availability of grants from public funds to meet the expense of the measures required.

5.21   In addition to the duty to adapt premises, there are other measures which could be taken to promote equality of opportunity for disabled workers. These include statutory rights to time off work. In our view there should be a new right to paid disability leave for those workers who become seriously ill or disabled on the job or while in employment. During this minimum period of paid disability leave it would be an automatically unfair dismissal for an employer to terminate the contract of employment and such termination would be void. After the minimum period of paid disability leave the worker could only be dismissed in accordance with the principles of unfair dismissal outlined in chapter 9. The employer would first have to satisfy the duty to make reasonable accommodation in any event. In the case of job-related illness or disability, there might be a case for a longer period of paid (or unpaid) disability leave before the employer could consider a fair dismissal.

5.22 The working rights of carers or partners of disabled persons also warrant special protection. We propose that they should be protected from discrimination by association with a disabled person. Furthermore, we propose that a carer or partner would be enabled to enjoy the benefits of a right to reasonable accommodation such as adjustments to working time. There might also be a case for a right to carers' leave commensurate with any right to parental leave, on which see paragraph 5.60 below. Initiatives for parental and family leave are considered below where we propose the introduction of time off work with pay for parents and for other workers with dependent children. We propose that the scheme be adapted to extend a similar benefit to workers with disabled dependants. We also propose that these measures be adapted to deal with the needs of parents with disabled children for whom more flexible provision may be necessary.

5.23 As noted above the current law lacks an adequate strategy for the enforcement of disability rights for workers. While the National Disability Council was established under the Disability Discrimination Act 1995, its function is only that of an advisory body. In order to strengthen the proposed statutory rights for disabled workers, we propose that a Disability Rights Commission (DRC) should be established, with comparable powers to those of the Equal Opportunities Commission and the Commission for Racial Equality. The Commission should be charged with the general duty to work towards the elimination of discrimination, to promote equality of opportunity for disabled persons and to review the operation of all disability legislation. The Commission should also have the power to assist individuals or groups in bringing complaints under disability legislation; and to investigate cases of disability discrimination, or failures by employers to provide reasonable accommodation for disabled workers. This is a matter to which we return in chapter 10.

Sex Discrimination and Sexual Orientation

5.24 The current legislation prohibiting discrimination on the grounds of sex was introduced in 1975. Under the Sex Discrimination Act, it is unlawful for an employer (though the Act applies to activities other than employment and to persons other than employers) to discriminate against a worker on the grounds of sex in relation to a range of matters dealing with the employment relationship. Discrimination is defined to include direct and indirect discrimination, and the Act applies not only to discrimination against women, but also against men, married persons in employment, and people who have been victimised for bringing a complaint under the Act. Direct discrimination means less favourable treatment on grounds on grounds of sex, whereas indirect discrimination means discrimination arising from the common application of a rule or practice, which is neutral on its face, but which has a disproportionate effect upon the members of one sex, and which cannot be justified by the employer.

(a) Reforming the Sex Discrimination Act 1975

5.25 The Sex Discrimination Act 1975 applies to prohibit discrimination against women, or against men, or against married persons in the employment field. We propose that in principle legislation should continue to apply to these categories but that it should be expanded. We also propose in particular that the provisions concerning the discrimination against married persons in the employment field should be altered to outlaw discrimination on the grounds of 'marital and family status'. This would bring national law into line with Article 2(1) of the EC Equal Treatment Directive (76/207/EC). We also propose that the statutory protection against victimisation should be amended, as a result of the decision in *Cornelius v University College Swansea* [1987] IRLR 141 where it was indicated that it was not sufficient for complainants to show that they were victimised because they brought proceedings under the 1975 Act; they also had to show that they would not have been victimised for bringing proceedings under a different statute.

5.26 The EOC has recommended that 'any persons suffering detriment as a result of anything done under or by reference to, the Sex Discrimination Act or the Equal Pay Act shall be the victim of unlawful victimisation'. The Government, in its response, has agreed that a victimisation claim should succeed if: (a) the act of the victim was done under or by reference to the legislation; (b) the discriminator treated the victim as he or she did because the victim did the act; and (c) that treatment was less favourable than would have been given if the victim had not done that act. In addition, the Government has agreed that it should be irrelevant whether the discriminator was influenced by the connection with the legislation and also that passive participants in cases (e.g. comparators) should have protection. We propose that these recommendations should be implemented and they should also be applied to discrimination on grounds of race, sexual orientation and disability.

5.27 In terms of the definition of discrimination in the Sex Discrimination Act 1975, we propose that the definition of direct discrimination should remain unaltered. So far as indirect discrimination is concerned, the current definition has caused three problems for complainants. First, they have had difficulty in identifying a discriminatory 'requirement or condition' (especially if the requirement is composite e.g. age, qualifications and experience), and secondly, they are faced by a narrow judicial interpretation of the phrase. In *Perera v Civil Service Commission* [1983] ICR 428 the Court of Appeal held that a 'requirement or a condition' could only exist if it amounted to a complete bar if not met. This means that the widespread use by employers of 'preferences' - practices which are relevant in a particular situation but which are not decisive - cannot form the basis of a claim. We propose that the definition should be amended to make it clear that it includes any practice or policy as well as any requirement or condition which has a disproportionate impact on the members of a particular sex. Thirdly, the definition is restrictive as it provides that a requirement or condition will only be unlawful if a 'considerably smaller' proportion of the disadvantaged group can comply with it. We propose that it should be enough only that a 'smaller' proportion can comply.

5.28 The other problem with the current definition of indirect discrimination relates to the question of justification. The difficulty arises partly as a result of the interpretation which the courts placed on this defence in *Ojutiku v Manpower Services Commission* [1982] ICR 661 where the Court of Appeal said that the employer did not need to prove that the requirement was necessary for the good of the business but rather that 'if a person produces reasons for doing something which would be acceptable to right thinking people as sound and tolerable reasons for so doing then he has justified his conduct.' Since, the ECJ's ruling in *Bilka-Kaufhaus GmbH v Weber von Hartz* [1986] IRLR 317, the domestic courts have adopted a stricter interpretation of justifiability. In line with these decisions, we propose the introduction of a statutory provision which adopts a stricter approach to justifiability which would require the employer to show that there was no alternative non-discriminatory way to meet the business needs of the enterprise, and that the means chosen had the smallest burden possible on women (or men, as the case may be).

5.29   As a result of the foregoing we propose that the definition of discrimination in the Sex Discrimination Act 1975 should be amended as follows:

(1) A person discriminates against a woman in any circumstances relevant for the purposes of any provision of this Act if: (a) on the ground of her sex he treats her less favourably than he treats or would treat a man, or (b) he applies to her a requirement, condition, policy or practice which he applies or would apply to a man but -

   (i) which is such that the proportion of women who can comply with it is smaller than the proportion of men who can comply with it;

   (ii) which is to her detriment because she cannot comply with it; and

   (iii) which the employer cannot show to be justifiable irrespective of the sex of the person to which it is applied.

(2) In order to establish that a requirement, condition, policy or practice is justifiable, the employer must show that the means corresponded to an essential need on the part of the undertaking, that it was narrowly tailored to that objective, and that there was no non-discriminatory alternative way of achieving that objective.

5.30   Turning from questions of definition of discrimination and the scope of the Act to the areas of activity to which it applies, this is dealt with principally by section 6 of the Act, at least so far as discrimination by employers against applicants and workers is concerned. Currently, victims of sexual harassment must rely on section 6 for protection. Sexual harassment has not been satisfactorily dealt with by this provision and we propose that a specific statutory right not to be sexually harassed should be created (see paragraphs 5.94 - 5.98). We also propose that section 6 should be amended to deal specifically with the omission of pay, currently excluded because of the overlap with the Equal Pay Act 1970. In our view this exclusion should be removed, thereby applying the existing regime to cases of individual women who have a complaint about discrimination in pay and conditions. Consequently, women who consider they are paid less than men either on recruitment or subsequently during the employment would be able to argue that they have either been directly or indirectly discriminated against on the grounds of their sex, applying the tests laid down in the legislation. This proposal is without prejudice to our wider proposals on 'pay equity' developed below and would be complementary to any such changes.

5.31 We therefore propose that the scope of the legislation relating to discrimination on the grounds of sex should be expanded as follows:

(1) It is unlawful for persons in relation to employment by them at an establishment in Great Britain, to discriminate against a woman -
  (a) in the arrangements they make for the purpose of determining who should be offered that employment, or
  (b) in the terms on which they offer her that employment, including the rate of pay and other aspects of the remuneration package, or
  (c) by refusing or deliberately omitting to offer her that employment.
(2) It is unlawful for persons, in the case of a woman employed by them at an establishment in Great Britain, to discriminate against her -
  (a) in the way they afford her access to opportunities for promotion, transfer or training, or to any other benefits, facilities or services, or by refusing or deliberately omitting to afford her access to them, or
  (b) in the method, rate and composition of payment, or
  (c) by dismissing her, or taking any other action against her, or by subjecting her to any other detriment.

(b) Sexual Orientation: Extending the Frontiers of the 1975 Act
5.32 Discrimination against lesbian and gay workers in Britain is widespread and manifests itself in many varied forms. A report published by Stonewall in 1993, based on a survey of 1,845 lesbians and gay men, revealed that 48 per cent of respondents had been harassed at work because they were known or suspected to be lesbian or gay. When asked whether they had been refused a job or promotion for the same reason, 22 per cent and 24 per cent respectively said that they either knew or suspected they had, whilst 8 per cent said they had been dismissed because of their sexuality. The Stonewall

survey also revealed that 68 per cent of respondents hid their sexuality from some or all of the people with whom they worked for fear of the victimisation or discrimination which might follow. The disadvantage experienced by gay men and lesbians also extends to the issues of pay and other bonuses. In some workplaces homosexual relationships are not considered to be of "equal value" to heterosexual relationships, as demonstrated in the fact that gay men and lesbians are often paid less in terms of pensions, travel bonuses, health insurance and other benefits as compared with their heterosexual colleagues.

5.33   The law currently provides little, if any, protection for gay men and lesbians in the workplace. In recent years the Government has fiercely resisted a series of measures designed to prohibit unequal treatment at work on the grounds of sexual orientation. As proposed in Baroness Turner's Sexual Orientation Discrimination Bill, we believe that the Sex Discrimination Act 1975 should be extended to provide that it is not only unlawful to discriminate against men and women on the grounds of sex, but also to discriminate against men and women on the grounds of sexual orientation. Applying the definition used in the New Zealand Human Rights Act 1993, the term sexual orientation should be understood for these purposes to mean a person's heterosexual, homosexual, lesbian or bisexual orientation. The Sex Discrimination Act 1975 also prohibits discrimination against married persons, which we propose above should be extended to family status. For this purpose family status should be understood to encompass both heterosexual and homosexual relationships. We also propose that the definition should be wide enough to include transsexuals.

5.34   Turning to the meaning of discrimination, we propose that the definition of discrimination on grounds of sexual orientation should apply to both direct and indirect discrimination. We also propose that direct discrimination on grounds of supposed sexual orientation should be prohibited in order to protect individuals who may experience anti-homosexual discrimination, but who are in fact neither gay nor lesbian. In line with existing anti-discrimination legislation, the prohibition against discrimination by employers on grounds of sexuality should apply to all aspects of the employment relationship. We propose therefore that it should be unlawful for an employer to discriminate on the grounds of sexual orientation, in relation to employment at an establishment in Britain, in the selection or candidates for appointment, in the terms under which employment is offered, and by refusing or deliberately omitting to offer someone employment. It should also be unlawful to discriminate on grounds of sexuality in matters such as access to promotion, transfer or training; the terms and conditions of employment (including pay); or subjecting the worker to any other detriment.

5.35 Equally, it is important that an employer should be prohibited from terminating the employment relationship on the grounds of sexual orientation. Whilst employees, with two years' continuous service, who suspect that they have been dismissed because of their sexuality, may currently claim unfair dismissal, the likelihood of success is minimal. This is largely because the tribunals and courts may to give considerable weight to the argument that it is reasonable for employers to act upon the actual, or even presumed, feelings and prejudices of their clients or other employees. This is the case even if those feelings or prejudices appear unreasonable when assessed objectively. We propose that the law should clearly provide that it is unlawful for an employer to discriminate against a worker by dismissing him or her on grounds of sexual orientation. We further propose that dismissal on grounds of sexual orientation should be automatically unfair under general legislation on dismissal, on which see paragraph 9.34 below. Finally, it should be unlawful to harass a worker either directly on grounds of sexuality, or indirectly, because of stereotypes relating to HIV seropositivity. We propose that a specific statutory right not to be harassed should be provided (see paragraphs 5.94-5.98).

Sex Discrimination, Equal Pay and Pay Equity

5.36 The current equal pay legislation has been in place for almost twenty years, and equal value claims have been available for eleven. Prior to the implementation of the equal value amendments in 1983, the progress which had been made in women's relative pay had ground to a halt. While full-time women's hourly wages increased by 12 percentage points between 1970 and 1977 (63 per cent to 75 per cent), in 1978 the figure fell and remained at around 73-74 per cent thereafter. Substantial progress did not begin to be made again until 1987. Since then the 'headline' rate has increased to 79.6 per cent but progress has slowed over the last few years and the hourly earnings of manual and non-manual women workers relative to equivalent men, and of part-time women workers, remain very much lower than 79.6 per cent (standing, in 1995, at 72.8 per cent, 69.2 per cent and 59.6 per cent respectively). Women's weekly earnings are lower still.

5.37 The gap between men's wages and those of women comes

about in a number of ways. In the first place, women are segregated both occupationally and in terms of establishment. Predominantly female occupations attract lower rates of pay than do those in which men work and even where men and women are doing the same kinds of jobs (but in different workplaces, for different employers) women's wages are lower. This is particularly true where the women are working part-time. Secondly, even where men and women do the same kinds of work in the same organisation, men tend to attract higher wages for reasons associated with women's concentration in lower-paying specialisms, occupation of lower status jobs and the operation of payment systems which impact differently on men and women (by, for example, rewarding 'seniority' or 'flexibility', or by awarding performance-related pay predominantly in male-dominated jobs or on the basis of characteristics stereotypically associated with men).

5.38 Women's wages are held down by direct and indirect sex discrimination in terms of access to jobs (in particular, by problems associated with motherhood) and in relation to payment itself (the undervaluation of female jobs for reasons associated with sex as well as the indirectly discriminatory factors already mentioned above). It is clear that the current individualised system for enforcing the principle of equal value used in sex discrimination cases is not workable or effective. There are three reasons for this. First, equal value can only be established if a complainant can find a man in the same establishment doing work of equal value. In highly segregated establishments such a man may not exist. Secondly, equal value requires that the two jobs be equal in value. This means that disproportionate differentials between jobs of admittedly different value cannot be challenged. Thirdly, the notion of 'value' is too indeterminate, running a high risk of being re-imbued with the stereotypes currently associated with women's work. We propose therefore that measures should be introduced which aim to deal with disparities in pay based on sex as a collective issue, spanning different establishments, and avoiding the problem of value.

5.39 In order to achieve pay equity, defined as a situation in which inequalities in pay are distributed evenly throughout the population, rather than being closely correlated with gender, race, ethnicity or a combination of these, we propose that a threefold strategy is required. In the first place there is a need for a statutory minimum wage which, as we point out in paragraph 5.2 above, would go some way towards addressing the problem of extremely poor wages earned by many women, particularly women of colour, part-time workers, homeworkers, and by some black men. To be effective for this purpose, the minimum wage would have to be set at a level which excludes the possibility of poverty wages. It is important also that the minimum wage, together with other statutory employment rights, be extended to all workers, not those currently working under what is recognised as a 'contract of employment'. Otherwise there is a danger that those most in need of protection (that is to say the vulnerable groups already identified) would be excluded from the protection on the ground that they were regarded as self employed rather than employed. This is a matter more fully discussed in chapter 2 above.

5.40 Secondly there is a need for more centralised bargaining arrangements. The evidence made available to us from other countries tends to point unequivocally in the direction of a lower gender pay gap in industrial relations systems with more centralised bargaining arrangements. This is true, for example, of Australia, Germany and Denmark. In this context our proposals in chapter 3 are thus particularly important. Although they are justifiable and desirable on other grounds, the arguments are powerfully reinforced by our concern to promote pay equity. Where sectoral bargaining machinery is in place, it should be the duty of all parties to give due consideration to the advancement of pay equity.

5.41 We are not suggesting that a statutory minimum wage and sectoral bargaining would be enough to secure the elimination of pay discrimination. Although such devices might help, there is also a role for a third strategy employing arbitral methods in the form of the Central Arbitration Committee (CAC), which has already demonstrated its prowess in this area. We anticipate that it should be possible to refer a sectoral employment agreement or an enterprise based collective agreement to the CAC on the ground that it perpetuates pay inequity or fails to make sufficient progress towards pay equity. We propose that the reference could be made by any worker covered by the agreement, a trade union, the CRE or EOC, or any public interest group with sufficient standing in the area. Where there is no collective bargaining at all we propose that anyone with standing should be able to refer an employer's pay structure to the CAC on the ground that it perpetuates pay inequity, or fails to make sufficient progress towards pay equity. A worker who is concerned in case he or she might be victimised, should be permitted to make an anonymous reference.

5.42 On receiving a collective agreement or payment structure, the CAC would be required to examine its terms with a view to determining whether more needs to be done in terms of a strategy to advance pay equity. It would have regard to a variety of factors, including the content of the jobs in the agreement or payment structure (examining the demands made on the worker, in terms of skill, responsibility, etc.), their value to the enterprise, the levels of pay for comparable jobs in other enterprises, internal relativities, and the history of the job at issue, particularly if it has recently moved from a male dominated to a female dominated profession. Having examined the payment structure, the CAC would have the power to amend or adjust it in order to advance pay equity, having particular regard to the correction of disproportionate differentials, and the role of bonus payments. Affordability to the enterprise would be a relevant factor to be taken into account only in terms of permitting an award to be phased in.

5.43 The CAC would be empowered to determine its own procedure, having regard to the interests of fairness and the aim of achieving a result by means of an arbitral rather than a judicial procedure. It should be empowered to require the production of any relevant information, which the employer would be required to disclose, subject to guarantees of confidentiality. There would be no appeal from an award of the CAC, but judicial review by the Labour Court would be available on the grounds referred to in chapter 10. Any award made by the CAC could be extended to other comparable occupations. Anyone with standing, as defined above, could apply to the CAC for an order applying the award to the workers in that establishment. Awards by the CAC would be policed by the Labour Inspectorate, the establishment of which is proposed in chapter 10, armed with powers which we deal with more fully in chapter 10 below. The Labour Inspectorate could also alert the EOC to conditions of pay inequity in any workplace it inspects, for whatever reason.

5.44 Although the primary route to pay equity which we propose is a threefold one, based on a statutory minimum wage, sectoral bargaining and reference to the CAC, there is also a role for individual complaints. Indeed it would be difficult to contemplate the exclusion of this option, not least because such a right of individual complainants is probably required by Article 119 of the EC Treaty. We therefore propose that any individual who wishes to assert her right to equal pay may apply to the proposed Labour Court which, except in cases of like work or work rated as equivalent, would be required to refer the claim to the CAC for a determination. Once the CAC had made the appropriate amendments to the payment structure of the enterprise at which the applicant worked, the matter would be returned to the Labour Court which would be required to assess compensation payable to the applicant. The levels of compensation would at the discretion of the Labour Court, in accordance with the principles referred to in chapter 10 below.

Workers with Parenting and Family Responsibilities

5.45 So far as opportunities for women are concerned, it is clear from recent statistical research that one of the major contributory factors to women's continuing disadvantage in the paid workforce is the fact that they remain primarily responsible for child-care. Indeed, it has been estimated that a woman with children in Britain loses as much as 57 per cent of lifetime earnings after age 25 compared to her childless counterpart. This is in part due to continuing prejudice and direct discrimination against pregnant women in the paid workforce; and in part due to deep-seated structural factors which favour workers who do not have child-care obligations. Since the majority of women will have children, this is one of the key areas on which reform should focus.

5.46 Current law offers two alternative routes to reform: one via the equal treatment principle found in anti-discrimination law and one based on specific employment protection rights. Both avenues have pitfalls. The equality principle is expressly based on a male norm, and is therefore particularly clumsy in relation to pregnancy, since there is no appropriate male comparator. Nor is it sufficiently focused to play a prescriptive role in respect of leave after childbirth. Specific rights have greater potential, since they do not depend explicitly on a male comparator. However, rights are only as good as their content and the method by which they can be enforced. The current package of rights relates to ante natal care, maternity leave and a right to return, and protection against discrimination. But although clearly important, by granting parenting rights to mothers only, they tend to perpetuate women's primary responsibility for child-care.

5.47 The reform package proposed here seeks to break away from exclusive reliance on the equal treatment principle (without denying its importance in areas where it is clearly relevant) and relies instead on specific rights and resource input from the State in order more effectively to promote equality of opportunity. The nature of these rights is, however, different from the current law. A central principle behind our proposals is the distinction drawn between pregnancy and parenthood. Pregnancy and breast-feeding are genuinely unique to women, and it is therefore appropriate to grant special rights to pregnant and breast-feeding women. But this is not true for parenthood, which should be recognised as a shared responsibility of mothers and fathers. If the law is to contribute to a genuine improvement of the position of women with children, it is crucial to ensure that parenting rights are extended to both parents. There may also be a case for seeking to use the law to encourage both parents to assume full responsibility for parenting.

5.48 A chief element in the reform strategy is the need to provide properly funded and easily accessible child-care. However, this is not the full solution: many parents justifiably wish to participate in the care of their own children without being forced to retire from the paid work-force or to accept low status, low paid work simply because the hours are suitable. It is therefore important for workers to require employers to restructure working time to allow both parents to participate in care of their children if they so desire. Also central to a reform package is the need to spread the costs. Costs of parenting should not be born entirely by the parents, nor entirely by the employer. Instead the costs should be born by a fund partially funded by employers' National Insurance contributions, and partially from general taxation. Parents themselves can be expected to bear part of the cost. We now consider in more detail some of the issues raised in the foregoing paragraphs.

(a) Pregnancy

5.49 The Employment Rights Act 1996 currently gives women the right not to be unfairly dismissed on grounds of pregnancy. But there is no specific protection against discrimination in recruitment or promotion or training, unless a woman can successfully argue that she has been discriminated against on grounds of sex. In our view there should be protection in such cases without the need to prove less favourable treatment than a relevant male, thus overcoming many of the problems of associated with the adaptation of the equality principle in this area. We therefore propose that it should be unlawful to (a) refuse to appoint or to promote or offer training opportunities to a woman on the grounds of her pregnancy; or (b) terminate the employment of a woman at any time on the grounds of her pregnancy; or (c) subject a woman to any other detriment on the grounds of her pregnancy, except as permitted by the health and safety legislation.

5.50 Like the provisions of the Sex Discrimination Act 1975 these protections would apply to workers rather than employees, thus including in its scope homeworkers and other marginal workers. In terms of the burden of proof, however, we go beyond the current provisions of the 1975 Act, proposing that the burden of proof be reversed, thus making it less difficult for women to assert their rights. Thus we propose that it should be presumed that any detrimental treatment was for reasons connected with breast feeding or pregnancy unless the employer proves on the basis of facts known to him or her at the relevant time that the detrimental treatment was objectively justified on grounds unconnected with the worker's breast feeding or pregnancy. The remedies available in cases of this kind would be the same as in cases relating to sex discrimination, and questions of standing to enforce these rights would be governed by the proposals in chapter 10.

(b) Maternity and Paternity Leave

5.51   Our second concern is to ensure that a mother has leave specifically to assist her to recover from childbirth and to breast-feed the baby. We propose that the period be set at 18 weeks because it is intended to be conjoined with a much longer period of parental leave, which is available to both parents. With her parental leave, a mother should be able to take a total of over 8 months leave after the birth, and the father should be entitled to a further four months, thus ensuring that at least one parent can care for the child for the whole of its first year of life. The maternity leave would be with full pay, although we propose below that the costs should not be born by the individual employer alone.

5.52   We therefore propose that legislation should provide as a minimum that (a) a woman worker should be entitled to 18 weeks leave in respect of childbirth. The leave should begin at any time up to and including the date of childbirth, but should not begin more than six weeks before the expected date of childbirth; (b) where a pregnancy terminates in still-birth, the worker should be entitled to 18 weeks leave from the date of still-birth; (c) during the course of her leave, the woman should receive full pay and retain the benefit of all accrued rights during her period of absence. She should be entitled on payment of the relevant contributions to continue to accrue pension rights.

5.53 We are also concerned to ensure that provision is made for paternity leave for fathers, to be taken at the time of child-birth, in order to participate in the early care, to establish primary bonding and to look after other children. It is essential that it be well paid in order to ensure fathers are financially able to make use of their rights. We therefore propose that in addition to maternity leave described above, and in addition to our proposals for parental leave in the following paragraph, as a general principle a father of a child should be entitled to four weeks paternity leave. Leave should begin no sooner than a period of two weeks before the expected date of childbirth and no later than the date of childbirth. In the case of still-birth, the father should be entitled to one weeks' leave. During the course of his leave, the worker would receive 90 per cent of earnings, with earnings based on the pay period during the month prior to the leave.

(c) Parental and Family Leave

5.54 In addition to our proposals for maternity and paternity leave, we also propose the introduction of a system of parental leave, as well as a system of family leave. The former aims to ensure that parents are able to provide primary care for their children in the first year of life. We propose that the parent of a child under 14 months old should be entitled to four months parental leave in order take care of the child. In the case of a mother, parental leave would begin on any date subsequent to the expiry of maternity leave. In the case of a father, parental leave would begin at any time after the birth of the child. In order to ensure that fathers take equal responsibility, the leave should be non-transferable. That is to say, if the father does not take his leave, it is lost. It should be expressly provided that it is unlawful for an employer to subject a worker to any detriment as a result of his or her decision to take parental leave. Although we do not propose any qualifying period for parental leave, we do propose the same qualifying conditions as operate for statutory sick pay, on which see paragraphs 4.17-4.18 above.

5.55 So provided the parent has earned more than the national insurance threshold for at least eight weeks in the previous 52 weeks, the parent would be entitled to 80 per cent of his or her earnings during the period of parental leave. For these purposes, 'earnings' means basic pay during the period of payment in the month preceding the leave. During the period of leave, the employer would continue to pay any employers' pensions contributions on behalf of the worker on leave, and the worker would be entitled to make the relevant contributions so as to protect his or her entitlements. The employer should, however, be entitled to recoup the earnings paid to someone on parental leave from a Parental Leave Fund, to which employers should contribute a percentage of their national insurance contributions to be determined from time to time by the Secretary of State. The amount thus attracted would be matched by the Secretary of State from general revenues.

5.56 So far as family leave is concerned, we propose the introduction of measures for parents to take care of sick children. The period, like parental leave, is not transferable between parents, thus creating an incentive for fathers to share the responsibility. Specifically we propose that a parent of a child under school-leaving age should be entitled to family leave in order to care for a child who is ill or otherwise requiring special care. The employer may require reasonable proof of the child's illness or other requirements. Each parent may take a maximum of 20 days family leave in any calendar year. Family leave would be fully paid and would be additional to a worker's normal sickness entitlements, the employer entitled to recoup the cost of family leave in full from the Parental Leave Fund. We also propose that the principle of Family Leave should be adapted to enable workers to take time off with pay to care for dependent relatives other than children, subject to the same maximum of 20 days.

(d) Flexible Working Arrangements

5.57 Although time off work is clearly important, so too is flexibility in terms of working time if parents are to participate in the parenting of their children without having to withdraw from the labour market or to take whatever part-time work they can find. The aim must be to build flexible working into the mainstream of the labour market, available to both parents, and with the prospect of returning to full-time working in the course of time. It should not be seen as a poorly paid ghetto for women with children. It is true that it may be possible to use the Sex Discrimination Act 1975 to remove barriers to more flexible working practices, as was demonstrated by the employee of London Underground who, as a single parent, successfully challenged her employer's decision to require her to work at weekends. The occasional success under the existing law is not, however, an adequate substitute for a carefully crafted provision dealing specifically with the problem of working time.

5.58 There is thus a need for a much clearer statutory lead than is provided by the Sex Discrimination Act 1975. We therefore propose that a parent of a child under school-leaving age shall be entitled to request that the employer consider permitting him or her to work according to agreed working hours which take into account the worker's family responsibilities. The employer should endeavour to agree suitable working hours and should in any event not demand a 'full-time working schedule' unless it can prove that this is necessary for the efficacy of the business and that no alternative schedules are available. 'Full-time working schedule' for these purposes means a working day beginning at nine in the morning (or earlier) and ending at five in the evening (or later) five or six days each week. We propose also that similar arrangements be made for workers with other dependent relatives.

5.59 Building on these proposals for flexible working arrangements is the additional question of career breaks for workers with family responsibilities. We propose that a parent of a child under school-leaving age should be entitled to request that the employer consider permitting him or her take a career break in order to fulfil his or her family responsibilities. A career break shall consist of a period of up to five years unpaid leave. At the end of the period, the worker shall be entitled to return to his or her previous job, or if the job is no longer in existence, to a comparable job, unless the employer can prove that had the worker not been absent on a career break he or she would have been made redundant. The fact that the worker is on a career break should not be a permissible consideration in determining who is to be selected for redundancy and the onus would be on the employer to rebut the proposed statutory presumption that anyone dismissed while absent because of a career break was dismissed because of the career break. An employer would normally be permitted to refuse a reasonable request for a career break.

(e) Child-Care

5.60 Our final concern in this section is to ensure the provision of properly resourced and supervised child-care facilities for working parents. There is a need to ensure not only pre-school care, but also after-school and vacation care. The absence of adequate after-school care has been shown to be a major cause of part-time or temporary working by mothers. In 1990, a third of mothers with a youngest child aged 5 - 11 worked only while their children were at school. We therefore propose that local authorities should have the duty to provide subsidised places for day-care for children under nursery school age in their areas. We also propose that funding should be shared between parents, employers and the general community. Thus although the duty to provide should be imposed upon local authorities, they would be entitled to recover part of the costs from employers (indirectly) and from workers using the facility.

5.61 In order to meet a proportion of the costs (perhaps one third) of such provision, local authorities should be entitled to claim from a proposed Child-Care Fund. All employers would be required to contribute a percentage of their national insurance contributions to the Fund, the percentage to be determined from time to time by the Secretary of State. Local authorities would also have the right to charge parents up to one third of the full cost of a child-care place. The other third of the cost would be provided from local taxation, whatever form that might take. Local authorities would have the duty to regulate the health and safety standards and the standards of care provided in day-centres as well as the working conditions (including pay) of child-care workers. It is crucial that child-care workers are properly remunerated. As an alternative to the provision of nursery care we propose that local authorities could discharge their obligations to provide child-care in part by providing financial support for registered child-minders in their areas, provided a proper system of supervision of such child-minders was in operation.

5.62 As already suggested the question of child-care is not confined to the pre-school child. There is the question also of after-school care in view of the fact that the school day does not always coincide with the working day. There is also the question of child-care in the vacations. In some cases it may be that parents would wish to adopt flexible working patterns as described. But this may not always be possible or indeed desired. We therefore propose that local authorities should be obliged to provide after-school care for school age children as appropriate at the premises of local primary and secondary schools. During term-time, after-school care would begin at the end of the school day and continue until at least the end of the ordinary working day. Out of term time, after-school care would begin a half-hour before the start of the ordinary working day and end not before the end of the ordinary working day. Local authorities would be entitled to charge parents up to one half of the cost of an after-school place and to apply to the Child-Care Fund to meet up to one half of the cost of an after-school place.

Race, Racial Discrimination and Equal Opportunities

5.63 The Race Relations Act 1976 was introduced with high expectations, which critics claim it has failed to fulfil. It is necessary to acknowledge, however, that any debate about the inadequacies of the 1976 Act must be viewed in the broader context of the debate about the limits of legal intervention. It would be disingenuous to believe that a redrafted and improved Race Relations Act 1976 would have the effect of solving all of the problems that currently exist in the field of race relations. There is, indeed, a great deal of validity in the argument that basic problems are structural in nature and that while the law has a role to play in achieving procedural equality it is likely to be less successful in achieving long term substantive equality. Nevertheless, the law does have a significant part to play - if only from a strategic point of view - and a revision of the Act should constitute a central component of any package of reform.

(a) Reforming the Race Relations Act 1976

5.64   The Race Relations Act 1976 currently applies to prohibit discrimination on racial grounds, a term defined to mean colour, race, nationality or ethnic or national origins. The current framework of race relations legislation in Britain thus does not make express allowance for discrimination on the basis of religion. This is in contrast to the situation in Northern Ireland where both discrimination on religious grounds and incitement to religious hatred are statutorily prohibited. Various factors, including the increase in the general levels of discrimination that took place against Muslims after the Rushdie affair in 1989 and the Gulf War in 1991, have led to a heightened awareness that discrimination may take place on the basis of religious identity to the same extent as discrimination on national origins. Consequently, calls to make religious discrimination unlawful have also significantly increased. We propose that specific provision should be introduced to make religious discrimination unlawful. We return to this issue later in paragraphs 5.75-5.80. The definition of discrimination in the 1976 Act includes acts of victimisation. We propose that protection from victimisation should be retained but that it should not only apply to cases where it can be shown that a comparable person would have been treated differently. This issue is dealt with more fully in the context of similar provisions of the Sex Discrimination Act 1975, in paragraphs 5.25-5.26 above.

5.65   In terms of the definition of discrimination in the Race Relations Act 1976, we propose that the definition of direct discrimination, which applies to the 'less favourable' treatment, should remain unaltered. So far as indirect discrimination is concerned, this applies where the employer applies a requirement or condition with which a considerably smaller proportion of the members of one racial group can comply and which cannot be shown

to be justifiable. As we have seen in paragraph 5.30, the words
'requirement or conditions' in the definition have been very
restrictively interpreted in a manner which prevents the courts from
considering whether a practice or policy is potentially discriminatory.
It has been acknowledged that this interpretation is inconsistent
with the spirit of anti-discrimination law and we propose that the
legislation should be amended to make it clear that the statutory
definition includes any policy or practice as well as a requirement or
condition which has a disproportionate impact on the members of a
particular racial group. As already pointed out, the requirement or
condition will be unlawful only if a considerably smaller proportion
of the disadvantaged group can comply with it. We propose that it
should be enough only that a smaller proportion can comply, thereby
giving the concept of indirect discrimination greater utility.

5.66   An employer may also be able to deflect a claim for indirect
discrimination if he or she can show the requirement or condition
applied was justifiable in the circumstances. The existing definition
of justifiability has proved troublesome, largely due to the
interpretation given to the term in *Ojutiku v Manpower Services
Commission* [1982] ICR 661 where the Court of Appeal decided that
the term implied 'a lower standard than the word "necessary".' This
decision was challenged in *Hampson v Department of Education and
Science* [1989] ICR 179, where the House of Lords applied a stricter
justifiability test based on the ECJ's ruling in *Bilka-Kaufhaus GmbH
v Weber von Hartz* [1986] IRLR 317. Building on this case and in line
with our proposals on sex discrimination, we propose that the
definition of indirect discrimination used in the Race Relations Act
1976 should be amended to adopt a strict approach to justifiability
which would require the employer to show that there was no
alternative non-discriminatory way to meet the business needs of
the enterprise, and that the means chosen had the smallest burden
possible on persons of the same racial group.

5.67   At the present time the Race Relations Act 1976 applies to
a wide range of employment practices and activities. Under the Act
it is unlawful for an employer to discriminate, in relation to an
employment at an establishment in Britain, in the selection of
candidates for appointment, in the terms under which employment
is offered, and by refusing or deliberately omitting to offer someone
employment. It is also unlawful to discriminate in matters such as
access to promotion, transfer or training; the terms and conditions
of employment; and dismissal or subjecting the worker to any other
detriment. Exceptions are made where being of a particular racial

group is a genuine occupational qualification, but the Act otherwise has a wide scope in the sense that it applies not only to employees (as is the normal practice for employment protection legislation) but also to people who might be regarded as being employed under a contract for services. One issue which needs further consideration is that of harassment. We are of the view that racial harassment cannot be adequately dealt with by anti-discrimination law, but should be the subject of separate statutory regulation (see paragraphs 5.94-5.98).

(b) Black Women and Multiple Discrimination

5.68 The unique nature of the experiences of black women highlights the specific and distinctly separate challenges black women face when subjected to both race and sex discrimination. Research indicates that the peculiarity of black women's labour market experience has two aspects. First, it is differentiated quite clearly from the experiences of white women, black men and white men. Second, the experiences of black women cannot always be assumed to be different from other categories of workers in all contexts. The complex interaction of factors such as class, age and disability as well as race and gender result in a multiplicity of discrimination.

5.69 Black women are more likely to work full-time, but to remain invisible in terms of official statistics because they participate in the family business or because they are homeworkers. They are also more likely to work in manual jobs, receive a lower income, work in differentiated industrial sectors and, where there is an increase in the number entering the professions, these will largely be restricted to work in the welfare state. Acknowledging that existing discrimination law fails to conceptualise a legal status for black women which sufficiently addresses the complexity of the interplay of race and gender, how can the law be transformed adequately to protect the interests of black women? One line of investigation has led to the holistic approach advanced by some commentators in the United States who argue that because of the particular nature of black women's experiences, both in employment and other areas, black women should be recognised as a distinct group deserving of legal protection; the means by which this could be achieved is by assigning to them a specific legal identity which is acquired by using the disadvantage of their multiple status.

5.70 In UK law, as it currently stands, black women are not recognised as a group entitled to protection as such. This may well lead to an absence of any protection: it may be impossible to show less favourable treatment on grounds of gender because white women are not subject to the same detrimental treatment as black women; and it may be equally impossible to demonstrate less favourable treatment on grounds of race because black men are not subjected to the same detrimental treatment as black women. We therefore propose that black women who suffer a synthesis of gender and race discrimination should be able to prove unlawful discrimination by demonstrating that they have been subjected to detrimental treatment because they are black women. For example, direct discrimination could be proved if a black women could show that she had been treated less favourably than a white woman, a black man or a white man. Similarly, indirect discrimination would be proved if a black woman could show a requirement, condition, practice or policy had the effect of excluding more black women than any other combination of race and gender, i.e. white women, black men or white men, and that it could not be justified on grounds unrelated to either race or sex.

5.71   Nor do we suggest that this analysis be limited to black women. Where multiple discrimination has taken place, we propose that anyone who claims to have been a victim of such discrimination, should have the right to demonstrate that the group of people sharing his or her characteristics is a group which warrants protection in its own right because it carries an inordinately large burden of disadvantage. For example, a gay disabled woman could bring a claim on the grounds of that status once she had shown that gay, disabled women are particularly disadvantaged in society. Similarly, a Bangladeshi woman might ground a claim on the grounds that Bangladeshi women are particularly disadvantaged, thus permitting comparisons between Bangladeshi women and women and men from any other ethnic group. Where a person claims to have suffered discrimination on grounds other than a combination of race and sex, he or she may bring a claim for discrimination on those grounds provided it can be shown that he or she belongs to a group which warrants protection because its members generally suffer similar multiple discrimination. In such cases, direct or indirect discrimination is demonstrated by drawing a comparison with individual members of the group apart from his or her own.

(c) Race and Pay

5.72   While there is a significant absence of any major national survey dealing with race and pay, there is a body of research which indicates that ethnic minority workers experience substantial pay discrimination. The average hourly earnings of men from ethnic minorities were 89 per cent of those of white men in Spring 1994, according to Labour Force Survey. The same survey suggested that women from the ethnic minorities earned about the same as white women. The accuracy of these figures, however, have been challenged by some commentators. In particular, Bruegel[1] has found that considerable earnings differentials, of up to 23 per cent, exist between black and white women when a number of factors were taken into account. These include the fact that black women are more likely to work full time and in shift work, the relative youth of the black female labour force, the fact that black women are more likely to be qualified, and that many work in London where wage rates tend to be higher. Contrary to common assumptions, Bruegel's work has also revealed that the differences between black women and black men in weekly pay, at 37 per cent, is greater than the difference between white men and women at 28 per cent. It is possible, therefore, that black women are not only disadvantaged in terms of race, but also gender.

5.73 The disparities in pay experienced by the racial minorities come about in a number of ways. The occupational distribution for white and non-white men is more varied than for white and non-white women. Men from the ethnic minorities, especially West Indian and Asian men, are more likely to work in sectors with low pay and poor conditions, such as distribution, hotels, catering and repairs. They are also less likely to hold supervisory positions than white men and more likely to be employed as manual workers and to do shift work. The causes for differences in black women's pay are very similar to those for women as a whole. Black women tend to be segregated by industrial sector, occupation and grade level. Recent developments in Government policy, such as the abolition of the wages councils and the entrenchment of compulsory competitive tendering, have had a disproportionately adverse effect on black women. Further the reform of the NHS pay structures have also proved detrimental to black women as it has particularly affected those grades where the racial minorities are concentrated.

5.74 We have made proposals in paragraphs 5.36- 5.44 above for the introduction of measures which would promote the principle of pay equity between men and women. We are of the view that it would be possible and desirable to adapt these procedures to deal with the position of pay equity between different ethnic groups. Thus we would

---

1   I. Bruegel, 'Sex and Race in the Labour Market' (1989) *Feminist Review*, 53.

hope that some progress would be made by the introduction of statutory minimum wage and by the re-establishment of more sectoral based collective bargaining, with those involved in the process being under clear and precise duties to have regard to pay equity not only between men and women, but also on racial grounds as well. It would also be possible to refer agreements or payment structures to the CAC not only on the ground that they reveal pay inequity between men and women and also because they reveal pay inequity between different ethnic groups or between say black women and white women, for example.

(d) Ethnic and Cultural Diversity: The Employer's Duty to Accommodate

5.75   The emphasis so far has been on the need to improve the Race Relations Act 1976 so far as it relates to discrimination. But this is not the only matter which requires attention. Also important is the need for legislation which respects the cultural diversity of the workforce and thereby removes barriers to full labour market participation. There is a need in particular to accept that, for reasons of conscience or religion, workers may not always be able to perform all the duties of office, whether these relate to clothing and appearance, working on certain days of the week, or performing tasks which may be incidental to the job for which the individual was hired. But there is a need also for employers to accommodate the practice by the individual worker of any obligation which may be imposed by his or her religion, so far as this can reasonably be done.

5.76   In this country, as the Commission for Racial Equality pointed out in 1980 (CRE, *Religious Observance by Muslim Employees* (1980)), the standard working week and provision for public holidays have been influenced by the traditions and religious needs of the majority culture. As was also pointed out, the provision of Sunday as a day of rest, and Christmas, Easter and Whitsuntide as public holidays is clearly linked to the importance which the Christian religion gives to these days. While many people within the majority culture do not attend church or engage in religious worship of any kind, it is nevertheless the case that the system has allowed Christians to practice their religion without conflict with the demands of their employment, although recent increases in Sunday working have to some extent limited this freedom. This contrasts with the position of workers who practice other religions who will find that there is no provision made by the law for the fact that their religious holy day falls on a day other then Sunday and whose religious festivals take part at times of the year not recognised by the traditional holidays in this country.

5.77 There is some evidence to suggest that in many workplaces Muslim employees in particular have found difficulty in reconciling their religious needs with the production requirements of the business for which they work. In some cases, it appears, workers as result have chosen particular job grades and shift patterns which impose fewer constraints on their religious practice. In others, feeling aggrieved and believing that management is insensitive, workers have unilaterally taken certain privileges, including time off for certain festivals and visits to Mosques. The problems were highlighted by a Court of Appeal decision in 1978 in which a schoolteacher resigned and claimed constructive dismissal because he was refused time off for Friday prayers at a nearby Mosque. The action failed, with one of the judges taking the view that the worker had no right 'to absent himself, for the purpose of religious worship, from his place of work during working hours and in breach of his contract of employment' (*Ahmad v Inner London Education Authority* [1977] ICR 490).

5.78 The starting point for any developments in this area is better education to make employers and other workers fully aware of the obligations and the nature of the obligations imposed by religions other than Christianity. It has been pointed out by the CRE, for example, that 'some employers do not understand Islamic requirements and hesitate to consider whether traditional industrial relations practices can reasonably be adapted to the needs of Muslim employees'. It has also been suggested, also by the CRE, that catering for the needs, in this case of Muslim employees, though it could be other employees, may be seen by other workers to entail favouritism and to cause resentment. This ignorance and these fears can only be overcome by education and awareness about the practice of other religions and the obligations which they impose on their members.

5.79 A clear commitment to raising levels of awareness must be accompanied by appropriate legal responsibilities. The duties on employers must, however, include sufficient flexibility to suit a variety of different religious as well as the employers' own operational requirements. We therefore propose that employers be under a duty to take such steps as are reasonable to accommodate the religious needs of their workers. A duty of accommodation includes adjusting time schedules, meeting dietary requirements, allowing time off for religious worship, and, where feasible, permitting the use of premises to conduct communal worship. A refusal by an employer to accommodate reasonable requests of workers should be unlawful unless it can be justified by reference to unavoidable business needs.

5.80 Finally in this section there is the question of dismissal and disadvantage which may be suffered by anyone who asserts any of the rights proposed above. The need for protection is demonstrated by case law in which it has been held to be fair to dismiss a worker for refusing to work overtime on a day which conflicted with his religious beliefs. To require the employer to roster overtime in a way which accommodated his religious beliefs was said to be 'wholly unreasonable' (*Esson v London Transport Executive* [1975] IRLR 48). We therefore propose that it should be unfair to dismiss or subject to any other detriment a worker who refuses to comply with any instruction (which is incidental to the principal duties of office) which are inconsistent with the requirements of his or her religion (which could be reasonably accommodated by the employer). We also propose that it should be unfair to dismiss a worker who exercises his or her rights to time off work for prayers or religious festivals, provided that reasonable notice is given to the employer.

(e) Immigration and Asylum

5.81 The introduction of the Immigration and Asylum Bill by the Government in 1995 presents one of the most serious challenges to the principle of equality of opportunity for ethnic minorities in the workplace. Of particular concern is Clause 8 of the Bill, which creates a new criminal offence for employers of employing an immigrant who has no entitlement to work in the UK. Employers who contravene this provision are subject to a maximum fine of £5,000 and the only defence allowed is that the employer has seen and obtained a copy of a document of a description specified in an order made by the Secretary of State, stating that the person can legitimately work. The introduction of this measure has been widely condemned. The TUC, the Association of British Chambers of Commerce, the Institute of Directors, the Federation of Small Businesses, the Institute of Personnel Development and Management and the Institute of Management all protested that 'the proposed legislation will do nothing to improve equal opportunities'.[2]

5.82 The concern expressed has focused on a number of issues. First, it is argued that immigration policing should not be the job of employers, but rather should be the responsibility of immigration officers, who are trained for the task. Secondly, employers are not equipped to understand the complexities of immigration rules and

---

2. *The Times*, 20 October 1995.

the different statuses which immigrants may have. A consultation document *Prevention of Illegal Working*, published by the Home Office in November 1995 suggested that the most straight forward check for employers would be based on National Insurance numbers. In practice, however, possession or otherwise of a National Insurance number will not always indicate a person's immigration status, as many people who are be legally entitled to work will not have a National Insurance number, especially those who have not worked before, while others who have a National Insurance number may not have the right to work, for instance because their Visa is out of date.

5.83   As a result, especially where no National Insurance number is available, according to the consultation document, an employer will have to have seen and obtained a copy of one of a range of documents which would demonstrate a worker's entitlement to live and work in the UK. These documents could include a British birth certificate or passport, an EEA passport or identity document, a passport or other identity document endorsed to show that the holder is settled in the UK or otherwise entitled to work here, or a certificate of registration or nationalisation as a British citizen. While in the majority of cases immigrants may be able to supply such documents, it is not difficult to foresee circumstances where this will not be possible, for example, in the case of a person appealing against a Home Office refusal of leave to remain, who is not restricted from taking employment, but who has an out of date stamp in their passport; or in the case of an asylum seeker, who at present is allowed to work if no decision has been taken or made or their application within six months, but who is unlikely to have the documents specified in the consultation document.

5.84   Overall, the proposals are likely to damage race relations as they will create an incentive for employers not to hire black or ethnic minority staff, or even people with foreign sounding names. According to the Labour Force Survey in Spring 1995, unemployment rates among black and ethnic minority workers are already high, at 18.8 per cent, which is more than double the rate for white workers at 8.1 per cent. Further black workers are far more likely to belong term unemployed than their white counterparts. 60 per cent of Afro-Caribbean workers classified as unemployed in Spring 1994 had been unemployed for over one year as compared with 44 per cent of white workers. The proposals can only make this situation worse. Further, employers are likely to concentrate their checks on ethnic minority employees, with potentially discriminatory effects. In the light of these concerns, we are of the view that employers should not be held criminally liable for employing people who are not entitled to work in the UK and that the responsibility should lie solely within the domain of qualified immigration officers.

(f) The European Dimension

5.85 While sex equality has been a central aspiration of the European Union since its formation, by virtue of the inclusion of Article 119 in the EC Treaty and of subsequent Directives, no corresponding provisions exist to prohibit discrimination on racial grounds. In recent years steps have been taken to rectify this situation. In July 1994, the Council of Ministers agreed to establish a Consultative Commission of eminent personalities, whose task it was to encourage tolerance and understanding, to develop a global strategy at the Union level aimed at combating acts of racial and xenophobic violence, and to set up training for officials in Member States. Reporting in April 1995, the Commission concluded that 'an explicit Treaty change confirming Community competence, will be the clearest expression of the European Union's real intention of combating, not merely protesting against the rising tide of racism and xenophobia' and that the question of such a Treaty amendment should be placed formally on the agenda of the 1996 Intergovernmental Conference. Since the publication of the Commission's report, two Resolutions have been adopted by the Council of Ministers dealing respectively with the fight against racism in the fields of employment and social affairs and the response of educational systems to the problems of racism and xenophobia. These measures, however, only constitute soft law and therefore create no rights for individual workers.

5.86 At the time of writing, further progress on the question of a Treaty amendment dealing with racial equality appears in doubt, due to fierce opposition from the British Government. Race relations legislation in the UK is probably the most comprehensive and advanced in Europe. It is difficult to understand, therefore, why the Government should resist efforts aimed at the harmonisation of racial anti-discrimination legislation in other Member States. We propose that steps should be taken to develop and implement a comprehensive strategy within Europe aimed at combating racism and xenophobia at work and harmonising anti-discrimination standards. As a starting point, in line with the conclusions of the EU Consultative Commission, an amendment should be made to the EC Treaty which provides that racial equality is a basic principle of Community law, which must be dealt with under the 'first pillar' at Treaty level, thereby giving the European Court of Justice the power to oversee compliance by national courts.

Promoting Fair Participation at Work

5.87 We have proposed so far that in the different areas that we have considered - disability, gender, sexual orientation, and race - two legal strategies should be adopted to promote equality of opportunity. These are respectively an anti-discrimination strategy on the one hand, and a strategy designed to remove barriers to effective equality of opportunity on the other. There is, however, a third strategy which we believe should be pursued. This we refer to as a strategy for fair participation at work, a strategy which we find recognised to some extent in the Fair Employment Act (Northern Ireland) 1989, which provides for 'fair participation' by the members of the two dominant religious communities in Northern Ireland. The Act provides that 'affirmative action' may be required to be taken to bring about 'fair participation' between the religious communities in the Province where an employer is not providing 'equality of opportunity'.

5.88 Much of what has been proposed in the foregoing paragraphs may be said to be designed to promote a fair participation strategy as well as eliminate discrimination and remove barriers to equality of opportunity. But we believe more needs to be done, though, at the time of writing, we are mindful of the fact that certain options for affirmative action may be foreclosed by EC law. We are mindful also that it may be necessary to limit clearly and precisely the scope of any exceptions to the principle of non-discrimination created to facilitate a movement towards 'fair participation', having regard to current U.S. experience which demonstrates that political support for equal opportunities could be lost and that there are dangers of moving too far in front of public opinion. Conversely, the quota established under the Disabled Persons Act 1944 did not give rise to controversy whilst the model disabled person was a wounded ex-serviceman or woman.

(a) Workplace Monitoring for Equal Opportunities

5.89 There is considerable support for the view that ethnic monitoring should be made a statutory requirement on all employers; the emphasis on voluntary compliance contained in the CRE Code of Practice does not have the necessary force to compel employers to adopt this practice. A useful model to consider is the Fair Employment

(Northern Ireland) Act 1989 which introduces the notion of compulsory monitoring in the private sector by creating a requirement that employers (defined as companies and organisations with over 25 employees for the first two years of the operation of the Act, and those with 10 or more employees thereafter) register with the Fair Employment Commission and monitor their workforce. Non-compliance with these measures is a criminal offence. The Act goes further by stipulating that public employers should also monitor applications for employment, an obligation imposed on private employers only if they have over 250 employees.

5.90 The basis of any move towards a duty to provide fair participation generally must be an assessment of the composition of the workforce. A wider obligation to monitor would provide a factual basis for subsequent discussion and development and a means whereby the effectiveness of any measures taken could be judged. Personnel planning is commonplace in management and what is proposed is no more than an extension of that process. We therefore propose that all employers should be under a statutory duty to monitor the composition of their workforce in terms of disability, race and gender. Where an employer fails to do so this would constitute a prima facie case of discrimination in relation to any worker who had thereby suffered a detriment. It is for consideration whether the obligation should also be reinforced by criminal penalties.

(b) Equal Opportunities Officers and Equal Opportunities Forums

5.91 As a further step in the strategy of promoting fair participation, employers (perhaps over a certain size, at least initially) should be under a duty to conduct their employment decisions with regard to the duty to provide fair participation. Specifically, employers should be required by legislation to create in each workplace an equal opportunities forum where equal opportunities issues could be discussed with the representatives of the different trade unions which may be recognised or represented at the workplace. The legislation could also provide in some detail what would be the duties of the forum. These are considered more fully below, but they would include a duty to develop and implement an equal opportunities policy for the workplace, taking account of local needs and conditions. Questions arise about workplaces in which there is no trade union representation. This is a matter which requires further consideration, along the lines proposed in paragraphs 7.65 - 7.68 below.

5.92 The duty of the employer would be to consult the equal opportunities forum about equal opportunities issues. There would be an obligation to draw up an equal opportunities plan, based on the employer's reasonable expectations of employment requirements, under which the enterprise could move towards a socially balanced workforce. There would be an obligation to disclose and discuss the results of the monitoring exercise annually and to make appropriate adjustments to the plan. The employer would be under a duty to consult the forum on any significant changes which are proposed to the composition of the workforce, by way of expansion, contraction, or reskilling in order to ensure that equal opportunities objectives were not thereby jeopardised. Where the employer fails to reach agreement with the equal opportunities forum, trade union representatives would have power to refer the matter to the appropriate commission (EOC, CRE, or the proposed Disability Rights Commission) for mediation or conciliation. If this fails, it is for consideration whether there should be a further right to refer the matter to the CAC for arbitration.

5.93 We also propose that employers should be under a duty to provide from among their workforce for the election or nomination of equal opportunities officers from recognised or representative trade unions. Where ther is no recognised or representative trade union, we propose that equal opportunities officers should be elected on the basis of our proposals in paragraph 7.62 below, with suitable adaptations as necessary. These officers would sit on the equal opportunities forum but would have additional duties in terms of implementing and monitoring equal opportunities issues in the workplace. They would also be the focus for complaints about equal opportunities grievances raised by workers in the enterprise and would liaise with equal opportunities officers in other plants. We propose that equal opportunities officers should be provided with statutory protection from discrimination and dismissal and that they should be entitled to time off work with pay to perform their duties but also to undergo training in these duties.

(c) The Working Environment: Dealing with Harassment

5.94 The questions of harassment are not dealt with satisfactorily by the equal treatment principle contained in anti-discrimination law. This is because it is artificial to base the right not to be harassed on a comparison between the way in which the person allegedly harassed is treated and the way in which a person of a different sex, race, sexual orientation or ability would have been treated. For example, an employer who can demonstrate that he would have sexually harassed both men and women is immune from challenge under the Sex Discrimination Act 1975. We, therefore, propose the introduction of separate statutory provisions protecting workers against harassment. We propose that it should be unlawful to harass, bully or otherwise assault the dignity of workers on grounds of their race, sex, sexual orientation, marital or family status or disability. Harassment should be defined as unwanted conduct based on any of the specified grounds which affects the dignity of women and men at work, including conduct of superiors and colleagues. This conduct may include unwelcome physical, verbal or non-verbal conduct and will be unacceptable if it is unwanted and offensive to the recipient; if it creates an intimidating, hostile or humiliating working environment for the recipient; and particularly in cases of sexual harassment, if a person's rejection of or submission to such conduct is used as a basis for a decision which affects that person's access to or terms or conditions of employment.

5.95 It is essential that the employer should be placed under a positive duty to create an environment free of harassment. Only in this way will real change occur. Yet current statutory provisions and case law permit the employer to avoid liability where he or she can show that, on common law principles of vicarious liability, an employee who harassed a fellow employee was thereby acting outside the course of employment. We propose that an employer should be under a duty to create and maintain a workplace which is so far as is reasonably possible free of unlawful harassment on grounds of race, sex, sexual orientation, marital or family status or disability. This would remove the matter from the common law of vicarious liability altogether, and the duty would include the establishment and publication of fair and effective procedures for dealing with complaints of harassment, as well as the institution of informal and confidential counselling or advice. Procedures should be developed in discussion with trade unions which may be recognised or represented in the workplace and would be a suitable matter for consideration by equal opportunities forum.

5.96 By way of example, we propose that protection from sexual harassment should be provided as follows. These provisions should be adapted to deal with harassment on grounds of race, sexual orientation, marital or family status or disability.

1 Sexual Harassment

(1) It is unlawful for an employer to permit sexual harassment to occur in the workplace.

(2) For the purposes of this section sexual harassment is unwanted conduct of a sexual nature, or other conduct based on sex affecting the dignity of women and men at work, including conduct of superiors and colleagues. This conduct may include unwelcome physical, verbal or non-verbal conduct. Such conduct is unacceptable if:

(a) it is unwanted and offensive to the recipient;

(b) a person's rejection of or submission to such conduct on the part of an employer or a fellow worker (including superiors and colleagues) is used explicitly or implicitly as a basis for a decision which affects that person's access to vocational training, access to employment, continued employment, promotion, salary or other employment decisions; and/or

(c) such conduct creates an intimidating, hostile or humiliating working environment for the recipient.

2 Liability of employers or principals

(1) Anything done by a person related to his or her employment shall be treated for the purposes of this Act as done by his employer as well as by him or her, whether or not it was done with the employer's knowledge or approval.

(2) In proceedings brought under this Act against any person in respect of an act alleged to have been done by a worker it shall be a defence for the employer to prove that he or she took all possible steps to prevent the worker from doing that act, or from doing acts of that description related to his or her employment.

3 Evidence

(1) The burden of proving on the balance of probabilities that an act of sexual harassment occurred lies with the applicant

(2) Evidence of an applicant's past sexual history is not admissible in legal proceedings under this Act.

(d) Contract Compliance and 'Fair Participation'

5.97 It is arguable that the principle of contract compliance should be adopted far more extensively than it is currently. The ability of both central and local government to use their economic power to facilitate equal opportunity has been under-utilised; a clear commitment is needed to redress a situation which has become more urgent by the entrenchment of CCT in the public sector. Once a notion of 'fair participation' is incorporated into the legislation, it would be possible to make compliance with the duty to ensure fair participation a condition for the award of central or local government contracts. We therefore propose the repeal of the current statutory provisions which impede the use of this particular strategy, but are conscious that there are problems arising under the EC Public Procurement Directives which may have to be overcome before this strategy can be confidently pursued.

5.98 We propose that these difficulties be investigated and that steps are taken to develop a framework which promotes the strategy of contract compliance as fully as possible in a manner consistent with EC law. We also propose that to the extent that it is possible under EC law, contract compliance should be developed as a strategy to eliminate discrimination, promote equality of opportunity, and develop the principle of fair participation at work in respect of disabled workers, workers from ethnic minority communities, and women. We further propose that, so far as consistent with EC law, the contract compliance strategy should be adopted as a compulsory measure in this area by central and local government as well as by all public bodies; it should also be encouraged by businesses operating in the private sector, with trade unions being particularly encouraged to persuade employers of the desirability of adopting this strategy.

(e) Affirmative Action

5.99 The other issue which arises here is the question of affirmative action. This may take several forms, though under current British law it is permitted to the limited extent of enabling employers to make special provision for advertising and training in situations where women or members of particular racial groups are under-represented. Otherwise affirmative action measures may be unlawful to the extent that benefits in favour of women or of the members of a particular racial group may be said to discriminate against men or the members of another racial group. It is also the case that the European Court of Justice has recently suggested the need for caution about affirmative action measures, taking the view that a preference for women over men, all other things being equal, was a breach of the Equal Treatment Directive (76/207/EEC). It has been suggested, however, that this does not undermine the validity of all affirmative action measures, including targets and quotas.

5.100 In Northern Ireland, the Fair Employment Act 1989 places emphasis on the introduction of affirmative action and as such serves as a useful model to consider. But although the Act introduces the concept of affirmative action, it fails to address important issues of definition and implementation. Any commitment to affirmative action must be couched in much clearer and more robust terms. Affirmative action needs to be clearly defined and clear guidance needs to be given to employers on the implementation of programmes. Thus there may be a case for saying that the legislation should be asymmetrical. In other words an employer could discriminate positively, for example, in favour of a disabled person or use disability as a qualification for an employment opportunity. Non-disabled persons would not be entitled to any cause of action, except in cases of discrimination by association or victimisation. However, employers could not discriminate between different disabilities or persons with different forms or degrees of disability. Consideration has to be given to the question of how far the principle of asymmetrically should extend.

5.101   There is also a need to consider the question of targets and quotas. Apart from questions of compatibility with EC law (at least in the area of gender) more difficult questions arise as to how far the strategy should go and how it could effectively be implemented. Equality targets are uncontroversial, for as the CRE has pointed out, they help establish what ought to happen in the absence of decision-making on racial grounds. If they are not met they may reveal a problem which needs investigation and resolution. The question of quotas is more controversial. But there may be, for example, a case for retaining alongside the anti-discrimination measures a new and enforceable quota scheme to assist severely disabled persons to enter the labour market and to secure employment or training opportunities. This may be especially important for workers with mental disabilities. But there may also be a case for an enforceable quota scheme or targets in other areas.

(f) Examples of Positive Action

5.102 Further to the discussion on affirmative action, it is important, if equality of opportunity is to be promoted, that the State should recognise a duty to fund projects aimed at enabling workers to overcome the social, cultural or physical barriers which can exclude them from the labour market. This suggests both the retention and strengthening of a number of existing projects and the extension and adaptation of such schemes to tackle the barriers faced by other disadvantaged groups. Examples of existing schemes include grants provided by the Home Office, under section 11 of the Local Government Act 1966, to enable local authorities to continue to employ additional staff for the purpose of helping members of communities of commonwealth origin to overcome linguistic or cultural barriers and thereby gain access to services and facilities. Since 1992, these grants have also been applied to assist members of ethnic minorities to gain employment and take up vocational training or to set up their own business. Further assistance is provided for ethnic minority workers via the City Action Teams and the Urban Programme and we propose that the funding for such schemes should be increased.

5.103 A further example is the Access to Work scheme, set up in June 1994, to replace previous provisions for disabled persons under Special Employment Schemes. The scheme pays for additional support which may be required by a disabled person to do a particular job. The scheme provides a variety of types of support including special aids to employment, adaptations to premises and equipment, assisted fares to work, adapted vehicles, personal readers, support workers, communicator support at interviews, and one off miscellaneous items of support. A report, sponsored jointly by the RNIB and RADAR in 1995, suggested that the scheme had been successful in improving employment support for disabled people to compete on an equal basis with their non-disabled colleagues 'by virtue of their skills and abilities without the employer having to worry about the additional costs involved'. Concern, however, has been raised at the imposition in 1996 of a levy on employers, requiring them to pay 20 per cent of costs over a threshold of £300. Any such levy would act as a tax on good practice and would be a disincentive to the employment of disabled people.

Conclusion

5.104 The notion of equality of treatment has gained a rightful pre-eminence and has recently come to form a cornerstone of the British constitutional system. As such, any statute which guarantees citizens the right not to be discriminated against guarantees a fundamental human right and should have priority over measures - both present and future - which conflict with it. There is a need for a clearer assertion of the superiority of such legislation (as is arguably secured by the Sex Discrimination Act 1975 as a result of EC law). In addition, the governmental principle of 'equal opportunity proofing' - whereby legislative and policy developments are, in theory, scrutinised in terms of equal opportunity matters - is not an adequate substitute for a clearer legal commitment to the same effect. This is a matter which requires further consideration.

5.105 Considerable scope exists to promote the realisation of equal opportunities, in the sense of improving the life chances of the more disadvantaged sections of society, by adopting a multi-faceted policy. First, appropriate macro-economic policies need to be pursued, allied to an effort to support and extend collective bargaining and to erect a firmer floor of general employment rights. Secondly, specific improvements need to be made to the structure of anti-discrimination law, while thirdly steps need to be taken to remove barriers to participation in the labour market by disabled workers, by ethnic minority workers and by women. Fourthly there is a need for a completely different approach to pay if the gender pay gap is to be closed, a need for an approach which rejects a complaints driven procedure as the principal vehicle for the carriage of an equal pay strategy. Finally, as outlined above there is a need also for a change of focus from anti-discrimination law towards placing a duty on employers to work towards the provision of 'fair participation'.

5.106 The foregoing does not yet deal with all the groups of workers in respect of whom statutory initiatives should be introduced. There is a need, for example, to consider more carefully the position of older workers. Whilst unemployment is highest in Britain amongst young people aged 16-24, and amongst young men in particular, the comparatively low figures for those aged over 45 disguise a substantial move out of the labour market by discouraged older workers. Thus whilst the young find difficulty in entering the labour market, the older worker is being forced out. Both of these trends have a serious impact upon life time earnings and the capacity of individuals to make financial commitments, such as house purchase. There is therefore a case to be made for legislation modelled upon the US Age Discrimination in Employment Act, though in addition to protecting the over 40's, the legislation might offer protection to the under 25's. The argument that young people should be 'priced into work' cannot be sustained, in that the growing inequalities have not stimulated employment for the unskilled, but simply impoverished them. This is a matter clearly in need of attention.

5.107 Nor does the foregoing exhaust the measures to be taken to promote equality of opportunity at work, in terms of strategies to be adopted. So far as the question of strategy is concerned, whilst developments in education in general lie outside the scope of this study, it is worth noting that educational attainments and the choice of specialism at school can have a long-term effect on the pattern of a person's working life, leading to so-called disadvantage before the labour market. Those responsible for education policy should be alive to the need to ensure the progress of all types of children and to offer appropriate support and/or remedial packages to those who are failing or whose horizons are limited. And in order to facilitate the transition of young people into the labour market and to reduce the inequalities associated with youth unemployment, consideration should be given to the institution of a right to education or training up to age 18 or even 21, without, however, the institution of 'workfare'. The task of promoting equality at work is thus one which requires a combination of economic, industrial relations, educational, and legal strategies if it is to be effectively realised.

Summary of Recommendations

(a) General

1   Legislation should proceed along three parallel paths: first it should seek to eliminate discriminatory employment practices; secondly, it should seek to remove barriers to effective labour market participation; and thirdly it should seek to promote the right of fair participation in work.

2   In developing these strategies, legislation should be specifically targeted to particular groups who suffer discrimination, disadvantage and exclusion. There is a need to recognise that the patterns of disadvantage and discrimination vary and that legislation can best respond by addressing the problems encountered by different victims of discrimination and disadvantage.

(b) Disability, Discrimination and Equality of Opportunity

3   There should be statutory protection against discrimination for disabled workers. To this end the definition of disability must be a broad and inclusive one based upon a social, rather than medical, model of disability.

4   Discrimination based upon a person's association with a member of the protected class must be unlawful; and the burden of proving that a complainant is not a member of the

protected class or has not suffered discrimination should be upon the party which asserts otherwise.

5 Discrimination should be defined to ensure that an employer shall not be permitted to discriminate against a disabled person who, with or without reasonable accommodation, can perform the essential functions of the employment position that such individual holds or desires.

6 Both direct and indirect discrimination should be prohibited and discrimination should, therefore, be defined as including both less favourable treatment by reason of disability and the application of any requirement, condition, policy or practice which has a disproportionate impact or effect upon persons with a disability.

7 The use of qualification standards, employment tests and selection criteria should be unlawful if they tend to screen out disabled persons, unless these can be shown to be essential to the job in question.

8 Indirect discrimination should only be defensible where the employer can objectively justify the use of a bona fide, job-related occupational requirement, condition or qualification or, exceptionally, an overriding business need.

9 All employers should be under a duty to make reasonable accommodation for disabled persons by making alterations to the workplace or by adjusting policies and practices that have a disproportionate effect upon disabled applicants or workers.

10 A failure to make reasonable accommodation would be subject to a defence of undue hardship and the burden of proving undue hardship should be on the employer, taking account of the nature and cost of the accommodation.

11 There should be a right to paid disability leave for those workers who become seriously ill or disabled on the job or while in employment, with protection against unfair dismissal for those on leave.

12 The carers or partners of disabled persons should be protected from discrimination by association with a disabled person. There should also be a right to carers' leave for workers with disabled dependants, commensurate with our proposals below for family and parental leave.

13 A Disability Rights Commission should be established, with comparable powers to those of the Equal Opportunities Commission and the Commission for Racial Equality. The Commission should be charged with the general duty to work towards the elimination of discrimination, to promote equality of opportunity for disabled persons and to review the operation of all disability legislation.

(c) Sex Discrimination and Sexual Orientation

14 The Sex Discrimination Act 1975 should be expanded to prohibit discrimination on the grounds of 'marital and family status', to cover both heterosexual and gay and lesbian relationships.

15 The Sex Discrimination Act 1975 should be amended to apply not only to discrimination against men and women on the grounds of sex, but also to discrimination against men and women on the grounds of sexual orientation. Transsexuals must also be protected from discrimination.

16 The definition of indirect discrimination in the Sex Discrimination Act 1975 should be expanded and it should be more difficult for an employer to justify indirectly discriminatory practices.

17 The scope of the legislation relating to discrimination on the grounds of sex should be expanded to apply to pay. It should also be unlawful for an employer to discriminate on pay on grounds of sexual orientation.

(d) Sex Discrimination, Equal Pay and Pay Equity

18 Where sectoral bargaining arrangements, as proposed in chapter 3, are in place, it should be the duty of all parties to give due consideration to the advancement of pay equity.

19 Sectoral Employment Agreements or collective agreements which perpetuate pay inequity, or which fail to make sufficient progress towards pay equity, should be referred to the CAC.

20 Where there is no collective agreement it should be possible to refer an employer's pay structure to the CAC on the grounds that it perpetuates pay inequity, or fails to make sufficient progress towards pay equity between men and women.

21 A reference to the CAC may be made by any worker covered by

the agreement or pay structure, any union or public interest group with an interest, or the EOC.

22 The CAC should be empowered to amend or adjust a collective agreement or pay structure in order to advance pay equity, having particular regard to the correction of disproportionate differentials, and the role of bonus payments.

23 The CAC should be empowered to determine its own procedure, having regard to the interests of fairness and the aim of achieving a result by means of an arbitral rather than a judicial procedure. There should be no appeal from an award of the CAC, but judicial review should be available in limited cases.

24 Any award made by the CAC should be extended to other comparable occupations. Anyone who has standing, as defined above, should be able to apply to the CAC for an order applying the award to the workers in that establishment.

25 Any individual who wishes to assert her right to pay for work of equal value under Article 119 of the EC Treaty should be able to apply to the Labour Court which must refer the claim to the CAC for a determination.

26 Once the CAC has made the appropriate amendments to the payment structure of the enterprise at which the applicant works, the matter would be returned to the proposed Labour Court which must assess compensation payable to the plaintiff. The levels of compensation are at the discretion of the Labour Court, provided the principles of true compensation and deterrence are adhered to.

27 Awards by the CAC would be policed by the labour inspectorate, which we propose in chapter 10 below. The labour inspectorate would also be empowered to alert the EOC to conditions of pay inequity in any workplace it inspects, for whatever reason.

(e) Workers with Parenting and Family Responsibilities

28 It should be unlawful to (a) refuse to appoint or to promote or offer training opportunities to a woman on the grounds of her pregnancy; or (b) terminate the employment of a woman at any time on the grounds of her pregnancy; or (c) subject a woman to any other detriment on the grounds of her pregnancy, except as permitted by the health and safety legislation.

29 Legislation should provide as a minimum that a woman worker shall be entitled to 18 weeks leave in respect of childbirth, during which she shall receive full pay and retain the benefit of all accrued rights, including pension contributions.

30 The father of a child should be entitled to four weeks paternity leave, during which he should be entitled to receive 90 per cent of earnings, where earnings are based on the pay period during the month prior to the leave.

31 The parent of a child under 14 months old should be entitled to four months parental leave in order take care of the child. In order to ensure that fathers take equal responsibility, the leave should be non-transferable, and it should be unlawful for an employer to subject a worker to any detriment as a result of his or her decision to take parental leave.

32 The parent of a child under school-leaving age should be entitled to family leave in order to care for a child who is ill or otherwise requiring of special care. The employer should be able to require reasonable proof of the child's illness or other requirements. Each parent should be able to take a maximum of 20 days family leave in any calendar year which should be non-transferable between parents.

33 Family leave would be fully paid and would be additional to a worker's normal sickness entitlements. The employer would be entitled to recoup the cost of family leave in full from the Parental Leave Fund.

34 Proposals for Family Leave should be adapted to enable workers to take time off with pay to care for dependent relatives other than children.

35 A parent of a child under school-leaving age should be entitled to request that the employer consider permitting him or her to work according to agreed working hours which take into account the worker's family responsibilities. Similar arrangements should be made for workers with other dependent relatives.

36 A parent of a child under school-leaving age should be entitled to request that the employer consider permitting him or her take a career break in order to fulfil his or her family responsibilities, which should consist of a period of up to five years unpaid leave.

37 At the end of a career break, the worker should be entitled to return to his or her previous job or if the job is no longer in existence, to a comparable job, unless the employer can prove that had the worker not been absent on a career break he or she would have been made redundant.

38 Local authorities should have the duty to provide subsidised places for day-care for children under nursery school age in their areas. Funding for child care should be shared between parents, employers and the general community.

39 As an alternative to the provision of nursery care local authorities could discharge their obligations to provide child-care in part by providing financial support for registered child-minders in their areas, provided a proper system of supervision of such child-minders is in operation.

40 Local authorities should be obliged to provide after-school care for school age children as appropriate at the premises of local primary and secondary schools.

(f) Race, Racial Discrimination and Equal Opportunity

41 Specific provision should be introduced to make religious discrimination unlawful.

42 The definition of indirect discrimination in the Race Relations Act 1976 should be expanded and it should be more difficult for an employer to justify indirectly discriminatory practices.

43 Multiple discrimination should be unlawful, where it can be demonstrated that a group of people sharing certain characteristics is a group which warrants protection in its own right because it carries an inordinately large burden of disadvantage. For example, it should be unlawful to discriminate against black women, who suffer a synthesis of gender and race discrimination.

44 It should be possible to refer sectoral employment agreements, collective agreements or payment structures to the CAC, not only on the ground that they reveal pay inequity between men and women, but also because they reveal inequity between different racial groups.

45 There is a need for a greater degree of education and awareness about the practice of other religions and the obligations which they impose on their members.

46 Employers should be under a duty to take such steps as are reasonable to accommodate the religious needs of their workers, including adjusting time schedules, meeting dietary requirements, allowing time off for religious worship, and where feasible permitting the use of premises to conduct communal worship.

47 It should be unfair to dismiss or subject to any other detriment a worker who exercises his or her rights to time off work for prayers or religious festivals, provided that reasonable notice is given to the employer.

48 Employers should not be held criminally liable for employing people who are not entitled to work in the UK and the responsibility of policing migrant workers should lie solely within the domain of qualified immigration officers.

49 Urgent steps should be taken develop and implement a comprehensive strategy within Europe aimed at combating racism and xenophobia at work and harmonising anti-discrimination standards. As a starting point, an amendment should be made to the EC Treaty which provides that racial equality is a basic principle of Community law.

(g) Promoting Fair Participation at Work

50 All employers should be under a statutory duty to monitor the composition of their workforce in terms of disability, race and gender.

51 Employers should be required by legislation to create in each workplace an equal opportunities forum where equal opportunities issues could be discussed with the representatives of the different trade unions which may be recognised or represented at the workplace.

52 Employers should be under a duty to provide from among their workforce for the election or nomination of equal opportunities officers from recognised or representative trade unions.

53 Equal opportunities officers should be provided with statutory protection from discrimination and dismissal and they should be entitled to time off work with pay to perform their duties but also to undergo training in these duties.

54 It should be unlawful to harass, bully or otherwise assault the dignity of workers on grounds of their race, sex, sexual orientation, marital or family status or disability, and employers should be placed under a positive duty to create a workplace free of harassment.

55 To the extent that it is possible under EC law, contract compliance should be developed as a strategy to eliminate discrimination, promote equality of opportunity, and develop the principle of fair participation at work in respect of disabled workers, workers from ethnic minority communities, and women.

TRADE UNIONS AND
THEIR MEMBERS

6.1   Trade unions are voluntary bodies designed to represent and protect the interests of their members. By acting collectively workers can help to overcome the great inequality which exists at the workplace and thereby begin to deal with the employer more effectively about matters of common interest between them. In other words, trade unions provide the means by which workers as a whole may have a voice at work and may participate in workplace decisions. The question for consideration in this chapter is to what extent the trade union as the collective expression of the interests of working people should be subject to regulation by law in matters of internal government. Are these questions to be left exclusively to the members and officials of the union, or does have the State have a legitimate interest in the way in which trade unions are governed? And if the State does have an interest, what is the nature of that interest, and what role does the law have to play in protecting its interest?

Trade Union Autonomy and Freedom of Association

6.2   The first question for consideration is whether the statutory regulation of trade union internal affairs can be justified. In our view there are two arguments from principle as well as an important practical consideration which create a presumption against such intervention. The first rests on the fact that trade unions are autonomous voluntary associations and that as such it is inappropriate they should be subject to detailed regulation by the State. The argument is all the stronger for the fact that, with the demise of the closed shop, workers are free to join and leave trade unions as they wish. Although the closed shop performs important functions, it is unlikely that we will ever see a return to the position where large numbers of workers will be required to be a trade union member or to join a trade union as a condition of employment. Quite apart from any other consideration, this is because the right to freedom of association, as protected by the

European Convention on Human Rights (by the terms of which governments in this country are bound) has been construed to include a freedom not to associate. This means in turn that, save in the most exceptional circumstances, closed shop arrangements will not be easy to justify, thereby diminishing any suggestion that trade unions are not truly voluntary bodies.

6.3   A second and perhaps a more compelling argument of principle is based on the right to freedom of association which is protected not only by ILO Convention 87 (the Right to Organise and Freedom of Association Convention, 1948), but also by the International Covenant on Civil and Political Rights, and as we have seen also by the European Convention on Human Rights. Applying the principle of freedom of association most generously, this would direct that workers should be free to associate with each other to promote their common interests and to determine the substance and content of the rules by which they wish their association to be governed. As such the principle embraces two quite distinct features: the first is the idea of *autonomy over membership* in the sense that workers and their organisations should be free to choose with whom they wish to associate and the conditions by which they wish to do so; and the second is the idea of *autonomy in membership* in the sense that workers should be free to determine how they wish their organisation to be governed and the objects and methods which they wish to pursue.

6.4   The third argument is the argument from practice and relates to the function which trade unions perform. Our concern is that detailed internal regulation of trade union internal affairs will inevitably undermine the strength and effectiveness of the organisation by directing energies and resources to the way in which the organisation is administered rather than what it can do for its members. The trade union thus becomes preoccupied with matters of internal administration rather than the representation of its members. Indeed this may in fact be the purpose of the statutory intervention since 1980, a conclusion which is supported by the weakness of the arguments which have been deployed to justify the legislation. Thus the two principal arguments have related to the closed shop and to the existence of the immunities from tortious liability for industrial action. The weakness of the argument relates to the fact that the extent of regulation of internal affairs has increased in direct proportion to the introduction of tighter controls on the operation of the closed shop on the one hand and the erosion of the immunities to the point of virtual extinction on the other.

Freedom of Association and Trade Union Members

6.5   But powerful although these considerations are, it does not follow that the State has no interest in the way in which trade unions are governed, or that trade union government should not be regulated by law. It is suggested, however, that these arguments must not be underestimated, and that they point unequivocally in the direction of a powerful presumption against internal State regulation, unless there are countervailing and overriding principles by which such regulation can be justified. One such consideration relates to the role which it is anticipated trade unions will perform in the implementation of the underlying principles of this document, and in particular the principle of workplace democracy. It may be argued, as others have done in the past, that if trade unions are to be the instrument through which workers will be empowered to participate in workplace decision making, then trade unions themselves must satisfy minimum standards of democracy. At the very least trade union structures should facilitate rather than inhibit membership participation in policy making and implementation, and the rules and procedures should be such that members are treated fairly and not arbitrarily by the administrative machinery of the union.

6.6   Consistently with the overriding commitment to freedom of association and the consequential commitment to trade union autonomy, we propose that that the relationship between the trade union and its members should comply with a number of principles, all of which we identify as principles which currently govern this relationship. These principles are as follows:

(i)   *Openness*, by which we mean that trade unions should not exclude applicants for membership without good cause.

(ii) *Transparency*, by which we mean that the members of trade unions should have the right of access to financial and other information relating to the way in which the union is governed.

(iii) *Participation*, by which we mean that members of the union should not, without good cause, be denied the opportunity to stand for election to office or as a delegate to the union's conference.

(iv) *Accountability*, by which we mean that those who exercise power in the union on behalf of the membership should be answerable to the membership for the way in which that power is used and for major decisions which may be taken.

(v)   *Fairness*, by which we mean that the members of the union individually should be treated fairly by the union, particularly in the exercise of any disciplinary powers, including expulsion from membership.

6.7   Yet although the State may have a legitimate interest in the way in which trade unions are governed, it does not follow that this necessarily means that there should be legal intervention of trade union internal affairs. Before any legal regulation can be justified, there must be clear evidence that there is a democratic deficit in the way in which trade unions are governed or clear evidence that trade unions treat their members arbitrarily and capriciously. And on this point it is necessary to be aware also that there is not necessarily any single definition of democracy for this purpose, and consequently no case for imposing a singular and one dimensional form of government on all trade unions regardless of their history, traditions and practices. At best the case for legislation can be made only if there is evidence that trade unions are not open, not transparent, discourage participation, are unaccountable to their members, or treat their members unfairly. Yet by any objective and historical standard, regardless of the impact of any law operating from time to time, trade unions must be regarded as one of the most democratic and participative organisations in our society.

Trade Unions and the Law: From Autonomy to State Control

6.8   Traditionally trade union government was subject to very little detailed control. The starting point of any regulation is the rule book of the union which forms the basis of the contract between the union and its members individually. With a few exceptions (applying to political funds and to amalgamations) until 1971 there was very little statutory regulation of trade union internal affairs or with the trade union rule book. The principal measure was the Trade Union Act 1871 which effectively required registered trade unions to have rules about prescribed issues, but did not in any way prescribe the content of these rules. Indeed the Trade Union Act 1871 went so far as to attempt to keep rule book disputes out of the courts, though the intention was never fully realised as the judges found ways to ensure that members with a rule book grievance had an opportunity to seek a judicial remedy. But for the most part the courts were empowered only to enforce the terms of the rule book, a power admittedly used from time to time in an unpredictable and hostile way. Nevertheless sporadic judicial creativity in the interpretation of trade union rules rather than direct and sustained statutory intervention was the only real legal threat to trade union autonomy.

6.9   The first major statutory intervention in trade union internal affairs was in the Industrial Relations Act 1971. This provided that organisations of workers were to comply with certain 'guiding principles' relating a broad range of matters, including admission to membership, participation in the electoral and decision making machinery of the union, and discipline and expulsion from membership. Unions which registered under the Act (and not many did) were also required to comply with a range of requirements laid down in Schedule 4. This contained fairly detailed measures which included a requirement that the rules made provision for the election of the governing body of the union and 'its re-election at reasonable intervals', and for the manner in which members of the governing body could be removed from office. Other requirements included an obligation to specify who was authorised to give instructions to take any kind of industrial action. These measures were repealed in 1974 along with the rest of the Act, though a number of the provisions regulating trade union membership were retained and were not eventually repealed until 1976.

6.10   Since 1979, however, the degree of regulation of trade union internal affairs has increased sharply, concentrating on several areas which undermine the autonomy of the union to govern its own affairs in accordance with the wishes of its members, as expressed by the rule book. A legal noose was thrown around the neck of the trade union movement in 1980, and this has been gradually tightened ever since. The first intervention was in the Employment Act 1980 which, consistently with the principle of trade union autonomy, but as a prelude to more authoritarian measures, introduced a public subsidy for prescribed ballots held by trade unions, including strike ballots and ballots of the members under the rules of the union. The same Act also introduced controls over trade union admissions and expulsions, though these were less intrusive than the corresponding provisions of the Industrial Relations Act 1971 in the sense that they applied only where a union membership agreement was in force and where, as a result of a refusal to admit or a decision to expel, a worker could be excluded from a particular employment and indeed a particular trade.

6.11   State intervention in trade union internal affairs was extended by the Trade Union Act 1984 which required trade unions to hold elections for the voting members of their principal executive committee at five yearly intervals. The same Act also introduced a requirement of strike ballots in the case of action authorised or endorsed by the union (though the obligation to ballot was enforceable by the employer rather than members of the union) and a requirement that trade unions with political objects should ballot their members every ten years for authority to continue to promote these objects. Additional obligations were introduced in the Employment Act 1988 which gave trade union members as well as employers the right to enforce the requirement to hold a ballot, introduced restrictions on the unions' right to discipline or expel members (particularly in the context of industrial action), provided members with a statutory right to inspect accounting records, prohibited unions from indemnifying members or officials for fines imposed in criminal proceedings, and significantly tightened the balloting procedures for union elections. The Act also introduced the Commissioner for the Rights of Trade Union Members.

6.12   Yet further erosion of the principle of trade union autonomy took place with the enactment of the Trade Union Reform and Employment Rights Act 1993. Apart from additional restrictions on industrial action, this measure imposed further obligations on trade union election procedures by extending the power of the scrutineer and by regulating the counting of votes in an election. The Act also introduced new controls on trade union admission and expulsion rules (designed mainly to frustrate the operation of the TUC's Bridlington procedures) so that an individual may not be excluded or expelled from a trade union 'unless the exclusion or expulsion' is for a reason 'permitted' by the Act. Only four grounds are permitted, the Act expressly excluding exclusion or expulsion because the individual in question is or was a member of another union. Remarkably the 1993 Act also withdrew the public subsidy from trade union ballots, remarkable because it was withdrawn at the very time the State was imposing even more financial and administrative burdens on trade unions.

International Labour Standards: Theory and Reality

6.13   How is the right to trade union autonomy protected in international labour law? As we have seen there are a number of instruments which are relevant, including the International Covenant on Civil and Political Rights and the European Convention on Human Rights. But perhaps the key text for this purpose (partly because it also helps to inform the interpretation of these other instruments) is ILO Convention 87 (the Right to Organise and Freedom of Association Convention, 1948), which on its face recognises two quite distinct aspects of the principle of trade union autonomy, the first of which is *autonomy over membership* of the organisation, that is to say who is eligible for membership and the persons whom the organisation is prepared to accept into its association. The other aspect of the principle of trade union autonomy is *autonomy in membership*, in the sense of autonomy over the way in which the association is governed and administered, and autonomy over the activities and objects which it wishes to promote.

6.14 There are three articles of Convention 87 which are particularly important. The first is Article 2 which seeks to establish the right of workers to join trade unions without interference but in doing so appears to recognise the right of trade union autonomy in terms of controlling who will be eligible for membership. Thus it is provided that 'Workers . . . shall have the right to establish and, subject only to the rules of the organisation concerned, to join organisations of their own choosing without previous authorisation'. Also important is Article 3 which appears to recognise the right of trade union autonomy in terms of the rules and procedures by which it is to be governed. Thus, Article 3 provides that 'Workers' and employers' organisations shall have the right to draw up their constitutions and rules, to elect their representatives in full freedom, to organise their administration and activities and to formulate their programmes'. Finally reference should be made to article 11 which provides that each member of the ILO for which the Convention is in force (and that includes Britain) 'undertakes to take all necessary and appropriate measures to ensure that workers and employers may exercise freely the right to organise'.

6.15 This gives a clear commitment to trade union autonomy in matters of internal government, but at least as far as the Committee of Experts is concerned, the commitment is not unequivocal. In what appears to be the first consideration of the 1980s legislation the Committee of Experts examined the Trade Union Act 1984, but found that the mandatory election of principal executive committees, mandatory strike ballots, and the periodic review of political objects did not violate the requirements of Convention 87. Although at first blush the legislation would appear unequivocally to undermine the 'full freedom' of workers' organisations to 'draw up their constitutions and rules', the Committee nevertheless observed, in the case of the mandatory elections for executive committees, that 'no violation of the principles of freedom of association is involved where legislation contains certain rules intended to promote democratic principles within trade union organisations or to ensure that the electoral procedure is conducted in a normal manner and with due respect for the rights of members in order to avoid any dispute arising as to the result of the election'.

6.16   In 1989 the Committee of Experts addressed a number of issues relating to British labour law in force at the time. Some of these concerned the internal affairs of trade unions. Again, however, the Committee considered that there was no incompatibility between Article 3 and a number of aspects of the legislation which was challenged. This was true of restrictions relating to (i) the election of union officers; (ii) the removal of union trustees; (iii) union members' right of access to accounting records; (iv) political expenditure by trade unions; (v) exclusion or expulsion from a trade union where a union membership agreement is in operation; (vi) access to the courts by union members who have a grievance against the union; (vii) ballots in respect of industrial action; and (viii) the role as then defined of the Commissioner of the Rights of Trade Union Members, though concern was expressed that some of these provisions (and particularly the last) could be applied in a manner which would be inconsistent with the letter or spirit of the Convention.

6.17   It is perhaps both disappointing and surprising that the Committee of Experts should have accepted such a wide range of restrictions on trade union autonomy, particularly in light of the clear language of the Convention. On the other hand, however, not all the restrictions introduced since 1980 were held to be compatible with Convention 87, the Committee drawing attention in particular to the restrictions on the right of trade unions to indemnify officials and the restrictions on the ability of trade unions to discipline and expel strike-breakers. In the case of the former they were said to be 'not compatible with the guarantees provided by Article 3 and should be repealed', though the Committee seemed unwilling subsequently to press the point. So far as the latter are concerned, however, the Committee was firmly of the view that 'proper respect for the guarantees provided by Article 3 requires that union members should be permitted, when drawing up their constitutions and rules, to determine whether or not it should be possible to discipline members who refuse to participate in lawful strikes and other industrial action or who seek to persuade fellow members to refuse to participate in such action'.

The Legal Status of Trade Unions

6.18   The first substantive question for consideration relates to the legal status of trade unions. Happily this is no longer a major issue of controversy, the underlying legal framework appropriate to the status and functions of trade unions being now largely in place. The recasting of the statute law in 1974-76, building on the foundations laid in 1871, contains the essential elements to protect trade unions against the doctrine of restraint of trade, and to preserve their status as voluntary associations. Although said to have 'quasi - corporate status', trade unions are not corporate bodies and are not to be treated as such except for specific purposes. They are thus free to own property, make contracts, conduct litigation and generally do all that is necessary to administer their affairs within the law on behalf of their members. There are undoubtedly anomalies and gaps in the current law which need to be addressed, one of which is the possible inability of a trade union to protect its reputation by suing for defamation (though it can be sued for defamation). We propose that the status of trade unions as provided in the 1974 legislation should be retained.

6.19   There is, however, one area where change is required. All trade union property is vested in trustees in trust for the union. In 1988 a statutory procedure was introduced for the removal of trustees, whereby a union member may apply to a court in certain circumstances, the court being empowered to issue an order which includes the removal of trustees. We accept that it should be possible to remove trustees with a minimum of formality on grounds of personal incapacity or unfitness for office. But, while we recognise the concern to protect trade union members and trade union funds from the actions of officials who may be acting contrary to the interests of the union, we are troubled by the fact that this important step can be taken without any greater formality in cases arising out of the conduct of industrial action. We therefore propose in such cases that (i) it should be possible to move an order for the removal of trustees only on the application of a prescribed number of members; (ii) an order for removal should be issued only after a ballot of the members of the union indicating support for this step; and (iii) the court should be required to appoint new trustees from within the union. Any such application should be made to the Labour Court proposed in chapter 10.

Trade Union Expenditure and the Use of Funds

(a) Indemnification of Members and Officials

6.20   It was recognised by the Trade Union Act 1871 that trade unions may have occasion to indemnify members or officials who incur liability while acting on union business. But rather than prevent trade union funds being used in this way the purpose of statutory intervention in 1871 was to keep disputes between the union and its members about such matters from the courts. Thus under the Act any agreement for the discharge of any fine imposed on any person was unenforceable, which meant that it if the union failed to reimburse any member or official, there was nothing they could do about it. Admittedly it does not follow from this that a rule which authorised the payment of a fine would be lawful and that any exercise of the power conferred by the rule would be lawful. Indeed the view was expressed by one leading authority that any such provision 'would probably be contrary to public policy and unenforceable'.[1]

6.21   The position is now governed by the Trade Union and Labour Relations (Consolidation) Act 1992, section 15, provisions first introduced by the Employment Act 1988. Making express what may have been implied, this provides that is unlawful for a union to use its funds to indemnify any individual for any fine imposed by a court on being found guilty of the commission of an offence or for contempt of court. The money is recoverable from the member and where the union fails to bring proceedings to recover the money, a member may apply to the court for an order authorising him or her to bring proceedings on the union's behalf and at the union's expense. Payments of this nature could also lead to the removal of trustees. Although this provision was initially condemned by the ILO Committee of Experts, as we have seen this is a conclusion from which they appeared subsequently to resile. Nevertheless we propose that this provision should be repealed and that a union should be permitted to reimburse or indemnify any member or official who is (i) acting on behalf of the union, (ii) in accordance with the rules and policy of the union, and (iii) in respect of any matter which does not involve violence to person or property.

(b) Political Activities

6.22   The regulation of political activities was first introduced by the Trade Union Act 1913. This requires trade unions to adopt

---

1   N. Citrine, *Trade Union Law,* (3rd ed by M.A. Hickling, 1967).

political fund rules, following a ballot of their members, if they wish to promote political objects. The rules must provide for the establishment of a separate political fund, to be funded by a separate political levy in respect of which members have a right to claim exemption. Exempt members must also be protected from discrimination on account of their non payment of the political levy, while any complaints of a breech of the political fund rules may be made to the Certification Officer. The legislation was amended in 1984, expanding the definition of political objects, which meant that there was a wider range of activities from which unions would be excluded if they did not have a political fund. The 1984 Act also required trade unions to hold ballots every ten years to renew the authority to promote political objects. So far no union has failed to renew its political objects.

6.23   The first question which arises for consideration here is whether it should be necessary for trade union political objects to be the subject of statutory regulation. Is this a matter for each union to determine in accordance with the terms of its own rule books, free to use general funds for political purposes if it so wishes, and free to have a separate political fund with or without a right to contract out, as the union wishes? It is well known that trade unions are subject to a quite exceptional degree of regulation of their political activities. Companies, in particular, are subject to no comparable controls, being required only to disclose political donations in excess of £200 in their annual reports to shareholders. It is not difficult to argue that if companies are to be free from legal regulation then so too should trade unions. On the other hand, it is open to question what benefits would be secured by removing the current regulation of trade unions which has operated well since 1913. We propose that, in the interests of equity between organisations, either the restrictions on trade union political expenditure should be removed, or companies should be subjected to the same degree of regulation as trade unions.

6.24   But if the current regime relating to trade union political expenditure is to be retained, it does not follow that the detail of the current law is satisfactory. The second question for consideration is whether the statutory definition of political objects is too wide. Are there items if political expenditure which unions should be permitted to finance from general funds? The main issue for consideration relates to paragraph (f) of the definition of political objects which applies to expenditure on the production, publication or distribution of any literature, document, film, sound recording or advertisement, the main purpose of which is to persuade any person to vote or not to vote for a particular political party or candidate. This prevents unions without a political fund from campaigning in elections not to support the Labour Party but to promote trade union issues such as the defence of public sector jobs. We propose that if the current framework is retained, the statutory definition of political objects should be amended to permit such expenditure and thereby confine the definition of political objects to expenditure of a genuinely party political nature. This would allow unions without political funds to incur expenditures from which they are currently precluded.

6.25   The third issue which arises in the context of trade union political funds relates to the mandatory ballots every ten years in order to renew political objects. We see no justification for this as a statutory obligation, though this is not to say that trade unions should not be free to decide that they wish to ballot their members in this way. But it should be a matter for each trade union and its members, rather than an obligation imposed by the State. The case for mandatory ballots on a regular basis would be more compelling if trade union members were required by the political fund rules of their union to pay the political levy whether they wished to do so or not. But the fact is that anyone can contract out and that no one can be compelled to contribute to the financing of political objects against their will. We are also persuaded by the fact that since the mandatory balloting requirement was implemented no trade union has failed to renew its political objects. The overwhelming majorities in most of these ballots is a clear indication that trade unions do not promote political objects without the consent of their members, further evidence of which is provided by the fact that generally only a small proportion of trade union members contract out of paying the levy in those unions which have political funds. We propose that, if the current regime is to be retained, the obligation to conduct political fund review ballots should be repealed.

Trade Union Government and the Election of Executive Committees

6.26   Until 1984 trade unions had almost complete autonomy over the election of officials. They were free to determine whether executive committees were to be elected or appointed, free to determine the method of election, and free to determine the length of tenure in office. Under the Trade Union Act 1871 registered trade unions were required simply to have rules providing for the appointment and removal of a general committee of management. The 1871 Act was repealed by the Industrial Relations Act 1971 which introduced a number of restrictions on trade union internal affairs. But compared to what we now live with these were modest intrusions on the principle of trade union autonomy. Unions were not to exclude members, by way of *arbitrary or unreasonable* discrimination, from being a candidate for or holding office in the organisation, nominating candidates for office, voting in any election or ballot of the members, or attending and taking part in meetings.

(a) Developments since 1980

6.27   The first intervention in trade union internal affairs was to be found in the Employment Act 1980, section 1. This provided public money for 'carrying out an election provided for by the rules of the trade union' and applied to elections for the national executive committee, the election of president, chairman, secretary or treasurer, and ballots for calling or ending industrial action. This measure did not in itself interfere with trade union autonomy, but reinforced it in the sense that the money was available (if the union wanted it) to finance elections in accordance with the union's own rules and procedures, provided that the rules met conditions laid down in The Funds for Trade Union Ballots Regulations 1980 (SI 1980/1252). Thus the scheme applied only to secret ballots in which the ballot paper was returned by post, while the Certification Officer (responsible for administering the scheme) had to be satisfied that other conditions were met including a requirement that those entitled to vote were to be allowed to do so without interference or constraint, that those entitled to vote had a fair opportunity of doing so, and that the votes were fairly counted.

6.28   The 1980 provisions were simply a prelude to what was to become, in the Trade Union Act 1984, the most significant and far reaching intervention in the government of trade unions ever seen in this country. Under the Act, every person who is a voting member of the principal executive committee of the union has to be elected and the elections are to be held every five years. The elections are held by secret ballot, but may be held by postal or workplace ballot and the votes are to be 'fairly and accurately counted'. In terms of who may be a candidate for election, the Act provided that no member of a trade union is to be unreasonably excluded from standing, and no candidate is to be required, whether directly or indirectly, to be a member of a political party. Where any member has a complaint that an election has not been held or that the statutory procedures have not been followed, he or she may refer the matter to the Certification

Officer or the High Court for a declaration.

6.29 The foundations built in 1984 now sustain a very heavy load in what has become an extraordinarily complex electoral process. A fresh layer of restriction introduced in the Employment Act 1988 extended the election requirement to include non-voting as well as voting members of the principal executive committee, as well as trade union general secretaries and presidents. Ballots were now to be postal with the option of workplace ballots having been repealed, and every candidate was to have an opportunity to prepare an election address which was to be distributed by the union, though not at the expense of the candidate. In addition trade unions were now required to appoint independent scrutineers who would have a number of duties under the Act, while just as controversial as any of the foregoing was the creation of the Commissioner of the Rights of Trade Union Members. And as we have seen, additional obligations still were introduced by the Trade Union Reform and Employment Rights Act 1993.

(b) The Balloting Options

6.30 The main question which arises for consideration here is whether legislation should prescribe any particular form of government for trade unions. We have already argued that trade unions should be accountable to the membership, both in terms of the general policy pursued by the union, and in terms also of major decisions taken on behalf of the membership. So far as the former issue is concerned, there was no attempt by legislation to impose any particular method of accountability on trade unions until the Trade Union Act 1984 imposed the requirement of mandatory ballots for executive committees. So far as the former issue is concerned, again there was little evidence of any prescribed statutory procedures to be followed before certain decisions could be taken, though it might be argued that the compulsory ballots before amalgamation and the compulsory ballots before political objects can be established are examples of such legislation.

6.31 The first issue which arises for consideration is whether there is a case for legislation requiring the periodic election of executive committees. The starting point is the right to freedom of association which implies not just a right to join with others to promote common interests, but a right also to determine with others how the group should be governed. It is true on the other hand that the right to freedom of association, as protected by ILO Convention 87, has not been taken to prevent the State from intervening to ensure that trade unions are run along democratic lines. But because the ILO sanctions interference of this kind, it does not follow that, in the absence of any clear and compelling evidence that trade unions are run on autocratic lines, the State should therefore intervene with legislation. The ILO jurisprudence permits State intervention to promote the interests of trade union democracy, but does not compel such intervention. And although the jurisprudence permits some form of intervention in trade union government, it does not direct the form which that intervention should take.

6.32 We recognise, nevertheless, that the mandatory election of executive committees is one which arouses strong passions within the trade union movement, and that not everyone is passionately opposed to either the principle or the practice. We are of the view that there is no obviously correct solution to this question and that public policy could equally adopt one of five solutions, by no means mutually consistent. These are as follows:

(a) A statutory requirement that trade unions should elect their executive committee on a regular basis; or

(b) A statutory requirement that trade union members should be entitled to trigger a ballot of the executive committee on a regular basis; or

(c) A statutory requirement that trade union rules should comply with model rules, including the election of the executive committee at regular intervals; or

(d) A statutory requirement that trade union rules should comply with a number of statutory principles, including the requirement that the executive committee should be elected; or

(e) No statutory regulation, with trade unions being free to determine the composition of their executive committee in accordance with the terms of the rule book.

(c) The Conduct of Ballots

6.33 So far as the conduct of ballots is concerned, the amount of detail has increased since mandatory ballots were first introduced for trade union political objects in the Trade Union Act 1913. Under the Act political fund ballots had to be taken in accordance with rules of the union which had to be approved by the Chief Registrar of Friendly Societies who had to be satisfied that 'every member has an equal right, and, if reasonably possible, a fair opportunity of voting, and that the secrecy of the ballot is properly secured'. Under the model ballot rules provision was made for ballots to be held from the general office of the union or in the branches. In the case of the former ballot papers were to be sent to members along with a copy of the ballot rules and an envelope addressed to the scrutineers. The scrutineers were to be three members of the union appointed by the national executive committee, and they had the responsibility of counting the papers in the presence of the national executive committee. They were then required to certify the result to the Chief Registrar of Friendly Societies and to seal the ballot papers which were to be retained for six months and were subject to inspection by the Registrar at any time. Modified rules existed for branch ballots.

6.34 The position is now very different under the current legislation relating to elections and ballots. A range of complex statutory obligations has gradually been built up since 1984 to regulate elections for executive committees, ballots before industrial action, and political fund ballots (which must now be held at ten yearly intervals). So far as the mandatory election of executive committees is concerned, the legislation regulates who may be a candidate at an election, requires election addresses to be produced at the union's expense and to be available equally to all candidates, and deals with the appointment and duties of an independent scrutineer, entitlement to vote, the method of voting, the content of the voting paper, the counting of votes by an 'independent' person, and the scrutineer's report. The law relating to the holding of political fund ballots has also been radically redrawn, there now being a much greater degree of statutory regulation of these ballots than was previously the case. An 'independent' scrutineer must now be appointed, the ballot must be conducted by post, and the votes are to be counted by an 'independent' person.

6.35 If the view is taken that one of models (a), (b), or (c) in paragraph 6.32 above is suitable, we would not propose that trade unions should be subjected to the degree of detailed regulation which is currently required by the Trade Union and Labour Relations (Consolidation) Act 1992. It is nevertheless difficult to resist the conclusion that if there is to be a requirement of mandatory elections that there should also be some regulation of the election procedure. There are several issues which would need to be considered: eligibility to stand for election, the right to circulate an election address, the independence of the union administration, and the provision of a scrutineer to supervise the process. It is also the case that if ballots are to be required directly or indirectly by the State, the cost of holding the ballot should be fully subsidised by the State. It is thus for consideration whether the reintroduction of the public subsidy for any union which chooses to apply for it should be a condition of any obligation directly or indirectly imposed on a union to hold elections or ballots for any prescribed purpose. Clearly, it should be expressly provided that no union is compelled to take advantage of the facility and that union officials will not be acting contrary to their duty to their members if they failed to apply for funding.

Trade Unions and their Members

6.36   So far as the rights of trade union members are concerned, we are mindful of the fact that we propose a critical role for trade unions in the development of rights at the workplace. In particular we see trade unions as the essential vehicle for ensuring that workers collectively have a voice in workplace decisions. From this a number of consequences flow in terms of the relationship between the trade union and its members. Above all, however, there is an interest in ensuring that trade unions are operated on democratic lines, for it would be difficult to sustain the argument in favour of trade unions as being the democratic voice in the enterprise if the unions themselves were closed and autocratic. We saw at paragraph 6.6, however, that the relationship between the trade union and its members should comply with a number of principles. We have no reason to believe that these principles are not generally followed by trade unions in this country, and in our view there is no need for comprehensive legislation to ensure their effective implementation. But this is not to say that there is no role for legislation or for other forms of guidance.

(a) Openness

6.37   So far as the principle of openness is concerned, the concern here is to ensure that people who wish to join a trade union for the protection of their interests should be free to do so, unless there is good reason for their exclusion. The issue was particularly controversial in workplaces where the closed shop operated, or where a union membership agreement was in force. The Employment Act 1980 addressed the question of admission to and expulsion from membership where a union membership agreement existed. Although the Act introduced a requirement to ballot for new union membership agreements (a requirement extended to existing agreements in 1982) and although the Act provided a wide right to claim exemption from union membership where a union membership agreement was in force, it also provided that an individual could not be unreasonably excluded or expelled from a trade union where such an agreement was in force. This provision lost much of its purpose when the Employment Act 1988 provided in effect that it would be automatically unfair to dismiss an employee because of non membership of a trade union (with the result that it became difficult to implement whatever agreements were in force) and was eventually repealed in 1993, though as we shall see other controls on admissions and expulsions survive.

6.38 The closed shop no longer presents a problem and no longer justifies State interference over trade union admission rules and policies. Unsurprisingly, however, there is no evidence that trade unions systematically exclude applicants from membership: it would hardly be in their interests to do so, for a variety of reasons. We do not wish to be taken to suggest, however, that trade unions should not be at liberty to exclude people where it is appropriate to do so, for as Lord Diplock said in *Cheall v APEX* [1983] 2 AC 180, at p 191 'freedom of association can only be mutual; there can be no right of an individual to associate with other individuals who are not willing to associate with him'. We therefore propose the repeal of the measures introduced by the Trade Union Reform and Employment Rights Act 1993, section 14. As already pointed out, aimed mainly at the TUC's Bridlington procedures, this authorises trade unions to exclude or expel from membership only on 'permitted' grounds. Self evidently it is inconsistent with the principle of freedom of association for the State to regulate trade union membership in such a manner. We see no objection in principle to trade unions deciding among themselves what steps must be taken to rationalise membership and recruitment patterns.

(b) Transparency

6.39 The right of trade union members to have access to financial information about the union was recognised by the Trade Union Act 1871 which provided that the rules of registered trade unions had to contain a rule providing for the inspection of the books of the union 'by every person having an interest in the funds of the union'. This provision survived for 100 years, giving rise to some, though not a great deal of litigation. In the leading case, *Norey v Keep* [1909] 1 Ch 561, it was held that members could ask that their accountant 'should have access to the books for the purpose of examining them'. This decision was followed in *Taylor v NUM (Derbyshire Area) (No 2)*

[1985] IRLR 65 where it was said by the judge that members 'must be entitled to the assistance of a trained accountant who can interpret the books and who will notice points which will give rise to enquiry if not suspicion'.

6.40 Similar provisions were introduced by the ill-fated Industrial Relations Act 1971, though they were not retained by the Trade Union and Labour Relations Act 1974 (as amended in 1976). Perhaps rather surprisingly, the 1974 Act simply required trade unions to keep accounting records and to file an annual return with the Certification Officer, a copy of which the trade union had to supply to any person on request either free of charge or on the payment of a reasonable fee. In 1988, however, the law relating to the members' right of access to financial information was extended so that unions must permit members to inspect accounting records and be accompanied by an accountant who can be required to agree to maintain confidentiality. There is no reason to believe that an obligation of this kind should not be retained, though it is unclear to us whether the law should be retained in its present form. This is a matter to which we return below. It is also for consideration whether the union should be entitled to impose conditions on access where the information is being sought to undermine the interests of the union.

(c) Participation

6.41 So far as participation is concerned, here we have in mind the right of members to stand for office, to nominate candidates for office, to attend meetings and to be elected as a delegate or representative to meetings of the union. Self evidently a union which sought to encourage participation amongst its members would not seek to exclude them from the normal policy making machinery or representative processes within the union. This has not been a major problem in the past though there are unions which have banned members of the Communist Party from standing for office, and there has been litigation about the fact that unions have required senior officers to be members of the Labour Party. There have also been occasional complaints about members being unreasonably excluded from office on other grounds, as in *Breen v AEU* [1971] 1 All ER 1148 where a shop steward was refused approval by a district committee on the basis of an unfounded allegation of financial impropriety against him. Concerns were expressed in that case about the procedures adopted by the District Committee before rejecting Breen who had been elected by his work-mates.

6.42   Until the Industrial Relations Act 1971, however, there was no direct statutory regulation of union rules and practices in this area. The 1971 Act provided that a member of a union should not, by way of arbitrary or unreasonable discrimination, be excluded from being a candidate for any office, nominating candidates for election, voting in any election, or attending and taking part in branch meetings. But these measures were short-lived and are not thought to have had much impact. The position is now governed by the Trade Union and Labour Relations (Consolidation) Act 1992 which provides in general terms that no member of a trade union 'shall be unreasonably excluded from standing as a candidate' and specifically that no candidate shall be required directly or indirectly to be a member of a political party. However, these provisions apply only in respect of elections, and then only executive committee elections, or elections for president or general secretary, which means that in other cases the matter will fall to be governed by the rule book unless any aggrieved member can demonstrate a possible breach of the Sex Discrimination Act 1975 or the Race Relations Act 1976.

(d) Accountability

6.43   How can the law best promote the principle of accountability? There are two issues here: the first is the general accountability of the national executive committee of the union for its conduct of union business; and the second is the specific accountability of union officials for particular decisions affecting members. So far as the former is concerned, this clearly could best be met by the regular election of the national executive committee. As we have seen it is for consideration, however, whether this should be left for trade unions themselves to deal with or whether it should be regulated by legislation, and if so whether the legislation should require mandatory ballots at regular intervals, or whether it should simply empower a prescribed number of members to requisition an election.

6.44   The other aspect of accountability is consultation with the membership before major decisions are taken. Into this category would fall three decisions: the first is the decision to adopt political objects. As we have already suggested the case for retaining this obligation is finely balanced, though we are less convinced of the need to retain the requirement of periodic ballots to renew political objects, particularly as trade union members have the right to claim exemption from the obligation to pay the political levy. The second decision to which the issue of mandatory ballots arises is our proposal in chapter 3 that trade unions should be empowered to derogate from a sectoral employment agreement as a result of a collective agreement at enterprise level. It is for consideration whether this should be done only after a ballot has been held of those members of the union who will be covered by the agreement. The third decision to which the issue of a mandatory ballot arises is the decision to call industrial action.

(e) Fairness

6.45 So far as the principle of fairness is concerned, this applies mainly in the context of the discipline and expulsion of members. Here two questions arise: the first is the reason for the discipline or expulsion, the question of substance; and the second is the procedure to be followed before discipline or expulsion, the procedural question. In terms of the grounds for expulsion, traditionally there has been little regulation of this question by the State. There was nothing in the 1871 Act restricting the power of discipline and expulsion and until 1971 the only significant intervention by legislation was the Trade Union Act 1913 which had the effect of prohibiting any discriminatory treatment on account of non payment of the political levy. The position changed in 1971, however, when the Industrial Relations Act introduced restrictions on 'unfair or unreasonable disciplinary action' which was defined to include disciplinary action for failing to take part in what was in effect unlawful industrial action. We see no reason why (with the exception of non payment of a political levy) the State should dictate the grounds on which trade unions may or may not discipline members. At present trade unions may not discipline or expel a member because he or she refused to take part in industrial action, even though the action was supported by a ballot. In our view this provision, which has been criticised as violating ILO Convention 87, ought to be repealed.

6.46 In terms of the procedures which should be followed before disciplinary action is taken, we take the view that the union should be required to adhere to the procedures in its rule book, and as at present should be required the apply the rules of natural justice. It is a matter for consideration, however, whether standards of procedural fairness should be set out in legislation as was done in the Industrial Relations Act 1971 which provided that trade union members could not be subjected to disciplinary action unless they had been given written notice of the charges brought against them, a reasonable time to prepare a defence, a full and fair hearing, a written statement of the findings resulting from the hearing, and the status quo maintained pending any appeal for which provision is made in the rule book. These obligations are already required in large measure by the rules of natural justice which supplement the rule book procedures of the unions. As a result it seems unnecessary to specify any additional obligations, though there may be some merit, in the interests of certainty and clarity, in developing a framework of good disciplinary procedure in a Code of Practice which if followed would absolve a trade union from any legal challenge based on the fairness of its procedures. The principles in question are essentially very simple, requiring no more than that the member should be given a fair hearing before an unbiased tribunal. This means that the individual in question should be given adequate notice of any charges, an opportunity to rebut the charges, and where appropriate an opportunity to be accompanied by a friend or legal representative.

A Residual Role for the Law

6.47   The question which now arises for consideration is how these principles can best be implemented. There are essentially three options. The first is to introduce a framework of legislation with which trade unions would have to comply regardless of the terms of the rule book. The second is to introduce a requirement whereby trade union rules must comply with certain minimum standards, a requirement which could apply to all trade unions or only to those seeking to take advantage of certain statutory benefits. The third is what might be referred to as the soft law option which is to have no mandatory standards of any kind, but perhaps a Code of Practice which prescribes certain minimum standards with which trade unions ought in principle to comply. The Code might be drafted by the Certification Officer or similar body and could be taken into account where appropriate in legal proceedings relating to the terms of the rule book.

6.48   On balance we prefer a modified version of the second option, which is in effect the approach pioneered in the Trade Union Act 1871. But apart from the attraction of historical continuity we are persuaded that this solution is the one which can most effectively combine our commitment to the principle of trade union autonomy with our commitment to ensure that trade union government complies with the principles identified in paragraph 6.6 above. What we have in mind is a procedure whereby trade unions would be listed with the Certification Officer, as is currently the case. In order to be eligible for listing the trade union in question would have to have rules which comply with certain prescribed standards. Only a listed union could apply for a certificate of independence, and only an independent trade union would be eligible to use the procedures which we propose in this text, relating in particular to Sectoral Employment Commissions in chapter 3, and to rights relating to trade union membership, organisation, representation, recognition and collective bargaining in chapter 7.

6.49 It is true that although based on an idea initially pioneered by the Trade Union Act 1871, this procedure develops some of the ideas promoted by the Donovan Royal Commission many years ago. We do not, however, see this as a source of weakness; indeed we believe the opposite to be the case. Although our model is not consciously modelled on Donovan, if people wish to draw comparisons, then in our view this should only serve to increase the scope for consensus in relation to these proposals. In any event the circumstances of the introduction of our proposals would be rather different from those existing in 1968, and there are also important differences which would distinguish our proposals from those measures which were proposed in 1968. Donovan proposed that eventually all trade unions should be 'registered' and a condition of doing so would be the adoption of satisfactory rules. It is crucial to our proposals, however, that trade unions would be free to choose to apply for listing or not as the case may be. Those which wish to do so would be required only to comply with certain minimum standards in the formulation of which their autonomy would be preserved.

6.50 The question for consideration then is what should be the conditions of listing? In our view trade union rules should include and deal with the following matters:

(i) The name and business address of the union
(ii) The full objects of the union
(iii) The method of making and amending the rules of the union
(iv) The governing body and the procedures for its re-election at regular intervals
(v) Eligibility for admission to the union
(vi) The inspection of the accounting records of the union by members of the union
(vii) Eligibility to nominate candidates for office, eligibility to stand for office, and eligibility to attend meetings or to be elected or nominated as a delegate to meetings
(viii) The rights of candidates in an election, the rules to secure that each candidate has an equal opportunity to issue an

election address, and the independence of the union administration

(ix) The appointment of an independent scrutineer to supervise the conduct of elections, with a clear statement of the scrutineer's duties

(x) The procedures for holding elections, including the issue and control of ballot papers, the method and supervision of voting, the counting and scrutiny of votes, and the declaration and notification of the result

(xi) The procedures to be adopted before industrial action is called, including the holding of ballots before industrial action, should the balloting option be adopted (on which see chapter 8)

(xii) The grounds for which any member of the union may be disciplined or expelled by the union (on which see chapter 8)

(xiii) The procedure which must be followed in the case of the discipline and expulsion of members and the range of penalties which may be imposed on any member for breach of the rules

(xiv) The right of appeal by anyone who has been disciplined in breach of the rules and for the status quo to be maintained pending the outcome of the appeal, unless there are exceptional circumstances.

We also propose that trade unions should be required, as at present, to submit an annual return to the Certification Officer.

The Resolution of Internal Disputes

6.51 At the present time trade union members who complain that the union has acted in breach of the rule book must take their complaint to the High Court. In other cases complaints may be made to the Certification Officer (for example in the case of alleged breaches of the political fund rules) and industrial tribunals (for example in the case of expulsion because of failure to participate in industrial action). In our view there is much to said for a more streamlined procedure which promotes autonomy and self regulation in the settlement of disputes and a unified and common procedure for the settlement of all disputes. So far as autonomy is concerned, we believe that disputes between trade unions and their members should be resolved where possible without the need for recourse to the courts. In this regard we are mindful of the TUC Independent Review Committee established in 1976 with a narrow jurisdiction to deal with disputes between trade unions and individual workers in cases where the worker in question had been excluded or expelled from the union where a closed shop operated. We propose the introduction of a similar such body with the power to investigate all complaints of alleged rule book breaches.

6.52 We are not suggesting, however, that this process should be compulsory on the part of the worker, nor are we suggesting that the worker in dispute with his or her union should be denied the right to have that dispute resolved by a judicial body. In our view it ought to be possible for a worker to choose to take the matter to a judicial body rather than to the TUC Independent Review Committee in the first place. Where, however, the worker chooses to proceed to the Independent Review Committee then in our view that decision should be binding subject only to a review jurisdiction on the part of the courts to intervene on the ground of illegality or procedural impropriety. But in the interests of a unified and common procedure we propose that both this original and review jurisdiction over disputes about trade union rules should lie with the Labour Court which we propose in chapter 10 below, though in these cases we also propose that the court should consist of a legally qualified chair and two representatives from a panel of persons nominated by trade unions, who would not have any connection with the union involved in the dispute.

Summary of Recommendations

1   The legal status of trade unions as provided in the 1974 legislation should be retained.

2   It should be possible to remove the trustees of a trade union with a minimum of formality on grounds of incapacity or unfitness for office.

3   In cases arising out of the conduct of industrial action, it should be possible to seek the removal of trustees only on the application of a prescribed number of members; only after a ballot of the members of the union indicating support for this step; and only after the court has appointed new trustees from within the union.

4   A union should be permitted to reimburse or indemnify any member or official who is (i) acting on behalf of the union, (ii) in accordance with the rules and policy of the union, and (iii) in

respect of any matter which does not involve violence to person or property.

5 Trade unions and companies should be treated the same way in matters relating to political activities, either by removing the controls on trade union political expenditure, or by subjecting companies to a similar regime.

6 If the principles of the Trade Union Act 1913 are retained, the current statutory definition of political objects should be amended to permit non party political expenditure to be financed from general funds.

7 If the principles of the Trade Union Act 1913 are retained, the current obligation to conduct political fund review ballots should be repealed.

8 Trade unions should be governed in a manner which promotes openness, transparency, participation, accountability and fairness.

9 Trade unions should be free to determine the content of their own rules and to apply for listing with the Certification Officer.

10 Trade unions which apply for listing should have rules which deal with prescribed matters, though it should be for the union to determine the content of these rules.

11 Trade unions should be required, as at present, to submit an annual return to the Certification Officer.

12 There should be re-established an independent review body by the TUC with jurisdiction to hear complaints from trade union members about the breach of the rules of the union.

13 Trade union members should have a right to choose to have any complaint about the breach of the rules of the union dealt with by the TUC Independent Review Committee or by the Labour Court, the creation of which is proposed in chapter 10 below.

14 If the worker chooses to have a matter examined by the Committee he or she should be permitted to refer the matter to the proposed Labour Court only on the ground of illegality or procedural impropriety by the Committee.

15 Where cases are heard by the proposed Labour Court, either as part of its original or review jurisdiction, for this purpose the court should consist of a legally qualified chair and two representatives from a panel of persons nominated by trade unions.

TRADE UNION MEMBERSHIP
TRADE UNION RECOGNITION AND
COLLECTIVE BARGAINING

7.1   One of the defining aims of the Conservative Party returning to government in 1979 was to reduce the power of the British trade union movement, and to undertake what it saw as the necessary re-balancing of the relationship between organised labour and employers. Whilst there will always be serious debate about how far the electorate actively supports Conservative notions of the employment relationship, successive general election victories have allowed the Government significantly to alter the balance of power at work. But in the period since 1979 the Government agenda has shifted from simply reducing trade union influence to developing a public policy that eschews any support for individual or collective representation in the workplace. During this period such limited advances in employment protection that have occured have largely resulted from pressure at a European Community level. However the Government's attitude is summed up by its ideological campaign to prevent ratification of the Social Chapter of the Maastricht Treaty and the resulting legislation.

7.2   Against this background of government hostility to the values of collective bargaining and representation, it is not surprising that the trade union movement has had regularly to re-evaluate its position on several issues, in particular the application of the law relating to industrial relations. There are few who would now argue that the law has no place in determining key aspects of the employment relationship. In the context of trade union recognition and collective bargaining, the law is now unquestionably an important method of ensuring that employers deal with representatives of their workforce. Whilst trade unions may historically have been able to rely on industrial muscle to convince employers to recognise them, it is difficult to see such options being available and effective in the future. This presents a serious challenge to those who wish to shape a future strategy for labour law which has at its heart a role for trade unions and collective bargaining. The legislative history in the UK in this respect is not encouraging. Consequently new ground will have to be broken in establishing a framework for recognition that works.

7.3   The conventional expression of freedom of association and representation at the workplace in the UK has been through membership and participation in independent trade unions. Few other effective channels of representation have evolved and despite the concerted attack upon the boundaries of trade union influence the case for representation at work cannot be quetioned. Whilst the Government may welcome the decline of collective bargaining, for the average worker this has not meant a corresponding increase in their ability as individuals to have a say in decision making within their companies. In fact, the most recent Workplace Industrial Relations Survey confirmed that where collective bargaining has been removed, a vacuum exists in terms of representation of employee interests. Moreover, the government's argument that individuals are in the best position to negotiate their terms and conditions of employment is absolutely hollow, when measured against the experience of working people.

7.4   The removal of collective bargaining and the imposition of personal contracts removes any prospect of co-determination at the workplace, detaches the individual from the support of fellow workers, and increases levels of stress, as job content and responsibility are expanded. The driving back of trade union influence has also undermined the ability of trade unions to act in their traditional role as a key element of a functioning democracy. Whereas in most European countries the participation of trade unionists in the various levels of Government and in the determination of social policy is accepted as legitimate, there are now few forums in this country in which the representatives of both sides of industry come together to debate important issues. It is also notable that a number of commentators are beginning to link the failure of key parts of the economy with growing insecurity at work, the key aspect of which has been the attack upon trade union representation.

7.5   It cannot be assumed, however, that because of growing insecurity at work the case for trade unionism and therefore individual and collective representation is automatically made. The changing composition of the British workforce, with the transfer of employment from manufacturing to service related industries and the growth of atypical forms of work, provides the greatest challenge to organisation and representation through a trade union. The question also has to be asked how far Government policy since 1979 has genuinely inculcated a culture of individualism, which will ignore all attempts to inspire collective decision-making. The answer to this question has a direct bearing upon whether a resurgence of trade union membership can be stimulated. If the concentration upon individualism is more a product of fear based upon insecurity, then the conditions exist whereby representation and collective bargaining can be sponsored by legal measures followed through by trade union organisation. On the other hand, if it is the case that individual relationships will be increasingly the norm at the workplace then a different framework of legal standards will be necessary. Nonetheless, the enforcement mechanism may well still be through an independent trade union.

7.6   We recognise also that we are bound to address one of the fundamental dilemmas which currently faces the trade union movement. That is how to reach an accommodation between the traditional approach to representation through the single channel of trade unionism, with the continental model of works councils, to which trade unions have rights of access, and which are woven into a positive framework of labour law. The manner in which this problem is resolved will, to a large extent, shape any redesign of the law underpinning freedom of association in this country. What does seem clear is that the framework of labour law which supports trade union rights and organisation in the future must be capable of recognising the diverse composition of British trade unions and the levels at which bargaining is carried out.

Trade Union Rights in British Law

7.7   In the 1970s trade unions could point to legislation which provided a legal basis for their activities. Employees had the right not to be dismissed or to suffer any other detriment on account of trade union membership or activities (provided in the case of the latter that they were conducted at an appropriate time). Trade unions had a right to recognition for the purposes of collective bargaining, with claims being made to ACAS which was empowered to make inquiries of the workers to whom the complaint related, and to make an appropriate recommendation. The representatives of a recognised trade union had the right to the disclosure of information, to time off work for trade union duties, and to be consulted about proposed redundancies (a provision extended in 1981 to include business transfers). Trade unions and employers were also free to enter into union membership agreements whereby employees covered by the agreement could be required as condition of employment (or continuing employment) to join and remain in membership of a specified trade union.

7.8   In the 1980s, much of this machinery was dismantled, as were some of the other techniques used by the State to encourage trade union recognition and collective bargaining. Thus the recognition legislation was repealed by the Employment Act 1980, after having been mauled by the Court of Appeal in particular, the government thereby removing the statutory right to a voice at work. 1980 also saw the beginning of the Government's relentless crusade against the closed shop, a campaign fuelled by the decision of the European Court of Human Rights in the British Rail case in which it was held that in some circumstances the mandatory membership of one of a number of specified trade unions was a violation of article 11 of the European Convention on Human Rights. The legislation first required new agreements to be supported in a ballot by 80 per cent of the workers to whom the agreement related, and then provided that employees in any event could not be required to join a union where they had some deeply held personal objection to union membership.

7.9   Steps were also taken in the 1980s to remove various other forms of state support, while legislation was also introduced to forbid the use of commercial pressure to promote trade unionism and collective bargaining. So far as the former is concerned, the two prominent examples of this were the revocation of the Fair Wages Resolution of 1946 and the repeal of Schedule 11 of the Employment Protection Act 1975. So far as the latter is concerned, the Employment Act 1982 provided that any term of a contract is void so far as it requires work to be done only by persons who are members of trade unions. Similarly a contractual term is void in so far as it purports to require a party to the contract to recognise one or more trade unions. So far as the closed shop or union membership agreements were concerned, further restrictions in the Employment Act 1982 required all agreements to be validated in a ballot at five yearly intervals, with either by 80 per cent of those eligible to vote or 85 per cent of those actually voting. In addition a new penal award of compensation was introduced for workers dismissed on account of non-membership of a union (though this was extended to the benefit of workers who were dismissed on account of union membership or activities).

7.10   The only significantly positive step taken under the Conservatives was in response to the decision of the European Court of Justice in *European Commission v UK* [1994] IRLR 392, 412. In that case it was held that British law failed to comply with the

Collective Redundancies Directive (75/129/EEC) and the Acquired Rights Directive (77/187/EEC). This is because under the terms of the Directives employers were required to consult with workers' representatives, which was translated in British law to mean the representatives of a recognised trade union. The omission here, and the one identified by the Court as constituting less than full compliance with the Directives, is that under domestic law employers were relieved of the duty to consult workers' representatives where there was no recognised trade union. But even this apparent triumph was turned by the Government into an anti-union measure, with the implementing regulations authorising the employer to consult with either the representatives of a recognised trade union or with non union representatives elected by the workforce as a whole. It is a reminder, nevertheless, of the need to confront the problem of representation in the non-union workplace.

International Labour Standards

7.11 How are trade union rights protected in international labour law? The basic texts for this purpose are ILO Conventions 87 (the Right to Organise and Freedom of Association Convention, 1948) and 98 (the Right to Organise and Collective Bargaining Convention, 1949). The former provides that 'Workers and employers, without distinction whatsoever, shall have the right to establish and, subject only to the rules of the organisation concerned, to join organisations of their own choosing without previous authorisation'. The Convention also provides that workers' and employers' organisations shall have the right to draw up their constitutions and rules, to elect their representatives in full freedom, to organise their administration and activities and to formulate their programmes. It is further provided that members of the ILO for which the Convention is in force undertake 'to take all necessary and appropriate measures to ensure that workers and employers may exercise freely the right to organise'.

7.12 It was the failure to comply with Convention 87 that led to the complaint to Geneva in the GCHQ case. It will be recalled that on 25 January 1984 the then Foreign Secretary announced in the House of Commons that staff employed at GCHQ would no longer be permitted to join or remain in membership of independent trade unions, but would be free only to join an officially approved departmental staff association. Both the Freedom of Association Committee and the Committee of Experts of the ILO concluded that the ban violated articles 2 and 11 of Convention 87, rejecting the government's claim that the case fell to be governed by Convention 151, the Labour Relations (Public Service) Convention, 1978 which allows for the exclusion of workers involved in confidential work. It was also concluded that the government's conduct could not be excused under article 9 of Convention 87 which allows exceptions to be made for members of the armed forces and the police.

7.13   So far as Convention 98 is concerned, this provides by article 1 that workers shall enjoy adequate protection against acts of anti-union discrimination in respect of their employment. This is to include protection against dismissal or other prejudice by reason of union membership or participation in union activities (outside working hours, or with the consent of the employer during working hours). These provisions were considered by the Freedom of Association Committee (and subsequently the Committee of Experts) in Geneva to raise doubts about the compatibility of section 13 of the Trade Union Reform and Employment Rights Act 1993 with Convention 98. This is the provision which permits employers, for example, to discriminate on matters of pay against trade union members who insist on having their working conditions governed by a collective agreement rather than a so-called personal contract. Convention 98 does not apply in respect of 'public servants engaged in the administration of the State', though they are covered by the parallel Convention 151, the Labour Relations (Public Service) Convention, 1978.

7.14   Paradoxically, however, there is no right to recognition in the ILO Conventions, although Convention 98, article 4 provides that 'Measures appropriate to national conditions shall be taken, where necessary, to encourage and promote the full development and utilisation of machinery for voluntary negotiation between employers or employers' organisations and workers' organisations, with a view to the regulation of terms and conditions of employment by means of collective agreements'. Although Convention 98 has been ratified by the British government, it is not thought to impose a duty on the part of ratifying states to have in place legislation which compels a reluctant employer to bargain with a union. This is because such compulsion would not be consistent with the obligation in article 4 for 'voluntary negotiation'. It is, however, reinforced by the Collective Bargaining Convention, 1981 (Convention 154) which provides that measures adapted to national conditions shall be taken to promote collective bargaining.

7.15   The other instruments which are relevant in this context are those which deal with the protection of workers' representatives. The first is the Workers' Representatives Convention, 1971 (Convention 135) which provides protection against prejudicial action, including dismissal, thereby overlapping to some extent with Convention 98. But it also provides that facilities should be made available to workers' representatives 'as may be appropriate in order to enable them to carry out their functions promptly and efficiently'. In determining what these facilities should be, account is to be taken of the needs, size and capabilities of the undertaking concerned, while the granting of facilities is not to impair the efficient operation of the undertaking concerned. These rather bald provisions are complemented by the Workers' Representatives Recommendation, 1971 (Recommendation 143) which contains more detailed measures for the protection of workers' representatives from hostile action by the employer, and makes more detailed provision for facilities to be afforded to workers' representatives. These are considered more fully below.

Trade Union Membership

7.16 At the present time employees are protected from dismissal and action short of dismissal on account of trade union membership or activities, provided in the case of trade union activities that these are conducted at 'an appropriate time'. Although there is a ceiling on the levels of permitted compensation for dismissal on these grounds, since 1982 it has been considerably higher than in the ordinary unfair dismissal case. Protection for trade union membership was extended in 1990 to prohibit the refusal to appoint someone on account of his or her trade union membership. Nevertheless there remain serious gaps in the statutory protection, these being identified in a number of cases which denied protection to casual workers on the ground that they were not 'employees', to factory workers dismissed in retaliation for a request made by their union for recognition, and notoriously to GCHQ staff from whom protection was arbitrarily removed on the ground of national security.

7.17 In our view the statutory protection against dismissal and action short of dismissal should apply to 'workers' and not only to 'employees'. This is discussed more fully in chapter 2 above and means that vulnerable groups such as casual workers, homeworkers or others in what might be referred to as an 'atypical' working relationship, are not excluded because they cannot show that they are engaged under a contract of service. We propose that the legislation should make it clear that the protection applies not only in respect of conduct by the individual in question, but also conduct of the trade union acting on behalf of its members; it should not be possible for an employer to take retaliatory action against individual workers for something which the union has done. We also propose that the ban at GCHQ should be revoked and that the power to revoke trade union membership rights, if it is to be retained, should be exercised strictly in accordance with ILO standards.

7.18 Most recently the limitations of the statutory protection were exposed in *Associated Newspapers Ltd v Wilson* [1995] 2 All ER 100 where *Daily Mail* journalists were offered a financial inducement to agree to have their employment conditions governed by 'personal contracts' rather than by a collective agreement for the time being in force. Reversing the Court of Appeal, the House of Lords held that it was not unlawful to withhold the payments from Mr Wilson who insisted on working under the collectively agreed terms. The employer's omission did not constitute action (short of dismissal), and in any event David Wilson had not been victimised on account of his trade union membership, a term narrowly defined by at least one of the judges (and perhaps more) to mean little more than a right not to suffer disadvantage for holding a union card. As such the decision indicates a clear and pressing need for legislation to protect not just the right to be a member and to take part in the activities of an independent trade union, but also to enjoy the benefits and facilities of trade union membership.

7.19 Following the decision of the Court of Appeal in the *Wilson* case (and before the decision of the House of Lords) the Government introduced what was to become the Trade Union Reform and Employment Rights Act 1993, section 13, this providing that an employer was free to discriminate against employees on the ground of their trade union membership and on matters relating to pay and other working conditions. The aim was to facilitate the introduction of personal contracts without incurring liability to other employees who refused to accept such a regime but insisted that their working conditions continue to be governed by a collective agreement. Although this measure was probably unnecessary after the Lords' decision in the *Wilson* case, it was widely condemned and has been called into question by the ILO Freedom of Association Committee and the ILO Committee of Experts which doubted whether it was consistent with the requirements of ILO Convention 87. This measure should be repealed and legislation should be introduced to reverse the *Wilson* decision by making it clear that workers are protected from discrimination not only on account of trade union membership or activities, but also where they take advantage of the benefits or facilities of trade union membership.

7.20   The proposals suggested in paragraphs 7.17 and 7.19 above would go some way to respond to some of the abuses which in recent times have blighted British workplaces. They do not, however, go all the way, for there is still the problem of hostile action against the known trade union activist. Although it is currently unlawful to refuse to employ someone on account of trade union membership, it is not unlawful to maintain lists of trade union activists to facilitate discriminatory treatment, nor is it always unlawful to refuse to employ someone because of previous trade union activism rather than membership. We therefore propose that it should be unlawful for anyone other than a trade union to maintain, distribute or provide access to lists of union members or activists except with the permission of the trade union. We also propose that it should be unlawful for an employer to refuse employment, to offer prejudicial terms of employment, or to take prejudicial action against an employed worker on account of current or previous union membership, participation or activities.

Trade Union Organisation

7.21   But it is important not only that the individual should be free to join a trade union and enjoy the benefits of membership. Equally important is the need to guarantee a floor of trade union organisational rights, a need recognised by ILO Convention 135 (the Workers' Representatives Convention, 1971) and ILO Recommendation 143 (the Workers' Representatives Recommendation, 1971). Under the Convention facilities are to be afforded to workers' representatives 'as may be appropriate in order to enable them to carry out their functions promptly and efficiently'. Under British law, however, trade union representatives are entitled only to paid time off for industrial relations duties or training in these duties, while trade union members are entitled only to time off without pay for trade union activities (though other facilities are recommended in the ACAS Code of Practice). In both cases (and the same is true of the Code of Practice) the facility is diminished by the fact that it is available only to the representatives of *recognised* trade unions.

7.22   If a trade union presence is to be built up and sustained at the workplace, it is necessary to extend the scope and content of these organisational rights, beyond time off for the officials and members of recognised unions. It ought to include first the right of access to an undertaking by full time and branch officials who may not be employed there; secondly, the right to post notices at the workplace at sites to which workers have easy access; and thirdly a duty on the part of management to make available such material facilities as may be necessary for workers' representatives to discharge their functions. Although not dealt with in the ILO Convention or Recommendation, it ought also to include the right to hold meetings on the premises, as well as the right to conduct elections. It is for consideration whether these rights should depend, not on the union being recognised by the employer, but on it being *represented* in the workplace, given that one important purpose of these measures is to build up strength in order to make an effective claim for recognition.

7.23   We therefore propose that a trade union with members in a workplace should be entitled to the following organisational facilities:

(a) the right of access to the premises at a reasonable time, on giving reasonable notice to the employer;
(b) the right to hold meetings on the premises at a suitable location provided by the employer, and at the expense of the employer;
(c) the right to hold elections and ballots on the premises at a suitable location provided by the employer, the expense of the venue (but not the expense of the election or ballot) to be met by the employer.

We propose also that the exercise of these rights should depend on the trade union having members in the workplace in question, though it is for consideration whether a prescribed number of members should be required before any or all of these rights crystallise.

7.24   The other organisational facility which is of benefit to trade unions is the deduction of contributions at source, sometimes referred to as the check off. As the law currently stands trade unions have no right to insist that employers provide this facility to those members who wish to pay their subscriptions in this way. Indeed the Trade Union Reform and Employment Rights Act 1993 conspires to make the practice unattractive to trade unions in the sense that it requires unions every three years to obtain the written authority of those employees whose subscriptions are paid in this way. We propose that this provision, which imposes an unnecessary administrative burden on trade unions, should be repealed. We propose also that workers should have the right to give their employer notice that they wish to have their trade union subscriptions deducted at source, and that workers should have the right to notify their employer that they would like the practice to be discontinued, after giving reasonable notice to both the union and the employer.

Trade Union Representation

7.25 So far as the question of trade union representation and recognition is concerned, it is one thing to express a 'commitment to the broad principle', when 'there is clear employee support', but something else to come up with a workable solution. One approach would be recognise that there is an important conceptual distinction between the union's right to recognition for the purpose of representing its *members* on the one hand, and its right to recognition for the purpose of representing the *workforce as a whole* in consultations and negotiations with management with a view to concluding a collective agreement on the other. In the former situation, where the union is seeking to act only on behalf of its members, its claim to act is established simply by the presence of at least one member in the enterprise. In the latter situation in contrast, where the union is seeking to act on behalf of the workforce as a whole, it may not be unreasonable for the union to demonstrate a measure of support within the group on behalf of whom it wishes to act.

7.26 We propose that a worker should have the right to be represented individually or collectively by a trade union in all matters relating to the employment relationship. We also propose that the nominated union should have the right to represent its members individually or collectively in all matters relating to the employment relationship. A union would thus have the right to represent workers individually on all matters relating to their employment, including in disciplinary and grievance procedures. It would also have the right to negotiate collectively on behalf of any group of workers who nominated it for the purpose of collective representation. Any agreement secured in this way would apply to the workers who had been represented in negotiations by the union, and would not necessarily be a collective agreement in the sense of extending to the workforce as a whole. But it would be open to the employer to apply the agreement universally within the enterprise, and in many cases this may well happen. In other cases the employer might well be required to do so because of the requirements of the Equal Pay Act 1970.

7.27   Clearly procedures would need to be introduced to deal with the fact that more than one union may wish to act on behalf of the same group of workers. We propose, however, that no trade union would be under any obligation to accept an individual into membership, and that a union would not be under any obligation to offer either individual or collective representation facilities. We have in mind the possibility that there may already be a union which is recognised for the purposes of collective bargaining, in which case we believe that it would be highly undesirable for another union to offer facilities of individual or collective representation where there are established bargaining arrangements. In order to minimise the risk of competition between unions we propose that the TUC should establish a Trade Union Representation and Recognition Unit to deal with differences between unions which might be seeking representation rights in the same establishment.

7.28   We recognise that there is some overlap in these proposals for trade union representation, and those which we develop below for trade union consultation and recognition. In our view, however, these proposals are complementary rather than contradictory and they are an acknowledgement that the solution to the recognition problem lies not in a single strategy but in a combination of strategies which provides a series of options for different unions to adopt at different times. A union which claimed rights of collective representation would not have the authority to seek consultation on behalf of the workforce as whole unless it had the prescribed level of support. Nor would it be entitled to collective bargaining rights unless it had the prescribed level of support for this purpose in the proposed bargaining unit. But a right of collective representation would give a union which had a large enough support to consultation rights on behalf of the workforce as a whole, the right also to negotiate at least on behalf of its members at the workplace. We thus see the right of collective representation as a desirable end in itself, but also as another step in the direction of full recognition of the trade union.

Trade Union Recognition

7.29   The difficulties of legislating for trade union recognition (with a view to collective bargaining leading to a collective agreement) are well known from the experience of the Employment Protection Act 1975 which introduced a procedure whereby trade unions could refer a recognition issue to ACAS if refused recognition by an employer. ACAS could make inquiries, which would include a ballot of the workers, and depending on the level of support, and other factors might recommend recognition. Failure on the part of the employer to comply with the recommendation could lead to a reference to the CAC, empowered unilaterally to vary the terms and conditions of employment of the workers to whom the recognition reference related. The legislation (which did seem to help directly and indirectly to encourage recognition) was repealed in 1980 following a letter by the Chairman of ACAS (Mr Jim Mortimer) to the Employment Secretary (Mr Jim Prior) in which he pointed out that in light of the increasing difficulties contributed in part by judicial review, ACAS could not 'satisfactorily operate the statutory recognition procedures as they stand'.

7.30 It does not follow, however, that there is no role for legislation to promote trade union recognition. But it does suggest a need to learn from past mistakes and to respond accordingly, in particular by the development of a strategy which, by building on trade union organisational and representation rights referred to above, enables trade unions to put down deep roots in an enterprise, thereby reducing the need to resort to bodies such as ACAS, and with it the danger of damaging judicial review. However, it is perhaps unavoidable that there should be in place a statutory procedure whereby a union with a sufficient level of support can seek a mandate to speak and act on behalf of the workforce as a whole (or a defined unit therein), either alone or in combination with other unions. North American experience as well as our own experience in the 1970s clearly points out that there are difficulties which such arrangements would have to overcome. But we should not diminish the significance of such a procedure which would offer a clear and unequivocal public commitment to the principle of collective bargaining.

7.31 We therefore propose that:

(a) A trade union should be entitled to recognition for the purposes of collective bargaining where it can show that it has the support of a prescribed number of workers in the proposed bargaining unit.

(b) A trade union should be entitled to consultation rights where it can show that it has the support of a prescribed number of workers in the proposed consultation unit. The right to consultation should apply to all matters relating to the employment relationship as well as to the matters prescribed by EC law.

(c) It should be possible for the union to demonstrate support for the purpose of either recognition or consultation rights by membership in one of a number of ways. The process of determining whether the prescribed level of support has been reached would be conducted by a public body to be called the Trade Union Representation and Recognition Agency (TURARA).

7.32   One of many difficulties associated with such system as that proposed in the foregoing paragraph is in determining whether the union has the acquired level of support in the appropriate representation unit. We believe that it ought to be possible for the union to be able to establish the prescribed level of support in one of two ways: by demonstrating membership of the prescribed number in the bargaining unit or by a petition supported by a prescribed number of workers in the appropriate bargaining unit. Where the union is unable to demonstrate the required method of support by either method, it should be entitled to call upon the Trade Union Representation and Recognition Agency to hold a ballot or conduct a survey of the workers concerned. Where, however, a ballot is called it should be held within a few days of being announced, in order to minimise the danger of damaging campaign tactics by the employer. The ballot should be held at the workplace, it should conducted by the Agency, and union officials should have a right of access to the workplace in order to address the workers who are to be balloted.

7.33   The other major difficulty which arises here is how to determine what will be the bargaining unit for the purposes of the ballot and possible future consultations or negotiations. We believe that the choice of bargaining unit should primarily reflect the organisation of the union. It should be for the union to decide whether to claim recognition rights in respect of the entire operations of a company throughout the country, in respect of a single site, or indeed in respect of a single department in the case of a union with a concentrated membership. The Trade Union Representation and Recognition Agency would be empowered to reject the union's proposed unit at the request of the employer or on its own volition only if the proposed unit is incapable of forming a rational basis for collective bargaining. We propose that the decision of the Agency to accept or reject the union's proposed unit would be reviewable by the Labour Court on the grounds proposed in paragraph 10.24.

7.34   The other question which arises for consideration relates to the appropriateness of the union. This is likely to be a problem particularly where more than one union makes a claim for recognition. We have already proposed in paragraph 7.27 that the TUC should establish a Representation and Recognition Unit which would seek to regulate conflicts between unions in cases of this kind. There may, however, be cases where differences cannot be resolved, or where one of the unions presenting itself for recognition is not affiliated to the TUC. In these cases it will be for the Agency to resolve inter-union conflicts, though we see no reason why any union should not have the right to have its claim for recognition taken seriously by the Agency. We anticipate that in the case of consultation rights there should be no objection to more than one union with the requisite level of support being awarded general consultation rights. We also anticipate that, where membership is shared between two or more unions, it ought to be possible for joint negotiation or consultation rights to be recommended by the Agency.

Remedies and Sanctions

7.35 The success of a statutory regime supporting individual and collective rights to representation will to a large extent be determined by the methods available to enforce decisions of those legal forums required to adjudicate upon the conflicts which will inevitably arise. In our view the remedies for non-compliance with statutory provisions should be effective, deterrent and proportionate. Yet achieving these aims for the mechanism underpinning the statutory route to representation is a demanding task, particularly in light of the experience with enforcement of trade union recognition under the terms of the Employment Protection Act 1975, to which we have already referred. But there are few other aspects of labour law which give rise to such expressions of antagonism by both sides of industry. The problems are likely only to be enhanced by virtue of the fact that since 1980 employers have enjoyed complete freedom to choose whether to allow their employees to be represented either individually or collectively.

7.36 Any curtailment of this freedom which employers have enjoyed is unlikely to be welcomed, particularly by those who have resisted such rights for employees in the past or have withdrawn them in the intervening period. As the penalties for failing to allow representation will be applied to employers of all types, their likely responses, industrial or legal, must be considered. A rough categorisation of employers would suggest that although there are many who will use the law to avoid recognition, there are also others who will never concede recognition whatever the law says, to the point of harming the business. This latter group will provide the sternest tests for the enforcement mechanism. The prospect of a multinational declining to invest in a new operation because of being required to bargain collectively, will be painted garishly as the product of intrusive labour laws inconsistent with international competitiveness. These are matters which will have to be addressed if the principle of a legal right to recognition is not to fall into disrepute and if it is to be a long term and accepted feature of UK labour law.

7.37   It is important then that any remedial framework in this as in other areas should inspire public confidence, and should be seen to be fair and reasonable. To some extent this reflects notions of proportionality, but in what can be a controversial area of labour relations attracting fierce media attention, the penalties must sit well with public awareness. Whilst the nature of public opinion is difficult to align with the design of a legal process, in this respect they are closely intertwined because the law would be giving effect to a political decision to promote representation at work, just as the current absence of legal support represents a political will operating against such provision. There is little doubt that the enforcement of trade union recognition presents far greater problems than the assertion of a statutory right to individual representation in the course of grievance or disciplinary procedures. However this is not to underestimate the potential impact of a right to representation upon all matters relating to the employment relationship, particularly where it impacts upon those which have a collective dimension such as working time.

7.38   So far as *the right of individual or collective representation* is concerned, we propose the following:

1) There should be a statutory requirement that employers take reasonable steps to draw to workers' attention their right to be represented by a trade union. This should be done by an amendment to section 1 of the Employment Rights Act 1996.

2) It should be unlawful for an employer to refuse to permit a worker to be represented by a trade union at any stage in the employment relationship, including matters relating to formation, variation and termination.

3) A variation of the terms of the employment relationship implemented without the worker being allowed access to representation could be invalidated on an application by a worker to a Labour Inspector, though, as we propose in

paragraph 4.81 above a *unilateral* variation of terms by the employer would in principle be void.

4) Any dismissal would be automatically unfair where either the right to representation is not made known, or is not permitted, the dismissal to be dealt with in accordance with the principles in paragraph 9.34 below.

5) It should be open to a worker (or his or her representative acting on his or her behalf) to seek a judicial order to compel an employer to permit representation, and to seek compensation for losses sustained as a result of any failure to permit such representation. There should also be a power on the part of the appropriate judicial body to award punitive compensation for any failure to allow representation.

7.39 Turning to the enforcement of the *right of trade union recognition*, we have in mind here consultation rights on the one hand and collective bargaining or negotiating rights on the other. Existing strategy regarding the former has concentrated on compensation as being the primary remedy while previous approaches to the latter have focused upon the incorporation of new terms into the contracts of employees by the Central Arbitration Committee. However experience of the last seventeen years has opened up the prospect of punitive financial and other sanctions being applied where aspects of the law are not observed, as trade unions are only too well aware. This has implications for both consultation and negotiating rights, for what is sauce for the goose is sauce for the gander. On the basis that these methods of enforcement can be said to have a measure of public support, we see the opportunity to make comparable remedies available in situations where employers flout a legal obligation to consult or negotiate with a trade union when under a legal duty to do so.

7.40 We propose that where an employer is under a duty to consult or engage in collective bargaining with a trade union:

1) The employer should be under an obligation to do so with a view to reaching an agreement.

2) It should be open to a trade union to challenge and restrain any decision which has been taken in breach of the duty to consult or the duty to engage in collective bargaining.

3) It should be open to a court to grant a mandatory order to require the employer to comply with his or her legal duty to consult or engage in collective bargaining and to award

compensation to both the union and the workers in respect of whom the duty to consult or bargain relates.

4) Failure on the part of the employer to comply with the duty to consult or engage in collective bargaining would be a contempt of court which would authorise the court to appoint officers from a panel of experts drawn up in advance to engage in consultations or bargaining with the union with a view to reaching an agreement.

5) Consideration should be given to the question whether the contempt should be marked by more coercive measures. These include the imposition of a fine with the size of the penalty being related to the size of the business. Consideration should also be given to the question of financial penalties being imposed upon the officers of the business.

Other Forms of State Support

(a) The Principle of Derogation

7.41 Apart from direct support for trade union recognition through the introduction of a cascade of membership, organisation, representation, and recognition rights, there is also a role for indirect forms of support designed to encourage employers to recognise trade unions for the purpose of collective bargaining. One way by which this can be done is by the principle of derogation whereby trade unions and employers are permitted by collective agreement to establish standards which differ from general standards. These general standards might be laid down in legislation or in orders of a sectoral employment commission, as proposed in chapter 3 above. The principle of derogation of the former kind is well known to our labour law, with arrangements being possible in respect, for example, of guaranteed payments and unfair dismissal procedures. It was also anticipated in the Bills which were introduced in the 1930s on working time, designed to implement ILO Convention 1 (the Hours of Work Convention, 1919).

7.42 We propose that this strategy should continue to be employed in the belief that in a more highly regulated labour market, it will provide incentives for employers to bargain and incentives for them to recognise trade unions. We are also of the view, however, that a derogation (to any extent) should only be through a qualifying collective agreement ('QCA'). An employer would be permitted to conclude a QCA only with an independent trade union (for the purpose of which the existing statutory definition should suffice) recognised by the employer for the purposes of collective bargaining. A QCA would have a binding effect on all workers to whom it related. It would not be possible for individual workers to agree less favourable terms, although it would be possible to modify the application of the QCA at local level by local QCAs with recognised trade unions. Individual workers would be free to negotiate improvements to qualifying collective agreements, but not reductions (though steps would have to be taken to ensure that any such individual agreements did not depart from the principles of equality outlined in chapter 5). The provisions of the QCA and any local QCA should apply to all relevant workers within that employment, whether or not they are union members.

(b) Contract Compliance

7.43   The second way by which the State may indirectly support the collective bargaining process is by a strategy of contract compliance. An example is provided by the Fair Wages Resolution of 1946 whereby government contractors were required to pay fair wages (as defined) but also to recognise the right of their workpeople to join trade unions. But this was revoked in 1982, and as we have seen measures have been introduced to prevent other public (or private) bodies adopting similar strategies. So a commercial contract may not specify that the contractor must recognise a union or employ union only labour. Similarly under the Local Government Act 1988, section 17 it is not lawful for local authorities to stipulate non commercial considerations in contracts, such as those relating to terms and conditions of employment, though special considerations apply to provisions relating to race relations in light of the statutory duty on local authorities under the Race Relations Act 1976.

7.44   In our view the foregoing statutory restrictions should be repealed. In their place we propose, so far as consistent with the uncertain terms of the EC Public Procurement Directives, the introduction of a statutory provision which provides that government departments and local authorities should contract only with approved contractors. An approved contractor would be defined in such a way to include only those tenderers which have in place procedures for the recognition (whether by way of negotiation or consultation) of trade unions, failing which procedures for the collective representation of trade union members, where there is a demand for such representation. A contractor which had no collective bargaining or collective reprentation procedures would be permitted on to an approved list, and it would be lawful to contract with a tenderer which had no collective bargaining or collective representation procedures, only if the company could establish that there was no support for trade union representation from amongst its workforce. We propose also that it should be open to private sector employers to impose similar contractual terms.

(c) Industrial Action

7.45 The third way by which the State can provide support for trade union recognition is by making it clear that industrial action may lawfully be taken by trade unions for this purpose. Before the Conservatives came to office the use of industrial action as a way of pressurising employers to recognise a union would in principle be protected by the immunities from liability in tort. The immunities have, however, been seriously eroded, although it is still permissible for industrial action to be taken by workers who have a recognition dispute with their own employer. But beyond that industrial action designed to promote recognition would invite legal proceedings at the suit of the employers affected by the action in question. So there is no immunity for solidarity or secondary action on behalf of a group of workers engaged in a recognition dispute, and there is no immunity for action by workers seeking to compel their own employer to contract only with businesses which recognise a trade union for the purposes of collective bargaining.

7.46 In our proposals for the right to strike in chapter 8, these restrictions would be swept away. Under our general proposals it would be permissible for industrial action to be taken in order to support and promote trade union recognition. For the avoidance of doubt, however, we also propose that it should be clearly indicated that it should be lawful for (a) a group of workers to take industrial action to seek to persuade their employer to recognise a trade union; (b) a group of workers to take industrial action against their own employer to seek to persuade him or her to contract only with third parties who recognise a trade union; and (c) a group of workers to take secondary industrial action in support of other workers engaged in a recognition dispute with their own employer. The industrial action would be conducted in accordance with the general proposals relating to industrial action outlined in chapter 8.

Facilities for Collective Bargaining

(a) Time Off Work

7.47 In order to assist union officials engaged in collective bargaining, it has been recognised that provision must be made to enable them to participate in the process effectively. Thus ILO Convention 135 (the Workers' Representatives Convention, 1971), provides that 'Such facilities in the undertaking shall be afforded to workers' representatives as may be appropriate in order for them to carry out their functions promptly and efficiently'. The accompanying Recommendation, ILO Recommendation 143 (the Workers' Representatives Recommendation, 1971) provides that workers' representatives should be afforded necessary time off work with pay for carrying out their representation functions in the undertaking; time off work with pay for attending trade union meetings and training courses; access to all workplaces in the undertaking to enable them to carry out their duties; the right to post trade union notices in the workplace in places agreed with management and to which workers have easy access; and the right to distribute union literature to workers employed in the undertaking, without prejudicing the orderly operation and tidiness of the undertaking.

7.48   Provision for time off is currently made in the Trade Union and Labour Relations (Consolidation) Act 1992, section 168. This is narrowly drawn and allows trade union officials time off work for the purpose of carrying out duties concerned with negotiations with the employer, or the performance on behalf of employees of functions related to or connected with matters which the employer has agreed may be performed by the union. The section also allows time off with pay to enable the official to undergo training in aspects of industrial relations which are relevant to the carrying out of his or her duties. The amount of time off which is permitted, the purposes for which, the occasions on which, and the conditions subject to which time off may be taken are those that are reasonable in all the circumstances, having regard to the ACAS Code of Practice. Provision is also made in section 170 to enable members of recognised trade unions to take time off work without pay to participate in the activities of the union, including activities in relation to which the employee is acting as a representative of the union.

7.49   In our view these provisions should be revised and expanded. In particular we are concerned to restore the original formula for time off with pay, that is to say the legislation which was in place before it was amended by the Employment Act 1989, prior to the 1992 consolidation. In our view an employer should permit a worker who is an official of a trade union recognised for the purposes of collective bargaining, in the absence of which a trade union with consultation rights, in the absence of which a trade union which has asserted rights of collective representation, to take time off work with pay for the purpose of carrying out his or her duties as an official which are concerned with industrial relations with the employer, and between any associated employer and their employees. We are also concerned to ensure that measures should be introduced to implement more clearly the other terms of ILO Recommendation 143. Thus we propose that there should be more explicit recognition of the right of trade union officials to (a) access to parts of the premises and to management where this is necessary to enable them to perform their duties, (b) post notices and distribute literature relating to normal union activities, and (c) material facilities to enable them to carry out their duties. This might properly be done by revising the ACAS Code of Practice.

(b) Disclosure of Information

7.50 The other major issue which it is convenient to deal with under the general rubric of facilities for collective bargaining is the disclosure of information. Provision is currently made in the Trade Union and Labour Relations (Consolidation) Act 1992 whereby an employer is required to disclose on request information to the representatives of a recognised trade union. The information to be disclosed is 'all information relating to the employer's undertaking which is in his possession' and it is information without which trade union representatives would be to a material extent impeded in carrying on collective bargaining, and which it would be in accordance with good industrial relations practice to disclose. But even if the information is covered by this formula, there are a number of exempted categories of information which need not be disclosed. This includes information the disclosure of which would be against the interests of national security, information which has been communicated to the employer in confidence, and information the disclosure of which would cause substantial injury to the undertaking for reasons other than its effect on collective bargaining.

7.51 It is a matter of some concern that these measures have been largely ineffective, and fail to provide access to the information which trade unions need for the purposes of collective bargaining. We are concerned to ensure that these measures are retained, but significantly improved. To this end we recommend that trade union representatives as referred to in paragraph 7.50 above should be entitled to any information about the undertaking which the employer has in his or her possession. It should not be necessary to show that failure to supply the information would to a material extent impede the union and that it would be in accordance with good practice to provide the information. In our view the starting point should be transparency: all information about a company should be disclosed to the representatives of those who work there unless there is some compelling reason for secrecy, which we accept there may be in some circumstances in respect of some information.

7.52 In our view, however, the protection of certain categories of information from disclosure is too widely drawn. We accept that there is a case in principle for not disclosing information which would damage national security, which could not be disclosed without breaching the terms of a statute, which relates to an individual (unless the individual agrees), or which has been obtained in connection with legal proceedings. But we are of the view that information should not be protected from even conditional disclosure on the ground that it has been communicated to or obtained by the employer in confidence. Similarly we propose that the exemption for information which would cause substantial injury to the undertaking may repay reconsideration with a view to the drafting of a narrower provision.

Collective Agreements

7.53 The question which now arises for consideration relates to the legal status of collective agreements. As matters presently stand, collective agreements are presumed not to be legally enforceable, though the parties are free to rebut this presumption by a clear statement in the agreement itself indicating that it is designed to be legally enforceable. This is not, however, a power which is widely used and it is indeed difficult to find examples of agreements which are legally enforceable under this provision. This does not mean that the terms of agreements will not acquire legal significance, for they may be incorporated into the contracts of employment of workers and be enforceable as such. Recent cases, dealing mainly with redundancy and job security agreements, have indicated, however, that it is not always easy to incorporate the terms of agreements into individual contracts in this way. There is also the problem that the enforcement of the agreement becomes the responsibility of individual workers rather than the unions which concluded them.

7.54 We believe that it may now be time to consider the possibility of revisiting the question of the legal enforceability of collective agreements, though we realise that there are dangers as well as possible benefits. The obvious disadvantages are that employers may be less reluctant to agree to terms in the knowledge that they are to be legally binding, and it is also a matter of concern that lawyers may inevitably be drawn into the bargaining process to a greater extent than is already the case, in order to scrutinise and advise on the drafting and content of agreements. There is the danger too that if legally enforceable, collective agreements would be enforceable by either party so that unions are as likely to be sued in the event of a breach as are employers. This would have important implications for industrial action called in breach of a dispute procedure agreement. It would be difficult in principle (but by no means impossible) to argue that these agreements should be immune from legal enforceability when the parts of the agreement dealing with substantive questions were not.

7.55 This is not to deny that there would be benefits of legally enforceable collective agreements at a time when trade union activity is being undermined in the workplace. There are perhaps three areas where benefits would arise. The first arises in the context of trade union recognition and facilities agreements which if legally enforceable would be more difficult to erode, though admittedly legal enforceability may serve only to delay rather than prevent the termination of an agreement. Secondly there is the problem of enforcing through the contract of employment the terms of those collective agreements clearly designed to have been for the benefit of employees, but which the courts decline to incorporate into the contract of employment. In these cases important provisions of important job security agreements remain unenforceable; although there are those who rightly wish to exclude the law industrial relations, we do not consider this to be a very happy state of affairs. Thirdly, there is the European dimension, including, for example problems associated with the transfer of undertakings which the legal enforceability of agreement might help to overcome.

7.56 Although there are thus clearly advantages which could flow from the legal enforceability of collective agreements, we are inclined to the view that the advantages do not outweigh the considerable disadvantages which would arise. We are mindful also that the parties are currently free to make their agreements legally enforceable if they wish and that few, if any, choose to do so. In our view the measures currently contained in the Trade Union and Labour Relations (Consolidation) Act 1992, 179 should be retained and the parties should continue to be free to conclude legally binding agreements if they so desire. But we see no reason for imposing on the collective parties obligations which they may neither want nor need, though we accept that even if a union wanted a particular agreement to be legally enforceable, in the current economic climate it may be difficult to persuade an employer to accept such a term, given that there may be few if any advantages in the rigidity which would arise.

7.57 But this is not to say that we should be complacent about some of the problems which we have identified above. Thus we propose that there should be a rebuttable statutory presumption that the terms of all collective agreements should be incorporated into the employment relationship of individual workers. Although this presumption might be easily rebutted in the case of recognition agreements, it would be less easy to rebut in the case of job security agreements. Although this does not deal with the problem of the vulnerability of recognition arrangements on the contracting out of work (should compulsory competitive tendering be retained, which we do not recommend) we are mindful here of our proposals above for trade union representation and recognition. If an employer were to terminate a recognition agreement, the workers affected would fall back on the statutory rights which give them through their union rights of collective representation, as well as rights of consultation and collective bargaining. We are also mindful that an employer in this situation would continue to be bound by any collective agreement or sectoral employment agreement or award (as propose in chapter 3 above) affecting the sector in question and that trade union recognition would be important in order to negotiate flexibility at local level.

7.58 So far as agreements derogating from statutory norms or sectoral employment agreements or awards are concerned, we see no need for these to be legally enforceable either, though it would be open to the parties to declare that they were intended to be legally enforceable in any particular case if they so wished. We would propose, however, that legislation should provide that any QCA, as described above, should be enforceable as part of the terms of the employment relationship of anyone to whom the terms of the agreement applied, and that they should apply to everyone within the bargaining unit in question, whether they are members of the union or not. Like other collective agreements, a QCA would thus become part of the terms of the employment relationship of the worker in question, but, unlike other agreements, the presumption would not be rebuttable, although it would be possible for workers individually to negotiate more favourable terms than those in the QCA, subject to concerns raised in paragraph 7.43 above about questions of equality of opportunity. As in the case of all other collective agreements enforcement should be at the suit of either the individual worker or a trade union which is a party to the agreement.

Works Councils and Workplace Consultation

7.59 Although the promotion of collective bargaining arrangements is a key priority, it does not follow that there is no room for other forms of workplace representation. There is some support in particular for the introduction of some form of works council, partly as a way of complying with EC law, partly as a result of the practice of other countries, and partly as a way of reducing the 'democratic deficit' in industry. There is a danger, however, that the works council could be seen as a rival to collective bargaining, and even to trade unionism itself, like the staff association in another era. It is true that collective bargaining and works councils appear to work in harmony and in an integrated way in Germany. But that is in the context of very different collective bargaining arrangements, with the works council operating at plant level to complement a process which may be conducted elsewhere. What price works councils in a system such as ours where collective bargaining is absent from many workplaces? Admittedly, the dangers associated with works councils would be much less acute if our proposal in chapter 3 for the reintroduction of national bargaining or sectoral employment commissions were to be implemented.

(a) Workplace Consultation and EC Law
7.60 Yet the works council is not something that can be ignored or avoided. The decision of the European Court of Justice in *European Commission v UK* [1994] IRLR 392, 412 suggests that it may be necessary to have in place a forum so that workers may be consulted at least about business transfers and collective redundancies. But it is far from clear precisely what the judgment of the court actually requires. The court was concerned that employers could frustrate the duty to consult by failing to recognise a union. Whether the decision requires employers to have in place a standing consultative body is uncertain, and whether it requires us to compromise our own practice of workplace representation through independent trade unions is controversial. But any proposal for a standing consultative body of the workforce as a whole, where there is no trade union recognised for consultation or negotiation, would as suggested be more acceptable in the context of more centralised bargaining arrangements.

7.61 We accept, however, that the decision of the ECJ does present a challenge to traditional forms of workplace representation. But in our view the works councils is, potentially, a Trojan Horse which is calculated in the long term to destroy trade unionism rather than promote it, though we accept that not everyone shares this view. We are thus concerned not to be seen too readily to embrace alternative forms of representation which will threaten representation by independent trade unions. Acknowledging nevertheless that there is a problem about consultation on redundancies and business transfers we propose that legislation should provide that this should take place with one of the following: (a) the representatives of a recognised trade union; in the absence of which (b) the representatives of a which has general consultative rights in accordance with the procedures as described above; in the absence of which (c) the representatives of a trade union which has asserted collective representation rights at the workplace.

7.62 There may of course be cases where at the time of the proposed redundancy or transfer there is no trade union presence in the workplace, arising in any of the above ways. In these cases we are of the view that the employer should be required to notify the Trade Union Representation and Recognition Agency which would then be under a duty to intervene on behalf of the workers who may be affected by the decision in question, and ask them to nominate a trade union to represent them in consultations about the proposed redundancy or transfer. The employer would then be under a duty to consult with the representatives of the designated trade union. If the workers declined to nominate one or more trade unions, the TURARA would be required to conduct a ballot for the designation of a representative from amongst the workforce. The status quo would be maintained pending the outcome of the representation designation process.

7.63 It is true that one drawback with the proposal is that it would cause delay for employers faced with redundancies or business transfers. But the problem, which is calculated to arise also with other proposals currently in circulation, is likely to arise only where the employer fails to recognise a trade union; the remedy thus lies in the employer's own hands. It is true also that another drawback is that there may not always be a trade union which has indicated a willingness to represent the workers in question. We would hope, however, that this is unlikely to be a common problem, but in cases where it did happen, the job of the Agency would be to supervise an election from among the workforce as a whole, provided of course that anyone was willing to assume the mantle of workers' representative. Our objective is thus to find a trade union solution to the problem of workplace representation, in whatever guise the problem presents itself.

(b) Health and Safety Representation

7.64 Under the Safety Representatives and Safety Committees (SRSC) Regulations 1977 (SI 1977/500), recognised unions have the right to appoint safety representatives and these representatives in turn are able to request the formation of safety committees. In many workplaces such safety representatives and committees have made an important contribution to improved standards of health and safety. At present no statutory rights of involvement exist in respect of workplaces where there is no recognised trade union, with the notable exception of off-shore installations covered by the Offshore Installations (Safety Representatives and Safety Committees) Regulations 1989 (SI 1989/971). As a result many workers are denied any right to be involved in health and safety issues in their workplace - a situation which seems unacceptable, given the given recent research that indicates that workplaces where health and safety issues are solely determined by management tend to have poorer incident records than those where this is not the case. The extension of representation rights to non-unionists therefore seems highly desirable. It would also seem to be required by the EC's Framework Directive (89/391/EEC).

7.65 Recently, the Health and Safety Commission has proposed draft regulations which would oblige employers to consult with those workers who are not covered by safety representatives appointed under the SRSC regulations. These regulations would undoubtedly represent an advance on the present situation. However, four of their features give rise to concern. First, employers are given the option of consulting workers directly rather than through representative structures. Secondly, where representatives are elected, they are not given any rights of inspection or powers relating to the establishment of safety committees. Thirdly, consultation of the type envisaged would take place with workers or representatives who do not have the support of any broader system of representation, both within and outside the workplace. Fourthly, there would be no effective means available by which workers could enforce the statutory requirements. The proposed approach effectively gives employers the freedom to choose the method of consultation which they view as the least threatening. Insofar as employers take advantage of this freedom, they are likely in practice to be undermining the potentially beneficial consequences that can flow from an expansion in worker involvement in health and safety matters.

7.66   A far better approach would therefore be to require safety representatives to be elected in all but the smallest workplaces. If this approach was adopted, then it becomes far more feasible to give such non-union representatives rights to conduct inspections and request the formation of safety committees, since employers would not have the ability to circumvent them by choosing to engage in direct consultations with workers. However, under such an approach workers would still confront the difficulties with enforcing their rights associated with the enforcement philosophy and resources of the HSC and the lack of support from broader systems of workplace representation. In part this can be resolved by providing both unionised and non-unionised workers with greater enforcement powers, independent of the statutory agencies. This in itself would, however, be unlikely to be sufficient given the vulnerable position of many non-union workers, even if they were to enjoy statutory protection against discrimination and dismissal. Consequently, we also propose that steps should be taken to ensure that such workers are given a more effective option of trade union representation over health and safety matters.

7.67   The best means of doing this would be to adopt an approach to representation similar to that proposed in respect of business transfers and redundancies. One way in which this could be done would be to amend the SRSC Regulations extending the right to appoint a safety representative to unions recognised for the purposes of collective bargaining, failing which unions which have general consultation rights, failing which unions which have asserted rights of collective representation. Where there is no such union it should be open to a worker to request an employer to make arrangements for the election of safety representatives of the workforce, under procedures to be supervised by TURARA described in paragraph 7.62. The safety representatives may but need not be employed by the employer, and the ballot should be conducted under the supervision of the Agency referred to in paragraph 7.31 above. If a union subsequently acquires bargaining or consultation rights, or subsequently asserts the right to collective representation, the elected safety representative would remain in office, but the union would be free also to appoint representatives.

(c) European Works Councils

7.68   Directive 94/95/EC on European Works Councils comes into effect on 22 September 1996. Although it does not yet apply to the United Kingdom (because of the Maastricht opt-out), it requires the establishment of a European Works Council (EWC) or a procedure for the purposes of informing or consulting employees. The enterprises affected are 'Community-scale undertakings' and a 'Community-scale group of undertakings' with at least 1000 employees in the Member States and at least 150 employees in each of at least two Member States. A TUC Report identified 2,677 UK subsidiaries owned by 588 different multinational companies subject to the Directive.[1] Three million British workers could eventually be covered by EWCs. The European Trade Union Institute has identified 106 UK-based companies affected.[2] It will also apply to continental-based multinational enterprises and non-EU based multinationals with establishments in the UK. Already, early voluntary agreements on EWCs by United Biscuits (1994) and Coats Viyella (early 1995) have been joined by more recent initiatives by BT, GKN, ICI, NatWest, Pilkington, Zeneca and Courtaulds.

7.69   UK multinationals establishing EWCs are unlikely to exclude their UK employees (often a majority) from participation in such EWCs. Industrial relations with workers' representatives from non-UK establishments will be more difficult if UK establishments are not represented. The European Trade Union Confederation finalised in February 1996 a Protocol of procedures on negotiations for the creation of EWCs. The involvement of the trade unions from the country where the European headquarters is located is mandatory (article 1). It is a prerequisite that 'where negotiations are opened in multinational companies with undertakings in the UK...., trade unions from (the UK) should become involved from the beginning in the process to set up an EWC' (article 3). The practice established so far indicates that EWC representatives from other Member States are selected following national procedures. For example, works councils in Germany select their representatives; trade unions in France nominate theirs. In the UK, however, where union representation depends on employers' voluntary recognition, there have been problems. The UK system of voluntary recognition, already under pressure from other EC law, now faces the Directive's

---

1.   TUC, *A Trade Unionist's Guide to European Works Councils* (1995).
2.   ETUI, *European Works Councils: Inventory of Affected Companies*, 1996.

requirements that EWCs must be established with rights of information and consultation.

7.70 The Directive imposes a legal requirement on the management of transnational enterprises to recognise worker representatives for purposes of information and consultation as a matter of principle. This requirement is to be implemented as follows: (i) the mandatory creation of a Special Negotiation Body (SNB); (ii) negotiations by the SNB with central management on the creation of an EWC; and (iii) in the event of failure to agree on the creation of an EWC, the mandatory establishment of an EWC in line with the 'subsidiarity requirements' contained in the Annex to the Directive, which may also be adopted by the agreement of the parties in lieu of anything else. The creation of an SNB is triggered by the initiative of the management, or at the written request of at least 100 employees or their representative in at least two undertakings or establishments in at least two diffferent Member States (article 5(1)). The next step is that 'With a view to the conclusion of an agreement in accordance with article 6, the central management shall convene a meeting with the SNB...'. And article 6(1) states: 'The central management and the SNB must negotiate in a spirit of co-operation with a view to reaching an agreement...'.

7.71 Where there is a failure to negotiate or agree, the Annex, paragraph 1(b), prescribes the creation of an EWC composed of employees 'elected or appointed from their number by the employees' representatives or, in the absence thereof, by the entire body of employees'. This mandatory EWC must be 'informed and consulted...on the progress of the business...and its prospects', and in particular 'the structure, economic and financial situation, the probable development of business and of production and sales, the situation and probable trend of employment, investments, and substantial changes concerning organisation, introduction of new working methods or production, mergers, cut-backs or closures of undertakings, establishments or important parts thereof, and collective redundancies'. The meaning of 'consultation' goes beyond the conventional limitations of the term and extends into the 'establishment of dialogue'. The process of consultation is not a mere 'exchange of views'. A static, formal, ad hoc, one-way process is incompatible with the purpose of the Directive. The nature of the process mandated by the Directive is encapsulated in the concept of 'dialogue': an active and continuous process of communication and interaction between the EWC and management. Management action is to be subject to procedures of information and consultation of the

EWC, enforced by effective EC law remedies.

7.72 On signing the Maastricht Social Chapter, transposition of this particular instrument will give rise to a number of complex questions, not all of which we can explore here. However, one important issue relates to the appointment of SNB members, both in cases where central management of the company in question is based in Britain, and also in cases where the central management is located eslewhere but workers in its British operations are entitled to be represented on the SNB. Particularly important is article 5 which provides for the election or appointment of a special negotiating body to determine with central management 'the scope, composition, functions, and terms of office of the European Works Council'. The Directive also provides that the Member States 'shall determine the method to be used for the election or appointment of the members of the special negotiating body'. In our view, implementing legislation in this country should be based on the principle of trade union representation as the principal vehicle for representation. Accordingly we propose that legislation should provide in the first instance that where there is a trade union recognised for the purposes of collective bargaining, the British representatives on an SNB should be appointed by the trade union. Where there is more than one union recognised by the employer the British representatives should be appointed by the unions jointly.

7.73 Where there is no recognised trade union, but a union with either consultation rights or collective representation rights, as described above, we propose in the first instance that that union (or where there is more than one union these unions jointly) should have the right to appoint an SNB representative. Where there is no union with recognition, consultation or collective representation rights, we propose that the TURARA should be required to supervise the nomination or election of a representative. In line with our proposals in paragraph 7.62 above, the workers should be asked whether they wish to be represented through the medium of a trade union, failing which a ballot should be held under the supervision of the Agency for the election of an SNB representative from the workforce as a whole, in which trade unions would have the right to nominate candidates. We propose a similar procedure for the composition of the European Works Council established on the basis of the Directive's subsidiary requirements according to article 7 in the Annex to the Directive, to be adopted where the central management and the special negotiating body fail to agree, or if they otherwise so decide.

7.74   Although the form of representation on the SNB and EWC is perhaps the most important question, it is clearly not the only one. Thus measures will have to be taken, for example, to comply with the requirements of article 10 of the Directive which requires protection for members of special negotiating bodies and EWCs, this to be the same as that provided for 'employees' representatives by national legislation'. Accordingly we propose that the current legislation protecting workers on account of trade union membership or activities should be extended to apply also to members of SNBs and EWCs, with appropriate modifications to ensure protection for those who stand for election (where an election is held), those who are members of either, and those who take part in the activities of either. We also propose that legislation be introduced to ensure that members of SNBs and EWCs are entitled to paid time off to engage in activities relating to their functions, and that the legislation should also deal with the question of employer financial contributions to the work of the SNBs and the EWCs. Finally consideration needs to be given to voluntary agreements under article 13 which provides that the obligations arising from the Directive do not apply whereby 22 September 1996 there is already in force 'an agreement, covering the entire workforce, providing for the transnational information and consultation of employees'. We propose that such agreements should be reviewed and that legislation introduced as necessary to ensure that they comply as far as representation is concerned with the principles outlined in paragraph 7.72 and 7.73 above.

Summary of Recommendations

1   The ban at GCHQ should be revoked and the power to revoke trade union membership rights, if it is to be retained, should be exercised strictly in accordance with ILO standards.

2   It should be unlawful for anyone other than a trade union to maintain, distribute or provide access to lists of union members or activists except with the permission of the trade union

3   It should be unlawful for an employer to refuse employment, to offer prejudicial terms of employment, or to take prejudicial action against an employed worker on account of current or previous union membership, participation or activities.

4 It should be unlawful for an employer to take prejudicial action against a worker not only on account of the worker's trade union membership or activities, but also where the worker has taken advantage of the benefits or facilities of trade union membership.

5 A trade union should be entitled to access to an employer's premises at a reasonable time in order to speak to members, to hold meetings, elections and ballots on the premises at a suitable location provided by the employer.

6 The exercise of the rights referred to in 5 above should depend on the trade union having members in the workplace in question, though it is for consideration whether a prescribed number of members should be required before any or all of these rights crystallise.

7 Workers should have the right to give their employer notice that they wish to have their trade union subscriptions deducted at source, and workers should have the right to notify their employer that they would like the practice to be discontinued, after giving reasonable notice.

8 A trade union should be entitled to represent its members individually and collectively on matters relating to working conditions, but a trade union should not be under any obligation to accept an individual into membership, nor offer representation facilities.

9 There should be a statutory requirement that employers take all reasonable steps to draw to the attention of workers their right of representation. This should be done by a suitable amendment to section 1 of the Employment Rights Act 1996.

10 It should be unlawful for an employer to refuse to permit a worker to be represented by a trade union at any stage in the employment relationship, including matters relating to formation, variation and termination.

11 A variation of the employment relationship implemented without the worker being allowed access to representation could be invalidated.

12 Any dismissal should be automatically unfair where either the right to representation is not made known, or is not permitted. This would be accompanied by mandatory reinstatement where sought by the applicant.

13 A trade union should be entitled to recognition for the purposes of collective bargaining where it can show that it has the support of a prescribed number of workers in the proposed bargaining unit.

14 A trade union should be entitled to consultation rights where it can show that it has the support of a prescribed number of workers in the proposed consultation unit. The right to consultation should apply to all matters relating to the employment relationship.

15 It should be possible for the union to demonstrate support for the purpose of either recognition or consultation rights in one of a number of ways. The process of determining whether the prescribed level of support has been reached would be conducted by a public body, to be called the Trade Union Representation and Recognition Agency.

16 Where an employer is under a duty to consult or engage in collective bargaining with a trade union, it should be required to do so with a view to reaching an agreement.

17 It should be open to a trade union to apply for a court order requiring an employer to comply with its legal duty to consult or bargain.

18 It should be possible for employers and trade unions to derogate from statutory standards and from sectoral employment agreements or awards by means of a qualifying collective agreement ('QCA').

19 An employer should be permitted to conclude a QCA only with an 'independent' trade union (for the purpose of which the existing statutory definition should suffice). A QCA would have a binding effect on all workers to whom it relates.

20 It should not be possible for individual workers to agree less favourable terms, although it would be possible to modify the application of the QCA at local level by local agreements with recognised unions within a framework set by the recognition arrangements in the company in question.

21 So far as consistent with the uncertain terms of the EC Public Procurement Directives, government departments and local authorities should contract only with approved contractors.

22 An approved contractor would be defined in such a way to include only those tenderers which comply or which undertake to comply with the recognition provisions referred to above; that is to say only those companies which have in place procedures for negotiation or consultation, depending on the level of worker support.

23 It should be lawful for a group of workers to take industrial action to seek to persuade their employer to recognise a trade union. The industrial action would be conducted in accordance with the general proposals relating to industrial action outlined in chapter 8.

24 It should be lawful for workers to take industrial action against their own employer to seek to persuade him or her to contract only with third parties who recognise a trade union, and for a group of workers to take secondary industrial action in support of other workers engaged in a recognition dispute with their own employer.

25 A worker who is an official of a recognised trade union should have the right to take time off work with pay to enable him or her to carry out his or her responsibilities as a trade union official.

26 There should be more explicit recognition of the right of trade union officials to (a) access to parts of the premises and to management where this is necessary to enable them to perform their duties, (b) post notices and distribute literature relating to normal union activities, and (c) material facilities to enable them to carry out their duties.

27 As a general principle, representatives of a recognised trade union should be entitled to any information about the undertaking which the employer has in his or her possession.

28 The measures currently contained in the Trade Union and Labour Relations (Consolidation) Act 1992, 179 should be retained and the parties should continue to be free to conclude legally binding agreements if they so desire.

29 There should be a rebuttable statutory presumption that the terms of all collective agreements should be incorporated into the terms of the employment relationship of individual workers to whom they relate.

30 Enforcement of a collective agreement should be at the suit of either the individual worker to whom it applies, or a trade union which is a party to the agreement.

31 Consultations on proposed redundancies or business transfers should take place with (a) the representatives of a recognised trade union; failing which (b) the representatives of a trade union which has consultation rights; failing which (c) the representatives of a trade union which has asserted collective representation rights at the workplace.

32 Where there is no such representative in place the employer should be required to notify the Trade Union Representation and Recognition Agency which would then be under a duty to intervene on behalf of the workers who may be affected by the decision in question, and ask them to nominate a trade union to represent them in consultations about the proposed redundancy or transfer.

33 The right to appoint a safety representative should apply to (a) unions recognised for the purposes of collective bargaining; failing which (b) unions which have general consultation rights; failing which (c) unions which have asserted rights of collective representation.

34 Where there is no such union it should be open to a worker to request an employer to make arrangements for the election of safety representatives of the workforce in accordance with the procedure in paragraph 32 above. The safety representatives may but need not be employed by the employer.

35 Legislation implementing the European Works Councils Directive should be based on the principle of trade union representation as the principal vehicle for representation. The legislation should provide in the first instance that where there is a trade union recognised for the purposes of collective bargaining, the British representatives on the Special Negotiating Body should be appointed by the trade union. Where there is more than one union recognised by the employer the British representative should be appointed by the unions jointly.

36 Where there is no recognised trade union, but a union which has either general consulation rights or has asserted collective representation rights, that union (or where there is more than one union these unions jointly) should have the right to appoint a SNB representative. Where there is no union with recognition, general consultation, or collective representation rights, the TURARA should be required to supervise the nomination or election of a representative (paragraph 7.73).

37 A similar procedure should be adopted in determining the composition of the European Works Council established on the basis of the Directive's subsidiary requirements according to article 7 in the Annex to the Directive, to be adopted where the central management and the special negotiating body fail to agree, or if they otherwise so decide.

THE RIGHT TO STRIKE

8.1   The right to strike is an indispensable requirement of a free society. As such it is recognised expressly (as in the case of the European Social Charter of 1961) or impliedly (as in the case of ILO Convention 87) in a number of international treaties to which this country is a party. It is also enshrined in the constitutions of a number of the Member States of the European Community, including the constitutions of France, Germany and Spain, while the Constitution of Sweden provides expressly that 'Any trade union ... shall be entitled to take strike ... action or any similar measure unless otherwise provided by law or arising out of an agreement'. Further recognition of the freedom to strike is to be found in the law and practice of probably all democratic regimes in the western liberal tradition; it has even been said by a court in the United States to be one of the 'fundamental human liberties'.

8.2   These different instruments reflect the fact that strike action will inevitably have a part to play in any developed system of industrial relations, no matter how unwilling trade unions may be to organise such action and no matter how reluctant workers may be to take part in it. Although no one is suggesting that there should be ready resort to strike action, even to the extent that it is permitted by the law, we should be mindful nevertheless that the right to take such action is to be defended in the strongest terms. It is necessary in the interests of personal liberty in the sense that people should not be compelled by the State to work when they have a grievance against their employer, another employer or indeed against the Government itself. But above all it is necessary in the interests of collective bargaining for without the right ultimately to withdraw their labour, workers would send their representatives to the bargaining table with no power to resist the imposition of terms by the employer.

8.3   Protection of the freedom to strike invites legal intervention to protect from discrimination or dismissal the individual worker who takes part in the strike, for otherwise the freedom would be rather empty of content. But it also means protecting from any potential legal liability both the trade union officials who organise the action and the trade unions on behalf of which they act and of which those participating in the action may be members. It does not follow, of course that this legal protection should be unlimited or unqualified, and there are indeed a number of possible restrictions which might be introduced, without necessarily violating international labour standards, or without deviating from the standards which have been adopted in legal systems which we might otherwise admire or seek to emulate. But like any other fundamental freedom any restrictions on the freedom to strike would have to be justified on the strongest grounds. And like any other fundamental freedom the onus is firmly on those who wish to impose controls.

8.4   In this section we begin by tracing the way in which the freedom to strike has been protected by a system of immunities from common law liability, and seek to indicate the nature and extent of the failure of the adopted strategy. We then proceed to give a brief account of how these immunities have been culled to the point of virtual extinction by the Conservative governments since 1979, thereby undermining the concerns that a freedom to strike based on immunities would be less vulnerable to attack by a hostile government than one built on rights. Moving from this inevitably brief and selective account of very complex statutory provisions, we assess the new restrictive regime in the light of international standards and in particular the jurisprudence of the ILO Committee of Experts. This indicates a compelling need to re-assert the legitimacy of industrial action in a free society and at the same time indicates the boundaries within which the discussion of any possible restraints may take place.

8.5   Our consideration of the jurisprudence of the ILO leads us to a consideration of how the freedom to strike should be protected in the future. Our starting point is that the existing statutory framework should be repealed and that we should start again with fresh legislation. In light of the foregoing, however, it will come as no surprise that we are not in favour to returning to the position which operated in the 1970s. There is a need for a fresh start, a fresh settlement, and a fresh approach to the use of the law in this area. We thus consider how the law should be used to protect both the individual striker and the trade union organisation. We also address the question of what, if any, controls should operate to restrain the freedom to strike, and consider in particular whether there ought to be any restrictions in terms of the purposes for which industrial action may be taken, in terms of the procedures to be followed before industrial action is taken, and in terms of the tactics which may be deployed in the course of a dispute.

Trade Union Immunities

8.6   Traditionally there has been no right to strike in British law. Industrial action would typically involve the commission of one or more torts and would therefore be unlawful at common law. The courts were inclined to say that industrial action constituted an actionable conspiracy against the employer, or that those who called the action were liable to the employer for inducing workers to break their contracts of employment. This led in 1906 to the introduction of immunities from tortious liability (extending an approach first adopted in 1875 which gave an immunity from certain criminal liabilities for acts done in contemplation or furtherance of a trade dispute). Under the Trade Disputes Act 1906 there would be no liability in tort for conspiracy or for inducing breach of a contract of employment if the acts were done in contemplation or furtherance of a trade dispute. It was also provided that an action against a trade union 'in respect of any tortious act alleged to have been committed by or on behalf of the trade union, shall not be entertained by any court of law.'

8.7   The 1906 Act survived until it was repealed by the Industrial Relations Act 1971. Following the failure of that Act and the election of a Labour Government, the immunities first introduced in 1906 were restored by the Trade Union and Labour Relations Act 1974 (as amended in 1976). An immunity was provided for specific heads of liability (conspiracy, inducing breach of contract, intimidation and interference with trade, business or employment of another person) for acts done in 'contemplation or furtherance of a trade dispute'. The term 'trade dispute' was widely defined in the legislation to mean any dispute between employers and workers, or workers and workers which was connected with an extensive range of matters which included, but was by no means confined to, terms and conditions of employment. A wider immunity was provided for trade unions, with section 14 enacting that no action in tort would lie against a trade union, with a number of carefully limited exceptions relating to negligence, nuisance and personal injury.

8.8   The immunity was thus in the most general terms, designed to withdraw the law from the conduct of trade disputes. There were no restrictions in terms of procedures to be followed before industrial action, in terms of the purposes for which industrial action might be taken (with one important caveat), and in terms of the tactics which might be employed in the course of a dispute. There were, for example, no restrictions on the right to take secondary or sympathy action, and the law knew no distinction between official and unofficial action. But this desire to exclude the law from trade disputes had weaknesses as well as strengths, for just as trade unions and their officials were protected from the legal consequences of their actions, so employers were protected from liability for unfair dismissal. This was achieved by denying the industrial tribunals jurisdiction to deal with unfair dismissal claims by employees dismissed while taking part in a strike, a protection for employers which would be lost only if the employer failed to dismiss everyone who was taking part or who had taken part in the action in question.

Trade Union Immunities under the Conservatives

8.9   Since 1980 these immunities have been significantly and substantially reduced. Although the language and form of immunity have been retained as the means for the protection of industrial action, the restrictions have made them much more difficult to operate. The process of erosion started in 1980 and has developed gradually over the intervening 17 years, with restrictive measures being contained in no fewer than six of the eight statutes (excluding the Trade Union and Labour Relations (Consolidation) Act 1992) dealing principally with labour law which have been passed at the time of writing since 1979. Thus important restrictions are to be found in the Employment Act 1980, the Employment Act 1982, the Trade Union Act 1984, the Employment Act 1988, the Employment Act 1990, and the Trade Union Reform and Employment Rights Act 1993. The cumulative impact of these measures has been enormous, leading to a number of violations of a number of international labour standards.

8.10   It is important to recall precisely the scope and extent of the new measures. The Employment Act 1980 can be identified as the start of the current policy on strike ballots, with section 1 introducing a State subsidy (since revoked) for strike (and other) ballots. Although the dangers of this measure were highlighted at the time, of more immediate concern were the restrictions (in line with decisions of the Court of Appeal in 1979) on the freedom to take secondary action in support of workers engaged in a trade dispute, and at the same time the monumentally important restraints on picketing. Although evidently designed to deal with the problem of secondary picketing, these restraints in fact go much wider by providing that workers may now picket only outside their own place of work. The restrictions (reinforced by a Code of Practice limiting the number of pickets at any one location to six) are so narrowly drawn that in the case of a multi-site employer workers in dispute may not picket the head office of the company by whom they are employed.

8.11 This was followed by the Employment Act 1982 which restricted the purposes for which industrial action might be taken, removed the immunity of trade unions for liability in tort, and facilitated the dismissal of workers who were engaged in industrial action. So far as the restricting the purposes for which industrial action might be taken, this was achieved by redefining the term 'trade dispute' on which the immunity depends, so that it would apply, for example, only to disputes between workers and their employer which related 'wholly or mainly' to one or more of the prescribed statutory purposes. The impact of this change was felt very quickly by the Post Office Engineering Union (as it then was) which found that it had no protection for industrial action in response to the proposed liberalisation and privatisation of the telephone system. Although almost certainly 'connected with', the union was unable to convince the courts that it related 'wholly or mainly to' any of the prescribed statutory purposes.

8.12 Apart from thus restricting the scope of the immunities, the 1982 Act also repealed the Trade Union and Labour Relations Act 1974, section 14, so that trade unions could now be sued in tort for industrial action outside the scope of the immunities which was authorised or endorsed by a 'responsible person'. Previously legal action had to be taken against the union official who induced the workers to break their contracts of employment, and any remedy would be granted against the official personally. The effect of the 1982 Act was that in practice injunctions and damages (admittedly subject to a statutory ceiling depending on the size of the union) could be granted or awarded in legal proceedings against a union rather than its officials. It also raised the spectre of contempt of court proceedings being instituted against a trade union in the event of an injunction not being complied with. This in fact led to the sequestration of the assets of a number of unions, including SOGAT and the NUS (as they then were).

8.13 Two years later the Trade Union Act 1984 introduced fresh conditions on the application of the immunities. Industrial action authorised or endorsed by a trade union would continue to enjoy immunity only if it was first supported by a secret ballot of those called upon to take the action in question. A union was required to ballot everyone likely to be called upon to take the action in question, but was not permitted to ballot anyone else. The ballot could be conducted at the workplace or by post, but the ballot paper had to include a question asking those balloted whether they were prepared to take industrial action in breach of their contracts of employment, a measure which seems designed deliberately to intimidate those to whom it was addressed. Industrial action had to be called within four weeks of the ballot being held. Failure to hold a ballot or failure to comply with the statutory procedures could lead to legal action against a trade union by the employer to whom the duty was owed.

8.14 The unions' obligation to consult their members under the 1984 Act was thus tied to their immunity from liability to the employer. In the Employment Act 1988, however, the right to sue to enforce the balloting requirements was extended so that trade union members could bring legal proceedings in the High Court to restrain industrial action unsupported by a ballot which complied with the statutory requirements. The Act also created the office of the Commissioner for the Rights of Trade Union Members to advise, assist and provide for the legal representation of trade union members in these and other cases. But apart from extending the range of people who could enforce the ballot requirements, the Act imposed further restrictions on the operation of the balloting rules, so that, for example, where those to be balloted had different places of work, in some cases separate ballots had to be held for each place of work.

8.15 Still further restrictions were introduced by the Employment Act 1990 which removed immunity from all secondary industrial action, and facilitated the selective dismissal of strikers engaged in an unofficial dispute. As suggested in paragraph 8.11 above, measures had already been introduced in 1982 to make it easier for employers to dismiss striking workers without the risk of liability. In further extending the employers' immunity from legal liability for unfair dismissal, the 1990 Act provided that industrial tribunals would not have jurisdiction to deal with complaints of unfair dismissal where the industrial action was taken without the authorisation or endorsement of a trade union, even though the employer had selectively dismissed anyone involved for a reason quite unrelated to the strike. The union could take steps to avoid the risk of selective dismissal by endorsing the action in question, but in so doing would thereby be exposed itself to the risk of liability given that the action is unlikely to have been supported by a ballot.

8.16 Even more restrictions have been imposed by the Trade Union Reform and Employment Rights Act 1993. This now requires all industrial action ballots to be conducted by post (the costs of which must now be met by the unions themselves, the State subsidy having been revoked), and provides that trade unions must also appoint an independent scrutineer to supervise the conduct of any ballot. Apart from these additional restrictions on the conduct of ballots, a number of new obligations were introduced whereby unions must give notice (within a period of 7 days before the ballot is due to start) to the employer stating that it intends to hold a ballot and (within 3 days of the start of the ballot) provide the employer with a copy of the voting paper. The union must also indicate to the employer the identity of those employees who are likely to be asked to participate in the ballot. After the ballot is held the union is required to notify every relevant employer of the result, and if industrial action is to be taken, give the employer at least seven days' notice of the proposed action.

8.17 The other novelty of the 1993 Act is the right of third parties in some circumstances to apply to the courts to restrain industrial action which is unprotected by the immunities. Under the Act the third parties' right arises where an effect or a likely effect of the industrial action is or will be to prevent or delay the supply of goods or services, or to reduce the quality of goods and services supplied. For the purpose of making an application 'it is immaterial whether or not the individual is entitled to be supplied with the goods or services in question'. An individual who is the party to such proceedings may apply to the newly created Commissioner for Protection Against Unlawful Industrial Action for assistance in relation to the proceedings. There is no reason to believe that the Commissioner (who holds her position jointly as Commissioner for the Rights of Trade Union Members) has been overwhelmed by complaints.

8.18 The cumulative effect of this piecemeal approach to legislation has been far reaching. In terms of the freedom to strike, we have seen restrictions imposed in terms of

* The procedures to be complied with before industrial action may take place;
* The purposes for which industrial action may be taken, even when these procedural obligations have been complied with;
* The tactics which may be deployed by trade unions involved in a dispute, even where the dispute is for a lawful purpose and even

though the procedural obligations have been met;
* The sanctions which may be imposed on a trade union which has authorised or endorsed industrial action which falls outside the scope of the receding immunities; and
* The liability to dismissal without the right to challenge the fairness of that dismissal on the part of individual workers participating in a strike or other industrial action.

In our view this legislation should be repealed and that a fresh start should be made in developing a new and fairer legal framework for industrial action.

International Labour Standards and the Right to Strike

8.19 It is quite clear, from a review of international labour standards, that in the period of post Conservative reconstruction, these far reaching restrictions will have to be modified, if we are to be seen to comply with our international obligations, and the rule of international law. The starting point is ILO Convention 87, the Freedom of Association and the Right to Organise Convention, 1948. As we have already seen, this provides by Article 3 that 'Workers and employers' organisations shall have the right to draw up their constitutions and rules, to elect their representatives in full freedom, to organise their administration and activities and to formulate their programmes'. Also important are Articles 8 and 10, the former providing that while trade unions are expected to comply with the law of the land, the law should not be such as to 'impair' the guarantees provided for in the Convention. The latter defines a workers' organisation as meaning 'any organisation of workers for furthering and defending the interests of workers. . .'.

8.20 Admittedly there is no express protection of the right to strike in ILO Convention 87, which is said to be one of the fundamental texts of the Organisation and as such binding on members, even though they have not ratified it. But as the Committee of Experts has pointed out, the right to strike is protected by implication, for it has 'always considered that the right to strike is one of the essential means available to workers and their organisations for the promotion and protection of their social and economic interests'. It does not follow from this, however, that there can be no limits on the scope and extent of the right. The jurisprudence of the Committee of Experts makes clear that a number of restrictions are permissible, including most notably from a British point of view a requirement for pre-strike ballots, which have been found on a number of occasions not to involve a violation of Convention 87.

8.21 On the other hand, however, it is quite clear that, in other respects, the legislation in this area introduced in this country since 1979 goes far beyond what is permissible. Indeed it is also clear that wide though the protection for industrial action may have been between 1974 and 1979, it was not wide enough. Thus in Observations published in 1989, the Committee of Experts drew attention to a number of areas where British law (originating both post and pre 1979) failed to comply with the standards set by the ILO. These related to the limited protection for the purposes for which industrial action might be taken; the restrictions on the scope of secondary and solidarity action; and the absence of effective protection for workers dismissed for taking part in a strike or industrial action. Questions were also raised about statutory restrictions on a union's power to discipline or expel members who refused to take part in a properly constituted strike.

8.22 So far as the first of these questions is concerned the Committee of Experts expressed concern that the amended definition of a trade dispute appears 'to deny protection to disputes where unions and their members have 'mixed' motives (for example, where they are pursuing both 'industrial' and 'political' or 'social' objectives)'. Concern was also expressed about the requirement that disputes must now be between workers and 'their' employer, thereby making it impossible for unions to take effective action in situations where the 'real' employer with whom they were in dispute was able to take refuge behind one or more subsidiary companies who were technically the employer of the workers concerned, but who lacked the capacity to take decisions which are capable of satisfactorily resolving the dispute. Further concern was revealed about the restrictions (introduced in 1982) on industrial action relating to matters occurring outside the United Kingdom.

8.23 More controversially perhaps were the Committee's Observations on the restrictions on secondary action, all the more interesting for the fact that they were made before the 1990 Act withdrew protection from secondary action altogether. Although the Committee of Experts had never previously expressed a decided view on the use of secondary action as an aspect of the right to strike, it had previously stated in the context of sympathy strikes that a general prohibition of this particular form of action 'could lead to abuse' and that 'workers should be able to take such action provided the initial strike they are supporting is itself lawful'. The opportunity was now taken to extend a similar analysis to secondary action. Thus in the view of the Committee 'where a boycott relates directly to the social and economic interests of the workers involved in either or both of the original dispute and the secondary action, and where the original dispute and the secondary action are not unlawful in themselves, then that boycott should be regarded as a legitimate exercise of the right to strike'.

8.24 The other major area highlighted by the Committee of Experts related to the lack of protection for strikers dismissed while taking part in a dispute. In the view of the Committee, it is inconsistent with the right to strike for an employer 'to be permitted to refuse to reinstate some or all of its employees at the conclusion of a strike, lock-out or other industrial action without those employees having the right to challenge the fairness of that dismissal before an independent court or tribunal'. Yet as we have seen an industrial tribunal has no jurisdiction to deal with a complaint of unfair dismissal if the complainant was dismissed for taking part in a strike or other industrial action, provided that everyone taking part in the action at the date of the complainant's dismissal was also dismissed. These observations were endorsed by the Freedom of Association Committee which, in a complaint from the seafarers' union, also condemned the amendments made in 1990 permitting the selective dismissal of 'unofficial' strikers.

8.25 The ILO supervisory agencies have thus recognised the existence of a right to strike as a feature of international labour law. So long as we remain in membership of the ILO, we are bound by this jurisprudence, however awkward it may be for those in government. Developing the content of the right to strike, the Committee of Experts has made it crystal clear that the right to strike need not be unlimited. But on the other hand both the Committee of Experts and the Freedom of Association Committee have made it equally clear that the purposes for which industrial action is to be permitted must not be too narrowly drawn, that it is not permissible to prohibit all forms of secondary and sympathy action, and that it is not acceptable to permit an employer to dismiss workers without providing them the opportunity to challenge the fairness of the dismissal. In our view the ILO standards should form the basis of future legislation on the right to strike.

A *Right* to Strike

8.26   Historically the freedom to strike has been protected in British law by a series of immunities from common law liabilities. This method of protection suffers, however, from a number of drawbacks and it is arguably of questionable effect. Most obviously, an immunity can only offer protection from liabilities which are known to exist at the time the legislation is passed. Yet the common law is not static, with the result that the immunities, and consequently the freedom to strike, can be seriously impaired by the emergence of new heads of liability. The immunities in the 1906 Act were undermined in 1964 by the discovery by the House of Lords of a new tort of intimidation, while the immunities in the 1974 Act were threatened by the principle of liability for procuring breach of a statutory duty, a matter of particular concern to trade unions in the public sector. There is a need for a response which is proactive rather than reactive, an approach which will seek to stop fresh controls being imposed by the common law, rather than one which simply invites such controls.

8.27   The alternative to an immunities-based protection for the freedom to strike is a rights-based approach, possibly in conjunction with an immunity, as was adopted in Australia in 1993. It is sometimes suggested by text book writers and others, however, that the way in which the freedom to strike is protected, whether by an immunity or a right, is merely a question of form. We believe this to be mistaken and to be based on a misapprehension. It is true that the right is as likely as an immunity to be undermined by a narrow interpretation by the courts. But the problem with the immunities is that they were subject to attack on two fronts: first by the emergence of new torts unprotected by the immunity and secondly by the misinterpretation of the immunity itself. The benefit of a properly drafted right is that it would overcome the first problem, clearly a benefit of substance even if the second problem remained untouched. We believe, however, that the form in which the law is drafted is relevant to the approach of the courts to its interpretation, also a matter of substance.

8.28   One of the points made time and again by the judges who indulged (gorged?) themselves in an orgy of destruction of the immunities was precisely that their action was justified because of the form of the protection adopted by Parliament. As Lord Denning pointed out by way of justification in *Express Newspapers Ltd v MacShane* [1979] ICR 210 'Parliament granted immunities to the leaders of trade unions, it did not give them any rights'. The language of immunity thus invites a restrictive interpretation of its terms, which would not be true of a legal protection cast in the language of rights. Although it is perfectly possible that the judges would still misinterpret the legislation and misread Parliament's intention, the responsibility of the legislator is to make it more difficult for the courts to do so, and part of that process concerns the choice of means used to achieve Parliament's goal. To the extent that the legal form may have a bearing on the integrity of the freedom, it is thus self evidently and unequivocally a matter of substance which it would be extraordinary to deny.

8.29 It is not suggested that a rights-based approach will avoid altogether the difficulties which have been encountered by the immunities, but it is likely that it would help to minimise these difficulties. It would not be possible for the courts to develop new heads of liability to circumvent the legislation: the right to strike would trump all common law liabilities whether already established or newly created. These and other considerations lead us to the firm view that the freedom to strike should be protected by a 'rights-based' system rather than one based wholly on immunities. We would also, however, propose the abolition of the principal torts by statute. These have been developed to deal specifically with trade unions, though they do have an application beyond labour law. However, the occasional reliance on these torts outside the labour law context is no justification for their retention. If the torts serve a useful purpose in other areas of the law, it would always be possible for Parliament to reintroduce the principles they embrace, but restrict their application to clearly identifiable areas of commercial or other activity.

8.30 The question arises whether it is necessary to define in legislation the meaning of the terms 'strike' or 'industrial action' for this purpose. There are examples of at least the first of these terms being defined in legislation, with the Trade Union and Labour Relations (Consolidation) Act 1992, providing in section 246 a wide definition for the purposes of that Act, a strike being defined to mean 'any concerted stoppage of work'. There are on the other hand examples of both these terms being used for other legislative purposes without the need apparently for either to be defined. The most obvious example of this is the legislation to deny jurisdiction to the industrial tribunals in the case of dismissals on the ground of participation in a strike or other industrial action, which until 1992 operated without a definition of either a strike or industrial action. Although the position is finely balanced we incline to the view that it is unnecessary in legislation to define what is meant by a strike or industrial action, which would serve only to encourage litigation on technical questions of statutory interpretation.

8.31 We are therefore proposing a new conceptual framework for the protection of the right to strike. It is no longer appropriate that the starting point of the law relating to industrial action should be based on a common law framework developed in a pre-democratic age. It is singularly appropriate that the legacy of the nineteenth century should be removed and that a fresh start should be made. It is therefore proposed that workers should have a right to strike and to engage in other forms of industrial action recognised and protected by law, within defined limits if appropriate. Those who exercise this right should not be regarded as having acted in breach of the employment relationship; they should be protected from dismissal; and those who organise industrial action should not be liable to the employer in tort or on any other ground.

The Scope and Content of the Right to Strike

8.32 Although there may be no need to define in legislation what is meant by the terms 'strike' or 'industrial action', there may be a need to identify the circumstances in which such action may be taken. Historically strike action in this country has been permitted in contemplation or furtherance of a trade dispute, defined at one time to mean a dispute between employers and workers or workers and workers which was connected with terms and conditions of employment and broadly related questions. A number of restrictions were imposed on the statutory definition by the courts, concerned that it should not be too widely exercised. This became a particular source of irritation in the 1970s in particular with the Court of Appeal holding that action to stop the transmission of the 1977 FA Cup Final was not action in furtherance of a trade dispute. But for the most part the definition was wide and permissive, a point emphasised by the House of Lords when the true intention was discovered.

8.33 Yet although clearly very widely drafted, there was one important limitation, even before the statutory amendments introduced since 1980, the definition excluding action designed to protest against the policies of government rather than in furtherance of a dispute with an employer. So in 1980 injunctions were granted to Express Newspapers to prevent the members of print unions taking part in a TUC Day of Action designed to protest against government economic policy. There is no reason in principle why there should be restrictions of this kind, and the reasons which might be used to defend them are fanciful at best. We are not suggesting that the strike weapon should be used to bring down or challenge the authority of a democratically elected government (something which has never been done in this country in the democratic age), for which there is in any event no evidence of any inclination on the part of workers or trade union officials. But we are suggesting that workers as citizens should be free to stop work in protest at the activities of government, particularly where these activities directly affect the well being of workers and their families.

8.34   In our view workers should have the right to take industrial action as a means of resolving any dispute which relates to their interests at work. This would include the list of items in the Trade Union and Labour Relations (Consolidation) Act 1992, section 244 , though we see no reason in principle why it should be confined to such matters, even if in practice the items listed cover most of the likely subjects of a dispute. In our view it is workers themselves, not the State, and not employers, who must determine the nature and extent of their own occupational interests. Therefore we propose that workers should be free to take industrial action to promote their occupational, social or economic interests. This would permit (1) action in furtherance of any dispute relating to the employment relationship; (2) action in furtherance of any dispute relating to the conduct of the business by which they are employed; and (3) action to protest about the social or economic policies of the government.

8.35   One area which calls for special protection is international solidarity action, which may not be covered by the terms of paragraph 8.34 above. Under the Trade Union and Labour Relations Act 1974 protection from liability was extended to a trade dispute even though it related to matters occurring outside Great Britain. This, however, was restricted in 1982 so that the protection applies only in respect of matters occurring outside the United Kingdom if those taking the action in this country are likely to be affected by the outcome of the dispute. It may be the case, however, that international solidarity action would now be caught by the general ban on secondary action introduced in 1990. The position is thus at best unclear, and was criticised by the ILO Committee of Experts which was concerned by the lack of protection 'for industrial action which was intended to protect or to improve the terms and conditions of employment of workers outside the United Kingdom, or to register disapproval of the social or racial policies of a government with whom the United Kingdom has trading or economic links'. We propose that legislation should clearly indicate that international solidarity action is not unlawful.

Limitations on the Right to Strike

8.36 Although we thus propose that workers should have a right to strike, for a wide range of purposes, it does not follow that it should operate without limitations. It is common practice in a number of countries in Europe and elsewhere to require limits on the use of the strike weapon. These are many and varied, though we are cautious in this field of seeking to follow too closely the practice elsewhere, partly because it is so variable, and partly because this is an area of the law where account has to be taken of the history, traditions and practices operating within a particular national system. There are, however, three grounds on which the right to strike might be limited. These arise from

* the agreement of the parties;
* the desire to ensure that workers have been consulted; and
* the concern about the impact and consequences of the action

It is to a consideration of each of these that we now turn.

(a) The Agreement of the Parties
8.37 The first ground on which it might be argued that the right to strike ought to be restricted is where workers through their trade union have agreed not to use the strike weapon, and agreed a different method for the resolution of disputes. It is established practice in a number of other countries that by virtue of what is sometimes referred to as a peace obligation, a strike will not take place during the currency of a collective agreement. The nature of the obligation varies from country to country, so that in some there is a virtual prohibition of all strikes during the life of the agreement; in some there is a prohibition only of strikes which relate to the matters covered in the agreement; and in others there may be exceptions to the obligation to permit defensive industrial action on behalf of workers.

8.38 This has not been the experience in this country. Although there may be procedure agreements for the resolution of disputes, they are presumed not to be legally binding. Indeed under the Trade Union and Labour Relations (Consolidation) Act 1992, section 179 a collective agreement is conclusively presumed not to be a legally enforceable contract unless it is in writing and contains a provision which states that the parties intend that it shall be a legally enforceable contract. The parties are thus free to enter into agreements which contain procedures for the resolution of disputes, to enter into no strike agreements, and to agree that the agreements in question shall be legally enforceable. We believe that trade unions and employers should continue to seek the resolution of their differences by methods other than industrial action, and propose that measures similar to those currently contained in the Trade Union and Labour Relations (Consolidation) Act 1992, section 179 should be retained.

(b) Consulting Trade Union Members

8.39 **Conflicting principles**. There is a strong argument in favour of the view that it is no business of the State to tell trade unions what procedures to adopt on behalf of their members in their dealings with employers. As a matter of principle, trade unions should be free 'to draw up their constitutions and rules' and the State should 'refrain from any interference which would restrict this right', as is clearly recognised by ILO Convention 87, article 3. Adopting the principle of freedom of association without qualification would mean that trade unions and their members would be free to develop their own constitutions, and this autonomy would include the freedom to determine the scope and content of the rules relating to the procedures to be adopted before a strike or other industrial action was called. The role of the State would thus be confined to providing machinery in the form of courts or tribunals to which trade union members could complain and seek relief if called upon to take industrial action in breach of any restriction contained in the union's constitution.

8.40   But although there is thus a strong case in favour of freedom of association and trade union autonomy, there is also a case for some qualification of the principle. This in fact has been recognised by the ILO Committee of Experts which has taken the view that mandatory strike ballots do not necessarily conflict with the principle of freedom of association embraced by Convention 87. According to the Committee, 'no violation of the principles of freedom of association is involved where legislation contains certain rules intended to promote democratic principles within trade union organisations'. As a result the Committee did not find that the balloting requirements of the Trade Union Act 1984 violated the freedom of association principles of Convention 87. It does not follow, of course, that because it is permissible under ILO Conventions to qualify the right to freedom of association, it is thereby necessary or even desirable to do so. The Committee of Experts does, however, indicate a tension between two complementary principles in the resolution of which there is no obviously 'right' answer.

8.41   The argument from democracy would accept that workers should be consulted in one way or another about major decisions which affect them, whether these decisions are taken by the employer or by the union. A decision by a union to call its members out on strike is a major decision in terms of its impact on the worker's income during the period of the stoppage, and in terms of the risk of dismissal. More to the point, perhaps, if the right to strike is to be seen as a right of the individual to act in combination with others, the individual has a strong claim to be consulted before being called upon to take action, the failure to participate in which may also affect his or her membership of the union (in the sense that strikebreaking may lead to expulsion) and consequently his or her right to participate through the union in workplace decisions which affect livelihood, and also his or her opportunity for protection by the union at the workplace.

8.42   **Questions of enforcement.** If the arguments relating to an obligation to ballot are finely balanced, there is perhaps less scope for a conflict of principles should a mandatory balloting regime be introduced. The first question for consideration is to whom any legal duty should be owed. In other words who would be entitled to sue to restrain industrial action which has been called without the support of the mandatory ballot? As matters currently stand under the Trade Union and Labour Relations (Consolidation) Act 1992 (as amended), proceedings may be instituted by an employer, by a trade union member (with the support of a State official), or in some cases by a disgruntled member of the public (also with the support of an officer of the State). The primary method of enforcement in practice, however, is the first, with the holding of a ballot in accordance with the detailed statutory procedures being a condition of immunity from tortious liability. The right of trade union members was added only in 1988 and that of members of the public in 1993. There have been few actions brought by individual members, and at the time of writing none instigated by a member of the public.

8.43   If the obligation to ballot is to be retained, it is a matter for consideration how any law should be drafted. Should it be a duty which the union owes to the employer, enforceable by the employer in the event of a failure to comply? Or should it be a duty which the union owes to its members, enforceable by the members in the event of a failure to comply? There are certain advantages in adopting either (or both) courses. So far as the first is concerned, it could be argued that it is more likely that any failure on the part of the union would be pursued. It will always be more difficult, for a number of obvious reasons, for a worker to take legal action against his or her union (particularly in the case of action which enjoys wide support) than it would for an employer. Apart from the question of the effective implementation of the law, there is also the fact that enforcement by a member may serve only to promote internal disruption whereas enforcement by the employer may be more calculated to promote internal cohesion in the face of an external challenge.

8.44 But although we recognise the strength of these arguments, nevertheless we incline to the view that if the a duty to ballot is to be imposed by the State, the failure to comply with the duty should be enforceable only by the members. There are two reasons for this. The first is that the right to be consulted is the right of the worker to be consulted before being called upon to exercise his or her individual right to take concerted action in combination with others. If it is the right of the individual which is at stake, it is the responsibility of the individual to enforce that right, which should not in turn depend for its enforcement on where the employer happens to perceive his or her interests to lie. Our second reason for proposing that any balloting obligation should be enforced by the individual is quite simply that in our view an employer has no legitimate interest in the relationship between the union and its members, any more than the union has in the relationship between the company and its shareholders. Therefore, we propose that if pre strike ballots are to be introduced or retained, the duty to ballot should be owed to and be enforceable by the trade union member only and not also by the employer.

8.45 **A flexible procedure.** We must always be mindful of the purpose for which a ballot is held. It is not to frustrate the right to take industrial action where there is a clear desire to do so by laying a number of trip wires over which unions will inevitably fall. Rather it is to determine whether there is genuinely support for the action which is being proposed. As a result we would reject the current framework of law, with its attendant technicalities in favour of a statutory procedure which is flexible and responsive to the position of each union. If there is to be a statutory duty, we propose that the framework legislation should simply require trade unions to have rules relating to ballots before industrial action, the rules in question to comply with the following conditions: the ballots should be secret; they should be conducted either at or near the workplace or by post (and could be either semi-postal or fully-postal); and they should indicate who is entitled to vote in the ballot.

8.46 Special consideration would have to be given to the question of whether a ballot should be required in all cases, if the balloting obligation were to be retained. In our view it is unfair to require a ballot in all cases, particularly in the case of spontaneous action in response to the victimisation of a shop steward or the unilateral variation of working conditions by the employer. Similarly we see no case for a ballot before workers refuse to cross a picket line established by other workers engaged in a dispute. In our view there should be no requirement of a ballot in these cases as a matter of law, though clearly it would be open to individual trade unions in their rules to require a ballot to be held in such cases. Special consideration also needs to be given to the possibility of unofficial action called without the authority of a ballot for reasons other than those specified. If the balloting obligation is retained, it is for consideration whether a union should have the opportunity formally to endorse the action by calling for a ballot within three days of the start of the unofficial action.

8.47 The rules would in turn have to be approved by the Certification Officer in line with our proposals in paragraphs 6.47-6.50. The Certification Officer would have the responsibility to ensure that the statutory principles, and any accompanying Code of Practice on the conduct of ballots, were complied with. In the event of the approval being unreasonably withheld, it would be possible for the union to appeal to the Labour Court which we propose in chapter 10. Once adopted the rules relating to ballots before industrial action would be enforceable as rules of the union, with complaints to be dealt with by the Labour Court. It is for consideration whether it ought to be necessary for the action to be launched only with the consent of a prescribed number of members to discourage frivolous applications. We also propose that it should not be lawful for a trade union to discipline or expel a member for failing to support a strike or industrial action which has not been conducted in accordance with the balloting rules, a point to which we return.

(c) The Impact and Consequences of Industrial Action

8.48 A third ground on which it could be argued that the exercise of the right to strike might be limited relates to the impact and consequences of the action. The Council of Europe's Social Charter provides that no restrictions or limitations may be imposed on the rights protected by the Charter except where these are prescribed by law and are necessary in a democratic society 'for the protection of the rights and freedoms of others or for the protection of the public interest, national security, public health or morals'. So it might be contended that there is a case for imposing limits where the harm caused by the action is out of all proportion to its objectives, whether to the employer or to third parties. This is an argument which could apply to the strike itself as well as any decision to extend the strike, for example by secondary action. As a matter of principle there would be nothing exceptional about a limit of this kind in the sense that there are few rights which are regarded as unlimited or unqualified.

8.49   In some respects it might be argued that a doctrine of proportionality is a rational one to the extent that it invites restricting specific strikes rather than the imposition of blanket restrictions to apply regardless of the impact of the dispute. We are, however, firmly opposed to the introduction of any such doctrine, for three reasons. First it would have the effect of denying the right to strike to some groups of workers whose action is always likely to have a significant impact and may not always be easy to justify on grounds of proportionality. Secondly there is the question of who is to decide whether a particular strike could be defended on grounds of proportionality. There are few trade unionists who would be sanguine about the prospect of this role being performed by the courts who would be asked to intervene on a case by case basis without adequate guidelines, creating confusion and uncertainty. And thirdly there is the fear that this doctrine would come close to saying that there is a right to strike, but only if does not cause inconvenience.

8.50   But although it would thus be difficult to justify a concept of proportionality as a basis for restricting the circumstances in which the strike weapon might be used, it does not follow that the principle has no application in relation to the tactics used in the course of the strike. If we look at the question of secondary action, and the extension of the dispute to the workers of other employers, it may be argued that the principle of proportionality invites some boundaries to be placed on the circumstances in which such action may be taken. Indeed one of the arguments about restricting the extension of a dispute to third parties is effectively a proportionality argument. Thus it is sometimes said that it is out of all proportion to the goal being pursued that 'innocent' third parties should be dragged into a matter in relation to which they bear no responsibility and over the outcome of which they have no control.

8.51   The question of secondary action is difficult and controversial, and there are a number of ways in which the law could be used in response. The first of essentially three options is that contained in the current law which has the effect of prohibiting all forms of secondary and sympathy action. This is not an option which we would support, for it is our view that workers must be free to support other workers engaged in a dispute with an employer. It is particularly galling that employers engaged in a dispute can call on the services of third parties, whether they be other workers or employers, but workers engaged in the same dispute may not. In any event this option is effectively foreclosed by the ILO Committee of Expert's Report in 1989 which requires secondary action to be permitted in an admittedly indeterminate range of circumstances.

8.52   The second option is for a limited right to take secondary action. Difficult questions will arise, however, in setting the boundaries of permissible action, though it is attempted in other jurisdictions. One possibility would be to permit what might be referred to as retaliatory secondary action, where the right is triggered by conduct of the employer which broadens out the dispute between the original parties, for example by hiring replacement labour. A second, and more permissive possibility would be to allow secondary action, within a defined range in terms of the third party employers whose workers could be called upon to take the action in question. A typical example would be to permit secondary action by workers engaged by the first customer or supplier of the employer in dispute, though steps would also have to be taken to permit the genuine display of solidarity where there is no commercial relationship of this kind.

8.53   The third option is the ILO option which would require secondary action to be permitted where both the primary dispute and the secondary action are otherwise lawful, and where it can be shown that 'the action relates directly to the social and economic interests of the workers involved in either or both of the original dispute and the secondary action'. There are three requirements here: the first is that the primary action should in itself be lawful; the second is that the secondary action should not be unlawful for reasons other than the fact that it is secondary action; and thirdly that the secondary action relates directly to the social and economic interests of the workers involved in either the primary or secondary action. Although clearly opaque, this is a widely drawn provision which would appear to preclude either of the two limited options referred to in paragraphs 8.51 and 8.52 above.

8.54   If we adopt the ILO formulation, as we feel obliged to, this would permit secondary action, but only in support of industrial action which is conducted for a lawful purpose, as defined in paragraph 8.34 above; and provided that the action in question is supported by a ballot should the balloting option be adopted; and provided also that the secondary action is itself supported by a ballot of the workers called upon to take the action should the balloting option be adopted. Although we are aware of the concerns in some quarters about the consequences of a legal power to take secondary action, a requirement that such action should be balloted should calm the nerves of those worried by a lifting of the current constraints, even if we were to accept that such fears were justified. On the other hand the requirement that a ballot should be enforceable at the suit of the members in the manner proposed in paragraph 8.44 above, would help to ensure that there was no ready resort to litigation. Therefore we propose that workers should be free in combination with others to take secondary action in support of other workers engaged in a dispute, and that they should be free to do so in line with ILO standards.

Picketing and Freedom of Assembly

8.55 Picketing in the course of a trade dispute has always given rise to difficulty and controversy, partly because of the uncertainty of the law and partly because of the wide discretion on the part of the police. The current law has its origins in legislation of 1875 and 1906. Under the Trade Disputes Act 1906, section 2, it was lawful in the course of a trade dispute to attend at or near a place where a person works or happens to be with a view peacefully to communicate information or peacefully persuade a person to work or abstain from working. The 1906 provisions were reintroduced with modifications in 1974, but the law was significantly amended in 1980 so that the immunity from liability applies only where the worker is picketing outside his or her own place of work, a term so narrowly defined that it would not be possible for a worker to picket the head office of the employer with whom he or she is in dispute unless this was the particular location of his or her employment. The legislation is also accompanied by a Code of Practice which recommends that no more than six people should picket at a single location, though it also states that in some circumstances a smaller number may be appropriate.

8.56 Even within its narrow constraints the current law offers only a very fragile protection for pickets. It is possible for members of a group as small as six to be arrested either for obstructing the highway, or for obstructing a police officer in the execution of his duty. This latter provision gives the police quite extraordinary powers to control the location, numbers and duration of a picket or assembly, and indeed to prevent people from gathering in the first place. The scope of the power was demonstrated during the miners' strike in 1984/85 when miners were prevented by police road blocks at motorway exits from travelling to working collieries. Those who refused to turn back were arrested and charged with obstruction. Further potential liabilities have been created by the Criminal Justice and Public Order Act 1994 which authorises the police to apply to a local authority for an order banning a 'trespassory assembly' (defined to include an assembly of 20 or more people to be held on a road), which it is believed may result in 'serious disruption to the life of the community'. It is an offence to take part in a prohibited assembly and the police are empowered to stop people travelling to what are reasonably believed to be prohibited assemblies.

8.57   In our view there is no convincing reason why pickets should be restricted in this way. It is already the case that workers (and others) may peacefully picket outside a shop to discourage consumers from buying products sold in the shop which are manufactured by an employer in dispute with his or her workers. This is lawful because the pickets are not persuading consumers to break contracts with the shop or with the employer engaged in the dispute; rather they are seeking to persuade people not to enter into contracts in the first place. We are bound to say that we find this distinction between picketing designed to prevent contracts being made on the one hand, and picketing designed to break contracts on the other, as extraordinarily formal and technical, if for no reason other than the fact that to persuade people not to buy products can be just as damaging to a business as persuading workers not to manufacture the products, or not to handle or supply materials which may be necessary in the manufacture of these products. We therefore propose that a worker should have the right to assemble in the course of industrial action outside a workplace, with a view to peacefully persuading people not to work or with a view to communicating information to people.

8.58   Alongside this removal of the restrictions on the location of peaceful picketing, we also recommend the removal of the arbitrary restriction on the numbers of people who may attend for this purpose, which we note has no formal parallel in terms of assemblies for purposes other than picketing. But although we propose the removal of arbitrary restraints on location and numbers we are not to be taken to propose that the law should protect action which (i) causes physical obstruction preventing access to the workplace, (ii) involves an act of violence or a threat of actual violence, or (iii) an act of violence to property or a threat of actual violence to property. We also propose, however, that (i) it should be the duty of the senior police officer present at an assembly to which these provisions apply to have regard to the right contained herein, and (ii) the senior police officer present should take whatever steps are reasonable in the circumstances to ensure that workers have an opportunity to communicate with individuals who are proposing to enter the premises in question. This would authorise the police, where necessary, to require the driver of any vehicle to stop in order to receive an approach from a picket. We also propose that there should be protection from dismissal for workers who refuse to cross a picket line.

Protection for the Individual from the Employer

(a) The Employment Relationship

8.59   As a general rule a worker who takes part in a strike or other industrial action will generally be regarded as having repudiated his or her contract of employment. At common law the employer is thereby free to terminate the contract without notice and the worker is thus denied any remedy in respect of wrongful dismissal. Attempts have been made in the past to suggest that it might be possible to regard the contract as suspended during the industrial action. But this has been largely discredited as a legal concept, and it is in any event of limited utility to the individual worker: it does not follow from the fact that the contract is suspended that it cannot be terminated with or without notice during or immediately after the period of suspension. Nevertheless it would be an odd right to strike which did not address the common law position. Therefore we recommend that participation in a strike or industrial action, within the boundaries of legality defined above, should not be regarded as constituting a breach of the employment relationship.

(b) Payment of Wages

8.60   But although the taking of strike or other forms of industrial action should not be regarded as a breach of the employment relationship, it does not follow that those taking part should continue to be paid. There is, however, a serious question here which relates to cases of industrial action short of a strike. The worker continues to offer some service, but not full performance of obligations arising under the employment relationship. As the law currently stands, employers appear to have at least three options. First, they may refuse to accept partial performance of the contract; secondly they may accept partial performance in which case they may have to make a partial payment; and thirdly they may accept partial performance as full performance and continue to pay as normal. Where the employer adopts the first option there will be no obligation to pay even though workers continue to work and provide benefit to the employer, as in the landmark case *Wiluszynski v Tower Hamlets LBC* [1989] ICR 493.

8.61 How should this matter be regulated by law? In answering this question we are mindful of the fact that workers who take action of this kind often do so in response to irregular, improper or unlawful conduct by the employer. In our view, however, it ought to be possible for an employer to refuse to accept partial performance of the employment relationship, except in cases where he or she has acted unlawfully. Where the employer does refuse to accept partial performance he or she must be under an obligation to communicate that fact clearly and unequivocally to every worker in question. Where workers provide only partial performance of the contract we are of the view that the employer should be required to pay for the value of any work done. It should not, however, be a matter for the employer unilaterally to determine what is the value of the work. We propose that in cases where an employer is entitled to make a deduction from wages (because of partial performance) it should be possible to do so only after the deduction has been authorised in advance by an appropriate public official, such as a Labour Inspector.

(c) Dismissal and Reinstatement

8.62 It follows from paragraph 8.31 above that as a general rule it should not be lawful to dismiss someone because he or she has taken part in a strike. Yet under the law as it presently stands a worker who is dismissed for taking part in a strike or other industrial action is unlikely to have a remedy for wrongful dismissal, and in only exceptional circumstances will a worker be able to bring an action for unfair dismissal. But although this lack of protection is unacceptable, the difficult question for consideration is what should replace the current law? Essentially there are three options for consideration. The first and arguably least radical option is simply to confer jurisdiction on the appropriate adjudicating agency to deal with the case in the same way as any other unfair dismissal case. The second option is to provide that the dismissal of strikers in some circumstances would be an automatically unfair dismissal. The third and most radical option is to provide that the dismissal of strikers would always be unfair regardless of the nature and circumstances of the dispute.

8.63   So far as the first option is concerned this would be achieved by repealing the current restriction in section 238 of the Trade Union and Labour Relations (Consolidation) Act 1992 which denies jurisdiction to the tribunals to deal with industrial action dismissals, a measure which is a legacy (though not in its current form) from the last Labour government. On this basis it would thus be possible to say that all industrial action dismissals could be challenged in the Labour Court (or whatever forum was thought suitable) in the ordinary way. The Court could be directed either by statute or a Code of Practice to have regard to a number of factors in determining whether or not the dismissal was fair, including (1) whether the strike or industrial action was in furtherance of the objectives in paragraph 8.34 above; (2) whether a ballot was held; (3) whether any collectively agreed procedures had been complied with; (4) whether the dismissal was for conduct other than the fact of going on strike; and (5) whether the complainant had been victimised. We regard this as the least that needs to be done.

8.64   So far as the second, and perhaps more radical option is concerned, on this basis it would be automatically unfair to dismiss a worker for taking part in industrial action which falls within the range of legality. In other cases it would be possible to challenge the fairness of the dismissal in the normal way. So it would be automatically unfair to dismiss someone taking part in a strike which was for a lawful purpose (as defined in paragraph 8.34 above) and supported by a ballot, should this be required (as provided in paragraphs 8.42-8.47 above). Where, however, there is no ballot (should this be required), as for example in the case of unofficial action, any subsequent dismissal would not be automatically unfair. Equally, however, any such dismissal would not be presumed to be fair, nor would the industrial tribunals be denied jurisdiction to deal with the case. These cases would be dealt with in the same way as cases would be dealt with under the first option.

8.65   So far as the third, and perhaps most radical option is concerned, this would be to say that it would always be unfair to dismiss someone because he or she has taken part in a strike or other industrial action, just in the same way as it is always unfair to dismiss someone on account of trade union membership. There is some merit in this option in the sense that there is a logical difficulty with both options one and two. Option one is not in our view consistent with any notion of a right to strike. There can be no right to strike, even within defined limits, if workers have no guaranteed protection against dismissal or victimisation. The first option leaves too much room for uncertainty and consequently the protection is much less secure than would be expected by the statutory recognition of a right to strike. It could also draw the adjudicating bodies into adjudicating on the merits of potentially all industrial disputes. Although it is true that this could happen to some extent under the second option where a ballot has not been held, there is much less scope for this than under the first option. Admittedly it is a matter of degree, but it is perhaps important to seek to minimise the need to entangle the courts in the relative merits of the claims and conduct of either side.

8.66 So far as option two is concerned the logical inconsistency relates to the fact that the duty to ballot proposed here is a domestic matter between the worker and his or her union. Why then should the rights of the worker in relation to his or her employer be made to depend on the performance of an obligation owed to the worker by a collateral party? The answer can only be by conceding that the employer has a legitimate interest in whether a ballot is held and in the way in which any ballot is conducted. This is because it would directly affect the employer's rights relating to dismissal, in the sense that it may be possible to dismiss if a ballot is not held, but it will not be possible to do so if one is held . In essence it would be to recognise that the ballot is not simply a matter between the union and its members, but is also a matter between the union and its members on the one hand and the employer on the other. This raises questions about whether the employer should therefore have the right to restrain unballoted industrial action, given that it will directly affect his or her liability in respect of dismissal. It also gives the employer a compelling claim to be provided with evidence that a ballot has been held and that the rules relating to the ballot have been complied with.

8.67 This is not to say that the third option is free from difficulty either. Some may see another logical inconsistency here: the right to engage in a strike or other industrial action would be wider than would be the right to engage in trade union activities. The latter are protected only if done at an appropriate time, which means a time outside working hours or a time during working hours with the consent of the employer. It would be absurd to suggest that a similar restraint should govern the right to strike, for obvious reasons. It may, however, be possible to say that the right to strike applies not at an appropriate time, but at any time except a time during which workers through their trade union have agreed not to take strike action, for example until prescribed procedures have been completed. It would be possible in these circumstances to say that dismissal for participation in a strike would be automatically unfair. But if so it ought to be possible for a dismissed worker to bring an action for unfair dismissal in the ordinary way in circumstances where industrial action has been called in breach of the agreed procedures.

8.68 In light of the foregoing, we propose that

(i)   Workers should be protected against dismissal for participation in a strike or industrial action.

(ii)   The protection should take one of three forms, as follows:
   (a) It should be possible for workers dismissed for participating in a strike or industrial action to challenge the fairness of that dismissal in the ordinary way in the appropriate forum;
   (b) It should be automatically unfair to dismiss a worker for participation in a strike or other industrial action falling with the margins of legality defined above. It should also be possible for workers dismissed for participating in a strike or industrial action falling outside the margins of legality defined above to challenge the fairness of the dismissal in the ordinary way in the appropriate forum;
   (c) It should be automatically unfair to dismiss a worker for participation in a strike or other industrial action.

(iii)   Workers should be entitled to be reinstated at the end of a dispute.

The Discipline and Expulsion of Members

8.69 Under the present law introduced in 1988, it is unlawful for a trade union to discipline or expel a member for non participation in a strike or industrial action. As we saw in paragraph 8.21 this measure has been challenged by the ILO Committee of Experts, on the ground that legislative incursion on trade autonomy must be limited, and that this particular measure denies trade unions the opportunity to give effect to their democratically determined rules. In our view it ought to be repealed. We propose that trade unions should be free to discipline and expel members in accordance with the rules of the union. The only requirement is that the disciplinary action should be conducted in accordance with powers laid down in the rule book and in accordance with the procedures in the rule book.

8.70 The only qualification to the our proposal in the foregoing paragraph relates to industrial action which falls outside the margin of legality discussed above. If, for example industrial action has been called or is being taken without the balloting rules being complied with (should a balloting requirement be retained), in our view no member of the union is or should be under any obligation to participate in that action, though he or she may wish to do so. Consequently we propose that a trade union member should have a right not to be disciplined or expelled from the union for failing to take part in industrial action which extends beyond the margins of legality. It would be a matter for each worker to decide whether or not to take part in such action. But a worker should be under no obligation to the union to do so and should not be disciplined or expelled for continuing to work, even if this means crossing picket lines.

8.71 The recommendation in the foregoing paragraph has implications for both unofficial and secondary action. As explained, in the case of the former an individual would be free to continue to work without the risk of expulsion from the union. The risk of divisions of this kind might thus place a premium on ensuring that all action is properly conducted by a ballot under the rules of the union. So far as secondary action is concerned, if the action has been supported by a ballot in circumstances where a ballot is required, those balloted would be under an obligation to the union to participate. But if the union merely requests its members to respect another picket line, its members would be free to do so, but they would be under no obligation to do so. If a member crossed a picket line in these circumstances he or she would not be liable to discipline or expulsion.

Trade Union Liability and the Protection of Funds

8.72 Turning from the question of individual liability in a strike to trade union liability, this too raises many thorny problems. But as a general principle it has to be accepted that there can be no meaningful right to strike vested in individual workers if the trade union organisation can be restrained from organising industrial action, or if its funds can be raided with impunity. So there is a need to protect from legal liability both the individual and the organisation of which he or she is a member, though it does not of course follow that the protection should be without boundaries. But we propose as a general principle that neither a trade union nor its officials should be liable for any acts done in the course of organising or participating in a strike or other industrial action within the margins of legality discussed above. Where, however, the action falls outside the scope of legality, we contemplate the possibility of legal action by an interested party to restrain the action in question.

8.73 Under the regime proposed here, however, the interested party will invariably be the trade union member. There is no common law liability to the employer, and the rights which are proposed to be created in terms of limitations on industrial action are rights of the members against the union. There is presumably no objection to legal proceedings against a union being instituted by its members (for example where there is a breach of the rules of the union). The more difficult question then relates to the remedies which might be secured. We recommend that all legal proceedings against trade unions should be commenced in the Labour Court which we propose in chapter 10, and that the Court would have no power to award common law remedies, though it would have the power to award statutory equivalent remedies. The Labour Court would thus have no power to issue injunctions or award damages, but it would have the power to issue restraining orders and to award compensation.

8.74 So far as restraining orders are concerned, we propose that it should not be possible for an applicant to obtain such relief on an ex parte basis. We also propose that the Court should have no power to issue interim orders (save in very exceptional circumstances) to restrain industrial action which would mean that an order could only be issued after a full trial of the issues. The Court would, of course, be empowered to give priority to certain cases over others and to move some cases to the top of its list. So far as compensation orders are concerned, we see no objection in principle to such orders being awarded against trade unions in favour of trade union members, but we would regard it as prudent to introduce the principle of limited liability, to depend on the number of members of the organisation in question.

8.75 The final questions for consideration here relate to the liability of a union for contempt of court in the event of any court order being breached. Given that this would be a new jurisdiction it does not follow that breach of such an order would attract the normal contempt liability. But we might want to anticipate the possibility of court orders being ignored, though it would be wrong to exaggerate this problem given that on the basis of the foregoing proposals these ought not to be major problems, as there is little room for employers to draw trade unions into court in the first place (though there could be at least contrived uncertainty). The issue is a tricky one. On the one hand we accept that the deliberate flouting of court orders should not go unpunished. But on the other hand it is difficult to argue that trade union members as a whole should be penalised because of the actions of their officials, yet difficult also to argue that trade union officials should be penalised for carrying out the wishes of their members.

8.76 This suggests then that there is no case for heavy financial penalties to be imposed on a union, or personal liability for trade union officials. The answer may lie in a *via media* which marks the union's failure but in a way which rejects the use of coercive or punitive sanctions. In practice, however, it may be that this is unlikely to be a serious problem. There is little evidence of court orders being disobeyed before 1980 (with the exception of the period under the Industrial Relations Act 1971). There is no reason to believe that trade unions would fail to obey the orders of the proposed Labour Court. It is for consideration whether there should be a reserve power to invoke contempt proceedings in exceptional cases, as we also propose in chapter 7 above, to introduce powers to permit proceedings to be brought for contempt against employers in exceptional cases for failure to comply with the duty to establish machinery for trade union recognition. If this exceptional power were to be adopted, there would have to be a carefully structured framework for the imposition of fines, based not only on the size of the union, but also the number of people involved in the action in question. It should not, however, be possible to sequestrate all the assets of the offending trade union.

Conclusion

8.77 By way of conclusion we are proposing a major refocusing of the law relating to industrial action. In essence what is contemplated here is nothing less than a complete break with the past in terms of the approach to protection, and a complete break with the last 16 years in terms of the content of the legislation. We propose that all common law liabilities should be abolished, and that the Conservative employment laws should be repealed, and not retained in whole or in part. We propose that workers and their trade unions should have a legally guaranteed right to strike which means essentially protection against dismissal on the one hand and protection against injunctions and damages on the other. We accept that there may be a case for some regulation of the circumstances in which the right to strike may be exercised and, although the arguments are finely balanced, accept in particular that there may be a case for the pre strike ballots, enforceable at the suit of the membership of the union.

8.78 In proposing the introduction of a more principled and rational approach to the question of industrial action we are mindful of the difficulties under which strikers would continue to labour. Those engaged in strike action would be under tremendous economic pressure due to the likely reduction of income during the period of the dispute. We are mindful also of the need for good procedures and a strong public agency in the shape of ACAS to both help prevent industrial action happening in the first place and to help engineer an effective and mutually agreeable resolution of the dispute when it does. We are firmly of the view, however, that the workplace should be governed on the basis of consensus and goodwill. Workers should not be coerced or intimidated by the law to accept intolerable working conditions or intolerable working practices. We need also to reflect hard on the fact that the economic circumstances which made the strike weapon a potent force in the past are not the economic circumstances of today in the context of which it is particularly appropriate to take steps to remove the chains which fetter the collective strength of working people.

Summary of Recommendations

1   The current legislation relating to trade disputes should be repealed and replaced with a fair and balanced framework of law.

2   The ILO standards should form the basis of future legislation on the right to strike.

3   Workers should have a right to strike and to engage in other forms of industrial action recognised and protected by law, within defined limits if appropriate.

4   Workers who exercise the right to strike (1) should not be regarded as having acted in breach of the employment relationship; (2) should be protected from dismissal; and (3) those who organise industrial action should not be liable to the employer in tort or on any other ground.

5   Workers should be free to take industrial action to promote their occupational, social or economic interests.

6   Workers should be free to take international solidarity action.

7 Trade unions and employers should continue to seek the resolution of their differences by methods other than industrial action. Measures such as those currently contained in the Trade Union and Labour Relations (Consolidation) Act 1992, section 179 should be retained.

6 Trade unions should be free to take industrial action in accordance with their rules and procedures, including pre-strike ballots in appropriate cases.

7 A ballot should not be required by law before industrial action in response to the victimisation of a trade union official, a unilateral variation of working conditions by the employer, or the refusal to cross a picket line.

8 Workers should be free in combination with others to take secondary action in support of other workers engaged in a dispute, and they should be free to do so in line with ILO standards.

9 Workers should be free in the course of a dispute to picket peacefully outside a place of work.

10 Workers should be protected against dismissal for participation in a strike or industrial action. Workers should be entitled to be reinstated at the end of a dispute.

11 Workers should be protected against dismissal for refusing to cross a picket line.

12 Trade unions should be free to discipline and expel members in accordance with the rules of the union. The disciplinary action should be conducted in accordance with powers laid down in the rule book and in accordance with the procedures in the rule book.

13 Neither a trade union nor its officials should be liable for any acts done in the course of organising or participating in a strike or other industrial action within the margins of legality discussed above.

14 All legal proceedings against trade unions should be commenced in the proposed Labour Court, which should have no power to award common law remedies, though it would have the power to award equivalent remedies.

15 It should not be possible for an applicant to obtain relief in the proposed Labour Court on an ex parte basis. The proposed Labour Court should have no power to issue interim orders to restrain industrial action (save in very exceptional circumstances).

JOB SECURITY AND
UNFAIR DISMISSAL

9.1   Legislation giving many employees a right not to be unfairly dismissed was enacted in the Industrial Relations Act 1971. This statutory right supplemented a common law right to claim wrongful dismissal for breach of contract which had become discredited, failing to provide workers with any substantial measure of protection. In some respects, such as the use of industrial tribunals for adjudication, this new right built upon earlier measures creating statutory rights to a minimum notice period and a redundancy payment. Despite many alterations in the detail of this legislation, the principle of a legal right not to be unfairly dismissed has persisted during a quarter of a century of rapid shifts in government policy regarding industrial relations and labour markets generally. The current law is now contained in Parts X and XI of the Employment Rights Act 1996, though amended in a number of significant respects.

9.2   Under the legislation employees who satisfy a qualifying period of employment may have a right to a redundancy payment and a right to claim unfair dismissal before an industrial tribunal. In response to a claim for unfair dismissal the employer is required to demonstrate the principal reason for dismissal, and to demonstrate also that it constitutes a substantial reason, such as the misconduct or lack of capability of the employee. The industrial tribunal is then charged with the task of determining whether a dismissal for that reason was 'reasonable' in all the circumstances. If the industrial tribunal finds for the employee, then it may either order reinstatement or re-engagement, or may order the employer to pay compensation. Where the reason for dismissal was plant closure or a reduction of the employer's requirements for employees to do work of a particular kind, then this constitutes a redundancy dismissal, for which the employer must pay compensation calculated by reference to the length of service of the employee. A redundancy dismissal may also be unfair, in which case the employee may be awarded compensation for unfair dismissal, or exceptionally reinstatement.

9.3   In many respects this legislation has proved successful. The risk of claims for unfair dismissal has compelled employers to adopt more careful investigations and fairer procedures prior to the termination of employment. This has reduced, though not eliminated entirely, the number of arbitrary or unjustified dismissals. Nevertheless, the legislation has been subjected to persistent criticisms, the more substantial of which include:

* The Industrial Tribunals permit many harsh dismissals to be regarded as fair due to their interpretation of the standard of 'reasonableness'
* The Industrial Tribunals rarely order reinstatement in successful claims for unfair dismissal
* The Industrial Tribunal system, despite its relative informality, can prove to be slow and expensive for litigants

9.4   Other criticisms relate to the remedies and in particular to the fact that the measure of compensation has slowly been eroded by inflation so that it fails to compensate adequately, and presents a reduced deterrent to employers. These concerns have been fuelled by recent statutory amendments which, though leaving the underlying principles of the legislation intact, have subtly eroded the impact of the law. For instance, the gradual extension of the qualifying period to claim unfair dismissal from six months to two years removed a substantial proportion of the workforce from coverage, though the two year qualifying period is subject to judicial review at the time of writing. Changes to the legislation also increased the opportunities for employers to insist that employees should agree to enter a contract which excluded their rights. The effect of such amendments has been to turn a universal right of employees into a privilege enjoyed only by some.

The Need for Legislation

9.5   In the light of these criticisms it is important to reassert the fundamental principles which justify the existence of a universal right of workers to be protected against unfair dismissal. All Member States of the European Union provide statutory protection against unfair dismissal, protection which has existed in some countries since 1919. Nevertheless, doubts continue to be expressed, especially in North America, about the justification for enacting a universal right for employees against unfair dismissal. On close inspection, however, both moral and economic arguments tend to support the case for some form of legal protection.

(a) Arguments for Protection

9.6   From a moral point of view, arbitrary and peremptory treatment of workers by an employer reveals a failure by the employer to treat workers with dignity and respect. Moreover, it becomes very difficult for workers to integrate work into a worthwhile set of plans for developing their own lives, if employers insist upon treating them as simply another commodity, to be bought and sold at will, without any regard for the interest of job security as part of a stable framework in which individuals can develop their lives. Given that the economic and social blow of losing a good job can easily be greater than unfair conduct by the State towards individuals, this vital interest should be regarded as equivalent to the rights of citizenship, in the securing and protection of which the State has a clear and compelling interest. It does not follow of course that this interest needs to be met by legislation if other methods of regulation, such as self-regulation or indeed the common law, can perform the task just as effectively.

9.7   From an economic perspective, it is arguable that employers can obtain the best commitment and co-operation from the workforce, if employers honour an implicit contract of rewarding hard work and loyalty to the firm by providing job security and worthwhile career avenues. It is possible to regard workers as stakeholders in a firm (in a politically neutral sense of that term), even if they do not own shares, for they make an investment in acquiring the firm-specific skills required to perform the tasks demanded by the employer, and on dismissal this investment may be lost if the skills are not transferable to another employer. At the same time, it should be recognised that employers need to have the managerial power to make adjustments in the workforce for the sake of improving efficiency and responding to alterations in the market for its products. But this power need not be an arbitrary power and can be used effectively whilst being constrained by fair procedures and accepted standards of reasonable behaviour.

(b) The Role of Legislation

9.8   These arguments support the need for protection of workers against unfair dismissal. But is there a need for this protection to be enacted in a statutory framework? Workers may benefit from equivalent protection to that afforded by statute as part of the internal rules of their employer's organisation. These organisational rules in turn may have been developed through collective bargaining between trade unions and employers. Yet whilst these contractual practices are to be encouraged, legislation remains essential. Statutory protection is needed in the first place for that large sector of the workforce which does not benefit from such private rules, where for example there may not be a significant trade union presence. Secondly, the common law has been clearly shown to be incapable of securing the enforcement of these private rules. Indeed even where workers do have contractual rights to protect them from arbitrary discharge, the courts have been reluctant to grant effective remedies to protect and enforce these rights. Thirdly, it is in any event clear that the presence of legislation establishing a minimum standard also serves to encourage employers and unions to develop fair internal disciplinary procedures for the firm.

9.9   Yet although there is thus a powerful case for protection from unfair dismissal and a strong case for legislation to provide that protection, we are nevertheless mindful that employers routinely complain that the law of unfair dismissal prevents any dismissals, even of those employees who are seriously damaging the business. We are also mindful of the argument that legislation of this kind imposes a cost on business, which reduces levels of employment in the economy and harms competitiveness. But there is no evidence to support these contentions. The legislation certainly encourages employers to be more careful in recruiting employees, but careful selection should improve productivity rather than prove a cost to employers. Employers will also be encouraged to train their workforce in order to cope with technological change, which is also a cost, but one which employers should be expected to share with the community as a whole.

(c) Guiding Considerations

9.10   Having established the need for legislation creating a general right to protection against unfair dismissal, the precise shape of any enactment will be guided by a number of further considerations. In the first place a major objective is to ensure compliance with relevant international standards, including those of the European Union and the International Labour Organisation, and protection of the basic rights and civil liberties of workers. So far as the former is concerned, the most significant of these for present purposes is ILO Convention 158 (the Termination of Employment Convention, 1982). So far as the latter is concerned, it is true that opinions will differ in some instances as to whether or not a dismissal was fair. However, the legislation should make it absolutely clear that dismissal on grounds which involve the violation of the basic rights of individuals will be automatically unfair and carry a heavy sanction.

9.11 A second objective, and perhaps the most important objective, is to reduce the number of dismissals to the minimum number compatible with the preservation of an efficient and competitive economy. Clearly it is not proposed that dismissals should be prevented altogether (for obvious reasons relating to the needs of the enterprise and indeed of other workers), but it is suggested that effective steps should be taken to deter dismissals unless the employer has a relevant and substantial reason. This policy supports measures designed to forestall dismissal decisions by employers, in order to prevent unjustifiable dismissals from occurring at all. It also leads inexorably to the conclusion that the legal rights required to protect individuals against unfair dismissal should in principle be inalienable, so that employers cannot purchase the right to dismiss unfairly. Although this policy does not rule out the possibility of settlements of claims, it does suggest that compensation agreements should be voluntary and objectively fair to the worker.

9.12 A third objective is what might be referred to as self regulation, that is to say to encourage employers to adopt fair internal rules for handling issues connected to the termination of employment. Where such rules exist they are likely to be followed by employers without the need for routine legal intervention. Provided that the rules are fair to workers, the general objective of the legislation will be obtained. What the law must seek to do is to induce employers to introduce rational procedures for making termination decisions, and to encourage mechanisms which are likely to ensure that these rules embrace fair substantive standards. These objectives can be achieved by a variety of techniques including the involvement of worker representation and education from official codes of practice. They can also be achieved in a way which supports other goals including in particular the greater involvement of trade unions in developing fair procedures at the workplace Perhaps the surest way to obtain fair internal rules of organisations is to have them produced as a result of discussion and negotiation with the workforce itself.

Institutions and Processes

9.13 These guiding considerations can only be implemented by substantial amendment of the current legislation. They suggest alterations both to the current substantive standards governing the determination of the unfairness of dismissals and to the procedures under which the right can be asserted. We examine first the types of institutions and processes required. Under the current law, employees who have been dismissed normally only have the option of bringing a claim for unfair dismissal before an industrial tribunal. Having submitted the claim, an ACAS conciliator will approach the parties with a view to achieving a settlement, a procedure which often results in a financial settlement precluding any further litigation. If no settlement can be reached, then the industrial tribunal may be called upon to determine the merits of the case, and if it upholds the claim for unfair dismissal it will normally award compensation to the dismissed employee.

(a) Conciliation.

9.14   At the present time the system of conciliation is aimed at avoiding a tribunal hearing by achieving a financial settlement. This is unsatisfactory in two respects. In the first place, the conciliation process commences too late to prevent dismissals from taking place, and secondly there is no protection for employees to ensure that the outcome of any settlement reflects the objective merits of the claim. In order to reduce unnecessary dismissals, a procedure is required which either compels or provides strong incentives for employers to investigate the facts of the matter prior to making a dismissal. In our view, an employer should be required to go through a conciliation process prior to making a dismissal. The conciliator would provide the employer with a certificate that conciliation had been attempted. Failure by the employer to comply with this obligation would result in the dismissal being legally ineffective, with the result that full wages would continue to be payable, and with the result also that the employer would be required to continue to provide work for the worker in question.

9.15   If the conciliation process leads to a proposed settlement of the dispute, other than full reinstatement, then it is important that the settlement is objectively fair to the worker in the light of the merits of the claim. Under the present arrangements, conciliators do not wish to intervene for this purpose, since this compromises their neutrality, which is perceived as important for the purpose of bringing the parties together. This creates the risk that dismissed employees may agree to unfavourable settlements due to the absence of legal advice. Employers will be reluctant to agree any settlement, however, unless they can be assured of the finality of the process. If, however, our proposal to make conciliation compulsory for employers prior to dismissal is accepted, the parties will have an incentive to negotiate with the help of the conciliator, so that the role of the conciliator can be altered in order to introduce a requirement that the conciliator ensures that any agreed settlement reflects the merits of the claim. We propose that any conciliated settlement can only achieve finality of the process if the conciliator not only certifies that an agreement has been reached but that also in the opinion of the conciliator the outcome of the settlement is reasonable in view of all the circumstances of the case.

(b) Arbitration

9.16   The use of alternative means of adjudication to courts and tribunals is attractive for two principal reasons. In the first place, there is a reasonable prospect that a form of private arbitration will prove more expeditious and less expensive, while secondly comparative evidence suggests that there is a greater chance that successful claimants will secure reinstatement. Nevertheless, there is a danger that private arbitration could operate unfairly for individual workers if it is primarily organised and paid for by the employer. This danger can be met by a requirement that private arbitration can only be an alternative to adjudication by courts and tribunals if the arbitration process has been established as part of a collective agreement with an independent trade union. The arbitration process could be unique to a single firm, or be applicable to a specific sector and include a number of employers. Arbitration would only be attractive to employers, however, if it could be quicker, cheaper, and promised a degree of finality. It would be unattractive if was simply another layer of litigation.

9.17   Arbitration could be attractive to the workforce if it was quicker, cheaper, and the arbitrator had their respect, and provided also that the outcomes were equivalent to those produced by courts and tribunals. The use of arbitration should also be used as a way of promoting collective bargaining over procedures and substantive disciplinary rules, if the arbitrator were normally bound to observe these rules. Trade unions could therefore find arbitration attractive for the purpose of securing greater control over the processes for handling disputes concerning grievances and managerial disciplinary decisions. Their participation in the process, however, would be influenced by their perceptions of the broader interests of the workforce as a whole. In our view, the private arbitration of disputes could provide an alternative to a formal legal claim where the arbitration process has been agreed between the employer and independent trade unions, either at sectoral or enterprise level. It should be open to a sectoral employment commission, as proposed in chapter 3 above, to conclude an arbitration agreement of this kind.

9.18 Any arbitration agreement of this kind should comply with certain minimum standards: it should provide for the identification and payment of the arbitrator, the procedure to be adopted, the criteria to be used in determining the fairness of dismissals, and the remedies available to the arbitrator. If such a private arbitration process were accepted, it would be necessary to specify its relation to the legal system. To achieve the desirable level of finality, the arbitration award would have to be immune from challenge except on the ground of illegality or procedural impropriety. It would also be necessary to provide an adequate legal method of enforcement of arbitration awards in the event that employer failed to comply with the award. There would, moreover, need to be a jurisdiction based in a court or tribunal to review awards on the grounds referred to above. We are also concerned, however, that arbitration should be voluntary on the part of individual workers who should have the right to choose the resolution of their dispute under an arbitration procedure or by adjudication.

(c) Adjudication

9.19 The need for State adjudication machinery remains necessary for the purpose of dealing with disputes about unfair dismissal. Indeed although we propose that arbitration should be available in principle, in practice we are of the view that most dismissed workers would continue to seek the resolution of their dispute by way of adjudication. As a result we are also of the view that the adjudication procedures should be adapted and be made more flexible. It does not follow in our view that all unfair dismissal disputes should be resolved (even by adjudication) in the same way, and in chapter 10 we explore the possibility of a more subtle system for the resolution of disputes in the employment sphere generally. This includes the creation of a new body of officers, Labour Adjudicators which together with the proposed tripartite Labour Court would have responsibility for hearing complaints of various kinds. We anticipate that both fora would have a role to play in unfair dismissal cases and that former would be particularly important in what we refer to below as disciplinary dismissals.

9.20 We also anticipate the creation of a Labour Inspectorate which in the specific context of unfair dismissal could perform a useful service in pre-empting disputes over dismissal, and more generally to offer guidance to employers in establishing disciplinary and grievance procedures. In order to reduce the number of dismissals, it is desirable that employers should operate fair procedures prior to termination of employment. We propose that Labour Inspectors should be empowered to certify that an employer's disciplinary procedure meets the standard of fairness and effectiveness required by the law. Such a certificate, if awarded, would prevent workers from bringing claims against the employer that the procedures were inadequate or unfair, unless the worker could demonstrate that the procedure had not been followed in a particular case.

9.21   The validation of procedures by the Labour Inspectorate would complement the present practice of using Codes of Practice to guide employers particularly in the case of disciplinary procedures.   These Codes would be particularly important for employers whose procedures had not been validated in the way we propose. Indeed we regard the continued operation of Codes of Practice in this area to be generally useful and therefore propose that there should be a multiplication of such guidance. Codes provide information about the necessary standards to be adopted in the context of termination of employment. We also propose the development of Codes of Practice not only in relation to procedural matters, but also for dealing with substantive issues (such as advice to employers on how to handle problems of long-term illness or suspected dishonesty) reasonably and fairly.

The Scope of the Legislation: Threshold Questions

9.22   Under the present law a worker who wishes to bring a claim for unfair dismissal must first cross a number of hurdles before the industrial tribunal can deal with the fairness or unfairness of the dismissal. If the claimant fails to do so the matter will be lost and the question of substance never resolved. The first of these questions is whether the claimant is an employee (that is to say whether he or she works under a contract of service) and whether he or she satisfies all of the many qualifying conditions imposed by the legislation, among the most notable of which is the requirement that he or she should have been continuously employed by the employer for at least two years. If the claimant negotiates this hurdle, he or she may stumble and fall at a second which is the requirement that he or she should have been 'dismissed'. Although the concept of dismissal is fairly widely defined in the legislation it is clear that it does not cover all the circumstances in which the contract of employment may be terminated other than voluntarily.

(a) 'Workers' and 'Employees'

9.23 In line with our recommendations in chapter 2 above we propose that the legislation should apply not only to employees, as presently narrowly defined, but to anyone engaged in an employment relationship, as that term is defined in chapter 2, failing which the legislation should apply to a wider category of 'employees' and 'workers', in the manner which we also discuss in chapter 2. We also propose in this context (although there is no reason in principle why the proposal should not apply more widely) that there should be a presumption that workers performing a service for another should be regarded as covered by the legislation. It would be possible for an employer to rebut the presumption by showing that the 'worker' in fact constitutes an independent business or an independent professional consultant, along the lines also discussed in chapter 2.

9.24 The decision to terminate employment is not always made by the person who is the other party to the contract of employment. In the case of agency workers, for instance, the employment may be terminated by the client of the agency who has no contractual relationship with the person providing the service. Similarly, in groups of companies, the decision to terminate the employment may be made in head office, though the contract of employment may be with a subsidiary company. In our view the identity of the employer should be determined by reference to the location of the decision to terminate the employment relationship. The effect of such a proposal will be to permit an investigation of the fairness of the decision to terminate employment no matter what the precise employment nexus may be between the parties. The employer may have the power to join other employers to the action in order to contest the location of the decision.

(b) Universality and the Question of Flexibility

9.25 Apart from the current restriction imposed by the requirement that an applicant must be an 'employee', UK law has always included certain restrictions on which employees are entitled to protection from unfair dismissal based upon such criteria as length of service, hours of work, and the nature of the employer. In our view such restrictions lack justification, for if the legislation is based upon both moral and economic considerations, then to deny the rights to a significant section of the working population appears both unjust and inefficient. Even worse, the exclusions are often discriminatory in their impact on women, for which reason they may be invalidated by EC law, as has already happened to the exclusion of part-time workers. In our view, there is no adequate justification for denying the universal application of the right not to be dismissed unfairly. We propose that there should be no restrictions on the universality of the right to claim unfair dismissal.

9.26 It does not follow from the foregoing that the right not to be unfairly dismissed should be universal in its application that there should be no scope for the flexible application of the law to reflect different working arrangements or the different needs of different employers, including small employers. Thus it would be perfectly possible to recognise that the test of fairness contains a degree of flexibility so that it can reflect all the circumstances of the case, and that this is a better way of proceeding than excluding workers from the protection of the law altogether. The test of fairness should recognise the relevance of the resources of the employer (as at present), in order to make some allowance for small employers in coping with the requirements of the law. Similarly, the test of fairness should recognise that it may be more reasonable for employers to terminate employment at the end of a probationary period if, despite adequate training, the worker is unable to perform the job required satisfactorily. And we have already indicated in chapter 2 how the legislation could be used to cope with flexibility with casual working practices.

(c) Termination of Employment

9.27 Under the current legislation, an employee who meets the various qualifying conditions may encounter a second problem which will prevent the industrial tribunal considering the fairness or unfairness of the dismissal. This is the requirement that he or she should have been dismissed, at first sight a perfectly straightforward and obvious requirement, but one which in practice it may be difficult in some circumstances to satisfy. It might be argued by the employer that the claimant left voluntarily (perhaps as a result of unreasonable though not repudiatory conduct by the employer), or it might be argued by the employer that the contract had been terminated by frustration, in the case for example of someone with long term illness. Although it is usually clear that an employee has been dismissed, this issue has given rise to considerable technicality in the law, which in some cases, presents a substantial obstacle to employees who have to prove that they have been dismissed.

9.28 In order to avoid most technical disputes about whether or not there has been a dismissal, we propose that the legislation should provide that whenever the employment relationship has terminated, the worker can bring a claim against the employer, unless the employer can demonstrate that the worker left voluntarily. This reverses the burden of proof, but raises the question of how the employer can satisfy this burden. A document signed by a worker that he or she has left voluntarily and accepts that he or she has consequently no right to claim remedies for unfair dismissal should normally suffice to satisfy the employer's burden of proof, unless the worker asserts that the signature was obtained by pressure or misrepresentation. In other cases it would be open to the employer to seek to convince the appropriate adjudicator that the worker in question voluntarily left the employment and that he or she had no just cause for doing so.

Procedures for Dismissals

9.29   As an important ingredient of the guiding consideration of minimizing dismissals, close attention has to be paid to the procedures which an employer will be required to follow in order to terminate employment. The objective here is prevention rather than cure, to establish procedures which are designed to prevent unfair dismissals rather than to compensate the worker when they take place. This consideration also influences the avenues through which the worker may pursue a claim, though here other factors designed to ensure the integrity of the process have an important bearing on the selection of the procedure adopted.

(a) Conciliation
9.30   We have already proposed that a conciliation stage should be introduced prior to every termination of employment. When contemplating a dismissal, the employer would be required to contact a conciliator, and would not be permitted to dismiss until a serious attempt at conciliation has been made and the conciliator certified that this has taken place. As already proposed, failure to obtain such a certificate prior to making a dismissal should render the purported dismissal ineffective, with the consequence that wages would continue to be payable. The employer would, however, be empowered to suspend the worker from performance or attendance at work pending the outcome of the conciliation process.

(b) The Reason for Dismissal
9.31   In order to determine the fairness of any dismissal, it is vital that the worker and any adjudicator should have access to a clearly stated reason for the dismissal, for without such a statement it becomes impossible to challenge the fairness of the decision. In

addition, by compelling employers to state the reason for dismissal in a formal manner, it is likely that they will give more careful consideration to the question whether or not the reason is sufficient and well-founded in fact, which may avoid some unfair terminations of employment. Following the conciliation process, if the employer decides to make the dismissal, we propose that the employer must give every dismissed worker a written statement of the reason or reasons for dismissal. The employer will be required also to state whether or not the reason for the dismissal is economic (redundancy).

(c) Categories of Dismissal

9.32 If the dismissal takes place despite these safeguards, we propose that the worker should be able to seek redress either before the Labour Adjudicator or in the Labour Court (on which see paragraph 9.19 above). Under the current law, the employee brings a claim before an industrial tribunal. Our proposals suggest that different procedures may be applicable in different types of case. These differences in procedure are desirable in order to ensure that the issues raised by the dismissal are addressed promptly, fairly, and efficiently. It is helpful for this purpose to divide the types of dismissal into three broad categories:

* **Public Rights Dismissals**. If the reason for the dismissal, or more likely if the worker thinks that the real reason for the dismissal, raises an issue of basic rights (an inadmissible reason), then the worker will bring the case straight before the Labour Court.
* **Economic Dismissals**. If the reason for dismissal is economic (redundancy), then a court or tribunal is not necessarily the best forum to consider some of the issues raised. In particular, the court or tribunal will encounter difficulty in assessing whether or not the economic dismissal was necessary on financial or business grounds for the employer. We propose that the worker should be able to refer the case to a Labour Inspector to examine its economic justification, in addition to a claim to a Labour Adjudicator or Labour Court for compensation.
* **Disciplinary Dismissals**. This is the residual (though potentially large) category, which would include dismissals on the ground of misconduct or incapacity, and where the procedure would normally be a hearing before a Labour Adjudicator if there is no applicable private arbitration agreement in accordance with our earlier proposals.

Public Rights Dismissals

9.33   One of the guiding considerations is to ensure that the basic rights of citizenship are respected in the workplace. The law should provide mechanisms for a decisive vindication of these rights and a substantial deterrence against violations. We propose that where the reason, the principal reason, or a subsidiary reason for dismissal involves the employer denying a worker certain basic rights at work, then the dismissal will be for an inadmissible reason and automatically unfair. We also propose that there should be an extensive list of inadmissible reasons, reflecting fully the demands of both international law on the one hand and EC law on the other.

(a) Inadmissible Reasons

9.34   In our view the category of inadmissible reasons should include:

* *sex discrimination*: dismissal on grounds of sex, marital or family status;
* *race discrimination*: dismissal on grounds of colour, race, nationality or ethnic or national origins;
* *pregnancy discrimination*: dismissal on ground of pregnancy
* *age discrimination*: dismissal on the ground that a person has reached a certain age, without regard to the worker's competence to perform the job or alternative available work;
* *disability discrimination*: dismissal on the ground that a person has a disability, without regard to the worker's competence to perform the job or alternative available work;
* *union membership discrimination*: dismissal on the ground that the worker is, or proposes to be, a member of an independent trade union, or that the worker has or is proposing to take part in the activities of an independent trade union;
* *trade union representation:* dismissal of a worker where the worker has been denied the right to be represented by a trade union official;
* *sexual orientation discrimination*: dismissal on the ground of the worker's sexual orientation;
* *family life*: dismissal where the alleged reason for alleged misconduct (such as absence from work) was the performance of an urgent and compelling family responsibility (such as a death of a close relative, or the sickness of a dependant);

* *freedom of speech*: dismissal for statements made by a worker, either orally or in writing, which are either unrelated to the employer's business, or if related to the business, then address a matter of public interest, as proposed in chapter 4;
* *exercise of legal rights*: dismissal on the ground of the worker exercising or seeking to exercise any statutory rights;
* *protection of legal rights*: dismissal on the ground that the worker refused to accept an unauthorised variation of working conditions;
* *political discrimination*: dismissal on the ground of the worker's political beliefs or membership of a political party or organisation;
* *religious discrimination*: dismissal on the ground of the worker's religious belief or that the worker is a member of a religious group, organisation, or church.

The precise details and qualifications of this list of inadmissible reasons would need to be elaborated further, with reference in particular to proposals made elsewhere in this report.

(b) Remedies

9.35   The primary objective of the remedies is to seek to prevent dismissals for inadmissible reasons altogether. Since employers are unlikely to admit the presence of inadmissible reasons, the burden of proof placed upon the worker should not be set too high, and there should be strong requirements of disclosure placed on the employer. One way in which to vindicate and protect rights is to provide an expedited procedure to secure reinstatement until the dispute is resolved. This is particularly important in the case of trade union membership, but we suggest that it should be extended to all instances of alleged dismissal for an 'inadmissible reason'. We therefore propose that pending the outcome of the hearing of the Labour Court on a case involving allegations of an 'inadmissible reason', the worker may apply to the Labour Court for a temporary reinstatement order, which should be granted whenever possible.

9.36   Where the Labour Court finds that a dismissal was for an inadmissible reason, we propose that it should be empowered to order either reinstatement or punitive damages after considering any representations from the parties. Reinstatement may be regarded as the primary remedy, though workers may not wish to pursue that remedy in the circumstances. The measure of punitive damages would be set at a significantly greater level than mere compensation for loss, with a minimum but no maximum. It should contain a substantial element to reflect the injury to dignity inflicted by the dismissal. The fear of victimisation may, however, deter claimants from seeking reinstatement as a remedy. Consequently we propose that in cases where reinstatement is ordered by an Labour Court, then any dismissal during a period of one year from the date of the order would have to be approved in advance by the Labour Court.

Economic Dismissals

9.37   Where the employer's reason for the dismissal is connected primarily to business considerations such as financial exigency, alterations in product demand, or changes in labour use required by the introduction of new technology, then the employer should be required to state this as the written reason for dismissal. The general objectives of the law in these circumstances should be to ensure that individual workers are treated fairly and to minimise the social cost of economic dismissals (which in some instances might permit a challenge to the dismissal itself). Economic dismissals cannot be regarded simply as a private decision of an employer, since they have such serious social and economic effects. Yet it must be recognised that some economic dismissals, though regrettable, are inevitable due to insolvency or new technologies.

(a) Justification
9.38   We propose that a procedure be introduced to require the employer to justify the need to make economic dismissals to a Labour Inspector. Thus if a worker believes that the economic dismissal is unnecessary, he or she should be able to challenge the managerial decision within a short space of time in order to test its plausibility. The worker could bring the case before the Labour Court or a Labour Adjudicator as a claim for unfair dismissal, requesting that the procedure for justification be followed. If satisfied that there may be a prima facie case, the Labour Court or Labour Adjudicator would refer the issue of justification to an expert drawn from the Labour Inspectorate. The employer would be required to explain to a Labour Inspector the reasons for the economic dismissals, and unless the inspector is satisfied that substantial reasons exist, the dismissal would be unfair. In determining whether there was adequate justification, the Labour Inspector would be directed to have regard to any consultation which took place before the dismissal. If the employer chooses not

to respond to the Labour Inspector's demand for justification, the dismissal would be automatically unfair.

(b) Consultation Procedure

9.39 An important objective is to require employers to adopt a fair procedure for consultation with the workforce and individual workers prior to the decision to make dismissals for economic reasons. The reasons for requiring such a procedure extend beyond the requirement to treat workers with respect, for the consultation process may suggest ways in which to minimise the number of dismissals by techniques such as training and job mobility. In principle, such a procedure for consultation should be established in advance of the problem arising. An essential element of such a procedure would be a duty to consult trade union or workers' representatives, in accordance with the principles in chapter 7. We propose that it should be open to a trade union or a worker to seek an order of the Labour Court to restrain an economic dismissal unless and until it is conducted according to either a consultation procedure agreed with the relevant recognised trade union, failing which a procedure approved by a Labour Inspector in accordance with guidelines laid down in a Code of Practice. We also propose that a dismissal in breach of any procedural obligations of the employer would be regarded as being automatically unfair, with workers entitled alternatively to seek reinstatement or compensation in accordance with the principles in paragraph 9.46 below.

(c) Remedies for Individual Workers

9.40 Under the present law, an employee dismissed for an economic reason may be awarded a redundancy payment. The level of this payment is fixed by reference to the length of service and rate of pay of the dismissed worker. We propose that redundancy payments should be retained in order to provide some assistance to workers faced with the economic dislocation of unemployment. The payments should not, however, disentitle the recipient from benefits under the social security system. In addition to a redundancy payment in some instances a more generous measure of compensation should be awarded in order to reflect the unfairness of the dismissal. We propose that the worker should be entitled to challenge the fairness of the dismissal on the ground not only that the redundancy procedures were not followed, but also that he or she was unfairly selected for dismissal compared to other workers. In the latter case the employer would be required to demonstrate that an objective and fair process of selection for dismissal was used, failing which the dismissal would be unfair and the worker entitled to reinstatement or compensation in accordance with the principles in paragraph 9.46 below. Some, though not all, of these cases will fall into the category of public rights dismissals and would therefore be automatically unfair.

Disciplinary Dismissals

9.41 If a dismissal is not otherwise dealt with as a public rights dismissal or an economic dismissal, it should be open to a worker to seek a remedy through either a private arbitration system, as described above, or through a Labour Adjudicator. Our proposals largely imitate the current law, but we suggest a number of detailed amendments.

(a) Unfair Procedure

9.42 The current law regarding the requirement that the employer should follow a fair procedure prior to dismissal is unsatisfactory for both employers and employees. The law requires the employer to follow a reasonable procedure, and although guidance is provided by a Code of Practice, the employer cannot be sure that any particular procedure will be regarded by a tribunal as fair. From the perspective of the employee the law is also unsatisfactory, since the requirement of a reasonable procedure can be interpreted by some tribunals and courts to require little or no procedure at all in the particular circumstances of the case. We think that the right to a fair procedure is an elementary requirement if workers are to be treated with dignity and respect. We therefore propose that the obligation to follow a fair procedure prior to dismissal should be mandatory.

9.43 In our view the legislation should state explicitly that failure to follow a fair procedure should result in an unfair dismissal, notwithstanding the possibility that a different procedure would not have affected the fairness or reasonableness of the decision. In order to assist employers in satisfying this requirement, we propose that if employers conform either to a collectively agreed disputes procedure which sets out requirements for a fair procedure, or to a procedure approved by a Labour Inspector guided by a Code of Practice, then the procedure should be regarded by a Labour Adjudicator as fair. In the absence of either of these settled procedures, then the employer would be advised to follow the Code of Practice, which will be used by Labour Adjudicators as a definitive guide to fairness. This gives employers an incentive either to agree the procedure with the relevant recognised trade union or to contact the Labour Inspector for approval in order to avoid the risk of disputes and litigation over the content of the procedures resulting in successful claims for unfair dismissal.

(b) The General Test of Fairness

9.44   It is, of course, difficult to provide a general test for the determination of the substantive merits of dismissal decisions, for each case must be considered in the light of all the circumstances and the conduct of the parties. The present law provides scant guidance, leaving the industrial tribunals principally to consider whether or not the dismissal was reasonable in the circumstances. We think it possible, however, to provide Labour Adjudicators with clearer guidance about the relevant considerations. We suggest that in approaching the question of the fairness of the dismissal, a Labour Adjudicator should be instructed to consider five dimensions of the issue. This general principle would be supplemented by codes of practice, breach of which would create a presumption of unfairness. We propose that there should be codes of practice on how to deal fairly with incompetence, sickness, and dishonesty.

9.45   We also propose that in considering the fairness of the dismissal, the Labour Adjudicator should be instructed to consider prescribed statutory criteria. The criteria which we have in mind include the following:

* *risk of harm to employers' business*: the employer must demonstrate the risk of serious harm to the business likely to result from continued employment of the worker.
* *resources of employer*: the standard of fairness should reflect the level of resources available to the employer;
* *proportionality*: the sanction of dismissal must not be excessive as a response to the misconduct, incompetence, or other ground
* *consistency*: the employer should treat similar cases in the same way;
* *reasonabless in all the circumstances*: the Adjudicator should have regard to all the circumstances of the case in reaching a decision that the employer's decision to dismiss was reasonable.

(c) Remedies

9.46   Labour Adjudicators should have the power to award reinstatement or compensation, following representations from the parties. The level of compensation to be awarded by a Labour Adjudicator should have no upper limit, but we propose a minimum level of compensation to be set by reference to a basic award equivalent to a redundancy payment. The present criteria for assessment of loss are unsatisfactory because they are confined to the economic loss caused to the worker. We propose that the Labour Adjudicator should calculate the measure of compensation by reference to the dual criteria of (a) the probable economic loss of the worker, and (b) the degree of culpability of the employer in dismissing unfairly, which could justify a measure of punitive damages. It is for consideration whether the Labour Adjudicator should have power to reduce compensation for contributory fault on the part of the worker, but not for efforts on the part of the worker to mitigate his or her loss.

Summary by Examples

9.47 It may be helpful to provide a crude summary of the foregoing ideas in an attempt to bring them to life.

Case 1: *Dismissal for Dishonesty. Here an employer proposes to dismiss a worker believed to be guilty of acts of dishonesty.*

The employer must follow any disciplinary procedure agreed with a recognised trade union or a Labour Inspector, otherwise the dismissal will be automatically unfair. If no such procedure exists then the employer should follow the requirements of a Code of Practice, breach of which will be presumptively unfair.

If the procedure confirms the decision to dismiss, the employer must call in a conciliator. Failure to comply with this obligation will result in the dismissal being legally ineffective, in which case the employer must continue to pay full wages and to provide work for the worker in question. Once called in, the conciliator will confirm whether a proper enquiry has been carried out and will try to achieve a settlement.

In the absence of a conciliated settlement, the employer must provide the worker with a written statement of the reason or reasons for the dismissal. The worker will then be able to bring a claim for unfair dismissal either before private arbitration, if an arbitration agreement has been collectively agreed for that workplace, or before a Labour Adjudicator.

The Adjudicator will determine fairness by reference to a general test of reasonableness and proportionality, taking into account the resources of the employer and the risk of harm to the employers' business and also taking into account conformity with any relevant codes of practice. If the employer has conformed to a collectively agreed disciplinary procedure or a procedure agreed by a Labour Inspector, then the worker will not be permitted to allege unfairness on the ground of unfair procedure, although he or she may argue that the procedure had not been fairly applied.

If the dismissal is held to be fair, the worker will only be able to appeal on a point of law to the Labour Court. If the dismissal is held to be unfair, the Adjudicator will have the power to order reinstatement or compensation. There would be no limit to the amount of compensation.

9.48 **Case 2:** *Dismissal for Business Reasons. Here the employer believes that he or she has some pressing business reason to reduce the labour force, perhaps provoked by a downturn in demand for a particular product.*

If dismissals take place, a dismissed worker will be able to challenge them in one of three ways:

(a) He or she may go to the Labour Inspector for a ruling that the dismissal was not economically necessary, and if such a ruling is given, he or she may then proceed to a Labour Adjudicator or to the Labour Court for an award of automatic unfair dismissal.

(b) The employer must follow any procedure agreed with a recognised trade union or a Labour Inspector otherwise the dismissal will be automatically unfair. If such a specified procedure is followed, however, it will not be possible to claim unfair dismissal on the ground of unfair procedure.

(c) If the procedure has been followed, the worker may claim that he or she had been unfairly selected for dismissal compared to other workers, in which case the employer must demonstrate an objective and fair process of selection, otherwise the dismissal would be unfair.

If the dismissal is unfair, the employer will be subject to the normal remedies for disciplinary dismissals, that is to say reinstatement or compensation. If the dismissal is fair, the employer may be required to pay the worker a redundancy payment, set with reference to his or her length of service and rate of pay.

9.49 **Case 3:** *Dismissal on Grounds of Age. Here the employer dismisses a person because she has reached the age of 63, at which age the employer always dismisses staff.*

The worker will be able to bring a claim before the Labour Court and establish that the dismissal was for this inadmissible reason (age).

If the worker establishes a prima facie case of the presence of an inadmissible reason, the worker will be able to ask the Labour Court for an interlocutory order against dismissal pending the hearing of the case.

If the claim is upheld on the facts, the Labour Court will have the power to order either reinstatement or punitive damages.

If reinstatement is ordered and the worker is dismissed again within a period of one year, the dismissal will be ineffective unless it was approved by the Labour Court in advance.

9.50 **Case 4:** *Expiration of a Fixed Term Contract. Here the employment relationship expires and is not renewed.*

There will be a presumption that this termination of the employment relationship is a dismissal by the employer.

The employer must decide whether or not this should be regarded as an economic dismissal. It will be an economic dismissal if, for instance, there is no more money to pay the worker. It will be a disciplinary dismissal if the employer decides not to renew the employment relationship, but to seek another worker instead who is expected to be more competent at the job.

If this is an economic dismissal, the employer must follow the procedure agreed with the recognised trade union or approved by the Labour Inspector. Failure to have such a procedure will lead to the dismissal being restrained or to a finding of unfair dismissal.

If this is a disciplinary dismissal, then the employer should follow any procedure agreed with a trade union or approved by a Labour Inspector, or in the absence of such a formal procedure, should follow the standards contained in the Code of Practice, otherwise the dismissal will be unfair.

If, having followed this procedure, the employer affirms its decision to dismiss the worker, he or she should engage in conciliation, and in the absence of a conciliated settlement he or she should issue the worker with a written statement of the reason for dismissal.

If the written statement states that the dismissal is for economic reasons, then the worker may insist that the employer justify the decision before a Labour Inspector. If the decision is justified, the worker may nevertheless challenge the dismissal on the ground that the procedures were not followed, or that he or she was unfairly selected.

If the written statement states that the dismissal is for misconduct or some other reason related to the conduct of the worker, then it will be handled as a disciplinary dismissal.

If the employer has an arbitration agreement with the union, then the case may be dealt with by the arbitrator, the award being enforceable by the Labour Court.

In the absence of an arbitration agreement, the worker will be able to claim reinstatement or compensation before a Labour Adjudicator, where the general test of reasonableness would apply.

Summary of Recommendations

1 Workers should have the right not to be unfairly dismissed.

2 Conciliation should be compulsory prior to dismissal, otherwise the dismissal would be unfair.

3 All workers should be entitled to claim unfair dismissal: there should no qualifying conditions

4 There should be a legal presumption, whenever an employment relationship is terminated, that a claim may be brought for unfair dismissal. The onus should be on the employer to show that the relationship was terminated voluntarily.

5 Where the reason, the principal reason, or a subsidiary reason for dismissal involves the employer denying a worker certain basic rights at work, then the dismissal will be for an inadmissible reason and automatically unfair.

6 An inadmissible reason should include dismissal on the ground of sex, race, disability, age, religion, political beliefs, and also for other basic rights such as freedom of speech and protection for family life.

7 It should be possible for a worker to apply to the Labour Court for interlocutory relief of temporary reinstatement, which should be granted whenever possible, in any case alleging dismissal for an inadmissible reason.

8 An employer should be required to justify the need to make economic dismissals to a Labour Inspector, and failure to do so would render any economic dismissal unfair.

9 An economic dismissal should be subject to restraint by an order from a Labour Court unless and until it is conducted according to either a consultation procedure agreed with the relevant recognised trade union, or a procedure approved by a Labour Inspector in accordance with guidelines laid down in a Code of Practice.

10 A worker should be entitled to challenge the fairness of an economic dismissal on the ground that there has been a failure to follow agreed or approved procedures, or that he or she was unfairly selected compared to other workers. Redundancy payments should continue to be available in cases of economic dismissal.

11 In the case of disciplinary dismissals, employers should be required to follow either a collectively agreed procedure, or a procedure approved by a Labour Inspector guided by a Code of Practice. A dismissal should be unfair if the employer fails to follow an approved procedure.

12 A disciplinary dismissal should be unfair even where an approved procedure has been followed if the dismissal cannot be justified on its merits. Complaints would normally be heard by a Labour Adjudicator.

13 In determining the fairness of a disciplinary dismissal consideration should be given to the risk of harm to employers'

business, the resources of the employer, proportionality, consistency, and reasonableness in all the circumstances.

14 The remedies for unfair dismissal should be reinstatement or compensation, though it should not be possible for an employer to frustrate an award of reinstatement.

15 The measure of compensation should be calculated by reference to the dual criteria of (a) the probable economic loss of the worker, and (b) the degree of culpability of the employer in dismissing unfairly, which could justify a punitive element.

THE ENFORCEMENT OF RIGHTS

10.1 Since the late 1960s, British labour law adjudication has been based upon a combination of specialist tribunals and the ordinary courts. The former are designed to offer a fast, cheap, informal and accessible method for the resolution of disputes while the latter retain a substantial residue of labour law adjudication, including many aspects of collective labour law such as internal trade union affairs and trade disputes. The industrial tribunals have grown into a form of labour court with substantial expertise in large areas of employment law, while highly controversial questions of collective labour law are adjudicated upon by judges with little or no appreciation of the legal and practical complexities of the issues before them. In our view this patchwork of tribunals and courts should be replaced by a comprehensive Labour Court system to which the vast bulk of employment-related disputes should be taken.

The Need for Reform

10.2 It is quite clear that there is a need for a radical overhaul of the system for the enforcement of employment rights. There are perhaps three reasons for this. The first is the chronic overloading of the current system, the second is the difficulty which some workers have in enforcing their rights in workplaces where there is no trade union presence (perhaps over half of the workplaces in the country), and the third is the pressure which the system is likely to face in the future with the introduction of a statutory minimum wage and the regulation of working time, to say nothing of the rest of the European Social Policy agenda and nothing about the implementation of some of the other more radical measures proposed elsewhere in this report. The number of applications to industrial tribunals has risen from 41,390 in 1976 to 90,078 in 1995. Of the latter a large number were settled by conciliation or were withdrawn. But there were still some 24,983 which proceeded to adjudication.

10.3 This enormous increase in the number of applications has taken place despite the current two year restriction on the bringing of unfair dismissal cases. The relaxation of that barrier, together with a more protective regime for 'atypical' workers, as well as the removal of the restraints on part time workers will inevitably see a significant increase in the number of applications. As already suggested the number of applications is likely to be swollen still further by the introduction of a statutory minimum wage and the transposition of the Working Time Directive (93/104/EC). It is true that it is unclear how the statutory minimum wage will be enforced and that it need not necessarily be by way of a complaint to the industrial tribunals. Indeed wages council orders (the antecedents of the statutory minimum wage) were enforced not by industrial tribunals but, insofar as they gave rise to a civil cause of action, in the civil courts. It would, however, make little sense to have cases involving a breach of the provisions introduced by the Wages Act 1986 (now Employment Rights Act 1996, Part II) to be heard in one forum, but actions to recover the minimum wage in another.

10.4 Although perhaps not a current problem, there is the additional fear of the role of the courts in the future, armed by judicial review with a capacity to liquidate any legislation designed to promote trade union recognition, and enabled by their role in the interpretation of statutes to undermine any liberalisation on the law relating to industrial action. It is true that the courts have been celebrated in some quarters recently for the new liberal spirit which some see as guiding their work. Indeed we have paid tribute to the path cut by the courts in the area of transfer of undertakings, and we are aware of the important developments made in the field of discrimination law where the Equal Treatment Directive (76/207/EEC) has been used in a most imaginative way, particularly to remove the restrictions on the right of part time workers to claim unfair dismissal. On the other hand, however, it is not at all clear how the ordinary courts would respond to a new progressive framework of labour law, in the sense that it is easy to appear liberal when the spirit of the legislation is pointing unequivocally in the other direction.

Guiding Principles

10.5 Although the industrial tribunals have made an important contribution to labour law, it is open to question whether they can satisfy all the demands which they now face. They are arguably ill-equipped to deal with 'complex' cases involving complicated questions of law such as those concerning equality law and sophisticated questions of EC law. On the other hand there is the danger of losing the attributes of speed, cheapness, informality and accessibility in 'simple' cases where legal technicality is at a minimum. Rather than tinker with the current arrangements, we believe that there is a need for radical reform and propose that there should be a greater degree of diversification in the enforcement of labour standards. Consequently we propose the introduction of a Labour Inspectorate with significant powers; the creation of a new office of Labour Adjudicator; and the development of a Labour Court.

10.6   In developing our proposals in this area we have been guided by a number of principles upon which a system for the protection of employment rights should be based. These are as follows:

*   accessibility - a 'simple justice' model, based upon 'Donovan' principles of cheapness, speed and informality, should be preferred for the resolution of disputes with low levels of evidential and substantive complexity;
*   appropriateness - a 'complex justice' model should be employed (with suitable levels of necessary specialisation) to resolve disputes with higher levels of substantive and procedural, including evidential, complexity;
*   adequacy of remedies - an effective and proportionate range of remedies, consistently applied, should be available to reflect the significance of the rights infringed and also to the seriousness of the breach.

10.7   In developing our proposals on adjudication, we are conscious of the fact that much dispute resolution takes place under the aegis, and by the intervention, of other bodies including ACAS, the Certification Officer, and the Central Arbitration Committee. It should be clear from discussions earlier in the text that we see a continuing role for such dispute resolution by such bodies within defined areas and on defined issues. Indeed we propose the introduction of other dispute resolution agencies such as the Trade Union Recognition and Representation Agency, considered in chapter 7. We also envisage that the existing functions of ACAS in relation to conciliation and mediation would continue to be performed in disputes within the Labour Court system, and indeed that this role might be enhanced and become part of the procedures of the Court, particularly in collective disputes. We also anticipate the possibility that cases which begin life as litigation in the Labour Court could be referred by that court to ACAS or the CAC as appropriate.

Labour Inspectorate

(a) Functions

10.8   The first institutional innovation which we propose in the enforcement field is the creation of a Labour Inspectorate, building on the traditions of the Health and Safety Inspectorate and the Wages Inspectorate. We are mindful also that the institution is to be found in many Member States of the European Union, including Belgium, France, Greece, Italy, Spain and Portugal, and we believe that it would be particularly important in this country for those workers who are not unionised and who as a result are likely to be among the most vulnerable members of the labour force. We anticipate that the Inspectorate would have 3 functions: to *inspect* for infractions of designated employment laws; to *enforce* those laws through the imposition of sanctions and referral to the Labour Court; and to *represent* the public interest within the Labour Court system. While having discretion to pursue individual infractions of employment rights, we also see its role as being largely strategic, performing these functions on the basis of 'employment protection' audits, particularly of non-unionised employers.

(b) Jurisdiction

10.9   The Labour Inspectorate should have jurisdiction over the enforcement of all individual employment rights conferred by statute. There is a case for restricting the jurisdiction to rights involving 'concrete entitlements', such as the minimum wage (as we propose in paragraph 4.7 above), which would be a transparent basis for enforcement, though it is the practice in other European countries for Labour Inspectors to have jurisdiction over a wide range of employment questions. It is also the case that in some European jurisdictions Labour Inspectors are empowered to ensure that collective agreements are applied, particularly those which are of general application, such as those extended by Royal Decree in Belgium (which actually gives them a legislative character). There would be a strong case for the proposition that if our proposals for Sectoral Employment Commissions were accepted, the jurisdiction of the Labour Inspectorate should be extended to ensure the enforcement of sectoral employment agreements and awards as well.

10.10   The position with regard to other terms of the employment relationship is more difficult. Nevertheless, there is clearly a public interest in the proper enforcement of employment rights, even of a technically private nature. We have already proposed (para 4.81) that the Labour Inspectorate should be empowered to intervene to restrain the unilateral variation of working conditions, and that the Labour Inspectorate should have a role to play in validating employers' grievance and disciplinary procedures (paragraphs 4.78 and 4.84), as well as policing awards relating to pay equity by the CAC (paragraph 5.43). There may also be a case for extending the jurisdiction of the Inspectorate still further to cover all terms of the employment relationship, including all non statutory terms. But however widely the jurisdiction of the Inspectorate is drawn, we accept that the inspectors are likely to gravitate towards the enforcement of cases of 'concrete entitlements', and that it would not be inappropriate for them to do so.

(c) Powers

10.11   It is crucial that workers should be made aware of the existence and powers of the Labour Inspector. We anticipate that all employers should be under a statutory duty prominently to display at the workplace information about the role of the inspector. We propose that the Labour Inspectorate should enjoy the wide powers, including a right to enter and inspect any workplace, either at his or her initiative or at the request of aggrieved workers or their representatives. The anonymity of the complainant would have to be permitted in order to avoid victimisation. The Inspectors would have an immediate right of entry to a place of employment, subject to possible exceptions on grounds of health and safety. They would be entitled to interview any worker employed there and inspect any documents, subject to the employer's right to withhold information on narrow and prescribed grounds of confidentiality.

10.12   In our view Labour Inspectors should have a range of sanctions at their disposal. Compensation orders would be appropriate, for example, in the case of non payment of the minimum wage (as we propose in paragraph 4.7). In cases of systematic non-compliance, the Inspectorate should have a power to make punitive compensation orders (perhaps a double compensation order) in order to ensure that the sanction is proportionate to the seriousness of the breach. Improvement notices and prohibition notices, broadly modelled upon the powers at present enjoyed by the Health and Safety Inspectorate, would be particularly important in the case of a wide-scale failure to comply with minimum standards. The Inspectors could in some cases have the immediate power to issue an improvement notice, setting a time limit within which breaches of employment rights had to be rectified.

In extreme circumstances, the Inspectorate could issue a prohibition notice as, for example, in the case of a failure to comply with the law on working time. We also propose that there should be a right of appeal against Labour Inspector orders to the Labour Court.

Labour Adjudicators and the Labour Court

(a) The Labour Adjudicator
   10.13   We propose that all litigation relating to the employment relationship should fall within the jurisdiction of the Labour Court. The first rung on the ladder would be the Labour Adjudicator, who would deal mainly with what might be referred to as 'simple' cases in the sense that they are concerned mainly with questions of fact (such as dismissal for reasons relating to capability or conduct) rather than complex questions of law. We envisage all cases being referred to the Labour Court office in the first instance, but that those coming within the categories on a devolved list (see paragraph 10.20 below) would be passed to a single Labour Adjudicator. In view of their inquisitorial role, often within the workplace, and in the interests of the objectives of speed and cheapness, we believe that it would be unnecessary to have tripartite Labour Adjudication, as we also believe that it would not be necessary for the Labour Adjudicator to be a lawyer, though we would not exclude the appointment of lawyers to this position, which could in fact be the first step in a career within the Labour Court system generally.
   10.14   We propose that Labour Adjudicator hearings should usually be held at the workplace and that normally such hearings should be private. A request by either party to hold the hearing, either privately or publicly, at a Labour Court office would be treated sympathetically by the Adjudicator, although the onus would be upon the party raising the objection to establish why the workplace was inappropriate in a particular case. Legal or other representation would be permitted but legal aid should not be available in a Labour Adjudicator hearing. There are arguments that lawyers would encourage 'legalism' in employment law cases. In our view, however, it is much more likely that it is the complexity of some labour law and the adversarial system which encourages legalism. Before the Labour Adjudicators, the legal questions should be less complicated and the inquisitorial approach should allow the Adjudicator to dictate the style of the proceedings, thereby minimising the respective benefit of legal representation and disadvantage of non representation.
   10.15   The Labour Adjudicator would be entitled to interrogate

any witness either at the invitation of the parties or of their own volition and inspect any documents, subject to the normal rules of confidentiality. We would anticipate an element of adversarialism at the end of each stage of the inquisitorial process in that the parties would, with the permission of the Adjudicator, be entitled to examine and cross-examine witnesses in relation to issues which they consider had not yet been fully explored. The Adjudicator would proceed beyond an investigation of the facts and would determine any questions of law raised during the adjudication. Appeals from the Labour Adjudicator to the Labour Court should be on questions of law, and findings of fact should only be open to appeal on grounds of perversity. We also anticipate that it should be possible for the Labour Adjudicator to refer a difficult or complex case to the Labour Court for disposal or to seek a reference to the Labour Court on a question of law.

(b) The Labour Court

10.16 We propose that the Labour Court should be tripartite and formally should be a division of the High Court. It may appear paradoxical that we should propose the use of lay members in cases involving complex legal questions, but not in more factually based cases likely to come before the Labour Adjudicator. We are conscious, however, that binding precedents on appeal from the Adjudicators will be established at the Labour Court level, and that the experience and expertise of the lay members will be most valuable. Secondly, the Labour Court will hear collective labour law as well as complex individual employment rights cases. It is most important that the views of lay persons are injected into the proceedings of this kind. We propose that the Labour Court should have an original jurisdiction to deal with prescribed matters; an appellate jurisdiction (from the Labour Adjudicator); and a review jurisdiction in respect of the various public agencies operating in the labour law field.

10.17 As a forum dealing with more complex issues of law, we propose that the Labour Court should operate with much of the procedures of a court of law, on an adversarial basis with a strong emphasis on written submissions. In particular, we propose that legal aid should be available and that full representation by lawyers or other parties should be permitted in the Labour Court. One particular problem concerns the awarding of costs before the Labour Court. It is easy to argue that the advent of legal aid leads inexorably to the awarding of costs also. We have come to the conclusion that the awarding of costs against an unsuccessful individual applicant to the Labour Court would be an unacceptable disincentive to the utilisation of the system. The arguments are less powerful but still persuasive in the great number of cases in which individuals would be supported by trade unions, agencies or other groups, as the risk of costs could provide a significant disincentive against organisational support for individual applications.

10.18 Given its focus upon legal issues it may be advisable to have a preliminary investigation of the facts. We propose that, as a prelude to a case on the 'reserved' list of cases to be heard before the Labour Court, a Labour Investigator, being an officer of the Court, should establish the facts of the case in order to focus the time and resources of the Labour Court upon the complex issues before it. We propose that the Labour Investigators should have the same rights of entry into the workplace, rights to take statements from witnesses and rights to inspect relevant documents as those enjoyed by the Labour Inspectorate and Labour Adjudicators. Investigators would be given a specified number of weeks within which to complete their investigations. A dossier of the facts would then be sent to the Labour Court prior to the hearing. It may be that the dividing line between fact-finding and questions of law would be more difficult to draw in some complex cases. However, it would still be open to the parties to reopen some findings of fact before the Labour Court.

(c) Division of Jurisdiction

10.19 As already suggested, we anticipate the establishment of a 'devolved' list of simpler cases which would be sent to an Adjudicator and a 'reserved' list of more complex cases which would be retained by the Labour Court. We also propose that categories of cases involving 'group' justice and significant 'public interest' would be placed on the reserved list. These lists would be based on broad categories of labour law disputes. Where a case was devolved, an Adjudicator, of his/her own volition or at the request of a party, could, at any stage in the proceedings, decide to transfer a devolved list case to the Labour Court rather than adjudicate upon it, on grounds that a substantial body of workers were affected by the dispute, or that the dispute raised questions of public interest, or issues of legal complexity, for example of European law. In those circumstances, the Adjudicator could take on the role of an Investigator for the purpose of the completion of the fact-finding process.

10.20 The Labour Court would be guided by a discretionary list of factors upon which it could decide to devolve cases to the Labour Adjudicators. On grounds of accessibility, we anticipate that the devolved list would include some unfair dismissal cases, particularly 'disciplinary dismissals' and perhaps also 'economic dismissals' (on which see chapter 9 above), as well as complaints about unfair disciplinary action, or complaints about unresolved grievances (on which see chapter 4 above). It would also follow that most statutory rights should be on the devolved list except, on grounds of appropriateness and group justice, for discrimination rights which would go on the reserved list. However, the Labour Court would be expected to exercise its discretion to devolve some direct discrimination cases to a Labour Adjudicator. For example, a sexual harassment case might well be most appropriately heard in private before an Adjudicator. On balance, most redundancy and transfers cases have significant 'group' justice aspects and often have a European dimension. They might therefore start on the 'reserved' list but with discretion on the part of the Labour Court to devolve them in simpler cases.

10.21   We anticipate that all collective disputes, including those relating to industrial action, freedom of association, information, consultation, support for collective bargaining, collective agreements, and trade union internal affairs, should go to the Labour Court. As mentioned above, individual cases with a strong 'group' justice aspect would stay with the Labour Court. Hearings on appeal from an order of the Labour Inspectorate would normally be made to the Labour Court as the most appropriate forum. Moreover, we propose that the exercise of the power of review of bodies such as the proposed Trade Union Recognition and Representation Unit, the Central Arbitration Committee or the proposed TUC Independent Review Committee should be only by the Labour Court. As already proposed in chapter 6, the Labour Court should sit with two trade unionists as lay members in any case involving the internal affairs of a trade union.

(d) Appeals

10.22   Although the new Labour Court system would replace the existing system of industrial tribunals and the Employment Appeal Tribunal, a question arises as to the scope for and the substance of appellate structures. We propose initially the establishment of a Labour Division in the Court of Appeal to which appeals on questions of law would lie from the Labour Court. In due course, we would propose an autonomous Labour Court of Appeal. Appeals would then lie to the House of Lords, sitting with two Labour Division or Labour Court of Appeal judges who had not sat in the lower court. Although there is much to be said for a totally insulated system on the German model, it is felt that the House of Lords should have a general jurisdiction including labour law questions of public importance, but that the Court of Appeal, as in a number of continental jurisdictions should have a specialist chamber for labour law appeals.

Administrative Agencies

10.23 As already indicated, there are a number of agencies currently operating in the field of labour law which we anticipate would continue to have a role to play in the enforcement and administration of labour standards. These include the Certification Officer, ACAS and the CAC, all set up in the 1970s, but with an important role to play in the future. However, we see no continuing role for either the Commissioner for the Rights of Trade Union Members (set up in 1988) or the Commissioner for Unlawful Industrial Action (set up in 1993). We have also proposed the creation of a number of new agencies, including the Industrial Relations Commission, Fair Wages Commission, the Trade Union Representation and Recognition Agency, and the Training Commission. In the case of some of these bodies, both existing (in light of the new powers which we propose they should have) and proposed, there is a very real danger of their work being disrupted by the power of judicial review, a fate which seriously limited almost all of the public agencies established in the 1970s. Given the rapid development of judicial review since 1980 this is a problem which is likely to become more rather than less acute in the future.

10.24 It is tempting to contemplate the possibility of a statutory provision which would exclude judicial review altogether and which would thereby permit all the agencies in the employment field to have total control over their own affairs. But we accept that this would not be easy to justify, for no matter how well intentioned, there is always the danger that the agencies would exceed the mandate conferred on them by Parliament, and that in such cases a remedy should be available to restrain them or to correct any error. This is not to say, however, that we are sanguine about the prospect of judicial review, though we would wish to ensure that any judicial review proceedings should be heard only in the Labour Court, and that the powers of the court to intervene should be carefully specified in the relevant legislation in order to prevent the policy goals of the legislation from being frustrated. With this in mind we would propose that the agencies should be directed by statute to have regard to a wide (but not exclusive) range of prescribed considerations, that the

Labour Court should be permitted to intervene only on the grounds of illegality or procedural impropriety, and that the Labour Court (and any appeal court) in dealing with any application should be specifically directed to have regard to the overall goals of the legislation as well as to the range of prescribed considerations to which the agencies must have regard. Just as important, however, is the need to ensure that the discretion of the statutory agencies is kept to a minimum if the mistakes of the 1970s are to be avoided.

10.25   In addition to the agencies referred to in paragraph 10.23 above, the Equal Opportunities Commission (EOC) and the Commission for Racial Equality (CRE), perform an important function in the enforcement of anti-discrimination law. As indicated in chapter five, we foresee a continuing role for these bodies in enforcing the law, but with their existing powers being strengthened and extended. As indicated in chapter 5, we also propose that a Disability Rights Commission (DRC) should be established, which is granted equivalent powers to those of the EOC and CRE. Currently, the EOC and the CRE are vested with a number of powers, including the power to provide assistance and advice to participants in legal proceedings, to initiate legal proceedings in cases involving advertising and instructions or pressure to discriminate, and to conduct formal investigations into discriminatory practices and issue non-discrimination notices. Each of these statutory powers is subject to a number of weaknesses and limitations, which need to be addressed.

10.26   First, we propose that unnecessary procedural requirements imposed on the Commissions' power to undertake formal investigations and to issue non-discrimination notices should be removed. In particular, we propose that the House of Lords decision in *Re Prestige Group plc* [1984] IRLR 166, which had the effect of requiring the Commissions to have sufficient evidence to found a belief that unlawful acts may have occurred prior to commencing an investigation against a named individual, should be reversed. Once an investigation is underway, the Commissions should be free to extend the boundaries of the investigation beyond those laid down in the stated terms of reference, provided that it is done for a purpose connected with their general statutory duties. We are also of the view that undue delay is caused by the extent of the opportunities provided for investigatees to make representations in relation to both formal investigations and possible non-discrimination notices. We propose that the right to make pre-investigation representations (which can assist the Commissions initially to reduce the scope of investigations) should be retained and extended to all persons named, but should be subject to a time limit of, for example, 28 days. In contrast, we are of the view that the right to make representations against a non-discrimination notice is unnecessary as it duplicates the appeal system and should be removed.

10.27 Secondly, where a formal investigation results in findings of unlawful discrimination, remedies should be provided for those individuals affected. Currently, such individuals are often denied redress as the time limit for taking a claim to an industrial tribunal will have passed by the time the Commission makes its findings. We therefore propose that an individual who considers that he or she has been the victim of any discrimination found in a Commission's report should be entitled to present a claim to the Labour Court within 3 months of the publication of the findings. The Labour Court should be required to take account of the findings of the Commission when considering the complaint. Thirdly, we propose that the scope of non-discrimination notice should be extended to provide not only that unlawful discrimination must cease, but also that the particular practices which have led to the discrimination, must be changed. Finally, we recommend that the CRE, the EOC and the DRC, should not be restricted to bring legal proceedings in their own name only in cases involving advertising, or an instruction or pressure to discriminate. Rather, the Commissions should be provided with a general power to bring legal proceedings in their own name wherever they believe that an unlawful discriminatory practice exists.

10.28 The CRE has proposed that their right to issue non-discrimination notices should be replaced by a power to gather evidence of discrimination and to put it before an independent discrimination tribunal which would then make the decision (after full opportunities for cross examination) as to whether discrimination has occurred and what remedies are appropriate. The EOC have reached a different conclusion and does not consider that there is an inevitable conflict between its investigative and law enforcement roles. The EOC is extremely careful to guard against the possibility or even appearance of pre-judgment by entrusting the conduct of investigations to officers and two nominated Commissioners leaving the full Commission to decide on subsequent enforcement action. The danger which the EOC foresees with any transfer of its right to make findings of discrimination in a formal investigation and to issue a non-discrimination notice is that the belief investigations (investigations into alleged unlawful acts), if not all investigations into named persons, would be conducted from the outset as litigation.

10.29 If this were the case the EOC would be prevented from examining issues and practices in a broad context and would in effect be restricted to establishing whether a prima facie case of discrimination existed for presentation to a tribunal/court. The presentation and examination of evidence would be prescribed and limited, making it unlikely that the tribunal/court would acquire a sufficient understanding of the issues to enable the tribunal/court to make anything other than the bare findings. Those who are being investigated might well take the view that a formal investigation was an exercise to find discrimination rather than an investigation to establish the facts. We propose that the three agencies in the discrimination field (EOC, CRE, and the proposed DRC) should have the power both to issue non discrimination notices or to apply to a court for an appropriate remedy to deal with evidence of discrimination. If would be a matter for each body to decide how it wished to proceed in any particular case. Any judicial review of the decision to issue a non discrimination notice should be undertaken by the Labour Court.

Access to Justice

10.30 In the UK, and indeed in most European jurisdictions, it has been traditional for access to justice to be restricted to those whose rights have allegedly been infringed, that is to say individuals in individual justice cases and unions in group justice cases such as redundancy consultation. However, some labour law questions raise complex questions which individuals may not have the expertise, resources or inclination fully to pursue or develop. More specifically many labour law questions are in theory, and most certainly in practice, group justice questions, in relation to which a particular individual may be less significant than the pooled concerns of all the members of the group. In some labour law cases indeed, the individual is therefore a highly valuable but vulnerable 'front person' for litigation between collective parties on group justice issues. Without removing the vital right of individual workers to bring grievances to the judicial process, we should nevertheless discard the charade whereby such cases can only be ventilated through the process of individual justice.

10.31 It is therefore important to consider the widening of standing, particularly before the Labour Court. The success of the EOC in judicial review proceedings is dramatic evidence of the potential of a more general standing for **public agencies**, not only against the illegality of public authorities through judicial review, but also against the illegality of both public and private sector employers. It might be argued that the agencies should only have standing where they can show that there is little or no prospect of an individual litigating or perhaps where none of the potential beneficiaries objects. But such restrictions might place unnecessary fetters upon the effectiveness of the enforcement system. Agencies are acting in the public interest and are invariably concerned with group justice cases. Such restrictions place an 'individual justice' gloss on the proceedings and leave the individual open to victimisation. However, it might be possible to frame standing criteria in terms of public interest/group justice objectives (such as a significant issue of law or a substantial group of workers affected), though it would be preferable if the agencies had an unfettered discretion whether to act.

10.32 It is difficult to resist the proposition that **trade unions** should enjoy general standing to litigate in their own name in cases in which their members' rights are alleged to be infringed. A most obvious example would be breach of terms of the employment relationship governed by a collective agreement, although unions might be expected to exploit further their participation in sex equality litigation, for example on questions of equal pay and indirect discrimination. Once again, there is no reason to place unnecessary fetters upon such standing. Union standing could, in particular, help to bring before the system infringements of collective interests, such as those relating to pay, which individuals would be unwilling themselves to undertake and in relation to which the union is, in any event, the most appropriate party to pursue a claim. We have already proposed (in paragraph 7.58) that a trade union should have standing to enforce the terms of a collective agreement to which it is a party, even though the agreement is not legally enforceable as such but nevertheless forms part of the terms of the employment relationship of any of its members.

10.33 It would be easy to argue that, in a system with individual standing, agency standing and union standing, there is no need for **interest group** standing. On the other hand, however, there is a strong argument that it would be preferable to institute the widest opportunities for standing, particularly once the public interest in social rights for workers is acknowledged. There may be cases in which one of a collection of law centres, advice agencies and other interest groups would litigate but where none of the other parties would have the resources or motivation to intervene. There are numerous situations in which law centres should be able to take any group justice labour law case or in which, for example, the Low Pay Unit, if inclined, could take a minimum wage case. We therefore propose standing for interest groups before the Labour Court, with interest groups being authorised to act where they consider it appropriate to do so.

10.34   The possibility of **class actions** is also a matter worthy of examination. This provides an opportunity for giving a group justice context to the pursuit of individual justice claims, for it broadens the potential resources available to the applicants and, through weight of numbers, it reduces to some extent the possibility of individual repercussions particularly for those in the course of employment. However, more explicitly group justice devices may, in many cases, be more appropriate and the threat of victimisation and personal discomfort will certainly not be eradicated merely through the coming together of a number of applicants. Nevertheless, the great number of armed forces pregnancy cases shows that there is much to be said for some form of class action device either to establish a point of principle or to deal with individual compensation claims after a point of principle has been established by way of earlier litigation, which conceivably might well have involved a single complainant.

Procedural Questions and the Judicial Process

(a) Time limits

10.35   The UK has some of the shortest time limits amongst European labour law systems, normally 3 months in employment law applications. In many jurisdictions, the Labour Court time limits correspond with ordinary private law limits. It is an arguable part of the 'Donovan' ethos of speedy justice that cases should be brought to the judicial process shortly after the events occur, while there is also something to be said for legal certainty in the application of time limits. There may also be a case for different time limits before the different adjudicating bodies which we propose. It is already the case that differential time limits operate in labour law, in the sense that the time limits for bringing cases before the ordinary courts is longer (considerably) than the time limits for bringing cases in the industrial tribunals. Indeed, in the case of the exclusion or expulsion from a trade union, applicants have six months in which to present a claim.

10.36   In any event three months is too short a period within which to expect a worker to react. Six months might be more appropriate and ample discretion should be expressly provided to the Labour Adjudicator, or perhaps the Labour Court itself, to extend the period, particularly where discretionary factors leave it uncertain whether the case would go to the Adjudicator or the Court or where difficult personal circumstances are in evidence. There are European precedents for the interesting proposition that an employment law time limit should only run from the date that a worker leaves the employment of the potential respondent. It might be necessary to place some ultimate restraint upon such a facility, but the proposition deals neatly with the significant threat of victimisation placed upon the shoulders of potential litigants during the course of their employment. It is for consideration whether a longer time limit still should apply in cases before the Labour Court, with the six months applying only in respect of the Adjudicator.

(b) Rights of Intervention

10.37   The questions of standing to bring cases to the Labour Court system should be distinguished from the question of a right to intervene in a case started by another party. It is certainly possible for a person or organisation to be an amicus curiae in ordinary civil proceedings, to help the court with its deliberations. It would be helpful if such a possibility was formally recognised within the Labour Court system, once again enriching the arguments before the Court. It is much more difficult to justify interventions before the Labour Adjudicators as such interventions would jeopardise the speedy justice which they are there to dispense, and may not in any event be appropriate to the type of case which typically would be dealt with in that particular forum. It would seem to be appropriate that public agencies, most obviously the Labour Inspectorate and the equality agencies, should have a right to intervene in Labour Court proceedings, at the discretion of the Court. It should also be open to trade unions to intervene in order to argue in their members' interests. So also if autonomous bodies such as law centres and interest groups are to be given standing in some cases before the Labour Court, they should also have the opportunity to intervene, perhaps at the invitation of the Court.

10.38   But apart from interventions in order to enrich the argument before the court, the situation could arise where an individual was being supported by an agency, a trade union or an interest group. An organisation which is supporting an individual is entitled to pursue group justice objectives, even though the initial basis of a case may be individual. Such a party should also be entitled to continue an action, even though the individual is offered an acceptable settlement. Although of general application, this principle is particularly appropriate in equality litigation where it may only be possible to pursue a complex justice case with external assistance. Rather than see a complex case, say on equal value or indirect discrimination, collapse because an individual complainant or a group of complainants have settled, we propose that such a supporting organisation should be able to seek a comprehensive settlement, or have the case continued and any question of law resolved after a settlement has been reached.

(c) Evidence and the Burden of Proof

10.39   A major complication in labour law cases is the collection of evidence. Given their position of authority in the workplace, it is inevitable that employers hold significant amounts of information which may be essential to the pursuit of litigation against them. Both in Labour Adjudication and also in the Labour Court, inquisitorial systems are proposed which will greatly facilitate the collection of information for the benefit of both levels of judicial process. Both workplace adjudication and the investigations of Labour Investigators would facilitate the speedy disclosure of relevant material. Nevertheless, applicants may well require disclosure of information prior to the initiation of proceedings. Applications could be made to the Labour Court which would decide, in accordance with the normal jurisdictional rules, whether the Court itself or a Labour Adjudicator should be responsible for orders of disclosure. Labour Court orders could be invoked against parties which failed to satisfy orders for relevant information and documents.

10.40   We have proposed elsewhere in the text that the burden of proof should be reversed in some cases, for example on termination of employment (see paragraph 9.28). On grounds of consistency, it is arguable that a more general reversal of the burden of proof may be considered, namely that when applicants have established a sufficient level of evidence of a breach of their employment rights, it is up to the employer to prove that the rights were not infringed. Since information is entirely within the domain of the employer, it is sensible to require the employer to carry the burden of establishing the reason and its legality. Indeed, such a reversal encourages employers to provide the information necessary to adjudicate upon the dispute. Nevertheless, reversal of the burden of proof raises controversial questions of imposing 'liability until proved innocent'. At present, the establishment of a prima facie case, in practice, requires the employer to satisfy the tribunal of the legality of its actions and a more inquisitorial approach in the Labour Court may provide as much information as is necessary to initiate, and adjudicate upon, applications. Regardless of the answer to this more general question, we would nevertheless propose that although the burden of proving the existence of discrimination on any of the stated grounds should rest with the applicant, where a prima facie case has been established, the burden should shift to the employer to rebut the presumption.

(d) Formal Advice

10.41   There are a number of ways in which the adjudicatory process might be enriched by formal advice to be given to the judicial process by an appropriate party. One possibility lies before the Labour Adjudicator. In some cases, an Adjudicator may wish to ask for formal advice from an ACAS official upon the Service's view of 'good practice' in a given situation. So also it is typical in a number of European jurisdictions to have a power whereby a court can seek an opinion from a suitable party in relation to an equality dispute, for example, the Belgian Ministry of Labour's Committee of Women and Work, the Dutch Equal Treatment Commission and the Spanish Institute of Women. It must be said that this judicial discretion is rarely exercised in these jurisdictions but in our view it should be open to Labour Adjudicators and the proposed Labour Court to invite such interventions.

10.42   A matter which also arises for consideration relates particularly to cases of specialist controversy which are likely to arise in the Labour Court, perhaps raising difficult questions of EC law. In the same way that Advocates General bring great expertise to bear upon questions before the ECJ, is there a role for a specialist officer (perhaps from the ranks of the junior judicial officials, that is to say the Investigators and Adjudicators) who could offer an opinion upon the case between the hearing and the judgment? If so this is a task which might be performed by the Labour Investigator who prepared the dossier of facts for the Court. Although it is true that the Labour Court would become highly expert in all aspects of its jurisdiction, the advice of specialist officers might be useful in some cases, particularly in the more difficult, esoteric and unusual cases likely to come before the court, and perhaps also in cases where the complainant is inadequately represented. Such an initiative may also help to provide a compromise between pressures for a specialist 'equality' division of the Labour Court and anxieties concerning over-specialisation within what would already be a specialist division of the High Court.

Remedies and Sanctions

(a) Effective Remedies

10.43 It goes without saying that effective remedies are vital for the protection of the social rights of workers. It is sometimes said, however, that in the social field, the law has a largely educational value or that the relationship is so personal that dramatic remedies are inappropriate. On the other hand, however, the educational value of strike law does not diminish a perceived need in some quarters for dramatic remedies to dissuade unions from unlawful action. It is also important to remember that the most draconian remedies in employment law, special awards in freedom of association cases, were introduced by a Conservative Government in order to place substantial penalties upon the shoulders of employers which defied the right of employees to 'disassociate'. The educational value of social rights will surely be enhanced by the knowledge that severe consequences will follow from their infringement. It is the very personal nature of many employment rights which makes their breach so objectionable and so worthy of effective protection.

(b) Compensation and Damages

10.44 Compensation has been the mainstay of the remedies available to industrial tribunals, despite the supposed pre-eminence of reinstatement orders in unfair dismissal law. It is inevitable that compensation will remain as a vitally important remedy despite new initiatives in relation to proactive remedies. It is part of the devaluation of social rights that the ordinary civil rules of assessment of damages only apply exceptionally to some areas of employment law (such as sex and race discrimination) but not to others (such as unfair dismissal). This limitation is exacerbated by the existence of statutory maxima, still generally applicable to compensation orders and upon components of compensation such as 'weekly wage'. There is no justification for a perpetuation of these limitations, and in chapter 9 we propose that there should be no limit on the level of unfair dismissal compensation. We propose that material losses, together with interest, should be fully compensable generally without limitation in terms of overall maximum or weekly wage where that is a component of the calculation of compensation.

10.45　More generally, compensation in employment law is limited by the general contractual rule that non-material loss is not compensable in relation to breach of employment contracts. The regime which applies to equality cases, compensation for injury to feelings and aggravated damages, should naturally apply to any breach of personal social rights. It is entirely appropriate that serious breaches of employment rights, such as a particularly insensitive dismissal, a case of victimisation or harassment or a breach of a fundamental social right, should be subjected to a punitive element. It might be arguable that the award of punitive element should not be made by Labour Adjudicators but could be recommended by them to the Labour Court for decision. We are of the view, however, that compensation for non material losses such as injury to feelings and punitive compensation should be generally available across the jurisdiction of the Labour Court system and that punitive compensation should also be available in appropriate cases at the discretion of the Adjudicator or the Court.

10.46　As a general rule compensation is usually available only to the party who brought the action in the first place. We are of the view, however, that where a finding is made against a respondent, the Adjudicator or Court should also have the power to award compensation to any other person(s) it finds to have been the victim of unlawful conduct either named or sufficiently identified, provided that such person(s) join(s) the proceedings within a prescribed time. This would be particularly important in cases of discrimination, but need not be confined to such cases. We also propose (as, for example, in paragraph 9.46) that in some cases a basic minimum award of compensation should be granted. A basic minimum award is appropriate in a number of situations, including unfair dismissal, but also in cases of unlawful discrimination (direct and indirect), though it is to be hoped that a specialist Labour Court would treat claims of this kind with a greater degree of urgency and seriousness than industrial tribunals have been inclined to do in the past, with higher levels of compensation which should in practice make the requirement of a minimum award unnecessary.

(c) Other Remedies and Sanctions

10.47　Although effective compensation is thus important, so too is the availability of a more effective range of remedies to enable the adjudicating bodies to respond sensitively and with flexibility to the problems which they may face. To this end we have already suggested at earlier points in this text a range of other remedies which might be made available. These include, in the case of recognition, powers to *restrain* decisions taken without consultation or negotiation, and to *order* or *compel* employers to comply with duties to consult or bargain. We have also suggested that in the case of unfair dismissal there should be more effective powers to recommend *reinstatement* and, in effect, to require the status quo to be maintained until procedural obligations (in terms of consultation in the case of redundancy have been complied with). And in this chapter we have proposed that there should be greater opportunity on the part of all the enforcement agencies to make use of prohibition and enforcement notices. Consistently with our desire to arm the Labour Court with a flexible range of remedies, we also propose that it should be able to order employers to offer a candidate who has not been appointed on grounds of disability, sexual orientation, race or sex the next suitable vacancy.

10.48   Varied though these possible remedies may be, even this does not exhaust the options which could be made available to the Court. A particularly attractive possibility would be to give the Labour Court a general power to make recommendations for the future conduct of the enterprise, to order an employer to discontinue unlawful practices, and to remove unlawful provisions in working conditions. In 'group' justice cases this could have wide-ranging implications for the enterprise as whole and not just a single individual employed therein. Where this problem does arise, because there would otherwise be a significant gap in the terms of the employment relationship in our view it should be open to the Labour Court to allow parties to collective agreements a period of negotiation to negotiate new terms to meet the objection of the court. It is also the case that in some cases the Labour Court may be required to substitute terms for those which have been declared unlawful, though this is a problem which is most likely to arise in discrimination cases and in cases relating to the transfer of undertakings.

Alternative Dispute Resolution

10.49   There are strong arguments currently being advanced for a move towards greater use of arbitration for the resolution of certain employment disputes. The possibility was canvassed in the Green Paper, *Resolving Employment Rights Disputes. Options for Reform* (Cm 2707 (1994)) as an optional and voluntary alternative to adjudication for the resolution of disputes. Although this would be an important innovation, and one which in chapter 9 we support in the context of unfair dismissal, we anticipate arbitration as complementing the proposals contained in this chapter for the radical overhaul of the system for the adjudication and resolution of disputes. There are, however, a number of reasons why it could not be seen as an adequate substitute for the reforms proposed. In the first place, arbitration would be unpredictable in its take up and it would be impossible to know how many cases would be absorbed in this way. Secondly and more importantly, voluntary arbitration would not necessarily be appropriate for the resolution of all employment based disputes, and would be particularly inappropriate for those disputes which give rise to difficult questions of law. In our view it would be better to have a coherent and rational system which directs different types of case to the appropriate channel for resolution.

10.50 In this way, through our proposal for a Labour Adjudicator, some of the goals underlying the arbitral option can best be met where it is appropriate. This is not to deny that there may be some merit in facilitating the resolution of disputes by arbitration where this is desired by the parties. The issues are more fully developed in chapter 9, though we are of the view generally that it should be possible to elect arbitration rather than adjudication of employment disputes in accordance with the terms of a procedure in a collective agreement, but that an individual worker should always have the right to choose adjudication even where the arbitral option is available. We anticipate that the arbitrator should sit alone and should adopt an inquisitorial style, should sit in an ACAS office if not at the workplace, and should apply 'industrial relations' criteria rather than legalistic ones. Arbitration awards should not be open to appeal in the traditional sense, though it is difficult to avoid the conclusion that they should be subject to judicial review in the Labour Court on the grounds proposed in paragraph 10.24, that is to say of illegality and procedural impropriety.

Summary of Recommendations

1   The existing machinery for the enforcement of employment rights should be replaced by a new framework based on three new agencies: a Labour Inspectorate with significant powers; a new office of Labour Adjudicator; and a Labour Court.

2   The Labour Inspectorate should have jurisdiction over the

enforcement of all individual employment rights conferred by statute.

3 There may also be a case for extending the jurisdiction of the Inspectorate still further to include all terms of the employment relationship, including all non statutory terms.

4 The Labour Inspectorate should enjoy wide powers, including a right to enter and inspect any workplace, either at his or her own initiative or at the request of aggrieved workers or their representatives.

5 Labour Inspectors should have a range of sanctions at their disposal, including compensation orders and prohibition and improvement notices. There should be a right of appeal against Labour Inspector orders to the Labour Court.

6 All litigation relating to the employment relationship should fall within the jurisdiction of the Labour Court.

7 The first rung on the ladder should be the Labour Adjudicator, who would deal mainly with a 'devolved' list containing what might be referred to as 'simple' cases in the sense that they are concerned mainly with questions of fact.

8 The Labour Court should have jurisdiction to deal with more complex cases raising difficult questions of law, but also cases involving 'group' justice and significant 'public interest' dimensions, which would both be placed on the 'reserved' list.

9 The Labour Court should have an original jurisdiction to hear cases on a 'reserved list', an appeal jurisdiction from the Labour Inspector and Labour Adjudicator, and a power to review the recommendations, orders and awards of public agencies operating in the field.

10 There should be a Labour Division in the Court of Appeal to which appeals on questions of law would lie from the Labour Court. In due course, there should be established an autonomous Labour Court of Appeal.

11 Material losses, together with interest, should be fully compensable without limitation in terms of overall maximum or weekly wage where that is a component of the calculation of compensation.

12 Compensation for non material losses such as injury to feelings

should be generally available across the jurisdiction of the Labour Court system and punitive awards should also be available.

13 There should be available a more effective range of remedies to enable the adjudicating bodies to respond sensitively and with flexibility to the problems which they may face.

14 It should be open to the Labour Adjudicator and the Labour Court in appropriate cases to issue restraining orders, to issue mandatory orders, and to order reinstatement.

15 It should be possible to elect arbitration rather than adjudication of employment disputes in accordance with the terms of a procedure in a collective agreement, but an individual worker should always have the right to choose adjudication even where the arbitral option is available.

SUMMARY OF
MAIN RECOMMENDATIONS

1. INTRODUCTION

(a) General

Labour law should be underpinned by five key principles which seek to promote equality of opportunity, social justice, workplace democracy, civil liberties, and fairness at work (paragraph 1.3).

(b) Labour Standards and Economic Efficiency

There is a need for re-regulation of the labour market in order to reverse the trend towards greater social and economic inequality, but also to promote economic efficiency (paragraphs 1.6 - 1.12).

High labour standards are necessary to promote productive efficiency, worker efficiency, consumption and employment growth (paragraphs 1.13 - 1.16).

(c) International Labour Standards

There is a need to ensure that British law complies with international standards established by the ILO and the Council of Europe, particularly ILO Conventions 87 and 98 (paragraphs 1.17 - 1.28).

There is a need to re-ratify ILO Conventions denounced since 1979 and to review the ILO Conventions made since 1979, with a view to increasing the number ratified by the UK (paragraph 1.19).

(d) European Social Policy

Britain must play a full part in the development of European Social Policy, and to this end must become a party to the Maastricht Agreement on Social Policy (paragraphs 1.39 - 1.40).

There is a need to ensure that British law complies with EC labour standards, and to this end measures such as the Working Time Directive should be implemented without delay (paragraph 1.39).

2. THE EMPLOYMENT RELATIONSHIP

(a) The Need for Reform

There is a need for a far-reaching reform in the way the employment relationship is constituted and regulated, in order to avoid the pitfalls of the traditional concept of the contract of employment (paragraphs 2.7 - 2.11).

The starting point for such a reform would be the notion of the worker's right as citizen which is recognised in the labour law systems of several other EC Member States, as well as increasingly within EC law itself (paragraphs 2.8 - 2.9).

(b) Categories of Workers Protected by Labour Law

Labour law should apply to an employment relationship defined for this purpose to mean anyone who undertakes personally to execute work or labour for another and is economically dependent on the business of the other (paragraph 2.14).

Labour law should not apply to the genuinely self-employed, that is to say those who contract to supply labour or services through a business of their own on which they are economically dependent, or those who contract to supply an end product without contracting to supply their own personal services or labour in producing or procuring it (paragraphs 2.14 per cent 2.18).

(c) Specific Regulation of Particular Forms of Employment

Specific regulation is required to deal with the growing variety of working arrangements which are developing and with the blurring of clear divisions between working time and private time, and between the workplace and the home (paragraphs 2.5 - 2.6, 2.17 - 2.32).

As a general principle, employment rights should apply from day 1 of the employment relationship. There may be a case for a short minimum threshold period to deal with residual cases of very short-term service (paragraph 2.16).

It should be clearly provided that all protective terms of the employment relationship (whatever their source) apply to all workers regardless of length of service and regardless of the number of hours worked. Where appropriate, benefits should be conferred pro rata on part-time workers and those with short term service (paragraph 2.21).

It should not be possible for workers to waive their statutory rights. Therefore it should not be possible to contract out of the legislation, whether the employment is for an indefinite duration or for a fixed term (paragraph 2.32).

Where workers are supplied by an agency there should be a statutory presumption that the worker in question is engaged in an employment relationship by both the agency and the client, the two of which will thus both be directly responsible jointly and severally for all liabilities arising (paragraph 2.26).

Express provision should be made to ensure that trainees and homeworkers are covered by any general definition of a worker for the purposes of the legislation (paragraph 2.14).

3. SETTING EMPLOYMENT STANDARDS

(a) General

Steps should be taken to re-establish multi-employer bargaining structures (paragraphs 3.14 - 3.17).

(b) Rebuilding Collective Bargaining Structures

Steps should be taken to promote the extension by voluntary means of Minimum Standards Agreements throughout different industrial sectors (paragraph 3.18).

When it is established that collectively agreed terms and conditions of employment are commonly applied in a particular sector, it should be possible for a trade union to seek the extension of the common terms to all workers in the sector in question (paragraph 3.19).

Policy for a statutory minimum wage should be adapted to permit the establishment of minimum rates of pay and the regulation of other issues (such as working time) on a sectoral basis. Any terms and conditions determined in this way should apply to all workers in the sector in question (paragraphs 3.20 - 3.21).

National pay bargaining should be required in all public sector activities, and sectoral bargaining should be required in the privatised utilities, such as water, electricity and gas. National agreements should apply automatically to all workers in the sector in question (paragraph 3.23).

In the longer term every worker in this country should be covered by a collective agreement concluded at the sectoral level. With this in mind there should be established by statute Sectoral Employment Commissions with responsibility to promote collective bargaining and to regulate minimum terms and conditions of employment within specific industrial sectors of the economy (paragraph 3.24).

(c) Sectoral Employment Commissions

The Sectoral Employment Commissions should be bipartite in nature with representatives of employers on the one hand and workers on the other. Employers' representatives would be nominated by representative employers' associations where these existed and workers' representatives would be nominated by trade unions in the sector in question (paragraphs 3.30 - 3.31).

Sectoral Employment Commissions would have responsibility for the following matters:

* The setting of minimum terms and conditions of employment

* The transposition of EC Directives

* The development of equal opportunities policies and strategies

* The training of people employed or intending to be employed in the industry

* The provision and regulation of pensions for those employed in the industry (paragraph 3.32).

The terms of any Sectoral Employment Agreement should apply automatically to govern the employment relationship of any worker employed in the sector to which the agreement relates. The terms would be enforceable as such by individual workers or by trade unions acting on their behalf. To the extent that a Sectoral Employment Agreement imposes obligations on employers which do not directly govern the employment relationship, these should be enforceable by the Labour Court at the suit of a worker, a trade union or another employer (paragraph 3.37).

The terms set by the Sectoral Employment Agreements would be minimum standards only. It would be possible for an employer and worker to agree to an improvement on the sectoral minimum in any respect. It would be possible to derogate downwards from the agreed minima to any extent, but only by a collective agreement with an independent trade union, in accordance with the procedure described in chapter 7 (paragraphs 3.38 - 3.39).

4. STATUTORY REGULATION OF THE EMPLOYMENT RELATIONSHIP

(a) General

A core of statutory rights in a number of areas should apply to every employment relationship as a matter of law. Derogations from statutory standards should be permitted only where they are the subject of collective bargaining at either sector, company or plant level, involving recognised or representative trade unions (paragraph 4.1).

(b) Wages and Remuneration

All workers should be entitled to a statutory minimum wage, with the Council of Europe decency threshold being a benchmark for the statutory minimum rate. The statutory minimum wage should be set and reviewed annually by government, following the recommendations of a Fair Wages Commission which would include representatives of the TUC and the CBI (paragraph 4.5).

Workers should be protected against arbitrary deductions from pay and legislation should seek to ensure that wages are paid on a regular periodic basis. Payment in kind should be strictly regulated (paragraph 4.12).

Workers should enjoy greater protection in the event of their employer's insolvency. The upper limit on the protection of workers' wages should be increased and workers should have a greater opportunity to recover outstanding sums owed by an insolvent employer from the National Insurance Fund (paragraphs 4.14 - 4.15).

(c) The Regulation of Working Time

Workers should have the right not to work for more than 48 hours a week. The limits on working time which are contained in the

Working Time Directive should be incorporated into domestic UK law, together with the Directive's provisions concerning the regulation of nightwork and shiftwork (paragraphs 4.23 - 4.27).

Workers should have the right to a statutory minimum of four weeks' holidays annually. This would be in addition to time off for family reasons or trade union activities (paragraph 4.24).

(d) A Safe and Healthy Working Environment

Employers should be required to have access to qualified occupational health and safety services in developing health and safety strategies, and legislation should prescribe in greater detail the minimum acceptable contents of employers' safety policies. Companies should be required to provide information in their annual reports on their health and safety arrangements, including details of cases where enforcement action has been taken against them (paragraphs 4.31 - 4.35).

A form of no-fault liability should be introduced for senior management and/or members of the board of directors where a company is found to have recklessly exposed workers to serious risk of personal injury. Criminal penalties under health and safety legislation should be made more rational, and it should be easier for workers and their trade unions to bring private proceedings (paragraphs 4.36 - 4.38).

(e) Civil Liberties at the Workplace

Workers should have the right to control the collection, storage, and use of personal data by employers and others, including data held manually. All workers should have the right to be informed by the employer of the personal data being processed about them, the purposes for which the data is held and the parties to whom it will be disclosed (paragraph 4.44).

Workers should have the right to speak out about malpractice in the workplace, in accordance with clear statutory guidance. Employers should be required to provide workers with a policy statement on the reporting of improprieties at work and the arrangements that exist for carrying out these policies (paragraphs 4.52 - 4.56).

(f) Training Opportunities at Work

Employers should be under a general training duty, to be developed in consultation with recognised or representative trade unions, to ensure that their workers are adequately trained and have the skills required for the jobs they are required to do.

Workers should have a statutory right (i) to time off with pay to undergo training in the job which they are employed to do, (ii) to reasonable time off from their employment in order to extend their skills and qualifications, and (iii) to time off to engage in training when faced with redundancy (paragraphs 4.69 - 4.73).

(g) Fairness at Work

Employers should be required to have a grievance procedure in place which must be either agreed with the representatives of a recognised or representative trade union, failing which a procedure approved by a Labour Inspector which should comply with minimum standards set down in a Code of Practice to be drafted by ACAS (paragraph 4.78).

Workers should have a right to a speedy remedy to prevent employers changing working conditions without agreement. It should be automatically unfair to dismiss someone because he or she refuses to agree to a variation of working conditions.

Workers should have the right to challenge a disciplinary decision against them on the ground that the action in question is unfair, whatever form the disciplinary sanction may take (paragraphs 4.81 - 4.84).

(h) Pensions: Income Security in Retirement

All workers should be guaranteed a minimum acceptable level of income in their retirement by means of a flat rate benefit paid at a level in excess of the present inadequate basic pension. This income should be provided by the State, paid to all workers as of right and increased in line with general living standards (paragraph 4.89).

All workers should be ensured of a reasonable income in their retirement which is above the basic level and is related to their income while at work. Alongside the restoration of SERPS there should be an expansion of private provision to ensure benefits in excess of the State's minimum. This should be provided by collectively agreed schemes negotiated and regulated at sectoral level (paragraphs 4.89 - 4.93).

(i) Transfer of Undertakings

The Transfer of Undertakings (Protection of Employment) Regulations 1981 should be amended and adapted to cover a change of ownership of a company, and a worker should be permitted to pursue an appropriate remedy under the regulations against either the transferee or the transferor (paragraph 4.102).

5. EQUAL OPPORTUNITIES

(a) General

Legislation should seek to eliminate discriminatory employment practices, to remove barriers to effective labour market participation, and to promote the right of fair participation in work (paragraph 5.4).

(b) Disability, Discrimination and Equality of Opportunity

There should be statutory protection against discrimination for disabled workers. To this end the definition of disability must be both broad and inclusive, based on a social, rather than medical, model of disability (paragraph 5.16).

Discrimination should be defined to ensure that an employer shall not be permitted to discriminate against a disabled person who, with or without reasonable accommodation, can perform the essential functions of the employment position that such individual holds or desires (paragraph 5.17).

Both direct and indirect discrimination should be prohibited and discrimination should, therefore, be defined to include both less favourable treatment by reason of disability and the application of any requirement, condition, policy or practice which has a disproportionate impact upon persons with a disability (paragraph 5.17).

All employers should be under a duty to make reasonable accommodation for disabled persons by making alterations to the workplace or by adjusting policies and practices that have a disproportionate effect upon disabled applicants or workers (paragraph 5.20).

There should be a right to paid disability leave for those workers who become seriously ill or disabled on the job or while in employment, with protection against unfair dismissal for those on leave. The carers or partners of disabled persons should be protected from discrimination by association with a disabled person (paragraph 5.21 - 5.22).

A Disability Rights Commission should be established, with comparable powers to those of the Equal Opportunities Commission and the Commission for Racial Equality. The Commission should be charged with the general duty to work towards the elimination of discrimination, to promote equality of opportunity for disabled persons and to review the operation of all disability legislation (paragraph 5.23).

(c) Sex Discrimination and Sexual Orientation

The Sex Discrimination Act 1975 should be expanded to prohibit discrimination on the grounds of 'marital and family status', to cover both heterosexual and gay and lesbian relationships (paragraphs 5.25 - 5.33).

The Sex Discrimination Act 1975 should be amended to apply not only to discrimination against men and women on the grounds of sex, but also to discrimination against men and women on the grounds of sexual orientation. Transsexuals should also be protected from discrimination (paragraph 5.33).

The definition of indirect discrimination in the Sex Discrimination Act 1975 should be expanded to include any 'practice or policy' as well as any 'requirement or condition' which has a disproportionate impact on members of a particular sex, and to apply where a 'smaller proportion' of the disadvantaged group can comply with the practice, policy, requirement or condition rather than a 'considerably smaller proportion' as currently required (paragraph 5.27).

An employer should only be able to justify indirectly discriminatory practices where there was no alternative non-discriminatory way to meet the business needs of the enterprise and where the means chosen had the smallest possible burden on the members of that sex (paragraphs 5.28 - 5.29).

The scope of the legislation relating to discrimination on the grounds of sex should be expanded to apply to pay, enabling women who consider they have paid less either on recruitment or during employment to argue they have either been directly or indirectly discriminated against on grounds of sex. This right should be complementary to the wider proposals on pay equity below (paragraph 5.30).

(d) Sex Discrimination, Equal Pay and Pay Equity

Sectoral employment agreements or collective agreements which perpetuate pay inequity, or fail to make sufficient progress towards pay equity, should be referable to the CAC (paragraph 5.41).

Where there is no collective agreement, it should be possible to refer an employer's pay structure to the CAC on the ground that it perpetuates pay inequity, or fails to make sufficient progress towards pay equity (paragraph 5.41).

It should be possible for a reference to be made by a worker, union, public interest group or the CRE/EOC. The CAC should be empowered to amend or adjust a collective agreement or pay structure in order to advance pay equity, having particular regard to the correction of disproportionate differentials, and the role of bonus payments (paragraph 5.41).

The CAC should be empowered to determine its own procedure, having regard to the interests of fairness and the aim of achieving a result by means of an arbitral rather than a judicial procedure. There should be no appeal from an award of the CAC, but judicial review by the Labour Court should be available in limited cases (paragraph 5.43).

Any individual who wishes to assert his or her right to pay for work of equal value under Article 119 of the Treaty of Rome should be able to apply to the Labour Court which would be required to refer the claim to the CAC for a determination (paragraph 5.44).

Once the CAC has made the appropriate amendments to the payment structure of the enterprise at which the applicant works, the matter would be returned to the Labour Court which must assess compensation payable to the plaintiff. The levels of compensation should be at the discretion of the Labour Court, provided the principles of true compensation and deterrence are followed (paragraph 5.44).

Awards by the CAC would be policed by the Labour Inspectorate. The Labour Inspectorate would also be empowered to alert the EOC to conditions of pay inequity in any workplace which it inspects (paragraph 5.43).

(e) Workers with Parenting and Family Responsibilities

It should be unlawful to (a) refuse to appoint or to promote or offer training opportunities to a woman on the grounds of her pregnancy; or (b) terminate the employment of a woman at any time on the grounds of her pregnancy; or (c) subject a woman to any other detriment on the grounds of her pregnancy, except as permitted by the health and safety legislation (paragraph 5.49).

Legislation should provide as a minimum that a woman worker shall be entitled to 18 weeks leave in respect of childbirth, during which she shall receive full pay and retain the benefit of all accrued rights, including pension contributions. The father of a child should be entitled to four weeks paternity leave, during which he should be entitled to receive 90 per cent of earnings, where earnings are based on the pay period during the month prior to the leave (paragraph 5.52 - 5.53).

The parent of a child under 14 months old should be entitled to four months parental leave in order take care of the child. In order to ensure that fathers take equal responsibility, the leave should be non-transferable, and it should be unlawful for an employer to subject a worker to any detriment as a result of his or her decision to take parental leave (paragraph 5.54).

The parent of a child under school-leaving age should be entitled to family leave in order to care for a child who is ill or otherwise requiring special care. The employer should be able to require reasonable proof of the child's illness or other requirements. Each parent should be able to take a maximum of 20 days family leave in any calendar year which should be non-transferable between parents (paragraph 5.56).

Proposals for Family Leave should be adapted to enable workers to take time off with pay to care for dependent relatives other than children (paragraph 5.56).

A parent of a child under school-leaving age should be entitled to request that the employer consider permitting him or her take a career break in order to fulfil his or her family responsibilities, which should consist of a period of up to five years unpaid leave. At the end of a career break, the worker should be entitled to return to his or her previous job, or to a comparable job, unless the employer can prove that had the worker not been absent on a

career break he or she would have been made redundant
(paragraph 5.59).

Local authorities should have the duty to provide subsidised places
for day-care for children under nursery school age in their areas.
Funding for child care should be shared between parents,
employers and the general community. As an alternative to the
provision of nursery care local authorities should be permitted to
discharge their obligations to provide child-care in part by
providing financial support for registered child-minders in their
areas, provided a proper system of supervision of such child-
minders is in operation (paragraph 5.60).

(f) Race, Racial Discrimination and Equal Opportunity

Specific provision should be introduced to make religious
discrimination unlawful (paragraph 5.64).

The definition of indirect discrimination in the Race Relations Act
1976 should be expanded in accordance with proposals on sex
discrimination above to include any 'practice or policy' as well as
any 'requirement or condition' which has a disproportionate
impact on members of a particular racial group. It should also be
enough that a 'smaller proportion' of the disadvantaged group can
comply with the practice, policy, requirement or condition and not
a 'considerably smaller proportion' as currently required
(paragraph 5.65).

An employer should only be able to justify indirectly
discriminatory practices, where there was no alternative non-
discriminatory way to meet the business needs of the enterprise
and where the means chosen had the smallest possible burden on
the members of the disadvantaged racial group (paragraph 5.66).

Multiple discrimination should be unlawful, where it can be
demonstrated that a group of people sharing certain
characteristics is a group which warrants protection in its own
right because it carries an inordinately large burden of
disadvantage. For example, it should be unlawful to discriminate
against black women, who suffer a synthesis of gender and race
discrimination (paragraphs 5.70 - 71).

It should be possible to refer sectoral employment agreements,
collective agreements or payment structures to the CAC not only

on the ground that they reveal pay inequity between men and women but also because that reveal pay inequity between different racial groups, for example, between black women and white women (paragraph 5.74).

Employers should be under a duty to take such steps as are reasonable to accommodate the religious needs of their workers, including adjusting time schedules, meeting dietary requirements, allowing time off for religious worship, and where feasible permitting the use of premises to conduct communal worship. It should be unfair to dismiss or subject to any other detriment a worker who exercises his or her rights to time off work for prayers or religious festivals, provided that reasonable notice is given to the employer (paragraph 5.79 - 5.80).

Employers should not be held criminally liable for employing people who are not entitled to work in the UK; the responsibility of policing should lie solely within the domain of qualified immigration officers (paragraph 5.84).

Urgent steps should be taken develop and implement a comprehensive strategy within Europe aimed at combating racism and xenophobia at work and harmonising anti-discrimination standards. As a starting point, an amendment should be made to the EC Treaty to provide that racial equality is a basic principle of Community law(paragraph 5.86).

(g) Promoting Fair Participation at Work

All employers should be under a statutory duty to monitor the composition of their workforce in terms of disability, race and gender (paragraph 5.90).

Employers should be required by legislation to create in each workplace an equal opportunities forum where equal opportunities issues can be discussed with the representatives of the different trade unions which may be recognised or represented at the workplace (paragraphs 5.91 - 5.92).

Employers should be under a duty to provide from among their workforce for the election or nomination of equal opportunities officers from recognised or representative trade unions. Equal opportunities officers should be provided with statutory protection from discrimination and dismissal, and they should be entitled to time off work with pay to perform their duties but also to undergo training in these duties (paragraph 5.93).

It should be unlawful to harass, bully or otherwise assault the dignity of workers on grounds of their race, sex, sexual orientation, marital or family status or disability, and employers should be placed under a positive duty to create a workplace free of harassment (paragraph 5.93 - 5.96).

To the extent that it is possible under EC law, contract compliance should be developed as a strategy to eliminate discrimination, promote equality of opportunity, and develop the principle of fair participation at work in respect of disabled workers, workers from ethnic minority communities, and women (paragraph 5.97 - 5.98).

6. TRADE UNIONS AND THEIR MEMBERS

(a) The Legal Status of Trade Unions

The legal status of trade unions as provided in the 1974 legislation should be retained (paragraph 6.18).

It should be possible to remove the trustees of a trade union with a minimum of formality on grounds of incapacity or unfitness for office. In cases arising out of the conduct of industrial action it should be possible to seek the removal of trustees only on the application of a prescribed number of members; only after a ballot of the members of the union indicating support for this step; and only after the court has appointed new trustees from within the union (paragraph 6.19).

(b) Trade Union Expenditure and the Use of Funds

A union should be permitted to reimburse or indemnify any member or official who is (i) acting on behalf of the union, (ii) in accordance with the rules and policy of the union, and (iii) in respect of any matter which does not involve violence to person or property (paragraph 6.21).

Trade unions and companies should be treated the same way in matters relating to political activities, either by removing the controls on trade union political expenditure, or by subjecting companies to a similar regime (paragraph 6.23).

If the restrictions on trade union political expenditure are retained, the current obligation to conduct political fund review ballots should be repealed, and the current statutory definition of political objects should be amended to permit non party political expenditure to be financed from general funds (paragraphs 6.24 - 6.25).

(c) Trade Unions and their Members

Trade unions should be governed in a manner which promotes openness, transparency, participation, accountability and fairness (paragraphs 6.37 - 6.46).

Trade unions which apply for listing with the Certification Officer should have rules which deal with the following prescribed list of matters:

(i)   The name and business address of the union

(ii)   The full objects of the union

(iii) The method of making and amending the rules of the union

(iv) The governing body and the procedures for its re-election at regular intervals

(v)   Eligibility for admission to the union

(vi) The inspection of the accounting records of the union by members of the union

(vii) Eligibility to nominate candidates for office, eligibility to stand for office, and eligibility to attend meetings or to be elected or nominated as a delegate to meetings

(viii)The rights of candidates in an election, the rules to secure that each candidate has an equal opportunity to issue an election address, and the independence of the union administration

(ix) The appointment of an independent scrutineer to supervise the conduct of elections, with a clear statement of the scrutineer's duties

(x)   The procedures for holding elections, including the issue and control of ballot papers, the method and supervision of voting, the counting and scrutiny of votes, and the declaration and notification of the result

(xi) The procedures to be adopted before industrial action is called, including the holding of ballots before industrial action, should the balloting option be adopted

(xii) The grounds for which any member of the union may be disciplined or expelled by the union

(xiii) The procedure which must be followed in the case of the discipline and expulsion of members and the range of penalties which may be imposed on any member for breach of the rules

(xiv) The right of appeal by anyone who has been disciplined in breach of the rules and for the status quo to be maintained pending the outcome of the appeal, unless there are exceptional circumstances (paragraphs 6.47 - 6.50).

It should be for unions to determine the content of the above rules. Trade unions should be required, as at present, to submit an annual return to the Certification Officer (paragraph 6.51).

(d) The Resolution of Internal Disputes

There should be re-established an independent review body by the TUC with jurisdiction to hear complaints from trade union members about the breach of the rules of the union (paragraph 6.51).

Trade union members should have a right to choose to have any complaint about the breach of the rules of their union dealt with by the TUC Independent Review Committee or by the Labour Court (paragraph 6.51).

If a worker chooses to have a matter examined by the TUC Independent Review Committee he or she should be permitted to refer the matter to the Labour Court only on the ground of illegality or procedural impropriety (paragraph 6.51).

Where cases are heard by the Labour Court, for this purpose the court should consist of a legally qualified chair and two representatives from a panel of persons nominated by trade unions, who would not have any connection with the union involved in the dispute (paragraph 6.51).

7. TRADE UNION MEMBERSHIP, TRADE UNION RECOGNITION AND COLLECTIVE BARGAINING

(a) Trade Union Membership

The ban at GCHQ should be revoked and the power to revoke trade union membership rights, if it is to be retained, should be exercised strictly in accordance with ILO standards (paragraph 7.17).

It should be unlawful for anyone other than a trade union to maintain, distribute or provide access to lists of union members or activists except with the permission of the trade union (paragraph 7.20).

It should be unlawful for an employer to refuse employment, to offer prejudicial terms of employment, or to take prejudicial action against an employed worker on account of current or previous trade union membership, participation or activities (paragraph 7.20).

It should be unlawful for an employer to take prejudicial action against a worker not only on account of the worker's trade union membership or activities, but also where the worker has taken advantage of the benefits or facilities of trade union membership (paragraph 7.19).

(b) Trade Union Organisation

A trade union should be entitled to have access to an employer's premises at a reasonable time in order to speak to members, to hold meetings, and to conduct elections and ballots on the premises, at a suitable location provided by the employer (paragraph 7.23).

The exercise of these rights should depend on the trade union having members in the workplace in question, though it is for consideration whether a prescribed number of members should be required before any or all of these rights crystallise (paragraph 7.23).

Workers should have the right to give their employer notice that they wish to have their trade union subscriptions deducted at source, and workers should have the right to notify their employer that they would like the practice to be discontinued, after giving reasonable notice (paragraph 7.24).

(d) Trade Union Representation

A trade union should be entitled to represent its members individually and collectively on matters relating to working conditions, but a trade union should not be under any obligation to accept an individual into membership, nor offer representation facilities (paragraph 7.26 - 7.27).

There should be a statutory requirement that employers take all reasonable steps to draw to the attention of workers their right of representation. This should be done by a suitable amendment to section 1 of the Employment Rights Act 1996 (paragraph 7.38).

It should be unlawful for an employer to refuse to permit a worker to be represented by a trade union at any stage in the employment relationship, including matters relating to formation, variation and termination (paragraph 7.38).

(d) Trade Union Recognition

A trade union should be entitled to recognition for the purposes of collective bargaining where it can show that it has the support of a prescribed number of workers in the proposed bargaining unit (paragraph 7.31).

A trade union should be entitled to consultation rights where it can show that it has the support of a prescribed number of workers in the proposed consultation unit. The right to consultation should apply to all matters relating to the employment relationship (paragraph 7.31).

It should be possible for the union to demonstrate support for the purpose of either recognition or consultation rights in one of a number of ways. The process of determining whether the prescribed level of support has been reached would be conducted by a public body, to be called the Trade Union Representation and Recognition Agency (paragraph 7.31).

Where an employer is under a duty to consult or engage in collective bargaining with a trade union, it should be required to do so with a view to reaching an agreement. It should be open to a trade union to apply for a court order requiring an employer to comply with its legal duty to consult or bargain (paragraph 7.40).

(e) Support for Collective Bargaining

It should be possible for employers and trade unions to derogate from statutory standards and from sectoral employment agreements or awards by means of a qualifying collective agreement ('QCA'). An employer should be permitted to conclude a QCA only with an independent trade union (paragraph 7.42).

A QCA would have a binding effect on all workers to whom it related. It would not be possible for individual workers to agree less favourable terms, although it would be possible to modify the application of the QCA at local level by local agreements with recognised unions within a framework set by the recognition arrangements in the company in question (paragraph 7.42).

So far as consistent with the terms of the EC Public Procurement Directives, there should be introduced a statutory provision which provides that government departments and local authorities should contract only with approved contractors (paragraph 7.44).

An approved contractor would be defined in such a way to include only those tenderers which comply or which undertake to comply with the recognition provisions referred to above; that is to say only those companies which have in place procedures for negotiation or consultation, depending on the level of worker support (paragraph 7.44).

It should be lawful for a group of workers to take industrial action to seek to persuade their employer to recognise a trade union. The industrial action would be conducted in accordance with the general proposals relating to industrial action outlined below (paragraph 7.46).

It should be lawful for workers to take industrial action against their own employer to seek to persuade him or her to contract only with third parties who recognise a trade union, and for a group of workers to take secondary industrial action in support of other workers engaged in a recognition dispute with their own employer (paragraph 7.46).

(f) Facilities for Collective Bargaining

There should be more explicit recognition of the right of trade union officials to (a) have access to parts of the premises and to management where this is necessary to enable them to perform their duties, (b) post notices and distribute literature relating to normal union activities, and (c) material facilities to enable them to carry out their duties (paragraph 7.48).

A worker who is an official of a recognised trade union should have the right to take time off work with pay to enable him or her to carry out his or her responsibilities. As a general principle, the representatives of a recognised trade union should be entitled to any information about the undertaking which the employer has in his or her possession (paragraph 7.49).

(g) Collective Agreements

There should continue to be a statutory presumption that collective agreements are not legally enforceable, but the parties to a collective agreement should continue to be free to conclude legally binding agreements if they so desire (paragraph 7.56).

There should be a rebuttable statutory presumption that the terms of all collective agreements are incorporated into the terms of the employment relationship of individual workers to whom they relate (paragraph 7.57). Enforcement of a collective agreement should be at the suit of either the individual worker to whom it applies, or a trade union which is a party to the agreement (paragraph 7.58).

(h) EC Law and Mandatory Consultation

Consultations on proposed redundancies or business transfers should take place with (a) the representatives of a recognised trade union; failing which (b) the representatives of a trade union which has general consultation rights; failing which (c) the representatives of a trade union which has asserted collective representation rights at the workplace (paragraph 7.61).

Where there is no such representative in place the employer should be required to notify the Trade Union Representation and Recognition Agency which would then be under a duty to intervene on behalf of the workers who may be affected by the decision in question, and ask them to nominate a trade union to represent them in consultations about the proposed redundancy or transfer (paragraph 7.62).

The right to appoint a safety representative should apply to unions recognised for the purposes of collective bargaining, failing which unions which have general consultation rights, failing which unions which have asserted rights of collective representation (paragraph 7.67).

Where there is no such union it should be open to a worker to request an employer to make arrangements for the election of safety representatives of the workforce. The safety representatives may but need not be employed by the employer in accordance with the procedures described above (paragraph 7,66).

(i) European Works Councils

Legislation implementing the European Works Councils Directive should be based on the principle of trade union representation as the principal vehicle for representation. The legislation should provide in the first instance that where there is a trade union recognised for the purposes of collective bargaining, the British representatives on the Special Negotiating Body should be appointed by the trade union. Where there is more than one union recognised by the employer the British representative should be appointed by the unions jointly (paragraph 7.72).

Where there is no recognised trade union, but a union with either consulation rights or collective representation rights, that union (or where there is more than one union these unions jointly) should have the right to appoint a SNB representative (paragraph 7.73).

Where there is no union with consultation or collective representation rights or where the appointment is not ratified in a ballot of the workforce, the TURARA should be required to supervise the election of the SNB representative from amongst the workforce as a whole and trade unions should have the right to nominate candidates in the election (paragraph 7.73).

A similar procedure should be adopted in determining the composition of the European Works Council established on the basis of the Directive's subsidiary requirements according to article 7 in the Annex to the Directive, to be adopted where the central management and the special negotiating body fail to agree, or if they otherwise so decide (paragraph 7.73)

8. THE RIGHT TO STRIKE

(a) General

The current legislation relating to trade disputes should be repealed and replaced with a fair and balanced framework of law (paragraph 8.18).

The ILO standards should form the basis of future legislation on the right to strike (paragraph 8.25).

(b) Scope and Content of the Right to Strike

Workers should have a right to strike and to engage in other forms of industrial action recognised and protected by law. Workers should be free to take industrial action to promote their occupational, social or economic interests. Workers should be free to take international solidarity action (paragraphs 8.31 - 8.35).

Workers who exercise the right to strike (1) should not be regarded as having acted in breach of the employment relationship; (2) they should be protected from dismissal; and (3) those who organise industrial action should not be liable to the employer in tort or on any other ground (paragraph 8.31).

(c) Limitations on the Right to Strike

Trade unions and employers should continue to seek the resolution of their differences by methods other than industrial action. There should continue to be a statutory presumption that collectively agreed disputes procedures are not legally enforceable, but the parties to a collective agreement should continue to be free to make such agreements legally binding (paragraph 8.38).

Trade unions should take industrial action in accordance with their rules and procedures, including pre-strike ballots in appropriate cases. A ballot should not be required by law before industrial action in response to the victimisation of a trade union official, a unilateral variation of working conditions by the employer, or the refusal to cross a picket line (paragraph 8.39 - 8.47).

Workers should be free in combination with others to take secondary action in support of other workers engaged in a dispute, and the power to do so should be limited only in accordance with ILO standards (paragraphs 8.50 - 8.54). Workers should be free in the course of a dispute to picket peacefully outside a place of work (paragraph 8.57).

(d) Protection for the Individual Striker

Workers should be protected against dismissal for participation in a strike or industrial action. Workers should be entitled to be reinstated at the end of a dispute. Workers should be protected against dismissal for refusing to cross a picket line (paragraphs 8.58 per cent 8.68).

(e) Discipline and Expulsion of Strike-Breakers

Trade unions should be free to discipline and expel members in accordance with the rules of the union. The disciplinary action should be conducted in accordance with powers and procedures laid down in the rule book (paragraph 8.70).

(f) Trade Union Liability and the Protection of Funds

Neither a trade union nor its officials should be liable for any acts done in the course of organising or participating in a strike or other industrial action within the margins of legality outlined above (paragraph 8.72).

All legal proceedings against trade unions should be commenced in the Labour Court, which should have no power to award common law remedies, though it would have the power to award equivalent remedies (paragraph 8.73).

It should not be possible for an applicant to obtain relief in the Labour Court on an ex parte basis. The Labour Court should have no power to issue interim orders to restrain industrial action (save in very exceptional circumstances) (paragraph 8.74).

9. JOB SECURITY AND UNFAIR DISMISSAL

(a) General

Workers should have the right not to be unfairly dismissed (paragraph 9.9).

Conciliation should be compulsory prior to dismissal, otherwise the dismissal will be unfair (paragraphs 9.14 - 9.15).

(b) Scope of the Legislation

All workers should be entitled to claim unfair dismissal: there should no qualifying conditions (paragraphs 9.23 - 25).

There should be a legal presumption that whenever an employment relationship is terminated, a claim may be brought for unfair dismissal. The onus should be on the employer to show that the relationship was terminated voluntarily (paragraph 9.28).

(c) 'Public Rights' Dismissals

Where the reason, the principal reason, or a subsidiary reason for dismissal involves the employer denying a worker certain basic rights at work, then the dismissal will be for an inadmissible reason and automatically unfair (paragraph 9.32).

An inadmissible reason should include dismissal on the ground of sex, race, disability, age, religion, political beliefs, and also for other basic rights such as freedom of speech and protection for family life (paragraph 9.33).

It should be possible for a worker to apply to the Labour Court for temporary reinstatement, which should be granted whenever possible, in any case alleging dismissal for an inadmissible reason (paragraph 9.35).

(d) 'Economic' Dismissals

An employer should be required to justify the need to make economic dismissals to a Labour Inspector, and failure to do so would render any economic dismissal unfair (paragraph 9.38).

An economic dismissal should be subject to restraint by an order from a Labour Court unless and until it is conducted according to either a consultation procedure agreed with the relevant recognised trade union, or a procedure approved by a Labour Inspector in accordance with guidelines laid down in a Code of Practice (paragraph 9.39).

A worker should be entitled to challenge the fairness of an economic dismissal on the ground that he or she was unfairly selected compared to other workers. Redundancy payments should continue to be available in cases of economic dismissal (paragraph 9.40).

(e) 'Disciplinary' Dismissals

In the case of disciplinary dismissals, employers should be required to follow either a collectively agreed procedure, or a procedure approved by a Labour Inspector guided by a Code of Practice. A dismissal should be unfair if the employer fails to follow an approved procedure (paragraph 9.42 - 9.43).

A disciplinary dismissal should be unfair where an approved

procedure has been followed if the dismissal cannot be justified on its merits. Complaints would normally be heard by a Labour Adjudicator (paragraph 9.44).

In determining the fairness of a disciplinary dismissal consideration should be given to the risk of harm to the employers' business, the resources of employer, proportionality, consistency, and reasonableness in all the circumstances (paragraph 9.45).

The remedies for unfair dismissal should be reinstatement or compensation, though it should not be possible for an employer to frustrate an award of reinstatement (paragraph 9.46).

The measure of compensation should be calculated by reference to (a) the probable economic loss of the worker, and (b) the degree of culpability of the employer in dismissing unfairly, which could justify a punitive element (paragraph 9.46).

10. THE ENFORCEMENT OF RIGHTS

(a) General

The existing machinery for the enforcement of employment rights should be replaced by a new framework based on three new agencies: a Labour Inspectorate with significant powers; a new office of Labour Adjudicator; and a Labour Court (paragraph 10.5).

(b) Labour Inspectorate

The Labour Inspectorate should have jurisdiction over the enforcement of all individual employment rights conferred by statute (paragraph 10.9).

There may also be a case for extending the jurisdiction of the Inspectorate still further to include all terms of the employment relationship, including all non statutory terms (paragraphs 10.9 - 10.10).

The Labour Inspectorate should enjoy the wide powers, including a right to enter and inspect any workplace, either at his or her own initiative or at the request of aggrieved workers or their representatives (paragraph 10.11).

Labour Inspectors should have a range of sanctions at their disposal, including compensation orders and prohibition and improvement notices. There should be a right of appeal against Labour Inspector orders to the Labour Court (paragraph 10.12).

(c) Labour Court

All litigation relating to the employment relationship should fall within the jurisdiction of the Labour Court (paragraph 10.13).

The first rung on the ladder should be the Labour Adjudicator, who would deal mainly with a 'devolved list' containing what might be referred to as 'simple' cases (paragraphs 10.13 - 10.19).

The Labour Court should have jurisdiction to deal with more complex cases raising difficult questions of law, but also cases involving a 'group' justice and significant 'public interest' dimensions, which would both be placed on the 'reserved list' (paragraph 10.19).

The Labour Court should have an original jurisdiction to hear cases on a 'reserved list', an appeal jurisdiction from the Labour Inspectors and Labour Adjudicators, and a power to review the recommendations or awards of public agencies operating in the field (paragraph 10.16).

There should be a Labour Division in the Court of Appeal to which appeals on questions of law would lie from the Labour Court. In due course, there should be established an autonomous Labour Court of Appeal (paragraph 10.22).

(d) Remedies and Sanctions

Material losses, together with interest, should be fully compensable without limitation. Compensation for non material losses such as injury to feelings and a punitive element should be available (paragraphs 10.44 - 10.45).

There should be available a more effective range of remedies to enable the adjudicating bodies to respond sensitively and with flexibility to the problems which they may face (paragraph 10.47).

It should be open to the Labour Adjudicator and the Labour Court in appropriate cases to issue restraining orders, to issue mandatory orders, and to order reinstatement (paragraph 10.47).

(e) Alternative Dispute Resolution

It should be possible to elect arbitration rather than adjudication of employment disputes in accordance with the terms of a procedure in a collective agreement, but an individual worker should always have the right to choose adjudication even where the arbitral option is available (paragraphs 10.49 - 10.50).

INDEX

A

B

C

E

EC 21, 85, 92-93, 97
  Consultative Commission 169
  directives 34, 64, 76, 82-83, 93
  Equal Treatment Directive 144
  Equitable Wage, Commission Opinion on the 134
  member states 44, 45, 58, 336 *see also* Denmark; France; Germany; Greece; Italy
  law 49, 51, 170, 175-177
  treaty 34, 169
  Works Councils Directive 38
European Court of Justice (ECJ) 328
economic 22, 25-26, 31, 174, 283, 298, 335
elections 223
Employment 50, 117, 129, 191-192, 196, 199, 203-204, 217, 292
  Act 191-192, 196, 199, 203-204, 217, 292
  Agencies Act 50
  Appeal Tribunal 117, 129
  Protection Act 69, 73, 78, 83, 85
  Rights Act, 1996 47, 50, 55-56, 89, 91, 107, 154, 192
  Training Act 112
employers 47, 50, 55-56, 62, 69, 75, 83-84, 89, 100-101, 117, 120, 125, 128-129, 131,
    142-143, 146, 148, 152, 156, 158, 161, 168, 180, 183, 184-185, 221, 228, 256, 260,
    264, 300-305, 310, 340, 347, 352, 358
enforcement 100, 359
enterprise 67, 152
entrenchment 39
equal opportunities 134, 186, 347,
    Commission (EOC) 139, 143, 321-323
Equal Pay Act 145, 146
Esson v London Transport Executive 167
ethnic minority workers 163, 168
European
  Community Charter of Fundamental Social Rights 85
  Convention of Human Rights and Fundamental Freedoms, 1950
  (ECHR) 31
    Social Charter, 1961 252
    Trade Union Confederation 243
    Union 35
    works councils 216, 243-245
Express Newspapers, 264
Express Newspapers Ltd v MacShane 230, 262

F

Factories Acts 42, 44
Fair Employment Act (Northern Ireland) 170
Fair Wages Commission 85, 320, 339
Family Credit 28
Federation of Small Businesses 167
Financial Times 69
Finland 61
fixed-term contracts 43, 56, 307
flexible working 158

T

U

W

X

Y

Z

Lawrence & Wishart

60 years of radical publishing

This year Lawrence & Wishart celebrates 60 years of radical publishing. To celebrate we will be having a prize draw at the end of the year. All respondents will be entered for the draw with a chance to **win £100 worth of L&W** books! You will also receive a free catalogue which includes details of our **anniversary free book offer**. Just answer the questions below (a photo copy or separate sheet will do) and send it to the address below.

NAME _____

ADDRESS _____

_____

_____ POSTCODE _____

OCCUPATION _____

I bought this book at _____

_____

I heard about this book from _____

_____

I have/have not bought Lawrence & Wishart books before (*please delete as necessary*)

If yes, please state which titles _____

_____

_____

Please send completed form to: Lawrence & Wishart 99a Wallis Road, London E9 5LN.
Tel: 0181 533 2506 Fax: 0181 533 7369

Offer ends 31.12.96 · Draw takes place 6.1.97 · Winner notified by post

WIN £100 OF L&W BOOKS!